Contents

Preface

The *ENOVIA V5-6R2017: DMU Navigator and Space Analysis* learning guide is an introduction to the DMU workbenches of the ENOVIA suite of products. Digital Mock-Up (DMU) is used primarily as a viewing and analysis tool for 3D CAD data. Students are introduced to the DMU interface by viewing, manipulating and analyzing 3D model geometry. Specific focus is on the Space Analysis workbench, which provides access to clash, sectioning, and comparison tools. Based on the results of these analyses, students will learn to create annotations directly on the 3D geometry in order to communicate information back to the designers.

Topics Covered:

- DMU user interface

- Model navigation and visualization

- File management

- Measurement tools

- Clash analysis

- Sectioning

- Distance and band analysis

- Compare products

- Arc through three points

- 3D annotations

- Annotation views

- Image capture

- Printing images

Note on Software Setup

This learning guide assumes a standard installation of the software using the default preferences during installation. Lectures and practices use the standard software templates and default options for the Content Libraries.

Lead Contributor: Scott Hendren

Scott Hendren has been a trainer and curriculum developer in the PLM industry for over 20 years, with experience on multiple CAD systems, including Pro/ENGINEER, Creo Parametric, and CATIA. Trained in Instructional Design, Scott uses his skills to develop instructor-led and web-based training products.

Scott has held training and development positions with several high profile PLM companies, and has been with the Ascent team since 2013.

Scott holds a Bachelor of Mechanical Engineering Degree as well as a Bachelor of Science in Mathematics from Dalhousie University, Nova Scotia, Canada.

Scott Hendren has been the Lead Contributor for *ENOVIA: DMU Navigator and Space Analysis* since 2013.

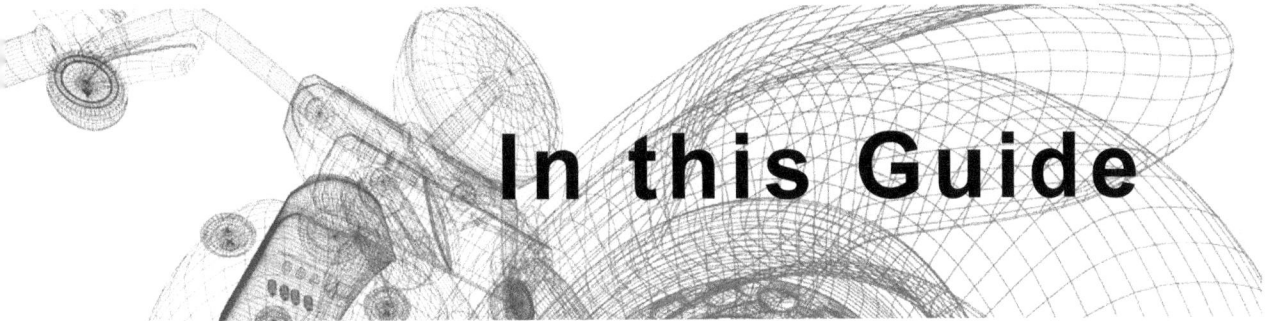

In this Guide

The following images highlight some of the features that can be found in this guide.

Practice Files

To download the practice files for this student guide, use the following steps:

1. Type the URL shown below into the address bar of your Internet browser. The URL must be typed **exactly as shown**. If you are using an ASCENT ebook, you can click on the link to download the file.

    Address bar

    http://www.ASCENTed.com/getfile?id=xxxxxxxx

    File Edit View Favorites Tools Help

2. Press <Enter> to download the .ZIP file that contains the Practice Files.

3. Once the download is complete, unzip the file to a local folder. The unzipped file contains an .EXE file.

4. Double-click on the .EXE file and follow the instructions to automatically install the Practice Files on the C:\ drive of your computer.

    Do not change the location in which the Practice Files folder is installed. Doing so can cause errors when completing the practices in this student guide.

    http://www.ASCENTed.com/getfile?id=xxxxxxxx

    Stay informed!
    Interested in receiving information about upcoming promotional offers, educational events, invitations to complimentary webcasts and discounts? If so, please visit www.ASCENTed.com/updates/

    Help us improve our product by completing the following survey:
    www.ASCENTed.com/feedback
    You can also contact us at: feedback@ASCENTed.com

Practice Files

The Practice Files page tells you how to download and install the practice files that are provided with this guide.

Link to the practice files

Chapter

1

Getting Started

In this chapter you learn how to start the AutoCAD® software, become familiar with the basic layout of the AutoCAD screen, how to access commands, use your pointing device, and understand the AutoCAD Cartesian workspace. You also learn how to open an existing drawing, view a drawing by zooming and panning, and save your work in the AutoCAD software.

Learning Objectives in this Chapter

- Launch the AutoCAD software and complete a basic initial setup of the drawing environment.
- Identify the basic layout and features of AutoCAD interface including the Ribbon, Drawing Window, and Application Menu.
- Locate commands and launch them using the Ribbon, shortcut menus, Application Menu and Quick Access Toolbar.
- Locate points in the AutoCAD Cartesian workspace.
- Open and close existing drawings and navigate to the location.
- Move around a drawing using the mouse, the **Zoom** and **Pan** commands, and the Navigation Bar.
- Save drawings in various formats and set the automatic save options using the Save commands.

Chapters

Each chapter begins with a brief introduction and a list of the chapter's Learning Objectives.

Learning Objectives for the chapter

Side notes

Side notes are hints or additional information for the current topic.

Instructional Content

Each chapter is split into a series of sections of instructional content on specific topics. These lectures include the descriptions, step-by-step procedures, figures, hints, and information you need to achieve the chapter's Learning Objectives.

Practice Objectives

Practices

Practices enable you to use the software to perform a hands-on review of a topic.

Some practices require you to use prepared practice files, which can be downloaded from the link found on the Practice Files page.

Practice Files

To download the practice files for this guide, use the following steps:

1. Type the URL shown below into the address bar of your Internet browser. The URL must be typed **exactly as shown**. If you are using an ASCENT ebook, you can click on the link to download the file.

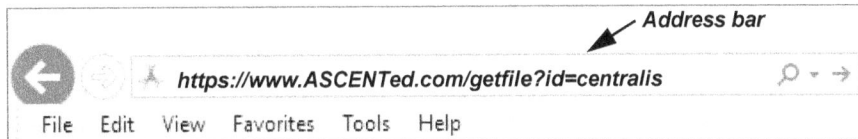

Address bar

https://www.ASCENTed.com/getfile?id=centralis

File   Edit   View   Favorites   Tools   Help

2. Press <Enter> to download the .ZIP file that contains the Practice Files.

3. Once the download is complete, unzip the file to a local folder. The unzipped file contains an .EXE file.

4. Double-click on the .EXE file and follow the instructions to automatically install the Practice Files on the C:\ drive of your computer.

   Do not change the location in which the Practice Files folder is installed. Doing so can cause errors when completing the practices.

https://www.ASCENTed.com/getfile?id=centralis

Stay Informed!

Interested in receiving information about upcoming promotional offers, educational events, invitations to complimentary webcasts, and discounts? If so, please visit:

www.ASCENTed.com/updates/

Help us improve our product by completing the following survey:

www.ASCENTed.com/feedback

You can also contact us at: *feedback@ASCENTed.com*

Introduction to DMU

This chapter provides an introduction to the Digital Mock-Up (DMU) workbenches of the ENOVIA suite of products. DMU is primarily used as a viewing and analysis tool for 3D CAD data. This chapter introduces you to the interface and methods of working in DMU.

Learning Objectives in this Chapter

- Understand the DMU product solution.
- Learn how to access the DMU Workbenches.
- Review the DMU user interface.
- Learn how to manipulate the DMU toolbars.
- Understand the fundamentals of solid modeling.

1.1 DMU Product Solution

ENOVIA is part of the PLM (Product Lifecycle Management) products that are used to manage and distribute developmental data and knowledge. Digital Mock-up (DMU) is part of the ENOVIA product line. It enables companies to collaborate, review, analyze, and simulate models created in Computer Aided Drafting (CAD) programs such as CATIA V5. The ENOVIA DMU workbenches are described as follows:

Workbench	Description
DMU Navigator	Navigator supplies the basic functions used in all workbenches, Viewing, Measuring, and annotation tools.
DMU Kinematics	Kinematics enables you to apply mechanisms to your assembly model to simulate motion. This provides the ability to analyze the motion and check for critical information such as interference and minimum distances.
DMU Space Analysis	Space Analysis enables you to cut sections, look for interferences, and perform complex measurements. 3D geometry comparisons can also be performed from this workbench.
DMU Fitting	Fitting Simulator provides the ability to create, record, and play back animations that simulate the assembly and disassembly of your products.
DMU Digital Plant and Ship Review	Digital Plant and Ship Review is similar to DMU Navigator but is dedicated to the Plant and Ship industry. It has tools to help locate, select, and analyze AEC objects.
DMU Tolerancing Review	Dimensioning & Tolerancing enables you to visualize, search, and filter dimensions and tolerances.
DMU Optimizer	Optimizer provides the ability to create alternate representations of products. It generates simplified representations that are reduced in size, but still accurate.
DMU 2D Viewer	2D viewer enables you to manipulate, annotate, import and export, and compare 2D documents.

1.2 Access Workbenches

A workbench is a set of tools used for completing certain tasks. The active workbench is indicated by an icon in your toolbar. By default, the icon is located in the upper right corner of the screen. Hover the cursor over the icon until the workbench name displays, as shown in Figure 1–1.

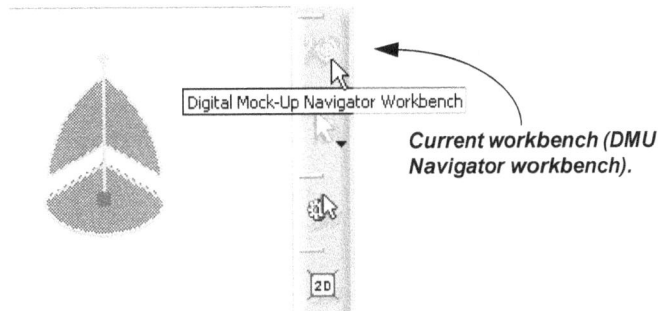

Digital Mock-Up Navigator Workbench

Current workbench (DMU Navigator workbench).

Figure 1–1

Accessing a workbench can be done using the following methods:

- **Start** menu

- Favorite Workbench

Start Menu

The **Start** menu contains all of the available workbenches that can be accessed. For example, to access the DMU Space Analysis workbench, select **Start>Digital Mockup>DMU Space Analysis**, as shown in Figure 1–2. The toolbars update for the active workbench.

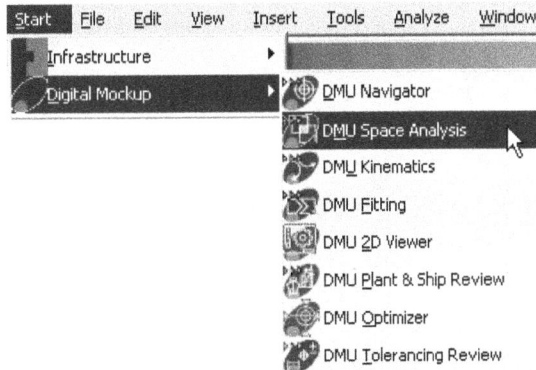

Figure 1–2

Favorite Workbenches

ENOVIA DMU can be customized to display the most commonly used workbenches by clicking the Workbench icon, as shown in Figure 1–1. The Welcome to ENOVIA PORTAL dialog box opens by default when you first click this icon, as shown in Figure 1–3.

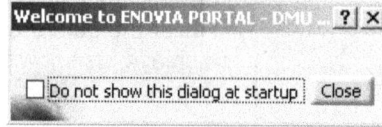

Figure 1–3

How To: Add a Workbench to the Welcome to ENOVIA PORTAL dialog box

1. Select **Tools>Customize** in the menu bar. The Customize dialog box opens, as shown in Figure 1–4.

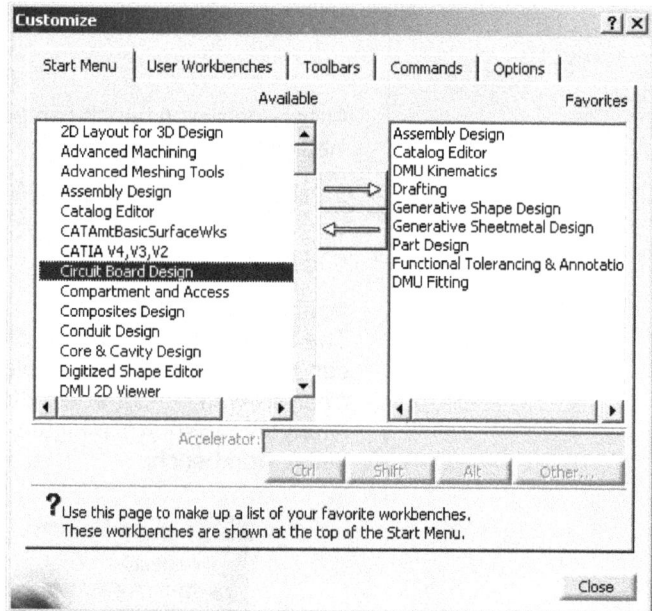

Figure 1–4

2. Select the required workbenches in the left column of the *Start Menu* tab.

3. Click ⟹ to add them to the "Favorites" column on the right.

4. The Favorites are automatically stored with the settings for ENOVIA. Click **Close** to complete the operation.

The next time the Workbench icon is clicked, the Welcome to ENOVIA dialog box opens the list of favorite workbenches, as shown in Figure 1–5.

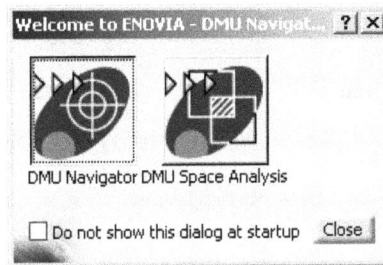

Figure 1–5

Click one of the workbench icons to switch Workbench modes. All toolbars update for functions specific to the selected workbench.

Once workbenches are customized, the list of favorites is also available for quick selection in the **Start** menu, as shown in Figure 1–6.

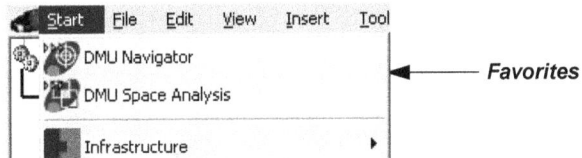

Figure 1–6

1.3 User Interface

When you open a model in the DMU Navigator workbench, the screen displays as shown in Figure 1–7. The major areas of the screen are labeled and described in this section.

Specification Tree   *Menu Bar*

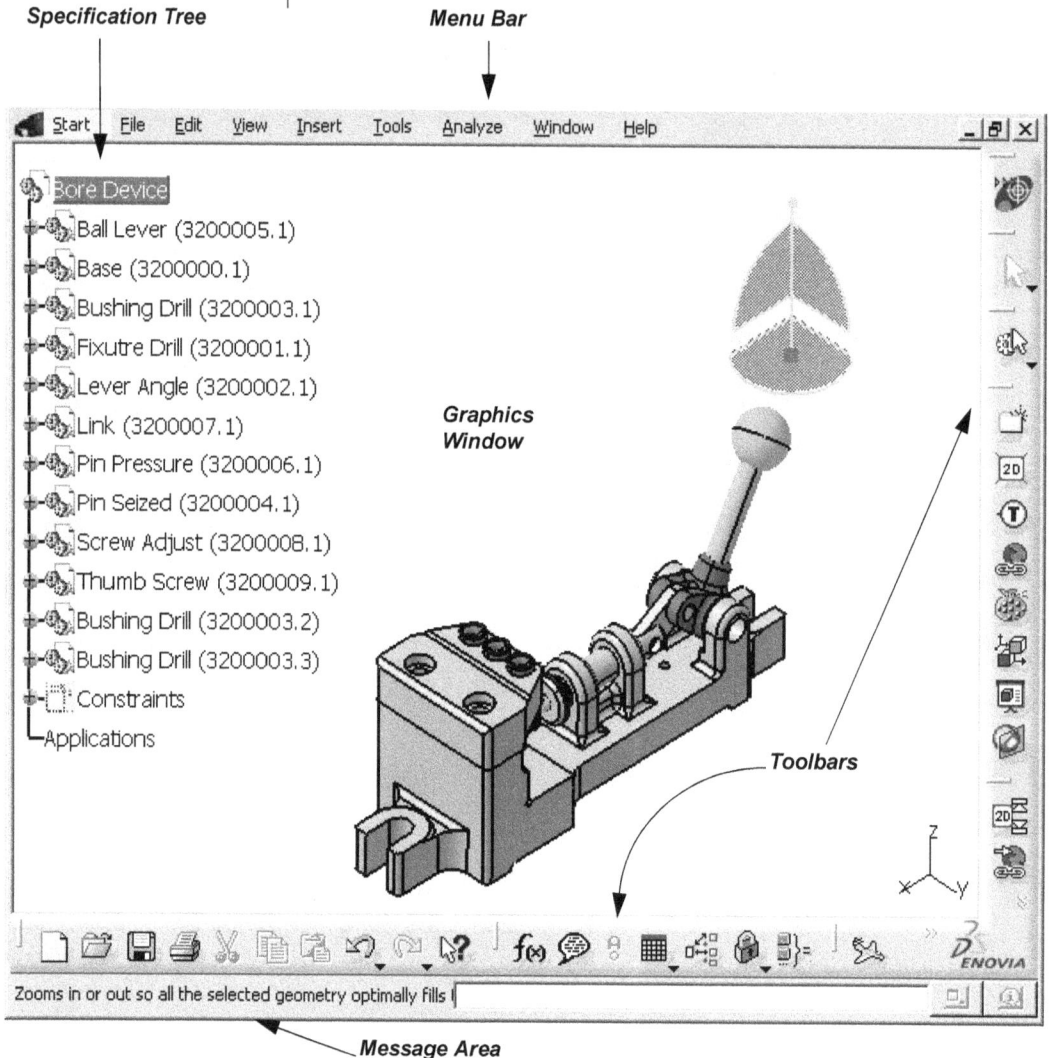

Figure 1–7

Toolbars & Menus

The primary way of interacting with the system is to click icons in the toolbars or select commands in the menu bar. You can customize the interface by arranging the location of the toolbars and selecting which icons to show.

In addition to the toolbars and menus, you can right-click to open a menu containing a list of appropriate options that can be used.

Message Area

In many cases, the system displays a single line prompt in the message area. This area of the screen is intended to guide you through the process of performing a certain task.

Specification Tree

The specification tree displays a variety of information about the model. The specification tree displays the features of the part in the order in which they were created. This is useful because it provides quick access to parameters, functions, materials, and commonly-used measurements.

1.4 Toolbar Manipulation

Depending on monitor size and screen resolution, your screen might not be able to display all of the toolbars. You can increase your productivity by understanding how to customize the toolbars so that more frequently used icons are easy to access.

Moving Toolbars

You can reposition toolbars on the screen with separators or double arrows.

Separators

Each toolbar contains a separator, as shown in Figure 1–8. To move the toolbar, simply select and drag the separator to a new position.

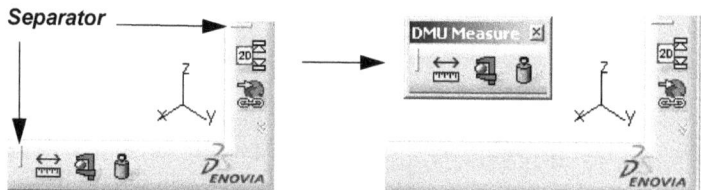

Figure 1–8

Double Arrows

If there is not enough room to display more toolbars, double arrows appear at the corner of the screen. The double arrows indicate that additional icons are present and not currently displayed.

The DMU Review Navigation toolbar is shown in Figure 1–9. The double arrows or the separators can both be used to move the toolbar.

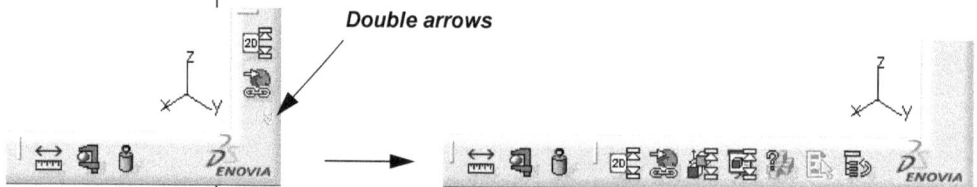

Figure 1–9

Toolbar Placement

Toolbars can be displayed in the following ways:

- Docking on the top, bottom, right, or left side of the screen.
- Floating away from the top, bottom, right, or left side of the screen.
- Stacking multiple levels on the top, bottom, right, or left side of the screen.

Some examples of toolbar placement are shown in Figure 1–10. Any combination of the placement methods can be used.

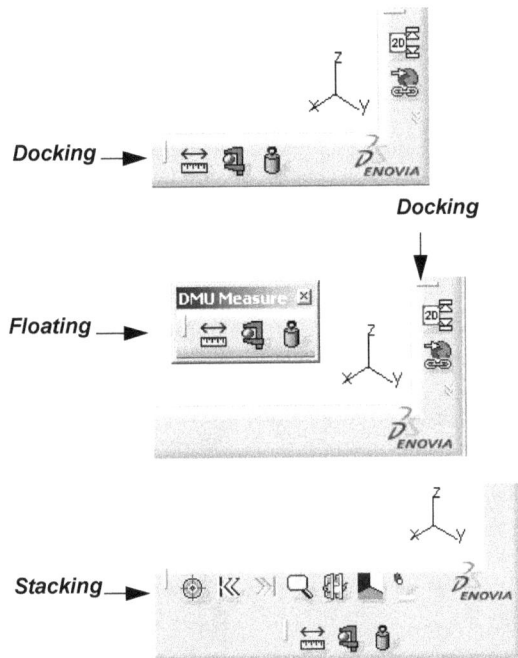

Figure 1–10

Add/Remove Toolbars

Toolbars can also be customized to display task-specific icons using one of the following methods:

- Select **View>Toolbars** and select the toolbar name so that ☑ displays to add a toolbar. Clear ☑ to remove the toolbar from the display.
- Right-click in an area of the toolbar and toggle on the toolbar name using ☑.

An example of the toolbar selection option box is shown in Figure 1–11.

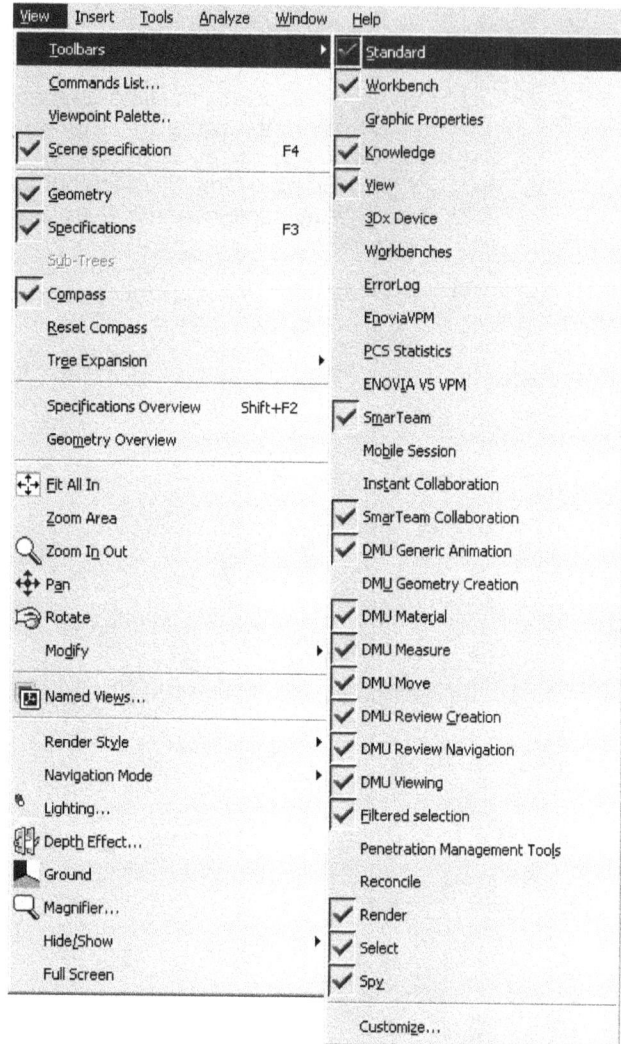

Figure 1–11

Expanding Flyouts

Some toolbar icons contain flyouts, which display additional icons when selected. For example, the Track, Clash Detection, and Reset Position operation icons contain flyouts, as shown in Figure 1–12.

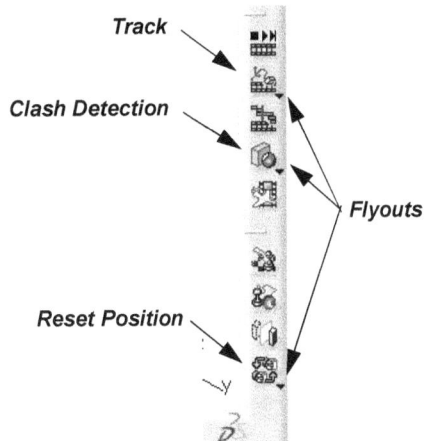

Figure 1–12

Selecting the flyout displays the additional icons, as shown in Figure 1–13. Flyout options are grouped by type.

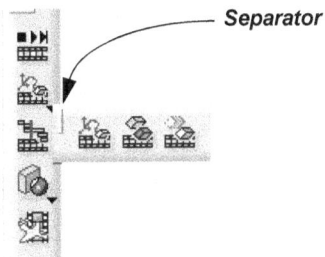

Figure 1–13

You can reposition the icons displayed in the flyout as their own toolbar instead of using the flyout. To show the flyout as a toolbar, drag the separator that displays for the flyout to a new position on the screen, as shown in Figure 1–14. You can position the flyout as a floating, docked, or stacked toolbar.

Creating a new toolbar from a flyout does not remove the original flyout icon.

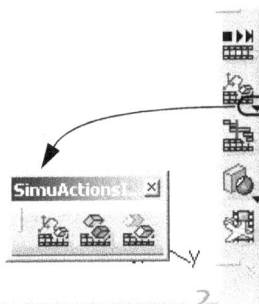

Figure 1–14

1.5 Modeling Fundamentals

ENOVIA DMU is a viewing and analysis tool that uses models created in a solid modeling CAD application such as CATIA. An understanding of the process used to make these models is useful when viewing and analyzing them. This section explains the qualities of these programs using CATIA V5 as the example.

Solid Modeling

CATIA can be used to create three-dimensional (3D) Solid Models. This means that the system understands that the model is "filled" with material. With a Solid Model, you can perform the following functions:

- Obtain the mass properties of a part.

- Determine whether components in an assembly interfere with one another.

- Create cross-sections of an assembly or display part cross-sections on a drawing.

It is important to understand that part models are also used to develop 2D Drawings. You do not need to manually "draw" the views in the drawing. You simply reference the part model to generate views and display the dimensions from the 3D geometry, as shown in Figure 1–15.

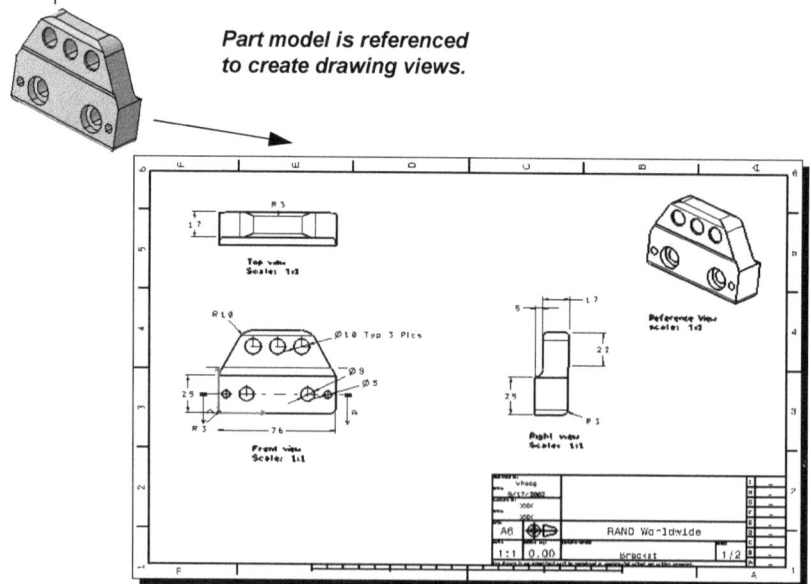

Part model is referenced to create drawing views.

Figure 1–15

This process is also true for assemblies, as shown in Figure 1–16. You can locate existing part and assembly models relative to one another. The assemblies can then be referenced by a drawing.

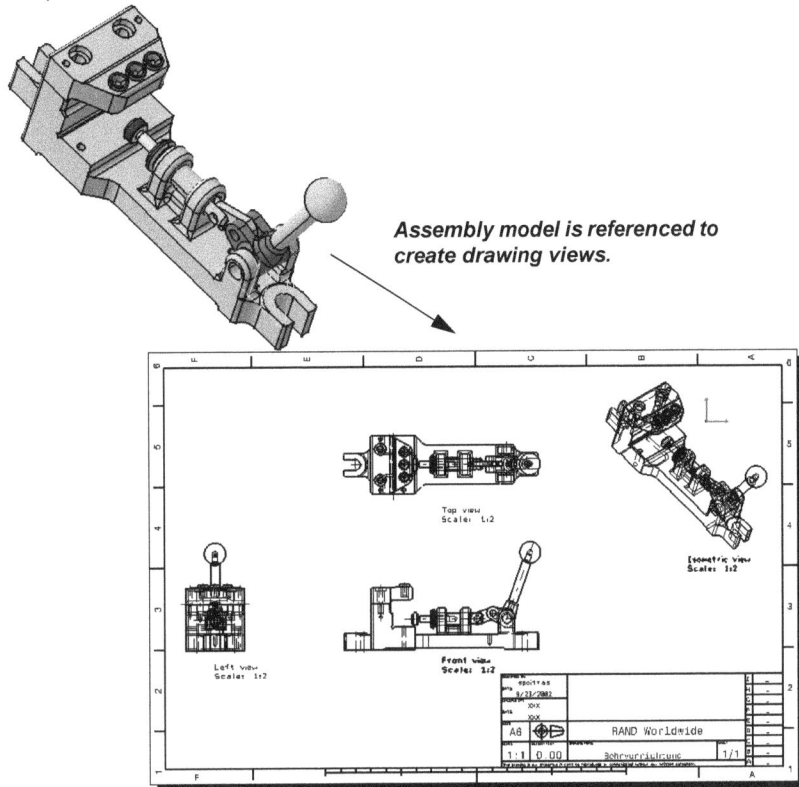

Assembly model is referenced to create drawing views.

Figure 1–16

Feature-Based

The solid model evolves by creating features, one by one, until the geometry is complete. The part model shown in Figure 1–17 is constructed by consecutively creating the following features:

1. Create a sketch.
2. Create a Pad feature.
3. Draft several walls of the part using the Draft feature.
4. Remove sharp edges of the geometry by creating a Fillet feature.
5. Create a Shell feature to hollow out the part.
6. Create another Pad feature to act as a cylindrical boss.
7. Center a Hole feature on the cylindrical Pad.

8. Duplicate the two features of the boss to create the second boss, as shown in Figure 1–17.

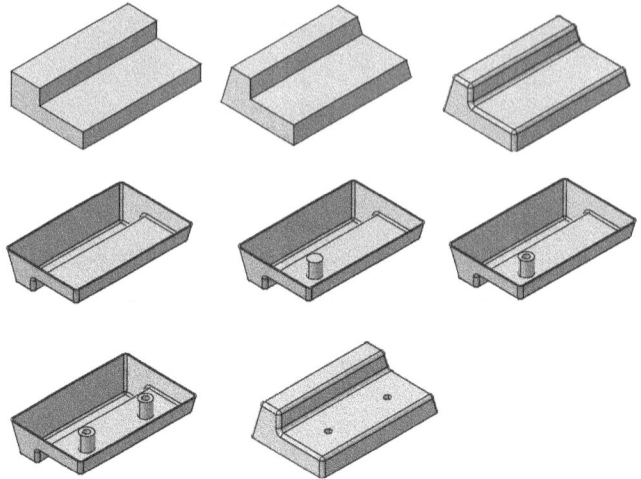

Figure 1–17

You typically organize the features based on your design intent. This process means that you begin with features that define the overall size and major geometric shape, leaving the small, finishing details until the end.

Parametric

Features that are created using CATIA are parametric. This means that all of the dimensional constraints you create to define a feature's shape are considered "parameters" and are accessible at any time. Simply double-click on a feature to display its dimensional constraints and change any of its values to alter the geometry.

The dimensional value that positions the Pocket feature shown in Figure 1–18 is changed. The position of the feature updates to reflect the design change.

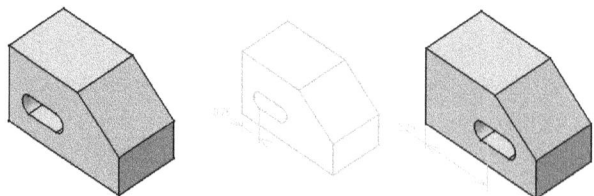

Figure 1–18

Associative

As mentioned, drawings are created by referencing a model. When the model is changed, any drawings of that model are automatically updated the next time they are opened. This case is the same with assemblies; changing a part model automatically reflects in the assembly. In addition, changes made in the assembly update throughout the other modes in CATIA, as shown in Figure 1–19.

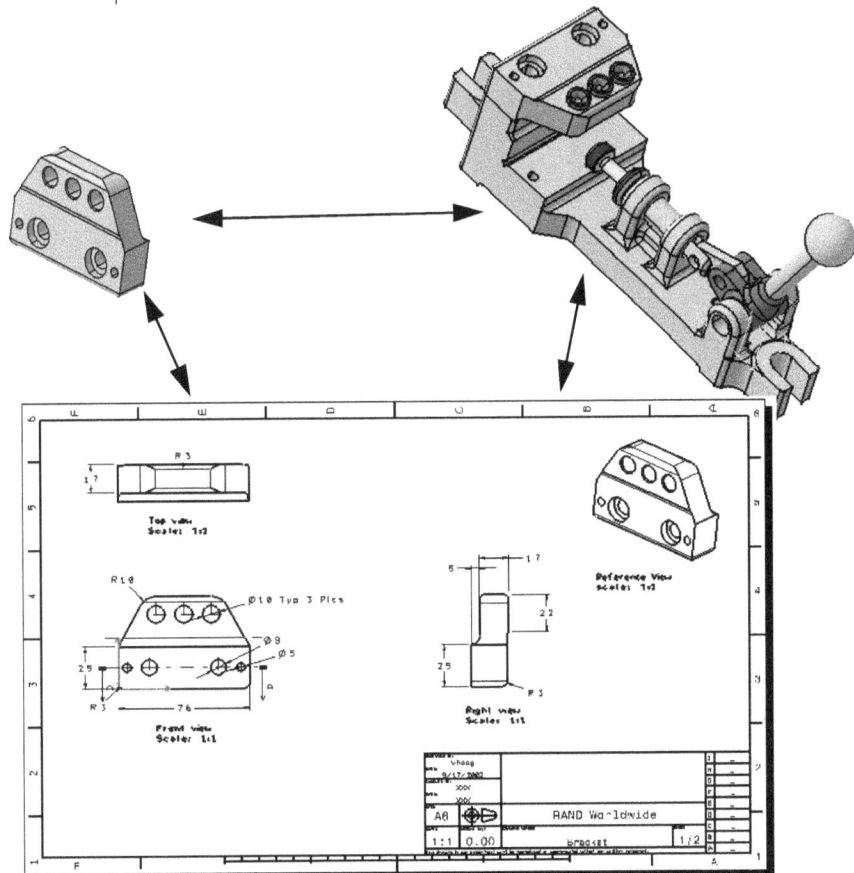

Figure 1–19

This associativity creates a dependency between models. The part models referenced by an assembly and/or drawing must be retrievable to work with the assembly and/or drawing.

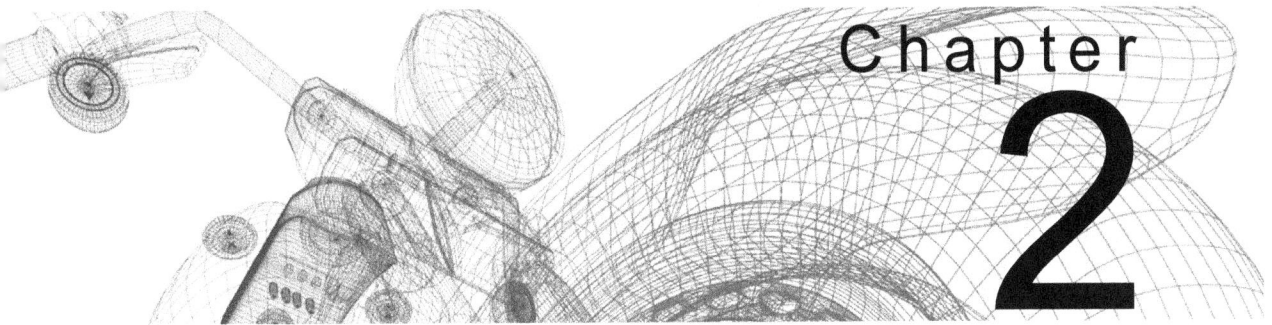

Chapter 2

Model Navigation

It is important to be able to correctly visualize the specific section of model geometry when viewing a 3D model. In this chapter, you learn how to navigate a 3D model within the DMU, and to control its visualization.

Learning Objectives in this Chapter

- Open existing models.
- Navigate a model.
- Use the model visualization tools.
- Learn how to use the Specification Tree.

© 2018, ASCENT - Center for Technical Knowledge®

2.1 Opening Existing Models

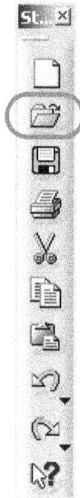

To open a model, click the [icon] (Open) icon in the Standard toolbar and select the model in the Open dialog box, as shown in Figure 2–1.

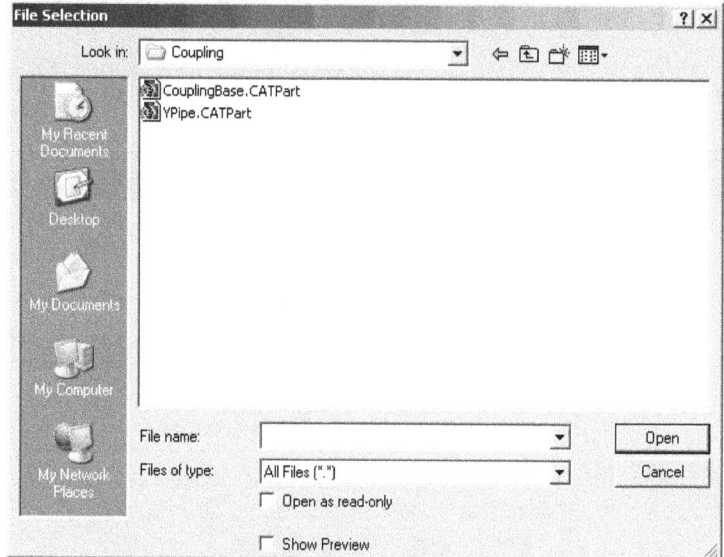

Figure 2–1

File formats that can be opened using DMU are listed below.

Object	File Extension
Bitmap Files	.bmp, .jpg, .rgb, .picture, .tiff
CATIA V4 Files	.model, .session, .library
CATIA V5 Files	.CATDrawing, .CATMaterial, .CATProduct
Standard Files	.igs, .wrl, .step, .stp
Vector Files	.cgm, .gl, .gl2, .hpgl
2D Standard Files	.dxf, .dwg
Data Files	.pdb

2.2 Navigating a Model

To inspect a model, you must understand how to reorient, zoom in and out, pan, and fly through a model. There are three methods to navigate a model:

- Examine mode

- Fly mode

- Walk mode

ENOVIA DMU also provides the ability to save important orientations (viewpoints) to recall later.

Examine Mode

Examine mode is the default navigation mode for DMU Navigator. It enables you to examine the model by panning, zooming, and rotating.

Standard Viewpoints

The Quick Views flyout contains predefined model orientations, enabling you to view the model from commonly used orientations. The available Standard Viewpoints are shown in Figure 2–2.

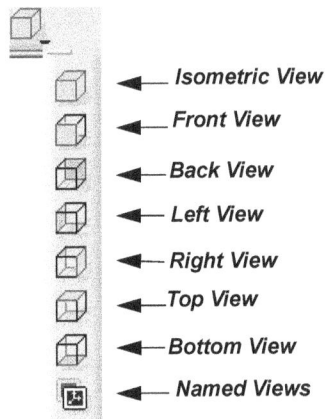

- Isometric View
- Front View
- Back View
- Left View
- Right View
- Top View
- Bottom View
- Named Views

Figure 2–2

Dynamic Orientation

To dynamically navigate around the model, you can use specific View toolbar icons, menu commands, or mouse shortcuts. The most commonly used navigation functions are listed as follows:

Function	Mouse Button	Menu	Icon
Pan	Hold Middle	**View>Pan**	✥
Rotate	Hold Middle + Right	**View>Rotate**	🔄
Zoom	Hold Middle + Click Right	**View>Zoom In/Out**	🔍 🔍
Zoom Area	N/A	**View>Zoom Area**	N/A
Fit All	N/A	**View>Fit All**	✛

Saved Viewpoints

To create a Saved Viewpoint, orient the model to the required orientation and select **View>Named Views.** The Named Views dialog box opens, as shown in Figure 2–3.

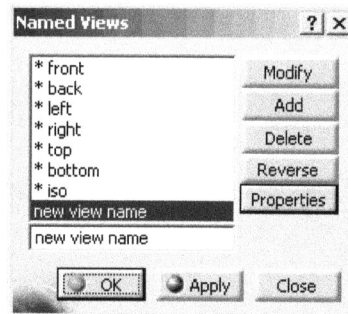

Figure 2–3

Click **Add**. The name defaults to Camera 1. Enter the required name and click **Apply**.

Fly Mode

Fly mode enables you to simulate flying around and through a model.

How To: Fly Through a Model

1. Activate Perspective mode. Select **View>Render Style> Perspective** to access a perspective view.
2. Activate Fly mode. Select **View>Navigation Mode>Fly**, or click the [icon] (Fly Mode) icon in the View toolbar. The View toolbar updates, as shown in Figure 2–4.

Figure 2–4

3. Define the Starting position. Click the [icon] (Turn Head) icon. Holding the left mouse button, drag the model to the direction from which you would like to start. Once in the required position, release the left mouse button.

4. Click the [icon] (Fly) icon to activate the Fly operation. Press the middle mouse button to define the initial horizontal plane. While keeping the middle mouse button pressed, move the cursor to pan the view to the correct starting direction.

5. Keeping the middle mouse button pressed, click the left mouse button to begin the flight. Move the cursor left and right, up and down to travel through the model. The further away you drag the cursor from the center of the view, the greater the change in direction. The green arrow at the bottom of the screen indicates the direction in which you are flying, as shown in Figure 2–5.

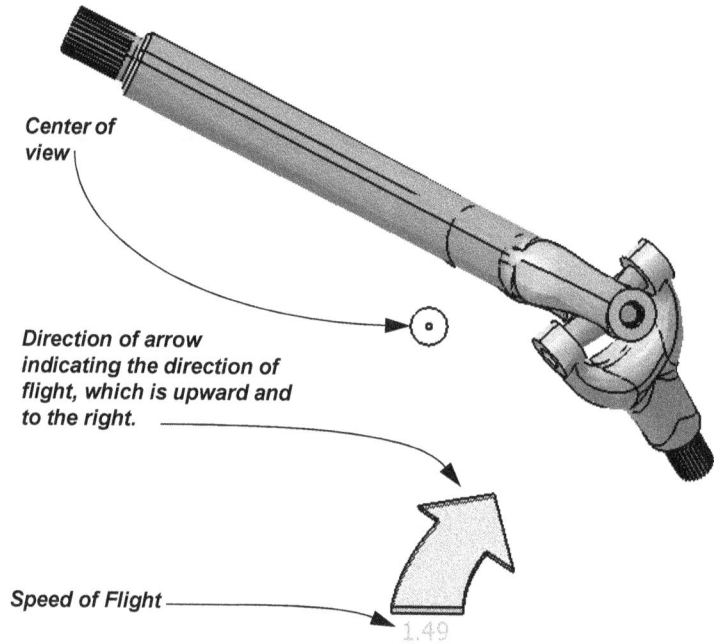

Center of view

Direction of arrow indicating the direction of flight, which is upward and to the right.

Speed of Flight

1.49

Figure 2–5

6. Toggle the direction of flight from forward to backward by clicking the left mouse button.
7. To increase or decrease the speed of flight during the fly through, press <Page Up> or <Page Down>, respectively.

   You can also click the (Accelerate) or (Decelerate) icon before starting the flight. Each click accelerates or decelerates the flight by approximately 40%.
8. To stop flying through the model, release the middle mouse button.

9. Click the (Examine Mode) icon to return to Examine mode.

Beginners Fly Mode

Beginners Fly mode is similar to the Fly mode already discussed, except that you do not have the ability to move backward or change speed during the flight. Beginners Fly mode is accessed the same way as Fly mode and uses the same method as Fly mode to set up a flight (click the [icon] (Fly) icon to begin the flight and hold the left mouse button to fly). While keeping the left mouse button depressed, move the cursor to change direction of flight (left, right, up, or down).

Walk Mode

Walk mode is another way of moving around and through the model. Like Fly mode, you can move left, right, forward, and backward. However, you cannot move up and down. In Walk mode, you are always on the same horizontal plane as you walk through the model. The procedure to use Walk mode is very similar to that used in Fly mode.

How To: View in Walk Mode

1. Activate Perspective mode. Select **View>Render Style> Perspective** to access a perspective view.
2. Activate Walk mode. Select **View>Navigation Mode>Walk**. The View toolbar updates, as shown in Figure 2–6.

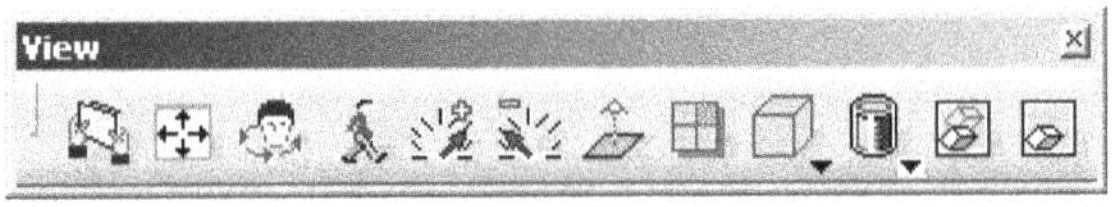

Figure 2–6

3. Define the Starting position. Click the [icon] (Turn Head) icon. Holding the left mouse button, drag the model to the direction from which you would like to start. Once in the required position, release the left mouse button.

4. Click the [icon] (Walk) icon to activate the Walk operation. Click the middle mouse button to define the horizontal plane. While keeping the middle mouse button pressed, move the cursor to pan the view to correct the starting direction.
5. Keeping the middle mouse button pressed, click the left mouse button. Move the cursor left and right to walk through the model. The further away you drag the cursor from the center of the view, the greater the change in direction.
6. Toggle the direction of the walk from forward to backward by clicking the left mouse button.

7. To increase or decrease the speed of the walk, press <Page Up> or <Page Down>, respectively. You can also click the (Accelerate) or (Decelerate) icon before starting the walk. Each click accelerates or decelerates the walk by approximately 40%.

8. To stop walking, release the middle mouse button.

9. Click the (Examine Mode) icon to return to Examine mode.

2.3 Model Visualization

Rendering a Model

Although you are working with a Solid Model, you can change how the geometry displays. These options can be accessed in the **View mode** flyout in the View toolbar, as shown in Figure 2–7.

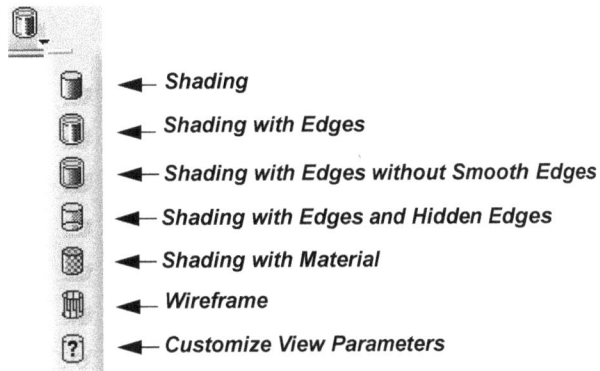

← *Shading*

← *Shading with Edges*

← *Shading with Edges without Smooth Edges*

← *Shading with Edges and Hidden Edges*

← *Shading with Material*

← *Wireframe*

← *Customize View Parameters*

Figure 2–7

An example of the first five options listed in the View mode toolbar is shown in Figure 2–8.

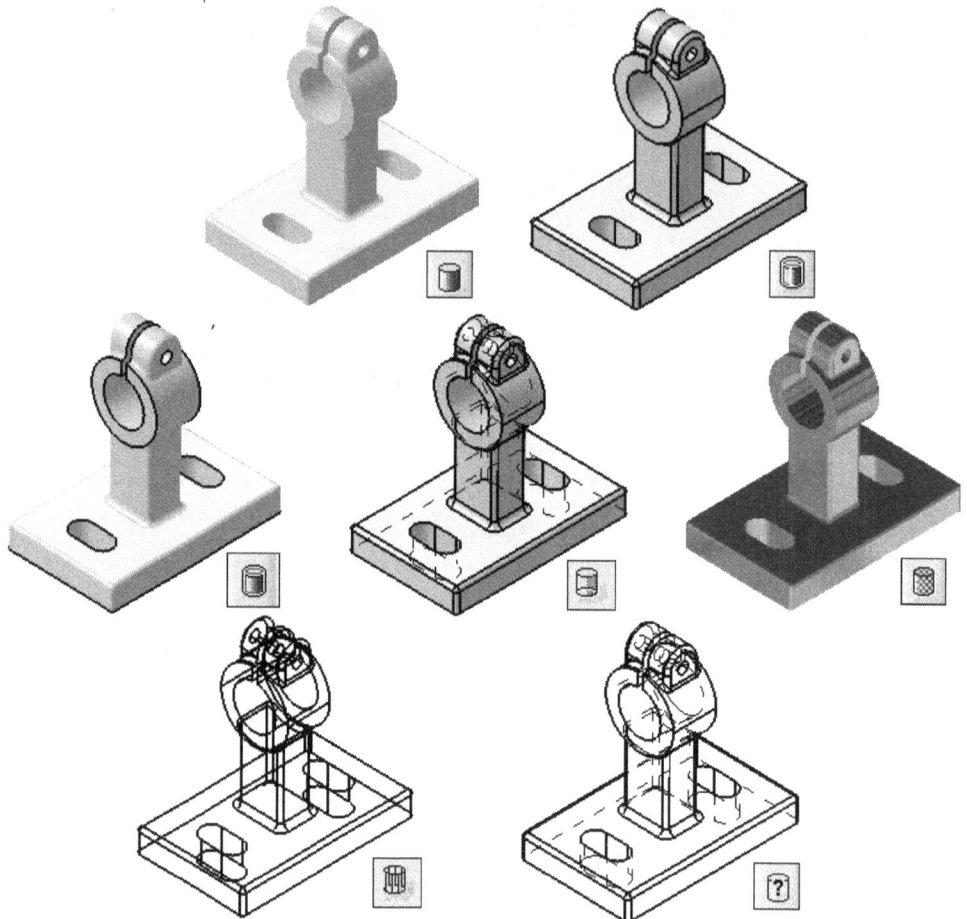

Figure 2–8

To change the customized view once one has been created, select View>Rendered Style>Customize View.

You can use customized Views to suit your preferences, such as displaying the model with hidden edges shown, with the material shown, or with faceted faces. To create an initial Customized view, click the ![icon] (Customized View Parameter) icon.

2.4 Specification Tree

The specification tree displays a variety of information about the model. It displays the parts that create the assembly and the features that combine to create each part. The components/features display in the order in which they were created. The specification tree also provides quick access to parameters, functions, material, and commonly-used measurements. The specification tree for a Coupling Assembly with three components is shown in Figure 2–9.

The specification tree can be quickly toggled on and off by pressing <F3>.

Click on the circle to expand/collapse parts of the tree. A ✚ symbol means that branch can be expanded. A ⬓ symbol means the branch can be collapsed.

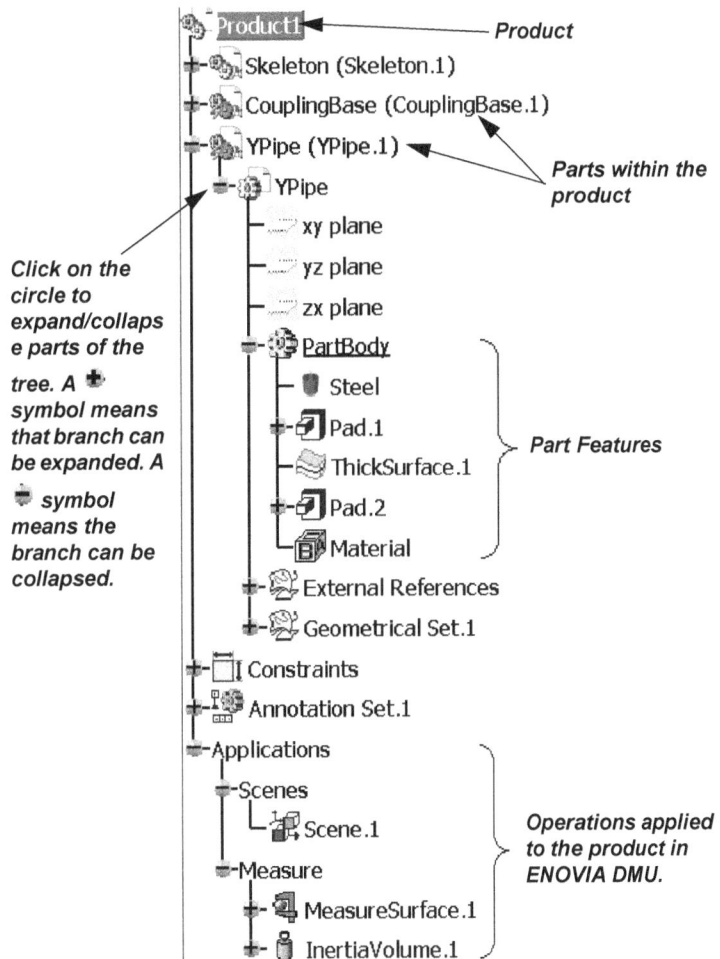

Figure 2–9

Hide/Show

CATIA enables you to hide or show certain elements on the model. Parts, annotations, measurements, or features can be hidden from display using the **Hide** and **Show** commands. Hiding a feature clarifies the display by placing it in an invisible work space.

To hide an item from display, select it in the specification tree, right-click and select **Hide/Show** as shown in Figure 2–10.

Alternatively, you can click the [icon] (Hide/Show) icon in the View toolbar. To redisplay the item, select the feature in the specification tree, right-click, and select **Hide/Show**.

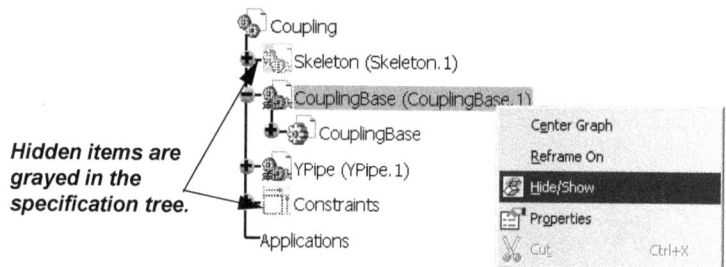

Hidden items are grayed in the specification tree.

Figure 2–10

To swap between the visible and invisible working spaces, click

the [icon] (Swap visible space) icon in the View toolbar. Any features that have been hidden are shown in a separate working space (invisible). Click the icon again to return to the visible working space.

Moving the Specification Tree

The specification tree can be panned and zoomed by clicking the left mouse button on a specification tree line segment, as shown in Figure 2–11. The model dims, indicating that the specification tree is active. Once the tree is active, mouse controls to pan and zoom the model affect the tree and not the model. Click the left mouse button again on a line segment of the specification tree to reactivate the model.

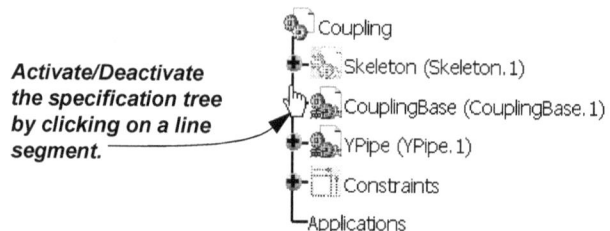

Activate/Deactivate the specification tree by clicking on a line segment.

Figure 2–11

Practice 2a

View a Part

Practice Objectives

- Open a model.
- View the model from different orientations.
- Use Fly mode.
- Change the display settings for the model.

In this practice, you will open a coupling assembly and visually examine the product. To examine the file, you will change the orientation of the model, use the Fly mode and adjust the visual display. Icons for the various tasks used in this practice are all found in the View toolbar shown in Figure 2–12.

Figure 2–12

Task 1 - Open the assembly.

The files for this practice can be found in the CouplingAssembly directory.

1. Click the ☞ (Open) icon in the Standard toolbar to open a model.

2. Select **CouplingAssembly.CATProduct**.

3. Click **Open**. The part displays as shown in Figure 2–13.

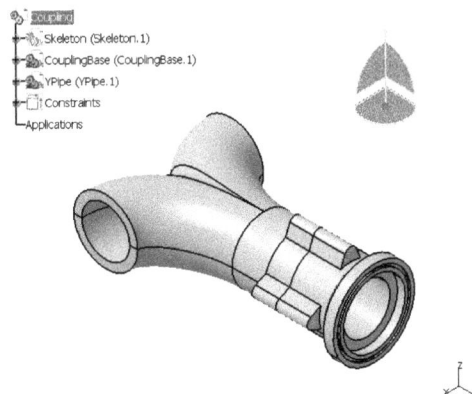

Figure 2–13

Task 2 - Change the display of the model.

1. Change the display to Shading by clicking the ▣ (Shading) icon in the **View mode** flyout, as shown in Figure 2–14.

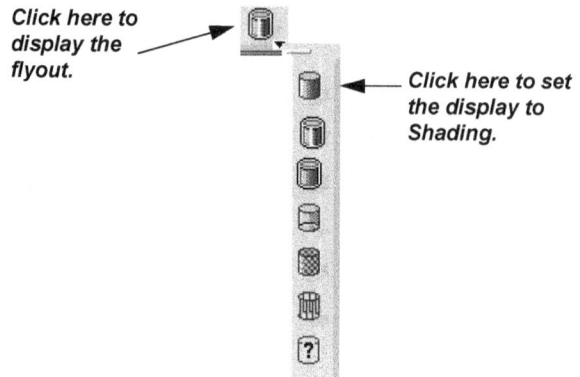

Click here to display the flyout.

Click here to set the display to Shading.

Figure 2–14

2. Repeat the above step to set the display to ▣ (Shading with Edges), ▣ (Shading with Edges without Smooth Edges), ▣ (Shading With Edges and Hidden Lines), and ▣ (Wireframe).

3. Set the display to [?] (Custom View).

4. Set the options as shown in Figure 2–15 and click **OK**.

*The Custom View Modes dialog box can also be accessed by selecting **View>Render Style>Customize View**.*

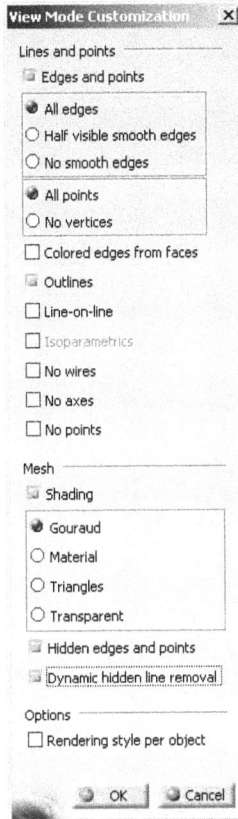

Figure 2–15

The model displays as shown in Figure 2–16.

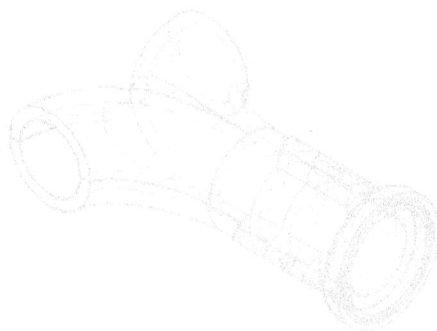

Figure 2–16

Task 3 - Use the Quick Views toolbar to change the model orientation.

1. Click the ⬭ (Shading With Edges without Smooth Edges) icon.

2. Change the display to Front by clicking the ⬭ (Front) icon in the **Quick View** flyout, as shown in Figure 2–17.

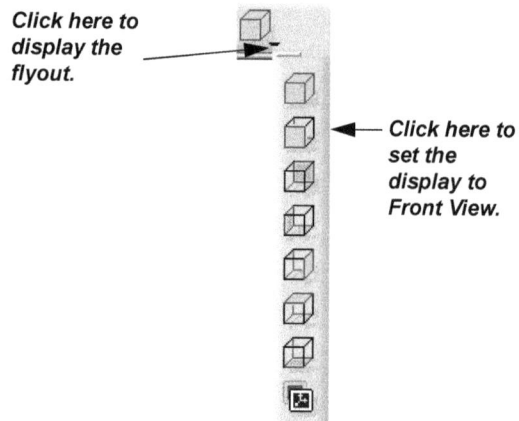

Click here to display the flyout.

Click here to set the display to Front View.

Figure 2–17

3. Repeat the above step for the ⬭ (Back), ⬭ (Right), ⬭ (Left), ⬭ (Top), and ⬭ (Bottom) quick views.

4. Return to the Isometric quick view.

Task 4 - Use the toolbar icons and menus to zoom, pan and spin the model.

1. Click the ⬭ (Zoom In) icon several times to zoom in.

2. Click the ⬭ (Fit All In) icon to fit the model in the window.

3. Click the ⬭ (Zoom Out) icon several times to zoom out.

4. Select **View>Zoom Area** in the menu bar. Use the left mouse button to draw a box around the area you want to zoom in on, as shown in Figure 2–18.

Click and hold here.

Release here.

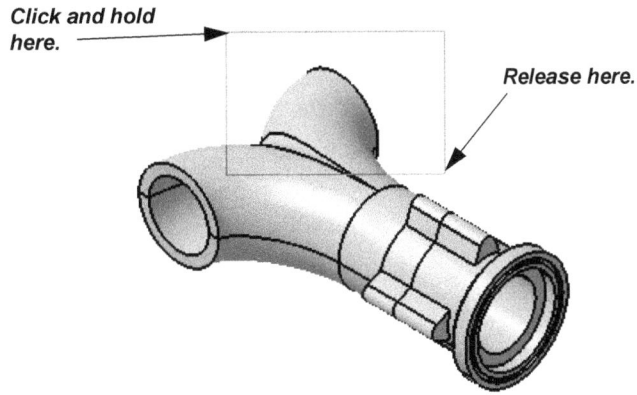

Figure 2–18

5. Click the ⊕ (Pan) icon. The icon turns orange to indicate that it is active.

6. Place the cursor near the bottom of the graphics window, hold the left mouse button, and drag the cursor to the top of the screen. You have panned the model up.

7. The ⊕ (Pan) icon no longer displays orange. This means you need to click this icon each time you want to pan.

8. Click the ⊕ (Fit All In) icon to fit the model in the window.

9. Click the ⟳ (Rotate) icon. Hold the left mouse button and move the cursor to rotate the model. The ⟳ (Rotate) icon behaves in the same manner as the ⊕ (Pan) icon, where you must click the icon each time you want to rotate the model.

To center your model in your graphics window,

click the [icon] *(Fit All In) icon.*

Try repeating these mouse shortcuts when possible.

Task 5 - Use the mouse to dynamically rotate, pan, and zoom the model.

1. Return to the Isometric quick view and fit the entire model in the window.

2. Hold the middle mouse button and move the cursor to pan the model.

3. Hold the middle mouse button and click the right mouse button once. Move the cursor up and down to zoom in and out.

4. Press and hold the middle mouse button, then press and hold the right mouse button and move the cursor to rotate the model.

Task 6 - Use the specification tree to review the model geometry.

1. In the specification tree, select **YPipe** (**YPipe.1**). The component highlights in orange in the tree and on the model, as shown in Figure 2–19.

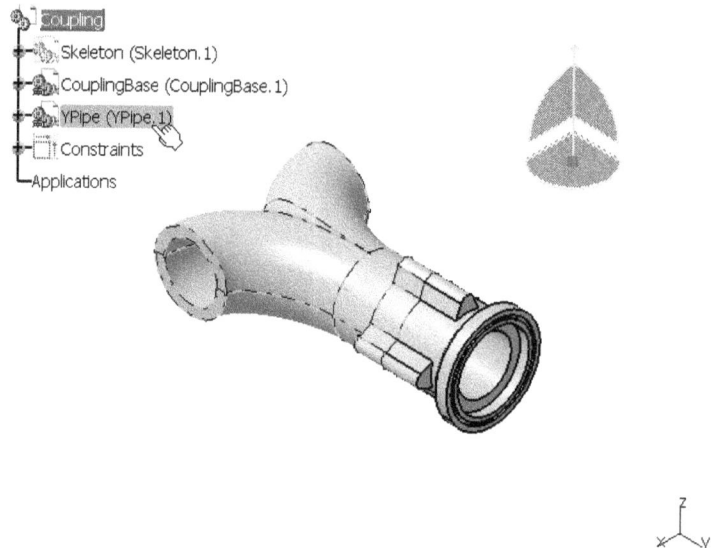

Figure 2–19

2. Highlight the other components in the model using the specification tree.

3. Expand the **CouplingBase** branch several times to display the features that combine to create the **CouplingBase** component.

4. Select **Pocket.1** in the specification tree, and the feature highlights on the model, as shown in Figure 2–20.

Click on the ✚ symbol beside the branch you want to expand. Click the ➖ symbol to collapse the branch again.

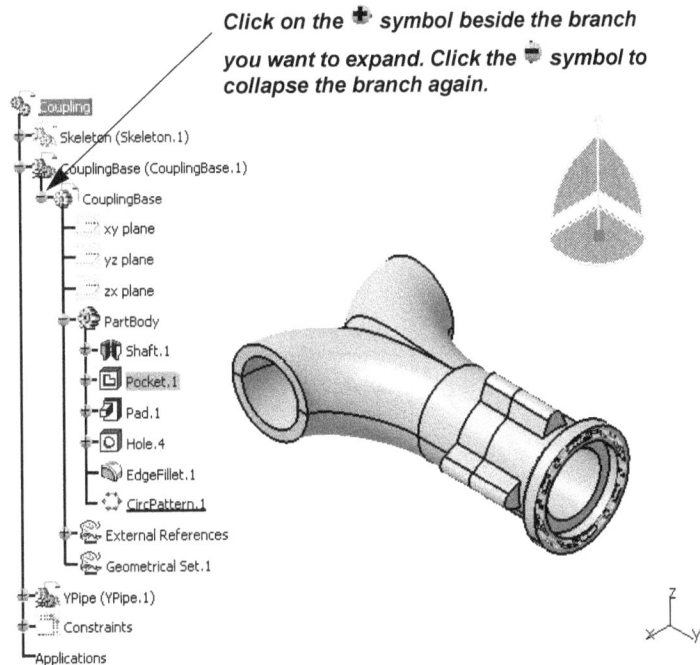

Figure 2–20

5. Select the coordinate system in the lower right corner of the screen, as shown in Figure 2–21. The model turns gray, indicating that it is inactive.

Figure 2–21

6. Select the coordinate system again to make it active.

7. Select a branch in the specification tree. This also activates the specification tree.

8. While the specification tree is active, press the middle mouse button to pan the specification tree.

9. Press the middle and left mouse buttons and zoom the specification tree in and out.

10. Select a branch in the specification tree again to reactivate the model.

11. Press <F3> several times to hide and show the specification tree.

Task 7 - Fly through the model.

To fly through a model, the view display must first be set to **Perspective**.

1. Select **View>Render Style>Perspective View** in the menu bar.

2. In the View toolbar, click the [icon] (Fly Mode) icon. The View toolbar changes to display the options available while in Fly mode, as shown in Figure 2–22.

Figure 2–22

3. Click the [icon] (Isometric View) icon to orient the model to the default Isometric view.

Design Considerations

Orienting the model while in Fly mode does not provide the same results as in Examine mode. If you want to start your fly through in a location other then those set up from the Quick Views or Named Views you might find it easier to orient the model before entering Fly mode.

4. Press the middle mouse button and pan the model to the position from which you want to start the fly through.

5. While still holding the middle mouse button, click the left mouse button to begin the fly through, as shown in Figure 2–23.

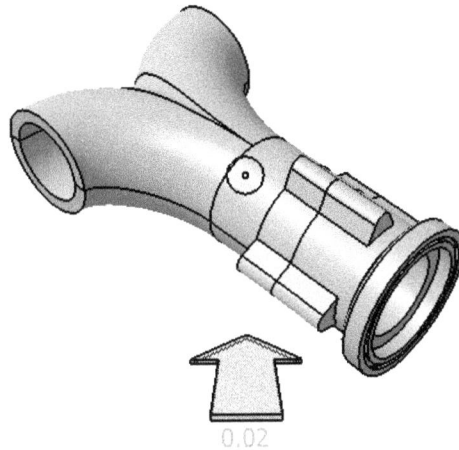

Figure 2–23

If the model flies off the screen, click the

 (Fit In All) icon to locate the model then repeat steps 4 and 5 to begin flying again.

6. Move the mouse up, down, left, and right to change the direction of the fly through.

7. Left-click to change the fly direction to backward. Left-click again to change direction to forward.

8. While flying, press <Page Up> and <Page Down> to change the speed of flight.

9. Release the middle mouse button to stop the fly through.

10. Click the (Examine Mode) icon to exit Fly mode.

Task 8 - Close the model.

1. Select **File>Close**.

2. If the system prompts you to save the changes to the model, click **No**.

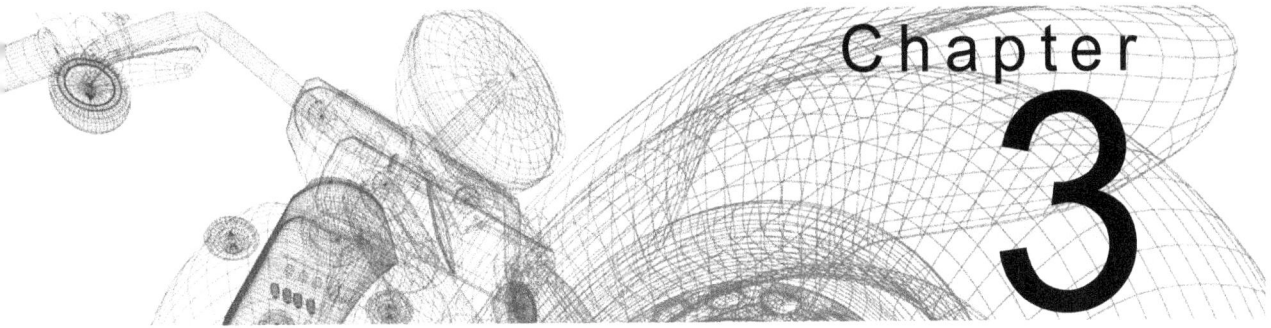

File Management

This chapter introduces the process of file management within ENOVIA DMU. Due to the associativity between a product and its components, ensuring that all modified data is saved is critical to working effectively in this workbench. In this chapter, you learn about **Save** operations and how to create a new product and manipulate its components.

Learning Objectives in this Chapter

- Understand the process for creating a new product structure.
- Learn how to use the compass.
- Understand the Save operations.

3.1 Creating a New Product Structure

New products can be created inside the DMU Navigator workbench. This enables you to assemble several files into one product for analysis. A variety of file formats can be added to the product.

General Steps

Use the following general steps to create a new product structure:

1. Create a new product.
2. Set properties on the product.
3. Add components to the product.

Step 1 - Create a new product.

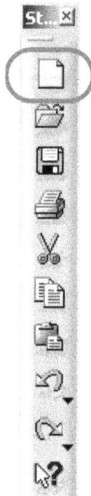

To create a new product, click the ⬜ (New) icon in the Standard toolbar. Select **Product** in the New dialog box, as shown in Figure 3–1, and click **OK**. A new empty product file is opened in the current DMU workbench.

Figure 3–1

Step 2 - Set properties on the product.

When a new product file is created, the system assigns a default filename and part number. The part number takes the form of Product#, where # is the number of new products in session.

To change the part number, select **Edit>Properties** in the menu bar. The Properties dialog box opens, as shown in Figure 3–2.

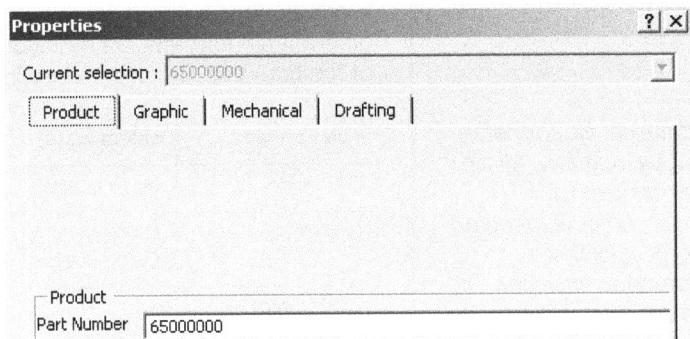

Figure 3–2

The part number is also the default filename of the CATProduct file. When you first save the model, you are prompted for a filename and a location on your computer for the file to reside. You can use different values for the part number and filename.

Step 3 - Add components to the product.

To add a component to the assembly, select the assembly in the specification tree, and select **Insert>Existing Component**. The File selection dialog box opens, as shown in Figure 3–3. To help locate the file more quickly, use the Files of Type drop-down list to filter out all files that are not of the correct format. Locate and select the file, and click **Open** to insert it.

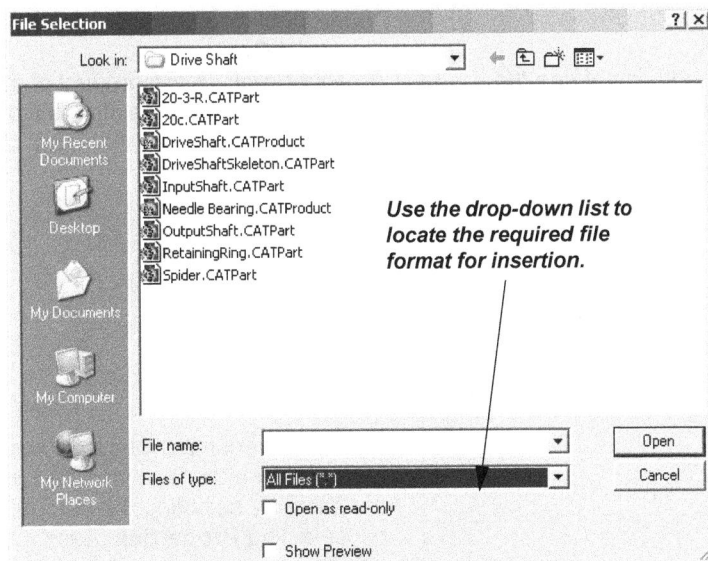

Figure 3–3

A component is an object that is added to an assembly. Many different file formats can be inserted into the Product file. Some of the common file formats are listed as follows:

Additional file formats can be inserted. All file formats can be accessed by expanding the Files of Type drop-down list in the File Selection dialog box, as shown in Figure 3–3.

File Format	Extension(s)
CATIA V4	.asm, .model
CATIA V5	.CATPart, .CATProduct, .CATAnalysis, .CATPSLayout, .CATShape, .cgr
Unigraphics	.prt
SolidWorks	.sldasm, .sldprtf
3D DXF	.dxf
Pro/ENGINEER	.asm, .prt
IDEAS	.iff, .mf, .mf1
SolidEdge	.par
ParaSolid	.x_b, .x_t
Neutral	.iges

Copy/Paste

Components that have already been inserted into the assembly can be duplicated using the **Copy** and **Paste** commands.

How To: Duplicate a Component

1. Right-click on the component in the specification tree and select **Copy**.
2. Right-click on the product in the specification tree and select **Paste**. An instance of the copied component displays at the end of the specification tree, as shown in Figure 3–4.

If you do not see the pasted component in the main window, it is probably on top of the original and needs to be moved.

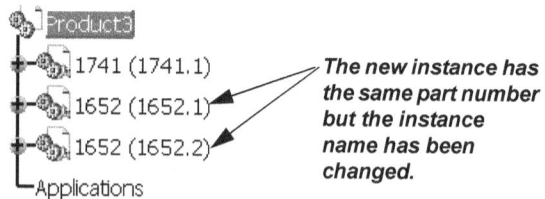

The new instance has the same part number but the instance name has been changed.

Figure 3–4

The Part number of the copied component remains the same but the instance name changes. You change the instance name by selecting the component, right-clicking and selecting **Properties**. Each instance must have a different instance name and the same part number.

3.2 Using the Compass

Once existing components are added to the assembly, they display in the default position and orientation. The compass is used to move components within the main window.

The compass displays in the upper right corner of the model window. When in the default assembly position, this tool can be used to perform the following functions:

- Freely rotate the model in all three directions.

- Rotate the model within a plane.

- Pan along one direction.

- Pan within a plane.

These functions are shown in Figure 3–5.

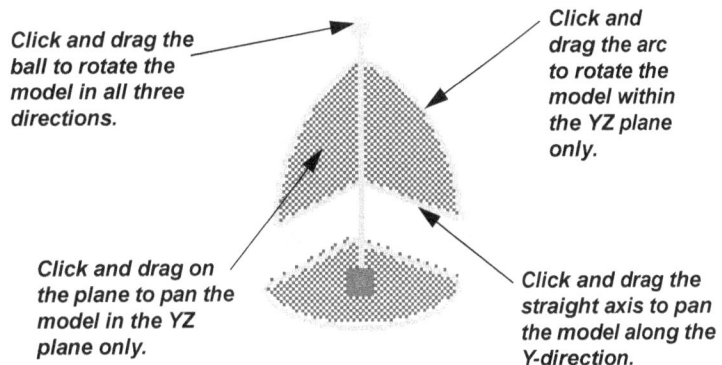

Click and drag the ball to rotate the model in all three directions.

Click and drag the arc to rotate the model within the YZ plane only.

Click and drag on the plane to pan the model in the YZ plane only.

Click and drag the straight axis to pan the model along the Y-direction.

Figure 3–5

The compass can also be used to move selected components relative to the rest of the assembly.

General Steps

Use the following general steps to move selected components with the compass:

1. Activate a component to move.
2. Move the component.
3. Complete the movement.

Step 1 - Activate a component to move.

Move the cursor over the red dot in the compass until it changes to a Move symbol, as shown in Figure 3–6. Once the Move symbol displays, hold the left mouse button to move the compass.

Once the Move symbol displays, press and hold the left mouse button to move the compass.

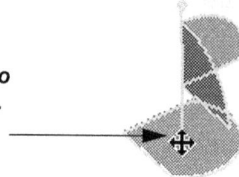

Figure 3–6

Drag the compass to the component to be moved. The compass snaps and reorients to the geometry belonging to the component, as shown in Figure 3–7. Once the orientation is correct, release the left mouse button to place the compass.

The Z-axis of the compass has snapped to the cylindrical features axis.

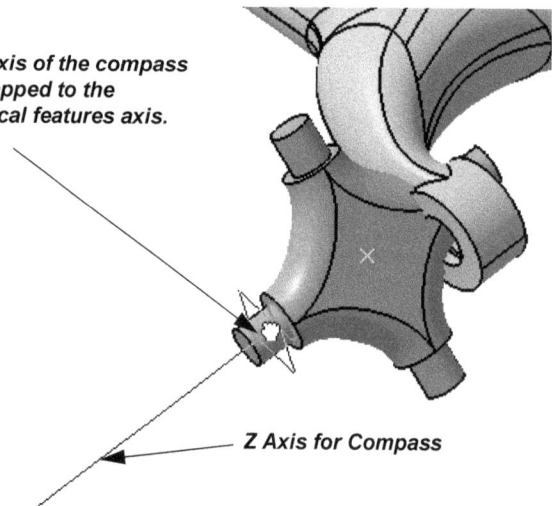

Z Axis for Compass

Figure 3–7

Once the compass has snapped to a component, the compass turns green. If the compass does not turn green, select the component from the model or specification tree to activate the movement of the selected component. You can activate any component for movement; it does not need to be the component the compass is snapped to. You can also activate multiple components by selecting them while holding <Ctrl>.

Automatic Snap

Toggle off this option after you have finished moving components.

You can automatically snap the compass to a selected object by right-clicking on the compass and selecting **Snap Automatically to Selected Object**, as shown in Figure 3–8.

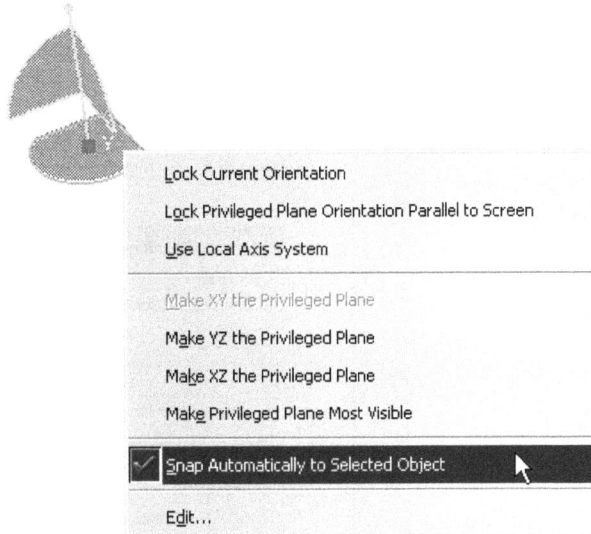

Lock Current Orientation
Lock Privileged Plane Orientation Parallel to Screen
Use Local Axis System

Make XY the Privileged Plane
Make YZ the Privileged Plane
Make XZ the Privileged Plane
Make Privileged Plane Most Visible

✓ Snap Automatically to Selected Object

Edit...

Figure 3–8

Once the option is activated, select the component you want to move from the model or specification tree. The compass automatically snaps to the selected component, as shown in Figure 3–9.

The system automatically selects the orientation of the compass based on the origin of the selected component.

The compass snaps to the selected component automatically and turns green.

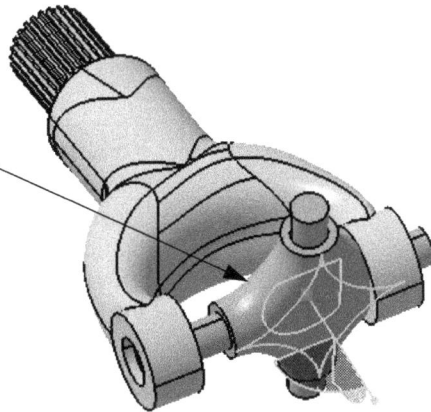

Figure 3–9

Step 2 - Move the component.

Once the compass is activated on the component, only compass movements control the selected component.

More precise movements of a component can be achieved by right-clicking on the compass and selecting **Edit**. The Parameters for Compass Manipulation dialog box, shown in Figure 3–10, enables you to enter exact translation or rotational increment values for precise movements.

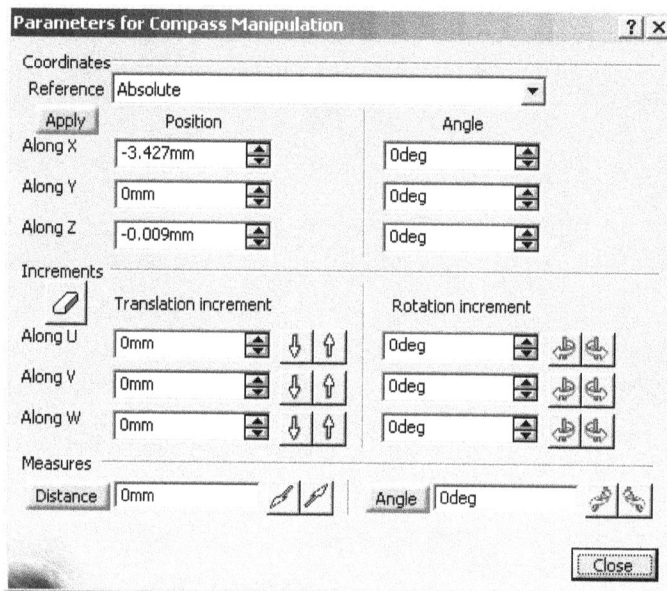

Figure 3–10

Step 3 - Complete the movement.

Once the component has been moved to the correct location, complete the movement by selecting another component to move. You can also click anywhere on the screen to deactivate the compass control of the component. The compass returns to its default color and control of the entire assembly. To return the compass back to the default position, select **View>Reset Compass**, or drag the compass off the model.

3.3 Save Operations

New or modified files should be saved frequently to prevent data loss. Files can be saved using a variety of options:

- Save
- Save As
- Save All
- Save Management
- Send To

Save

To save a file without renaming it, click the (Save) icon in the Standard toolbar or select **File>Save** in the menu bar. Using this option requires no further input from you.

Save As

If the file is being saved for the first time, the **Save As** option is performed automatically. You can also use this option to rename a file or save it to another format. Select **File>Save As** to open the Save As dialog box shown in Figure 3–11. The current name of the file displays in the *File name* field. To rename the file, enter a new name in the *File name* field. Click **Save** to save the file to the hard drive.

By default, the file is saved as a .CATProduct file. You can change the file formats by selecting it in the Save as type drop-down list.

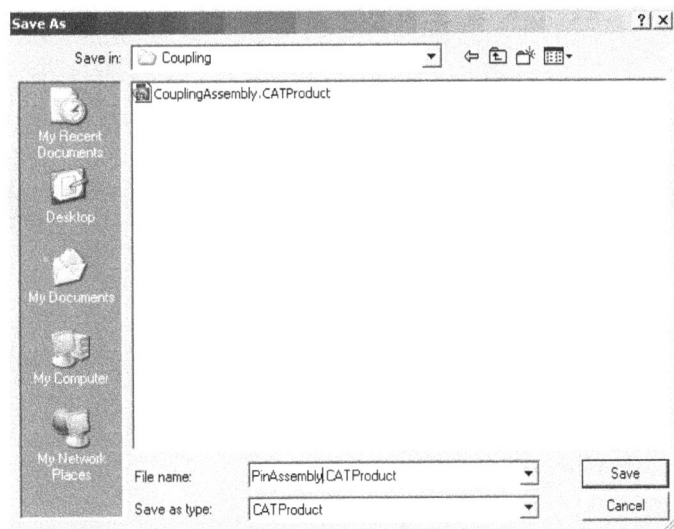

Figure 3–11

Save All

The **Save all** option performs the **Save** command on all open modified documents. This enables you to save several open documents simultaneously. To perform the operation, select **File>Save All**. If the **Save** operation can be performed on the documents without any user input, a prompt displays, as shown in Figure 3–12. Click **Yes** to save all modified open documents.

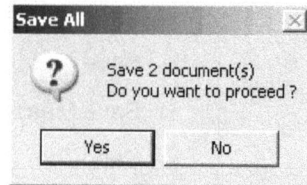

Figure 3–12

If any of the files to be saved require additional user input, the prompt shown in Figure 3–13 displays. Click **OK** to continue.

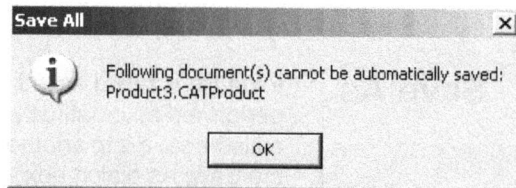

Figure 3–13

If documents cannot be saved automatically, the Save All dialog box opens. It lists all of the open modified files that require additional input to be saved. For example, in Figure 3–14, two files require additional input before they can be saved. The first file is a new file, indicating that it has never been saved to the hard drive before. The second file is a read-only file and cannot be saved to the same location with the same name. In both cases, select the file and click **Save As** to perform a **Save As** operation on the selected file. Once all files listed in the window have had a **Save As** performed on them, click **OK** to complete the **Save All**.

A Save As has already been performed on this file.

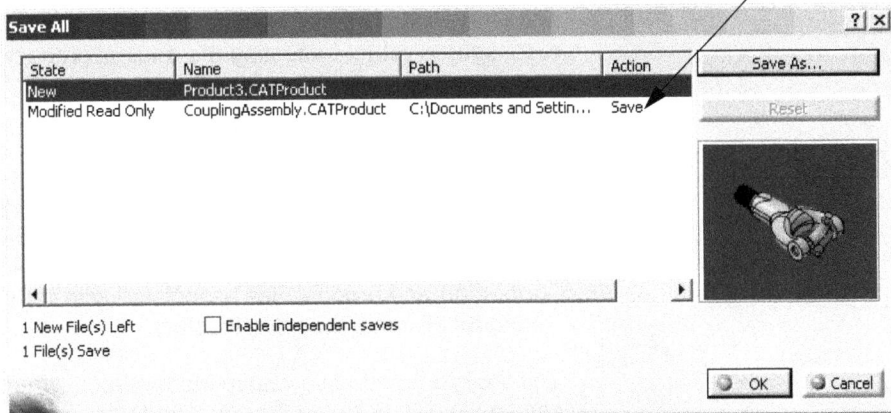

Figure 3–14

Save Management

The **Save Management** option enables you to control where all open files are saved. This option is useful when you need to rename multiple files.

How To: Rename the Part Files of a Product

1. Select **File>Save Management**.
2. Select the part file in the Save Management dialog box, as shown in Figure 3–15.

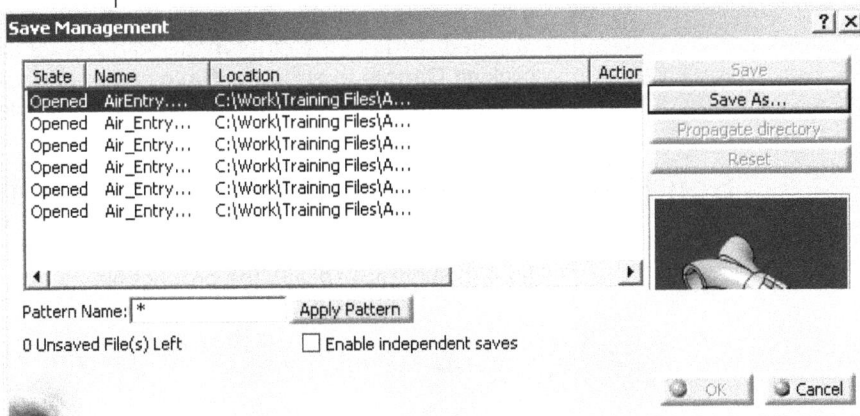

Figure 3–15

3. Click **Save As** and enter a new name for the part file.

Save Management is also useful for exploring alternative product development paths. **Propagate directory** enables you to create a copy of a complete assembly in a different directory. The part and product files in the new directory can then be modified and reconfigured without affecting the original product and part files.

How To: Propagate a Directory

1. Select a product file in the Save Management dialog box.
2. Click **Save As**. Specify a different directory in which to save the product file.
3. Click **Propagate directory**. The system saves a copy of all of the part and product files associated with the selected product file into the new directory.

You are prompted to use Save Management when attempting to save a file with links to other modified documents. For example, when a product being saved contains a part that has been altered, the prompt shown in Figure 3–16 displays.

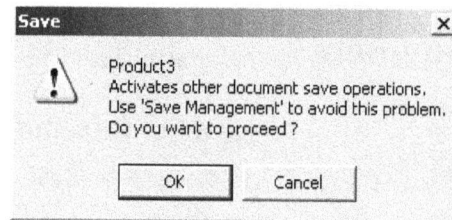

Figure 3–16

If you proceed with the **Save** option, only the selected document is saved, and not the other modified documents. Instead, try clicking **Cancel** to abort the **Save** option and using the **Save Management** or **Save All** option to avoid problems.

Send To

The **Send To** option copies a product and all linked files to a specified directory, or attaches them to an e-mail. This ensures that all of the files required to open a product file are included in an e-mail or moved with the product file.

In this example, **Send To Directory** was selected. The Send To Mail dialog box is the same, without the Copy To field at the bottom of the dialog box.

How To: Perform a Send To operation:

1. Select **File>Send To>Mail**, or **File>Send To>Directory**. The Send to Directory dialog box opens. The top window lists the selected product file and all files linked to it, as shown in Figure 3–17.

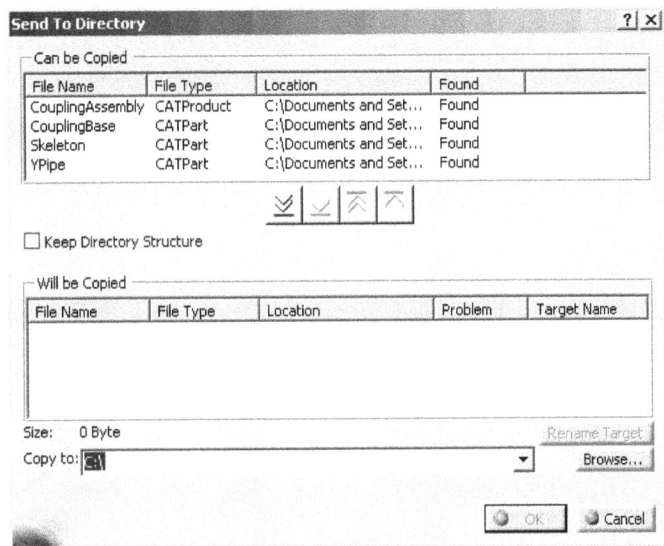

Figure 3–17

2. Click to copy the product and all of its associated files to the E-mail/directory. The files move from the top window to the bottom window, as shown in Figure 3–18.

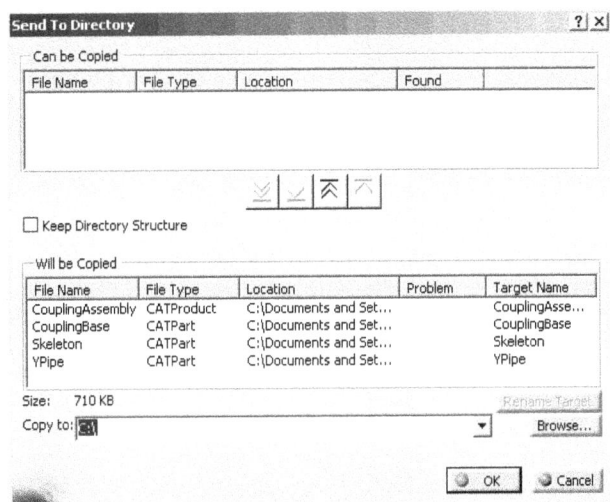

Figure 3–18

3. If the Send To Directory operation is performed, the files are copied to the directory indicated in the Copy To field. To change the directory, click **Browse** and locate the correct directory. The Copy To field updates to reflect the change.
4. Click **OK** to complete the copy.
5. If you have selected to **Send To Mail**, an e-mail displays with the copied files attached. If you have selected **Send To Directory**, a message window displays, notifying you that the copy was successful, as shown in Figure 3–19.

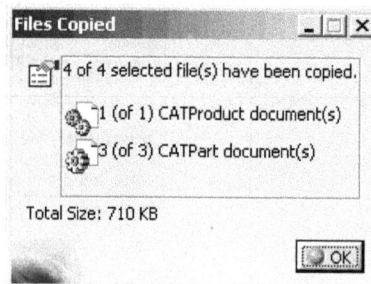

Figure 3–19

Practice 3a

File Creation

Practice Objectives

- Open a new product file.
- Insert components.
- Manipulate the components.
- Save the product file.

In this practice, you will create a new product file, insert two components, and position them using the compass. Typically, the files you will receive will be assembled using a CAD package so that each component is constrained correctly. There are times, however, when you might need to insert parts into a product file to run an analysis on them.

Task 1 - Create a new product file.

1. In the Standard toolbar, click the ⬜ (New) icon.

2. In the New dialog box select **Product**, as shown in Figure 3–20.

Figure 3–20

3. Click **OK**. The new product opens.

4. Right-click on **Product1** in the specification tree and select **Properties**, as shown in Figure 3–21.

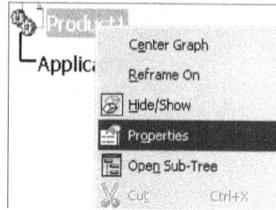

Figure 3–21

5. In the *Product* tab, change the name of the Part Number to **CouplingAssembly**.

6. Click **OK** to close the Properties dialog box and update the part number in the specification tree.

Task 2 - Insert the first component.

The files for this practice can be found in the **Coupling** directory.

1. Right-click on the Product in the specification tree and select **Components>Existing Component**.

2. Select **CouplingBase.CATPart** and click **Open**. The component is inserted into the assembly as shown in Figure 3–22.

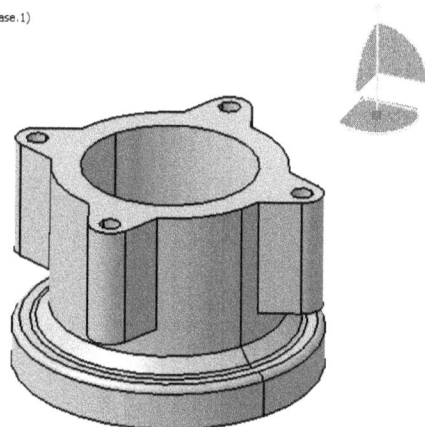

Figure 3–22

3. Use the compass to manipulate the model. Try each of the different compass movements to see how it moves the model, as shown in Figure 3–23.

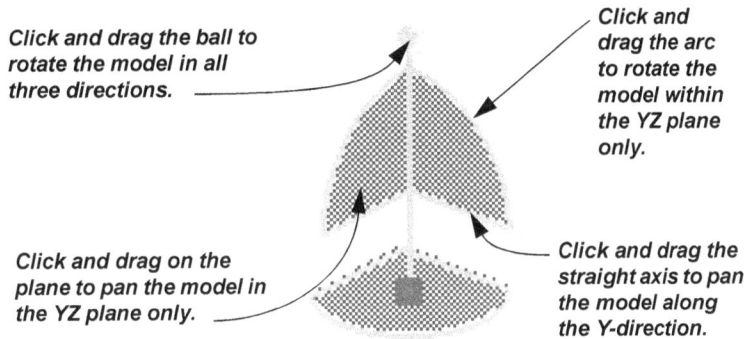

Click and drag the ball to rotate the model in all three directions.

Click and drag the arc to rotate the model within the YZ plane only.

Click and drag on the plane to pan the model in the YZ plane only.

Click and drag the straight axis to pan the model along the Y-direction.

Figure 3–23

4. Return to Isometric view using the **Quick View** flyout.

Task 3 - Insert the second component.

---

1. Select the CouplingAssembly in the specification tree. Select **Insert>Existing Component.**

2. In the Coupling directory, select **YPipe.CATPart** to insert. The model displays as shown in Figure 3–24.

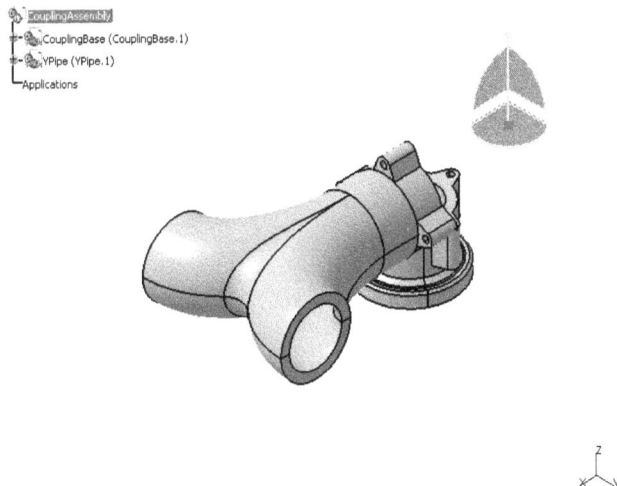

Figure 3–24

Task 4 - Manipulate the YPipe using the compass.

1. Use the compass again from its default location; both parts move.

2. Select the red dot in the center of the compass. While holding the left mouse button, drag the compass to a location anywhere on the YPipe. The compass snaps to the pipe, as shown in Figure 3–25. Release the left mouse button to place the compass and it turns green.

If the compass does not turn green after moving it to a location on the YPipe, select the YPipe in the specification tree.

Compass snaps to the geometry of the YPipe.

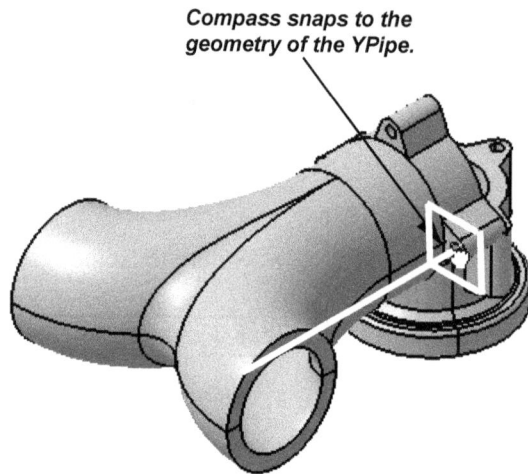

Figure 3–25

Task 5 - Edit compass manipulation.

1. Right-click on the compass and select **Snap Automatically to Select Object**.

2. Select the **YPipe** in the specification tree. The compass moves to the origin of the part, as shown in Figure 3–26.

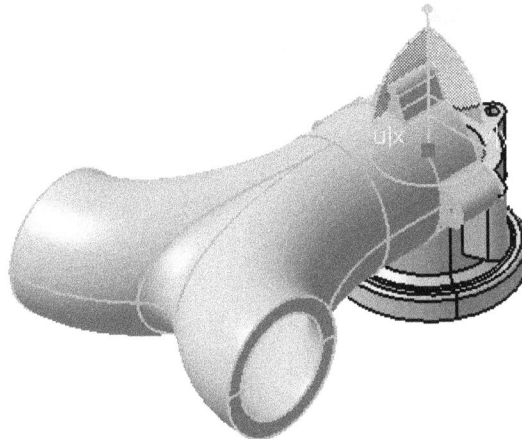

Figure 3–26

3. Right-click on the compass and select **Edit**.

4. Enter the position and angle values shown in Figure 3–27. Rotate the model **90°** about the Y-axis to place the part correctly.

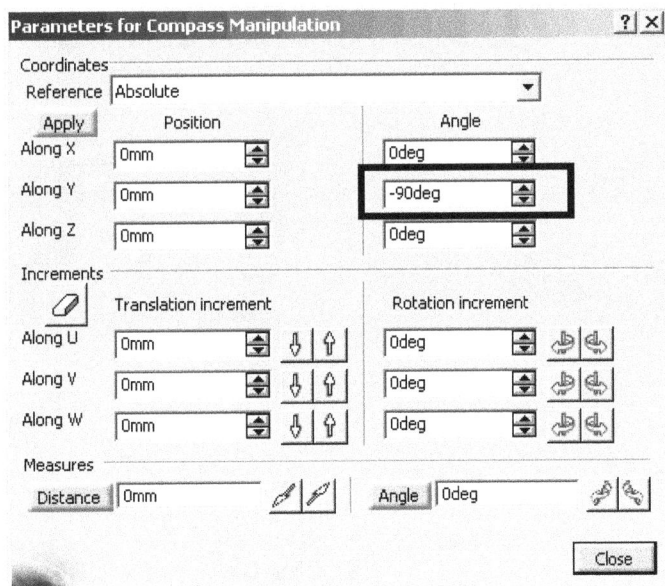

Figure 3–27

5. Click **Apply** to preview the move. The model displays as shown in Figure 3–28.

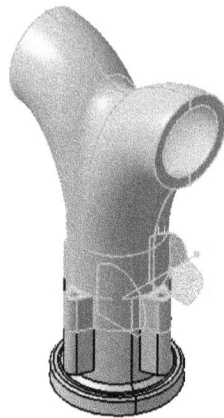

Figure 3–28

6. Change the rotation increment along the U-direction to **90°**, as shown in Figure 3–29.

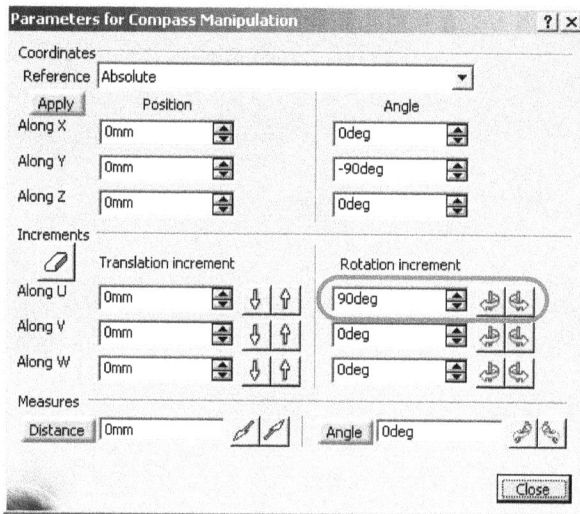

Figure 3–29

7. Click the ⬛ icon beside the rotation increment, as shown in Figure 3–29, to rotate the model 90°.

8. Click **Close** to complete the manipulation.

Task 6 - Reset the compass.

1. Select anywhere on the screen to deactivate the compass. The compass turns back to the default color.

2. Select **View>Reset Compass**. The compass moves back to the top right corner of the screen.

3. Right-click on the compass and ensure that no checkmark (✓) displays beside the **Snap Automatically to selected object** option. If there is a checkmark, reselect the option to toggle it off.

4. Use the compass again to manipulate the model; both components are once again moved with the compass.

Task 7 - Hide the reference plane.

A reference plane displays in the YPipe part and should not be displayed, so you will toggle it off.

1. Select the reference plane in the model to highlight it, as shown in Figure 3–30.

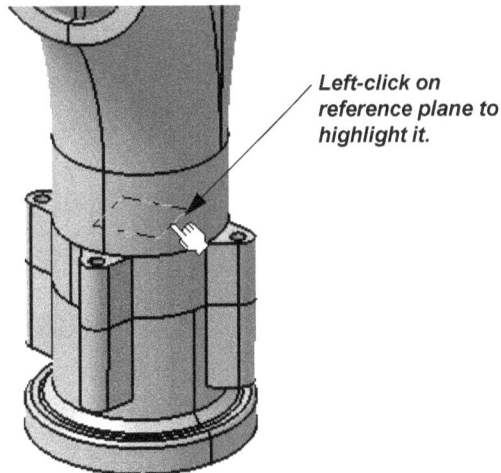

Left-click on reference plane to highlight it.

Figure 3–30

2. Right-click and select **Hide/Show**. The reference plane disappears from the display.

Task 8 - Save the assembly.

1. Click the ⊟ (Save) icon in the Standard toolbar. The Save As dialog box opens because this is the first time the document is saved.

2. Leave the default name of the file **CouplingAssembly** and click **Save**.

Design Considerations

A warning message displays as shown in Figure 3–31. It displays because the YPipe component was also changed (the reference plane was hidden). Because more then one model within this product requires saving, it is best to use the Save Management tool.

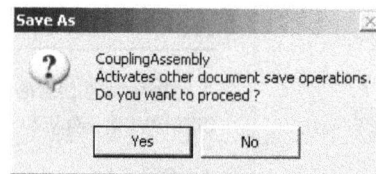

Figure 3–31

3. Click **No** in the warning message. Click **Cancel** in the Save As dialog box to abort the **Save**.

4. Select **File>Save Management**.

5. In the Save Management dialog box shown in Figure 3–32, the newly created product does not have a path to be saved to and the status of the YPipe is **Modified**.

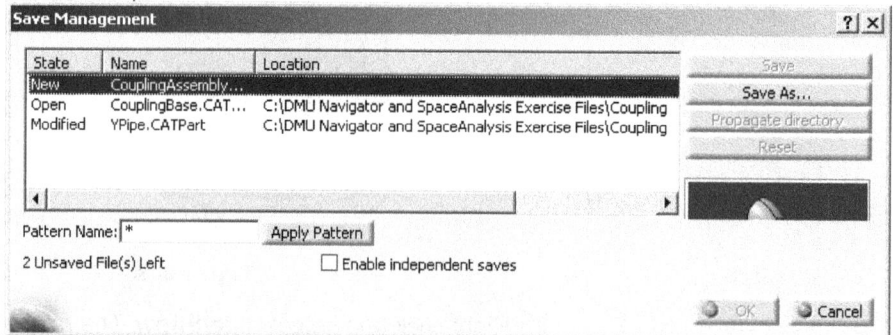

Figure 3–32

*If the New Folder name is not editable, select the new folder, right-click and select **Rename** to edit it again.*

6. Highlight **CouplingAssembly** in the Save Management dialog box and click **Save As**.

7. Leave the default filename.

8. Create a new directory inside the Coupling directory by clicking 🗂. Name the new folder **CouplingAssembly**.

9. Double-click on the new folder to save the file in this directory.

10. Click **Save**.

11. The Save Management dialog box updates to indicate the save path for the CouplingAssembly.

12. Since the YPipe and the CouplingBase components need to be saved to the same directory as their parent (the CouplingAssembly), click **Propagate directory**. The Save Management dialog box updates as shown in Figure 3–33.

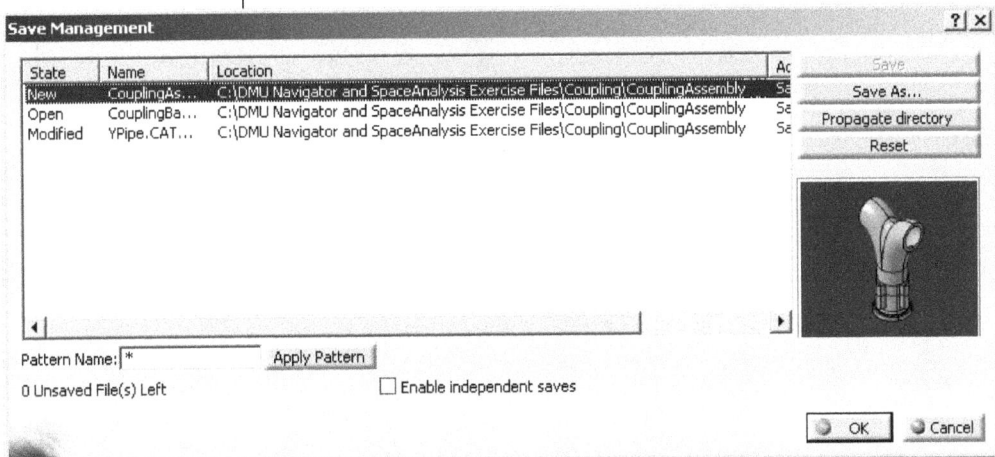

Figure 3–33

13. Click **OK** to save the files.

14. Close the file.

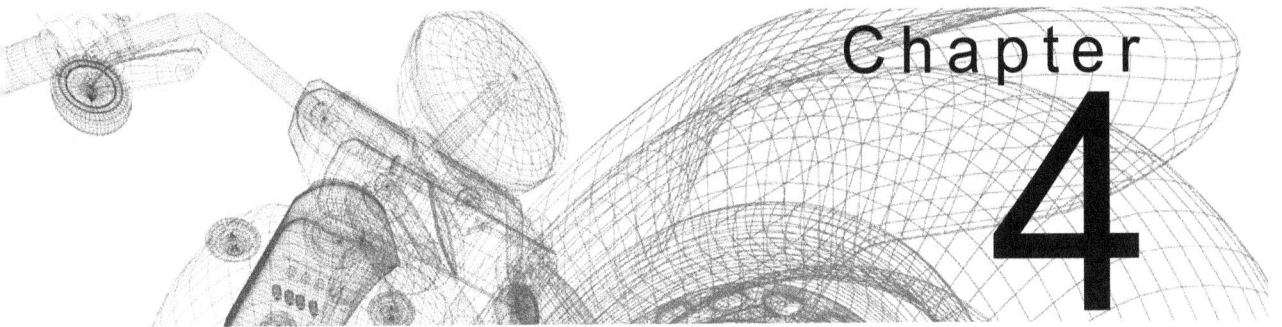

Measurement Tools

The DMU Navigator workbench contains three tools that can be used to extract measurements from a product file. This chapter introduces the process of using them to determine critical design information about an assembly or part.

Learning Objectives in this Chapter

- Learn how to measure objects.
- Learn how to measure inertia in a model.

4.1 Measuring an Item

The **Measure Item** operation enables you to measure properties of a single entity and save the measurements for future reference. You can select points, edges, surfaces, or part bodies from the specification tree or the screen to measure.

General Steps

Use the following general steps to create a measurement:

1. Activate the measurement operation.
2. Select the measurement type.
3. Customize the measurement, if required.
4. Select the feature to measure.
5. Save the measurement, if required.
6. Complete the measurement operation.

Step 1 - Activate the measurement operation.

Click the  (Measure Item) icon in the DMU Measure toolbar to open the Measure Item dialog box shown in Figure 4–1.

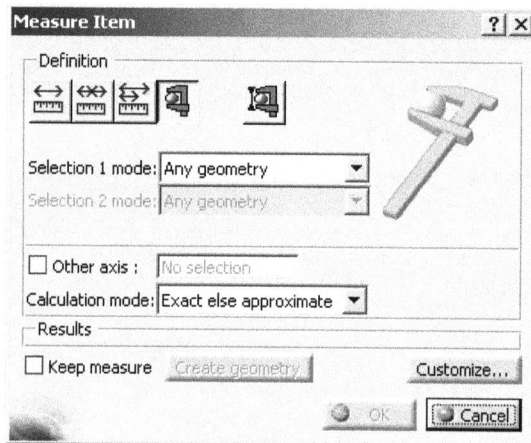

Figure 4–1

Standard Mode Measure Between

The ↔ (Measure Between) icon is the default Measure Between mode. It is a two-click measurement tool that enables you to measure between two selected items of the same or mixed types. You can select in the specification tree or directly from the model. The different selectable item types for the Measure Between tool are shown in Figure 4–2.

You can also access the standard Measure Between mode by

clicking the ↔ icon in the toolbar.

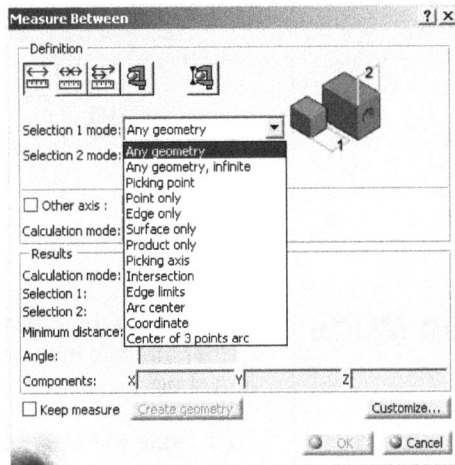

Figure 4–2

The Measure Between tool can be used to measure the distance or angle between items. An example of a measurement between two selected hole centers is shown in Figure 4–3.

The results can be customized using the same method as the Measure Item tool.

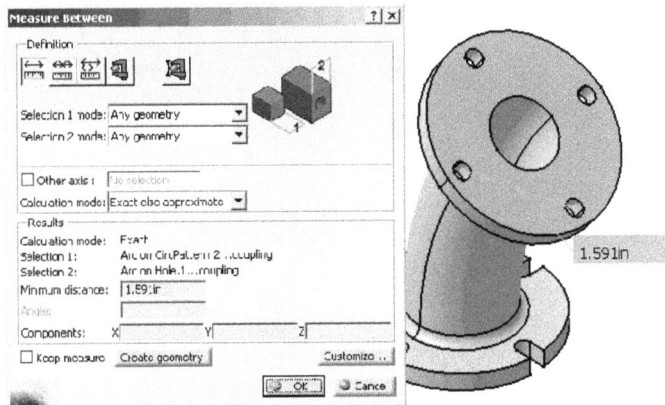

Figure 4–3

When selecting hole and arc centers, you can display an axis by moving the cursor over the approximate center of the hole and arc, as shown in Figure 4–4.

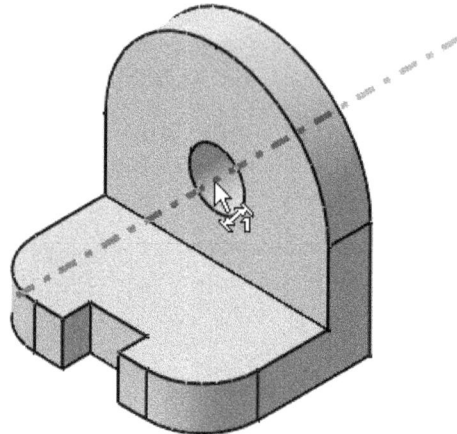

Figure 4–4

Chain Mode

The Measure Between in Chain Mode tool enables you to quickly gather multiple measurements between pairs of selected items in a chain.

To activate the Measure Between in Chain Mode tool, click the

 (Measure Between in Chain Mode) icon in the Measure Between dialog box. The three measurements shown in Figure 4–5 can be created using four item selections in Chain mode instead of six item selections in Standard mode.

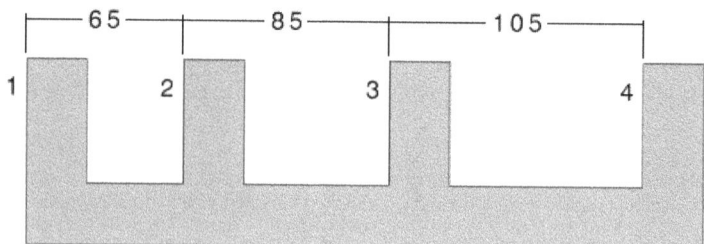

Figure 4–5

The results can be customized using the same method as the Measure Item tool.

Use the following steps to create the measurements shown in Figure 4–5 using Chain mode:

1. Select **Edge 1** and **Edge 2**. The measurement distance of 65 millimeters is created.

2. Select **Edge 3**. The measurement distance of 85 millimeters is created.

3. Select **Edge 4**. The measurement distance of 105 millimeters is created.

After the first measurement is created using Chain mode, the system creates measurements between any newly selected items and the last selected item.

Fan Mode

The Measure Between in Fan Mode tool enables you to quickly gather multiple measurements between one base item and any number of other items. To activate Fan mode, click the

[icon] (Measure between in Fan Mode) icon in the Measure Between dialog box.

The three measurements shown in Figure 4–6 can be created using four item selections in Fan mode instead of six item selections in Standard mode.

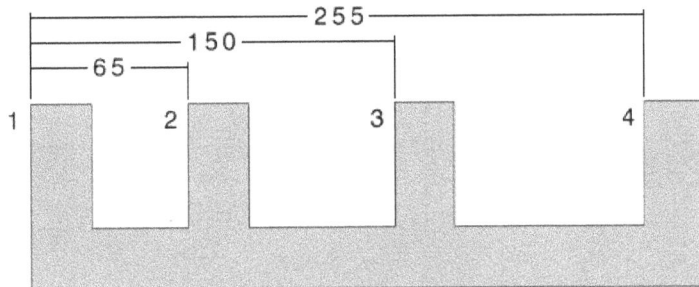

Figure 4–6

The results can be customized using the same method as the Measure Item tool.

Use the following steps to create the measurements shown in Figure 4–6 using Fan mode:

1. Select **Edge 1** and **Edge 2**. The measurement distance of 65 millimeters is created.

2. Select **Edge 3**. The measurement distance of 150 millimeters is created.

3. Select **Edge 4**. The measurement distance of 255 millimeters is created.

After the first measurement is created using Fan mode, the system creates measurements between any newly selected items and the first selected item (base item).

Measuring Thickness

The Thickness Measuring tool enables you to calculate the thickness of the model based on the selected face or edge. Thickness cannot be added to a measurement using the Customize dialog box. To calculate the thickness of a model, click the (Measure the thickness) icon in the Measure Item dialog box. An example of a thickness calculation is shown in Figure 4–7.

You must have license for DMU Space Analysis to use the Thickness Measurement tool. If you do not have a license, the Thickness icon does not appear in the Measure Item dialog box.

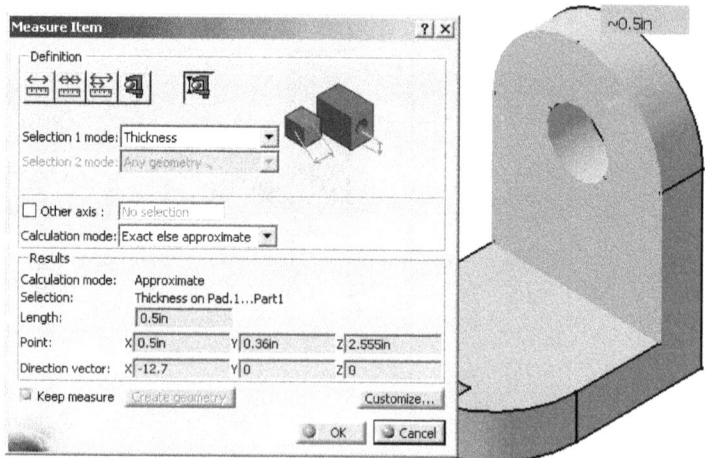

Thickness calculations are approximate.

Figure 4–7

Step 3 - Customize the measurement, if required.

The Measure Item results can be customized for a selected item by clicking **Customize**. The Measure Item Customization dialog box opens, as shown in Figure 4–8.

The default measurements can be changed by selecting and clearing options as required.

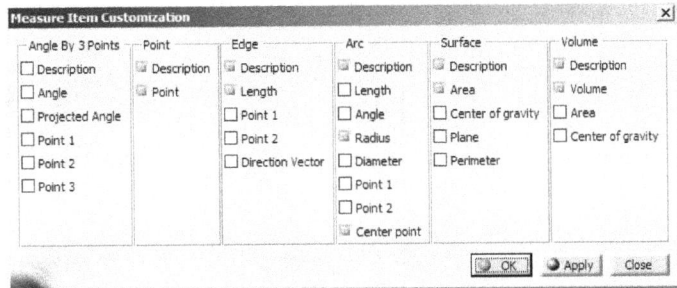

Figure 4–8

Step 4 - Select the feature to measure.

Select the element to measure in the specification tree, or directly on the model. The Measure Item dialog box updates to show the results of the calculation. Calculation results are also displayed on the model, as shown in Figure 4–9.

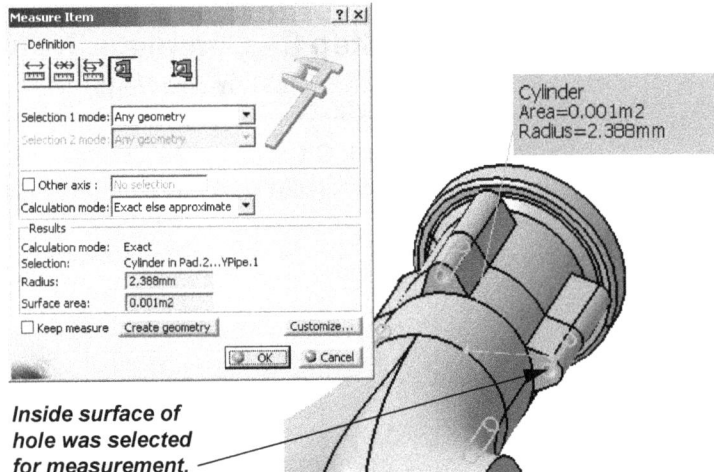

Inside surface of hole was selected for measurement.

Figure 4–9

Step 5 - Save the measurement, if required.

Once an item is measured, you can save the measurement with the model data. To save the measurement, select the **Keep Measure** option in the Measure Item dialog box, as shown in Figure 4–10.

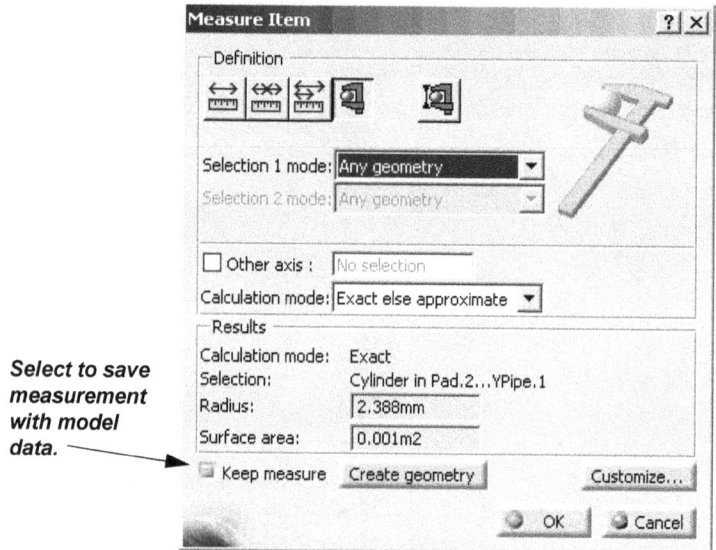

Select to save measurement with model data.

Figure 4–10

Step 6 - Complete the measurement operation.

Click **OK** to complete the measurement. It is added to the specification tree, as shown in Figure 4–11.

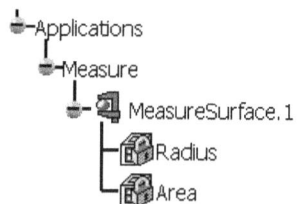

Figure 4–11

Updating Measurements

If modifications are made in the model that result in a change to a measured value (e.g., geometry change), the ⊚ symbol displays beside the measurement in the specification tree, indicating that the measured value is not updated.

Thickness calculations are not associative and cannot be updated.

To update the value, right-click on the measurement name and select **MeasureSurface.x object>Measure Update**, as shown in Figure 4–12.

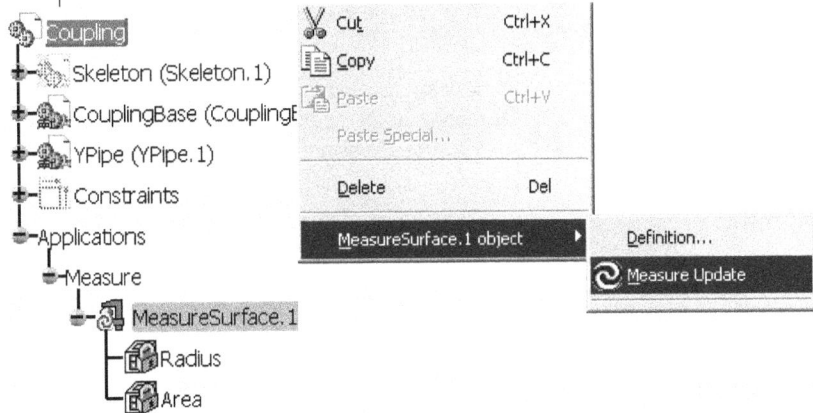

Figure 4–12

4.2 Measuring the Inertia of a Model

The Inertia tool calculates a model's mass properties based on a user-defined density. As with measurement calculations, the mass properties can be saved as features in the model.

Before measuring the inertia of the model, it is recommended that you first define the model's material properties.

Applying Material

When you apply a material to a model, the properties of the model (e.g., density and Young's Modulus) are defined. This ensures that accurate inertia values are computed for the model.

How To: Apply Material to a Part

Double-click on a graphic representing the required material in the Library dialog box to retrieve the material properties.

1. Click the [icon] (Apply Material) icon. The Material library opens as shown in Figure 4–13.

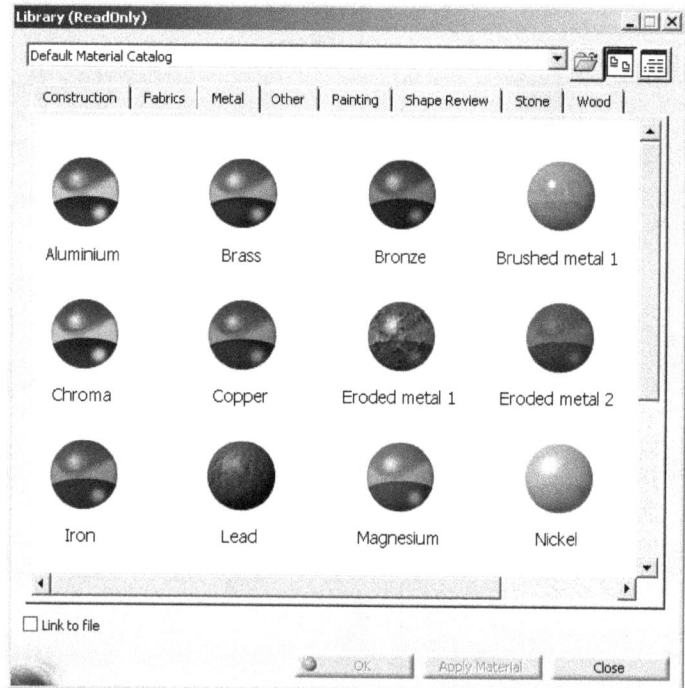

Figure 4–13

2. Select the material to apply. Material is categorized to make it simpler to locate the required type (e.g., fabrics, metal, or wood), as shown in Figure 4–13.
3. In the specification tree, select the part you want to apply selected material to and click **Apply Material**.
4. Repeat steps 2 and 3 for each part in the assembly.
5. Click **OK** to close the dialog box. The material applied to the part displays in the specification tree, as shown in Figure 4–14.

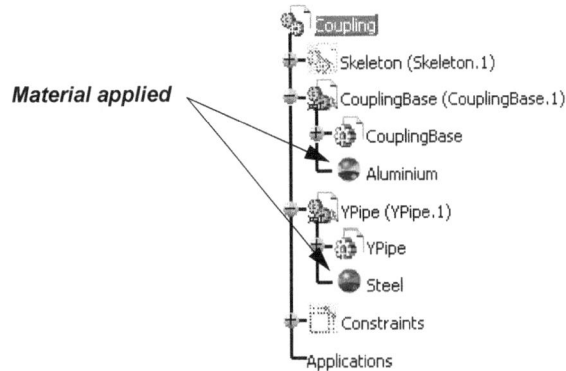

Material applied

Coupling
  Skeleton (Skeleton.1)
  CouplingBase (CouplingBase.1)
    CouplingBase
    Aluminium
  YPipe (YPipe.1)
    YPipe
    Steel
  Constraints
  Applications

Figure 4–14

Displaying Material on Model

Once material has been applied to a model, it can be displayed using the Shade with Material render mode, or with the **Customize View** option.

How To: Display Material with the Customize View Option

1. Select **View>Render Style>Customize View**.
2. In the View Mode Customization dialog box, select the **Material** and **Shading** options, as shown in Figure 4–15.

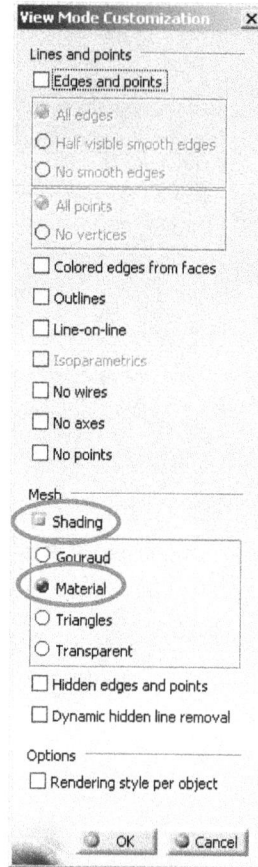

Figure 4–15

3. Click **OK** to close the View Mode Customization dialog box and apply the changes.

Inertia Measurement

Inertia calculations can be done on the entire assembly, assembly components, component features, or feature geometry - in this case, surface area is calculated (not volume).

How To: Compute Mass Properties

1. Select the items (i.e., assembly, components, or features) to perform a mass properties calculation. To avoid selecting the wrong items, select them directly in the specification tree. Select any geometry item (e.g., a face) from the screen. You can calculate the mass properties on more then one item at a time by holding <Ctrl> while selecting.

2. Click the [icon] (Measure Inertia) icon in the DMU Measure toolbar.

3. The results appear in the Measure Inertia dialog box as shown in Figure 4–16.

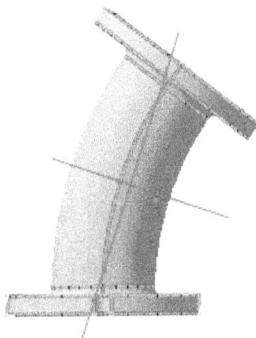

Measure Inertia ? x

Definition

Selection : Part2

Result

Calculation mode : Exact

Type : Volume

Characteristics

Volume	1.383e-005m3
Area	0.009m2
Mass	0.014kg
Density	1000kg_m3	◄——— *Enter new density here.*

Center Of Gravity (G)

Gx	1in
Gy	0.5in
Gz	0.419in

Inertia / G | Inertia / O | Inertia / P | Inertia / Axis | Inertia / Axis System

Inertia Matrix / G

| IoxG | 2.041e-006kgxm2 | IoyG | 4.768e-006kgxm2 | IozG | 5.083e-006kgxm2 |
| IxyG | 0kgxm2 | IxzG | 0kgxm2 | IyzG | 4.235e-022kgxm2 |

Principal Moments / G

| M1 | 2.041e-006kgxm2 | M2 | 4.768e-006kgxm2 | M3 | 5.083e-006kgxm2 |

☐ Keep measure   Create geometry   Export   Customize...

OK   Cancel

Figure 4–16

4. If a material was applied to the model, the density has been entered based upon the applied material. If no material has been applied, a default density is used and can be changed. To change the density of a part, enter the new density in the Density field and press <Enter>. When the density is changed, all of the measurements are recalculated.

5. To customize the results, click **Customize**. The results can be saved by selecting **Keep Measure**.

6. Click **OK** to complete the calculation. If the measurement was saved, the specification tree updates to display the new measurement.

Practice 4a | Taking Measurements

Practice Objectives

- Open an Assembly.
- Assign material to the part.
- Determine the mass, volume, and surface area of the part.
- Take a measurement.

In this practice, you will investigate a bore device. To determine the mass properties of the model, you will also need to apply material to the components.

Task 1 - Open the assembly.

1. Open **BoreDevice.CATProduct** in the BoreDevice directory. The assembly displays as shown in Figure 4–17.

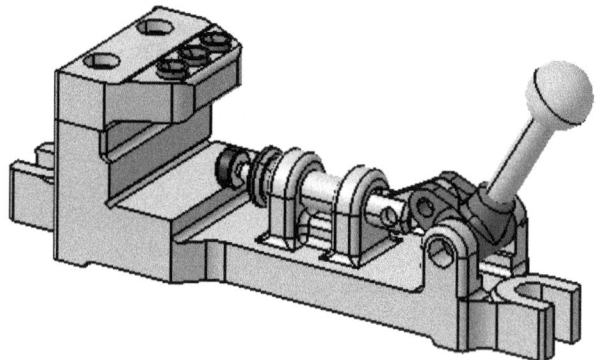

Figure 4–17

Task 2 - Assign material to parts in the assembly.

1. Click the (Apply Material) icon to open the material Library.

2. Select the *Other* tab and highlight the **Plastic** graphic.

3. Select the first component in the specification tree (Ball Lever).

4. Click **Apply Material**.

*To apply a material to an entire assembly, select the top-level assembly in the specification tree and click **Apply Material**.*

The other components in the model have already had material applied to them.

5. Select the **Lead** graphic in the *Metal* tab.

6. Select the second component in the specification tree (Base) and click **Apply Material**.

7. Close the Material library.

8. Expand the first component in the specification tree. The material has been added, as shown in Figure 4–18.

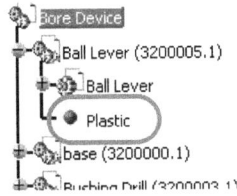

Figure 4–18

9. Right-click on the Plastic material in the specification tree and select **Properties**.

10. Select the *Analysis* tab and note the material properties of the plastic, as shown in Figure 4–19.

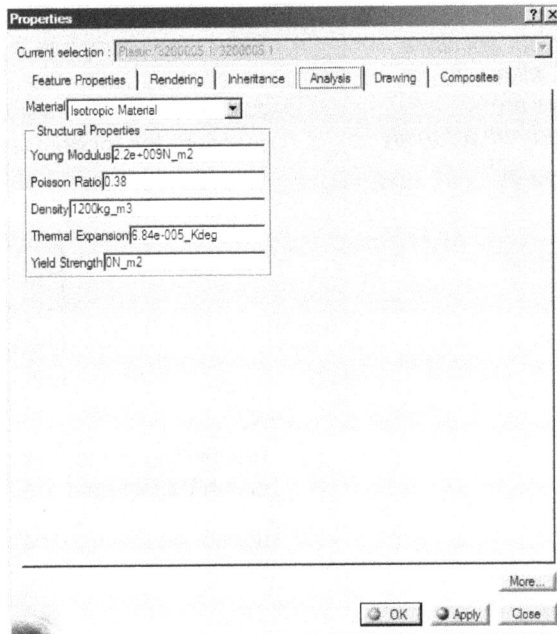

Figure 4–19

11. Close the Properties dialog box.

Task 3 - Set your display to render the model with material.

1. Click the [icon] (Shading with Material) icon in the **View Mode** flyout of the View toolbar. The model is rendered with the material applied to it, as shown in Figure 4–20.

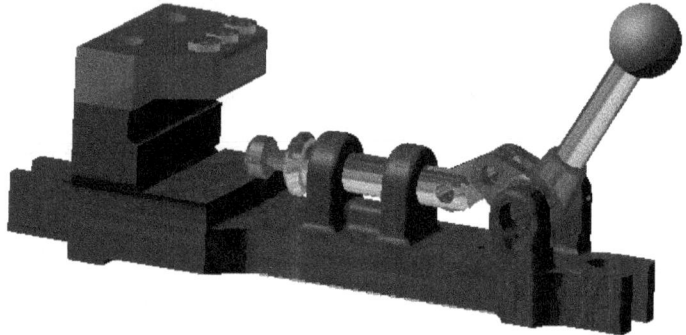

Figure 4–20

Task 4 - Calculate Inertia.

If you do not specify a material, all mass properties are calculated with a density of 1000 kg/m³.

1. Select the product in the specification tree, as shown in Figure 4–21, and click the [icon] (Measure Inertia) icon to measure the model inertia. The resulting data displays in the Measure Inertia dialog box.

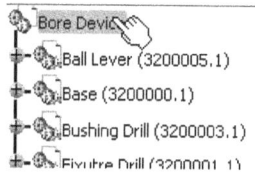

Figure 4–21

2. Review the measurements that are calculated and close the dialog box when done.

3. (Optional) Change the View mode back to Shading With Edges.

Task 5 - Take a series of one click measurements.

1. Click the ![icon] (Measure Item) icon to make some one-click measurements.

2. Select the cylindrical surface as shown in Figure 4–22. Both the *Area* and *Radius* display.

*If the units for the area calculation are incorrect, select **Tools>Options> Parameters and Measure**, select the Units tab and set the Area units to square meter.*

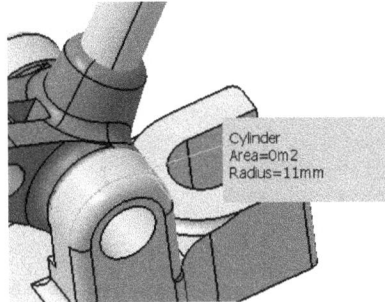

Cylinder
Area=0m2
Radius=11mm

Figure 4–22

Design Considerations

Note that you obtain an area of 0m^2. This is because the area of the cylindrical surface is relatively small. You can determine the correct area by changing the number of decimal places displayed for measurement.

3. Select **Tools>Options>Parameters and Measure**, and select the *Units* tab.

4. Select **Area** from the Units box.

5. Change the value in the **Decimal places for read/write numbers** field to **7**.

Decimal places cannot be set globally. You must individually set the number of decimal places for each type of unit.

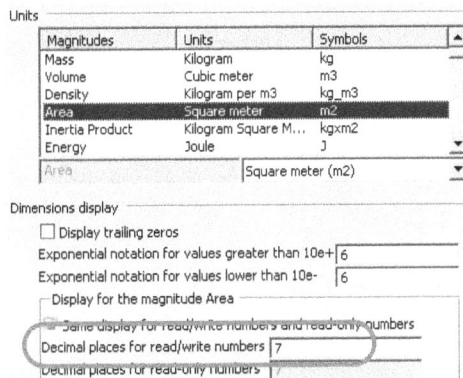

Magnitudes	Units	Symbols	
Mass	Kilogram	kg	
Volume	Cubic meter	m3	
Density	Kilogram per m3	kg_m3	
Area	Square meter	m2	
Inertia Product	Kilogram Square M...	kgxm2	
Energy	Joule	J	

Area	Square meter (m2)	

Dimensions display

☐ Display trailing zeros

Exponential notation for values greater than 10e+ [6]

Exponential notation for values lower than 10e- [6]

Display for the magnitude Area

Same display for read/write numbers and read-only numbers

Decimal places for read/write numbers [7]

Decimal places for read-only numbers [7]

Figure 4–23

6. Click **OK** to close the Options dialog box.

7. Repeat the measurement of the cylindrical surface. The results appear as shown in Figure 4–24.

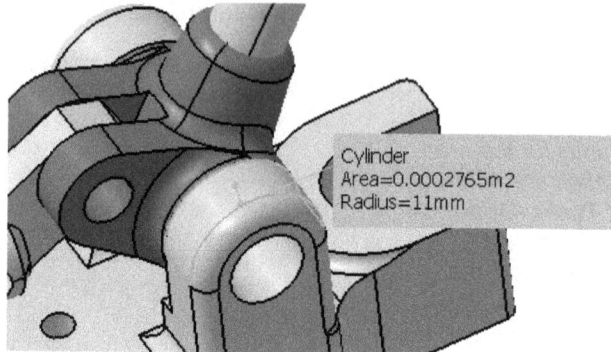

Cylinder
Area=0.0002765m2
Radius=11mm

Figure 4–24

8. Click **Customize** to customize the results.

9. Clear the **Area** option under the Surface element.

10. Click **Apply** and **OK**.

11. Repeat Step 2. for a different cylindrical surface. Only the radius is measured and displayed in the Measure Item dialog box.

12. Click **Customize** again to set the results to include the surface area measurement.

13. Close the Measure Item Customization dialog box.

14. Take additional one-click measure item measurements for different items in the model including flat surfaces, entire components, the entire product, and a vertex.

15. Click **OK** in the Measure Item dialog box when finished.

Task 6 - Take a series of measure between measurements.

1. Click the ↔ (Measure Between) icon to measure between measurements.

2. Activate the standard Measure Between mode by clicking the

    ↔ (Measure Between) icon.

3. Select the flat face and hole axis to measure between, as shown in Figure 4–25.

Locate the axis by moving the cursor over the area, the axis displays.

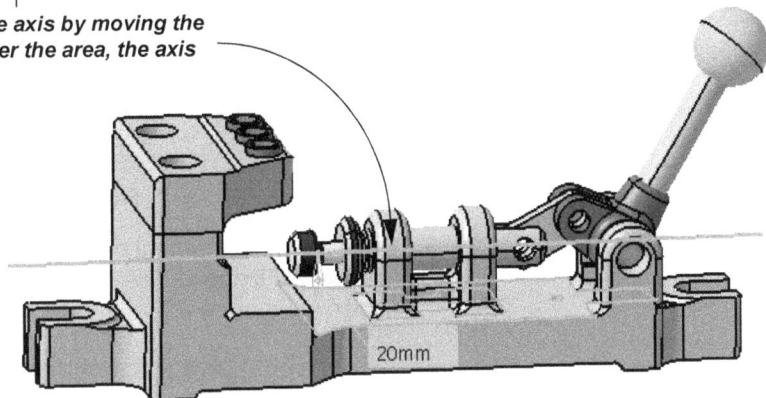

20mm

Figure 4–25

4. Practice making additional measurements using Standard mode.

5. Set the quick view to top by clicking the ⬚ (Top View) icon.

6. Activate the Measure Between in Chain Mode tool by clicking

    the ↔ (Measure Between in Chain Mode) icon in the Measure Between dialog box.

7. Select the **Keep Measure** option in the Measure Between dialog box to save the measurements with the model data.

Design Considerations

The **Keep measure** option saves measurement data to the part or product model file, and might be hidden from the visible space to maintain clarity in the display area. Kept measurements are an accurate way to record and convey design changes, or when used in conjunction with annotations, recommendations between members of a design team.

8. Select **Edge 1** and **Hole 1**, as shown in Figure 4–26.

Select the counterbore hole and not the inner hole (select the outer circle from the Top view).

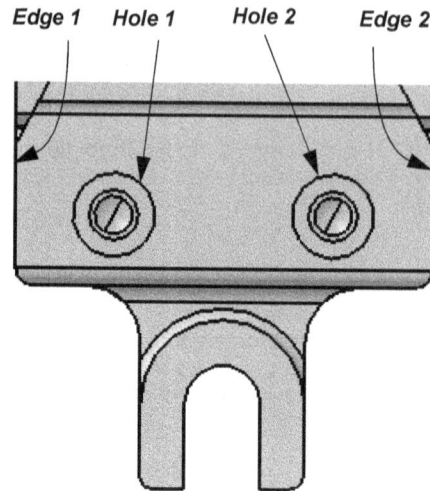

Edge 1   Hole 1   Hole 2   Edge 2

Figure 4–26

9. Once the measurement displays, continue to select **Hole 2**, followed by **Edge 2**. The measurements appear in order, as shown in Figure 4–27.

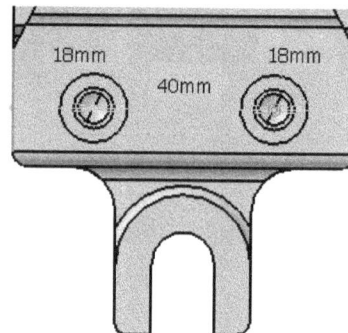

18mm   40mm   18mm

Figure 4–27

10. Click **OK** to complete the measurement.

11. Select the newly created parameters in the **Measure** node of the specification tree.

12. Right-click on one of the measurements and select **Hide/Show** to remove it from the model display.

13. Access the Measure Between tool again.

14. From the Measure Between dialog box, activate the Measure Between in Fan mode by selecting the ⇄ (Measure Between in Fan Mode) icon.

15. Repeat steps 8. to 9. and compare the results with the results in Figure 4–27.

16. Hide the parameters you have just created.

Task 7 - Take a series of thickness measurements.

1. Activate the thickness measurement tool by clicking the (Measures the thickness) icon in the Measure Item dialog box.

2. Select the face shown in Figure 4–28. The system measures the thickness of the model at this location.

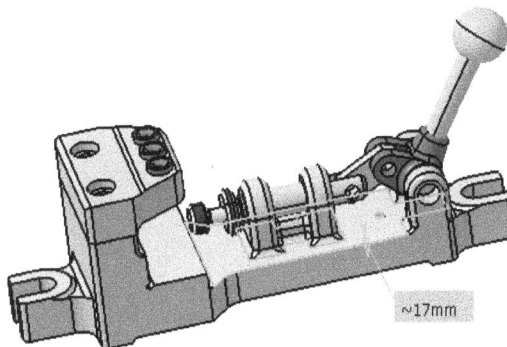

~17mm

Figure 4–28

3. Use the Measure Between tool to confirm the thickness measurement.

4. Perform additional measurements using the Thickness Measurement tool.

Task 8 - Save the part and close the window.

1. Click the (Save) icon in the Standard toolbar to save the model.

2. Select **File>Close**.

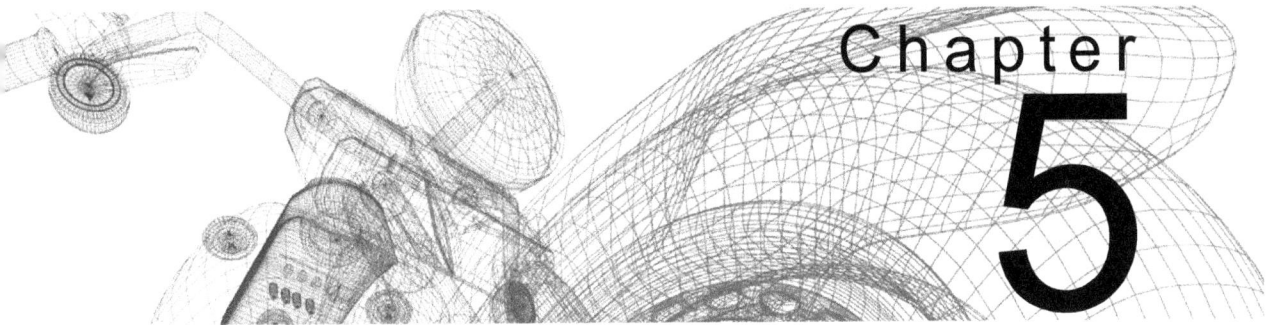

Chapter 5

DMU Space Analysis

Until this point, all work within DMU has been performed in the Navigator workbench. To perform additional types of model analyses, the Space Analysis workbench must be activated. This workbench contains the tools required to analyze engineering-critical information such as interference and revision changes.

Learning Objectives in this Chapter

- Understand the DMU Space Analysis workbench.
- Check for clash between objects in a product.
- Learn how to section a model.

5.1 DMU Space Analysis Workbench

The Space Analysis workbench is a Product level workbench with tools for analyzing assemblies. All models used in a CATIA V5 DMU session have a *.CATProduct file extension.

The icon for the DMU Space Analysis workbench is . Click **Start>Digital Mockup>DMU Space Analysis** to activate the Space Analysis workbench, as shown in Figure 5–1.

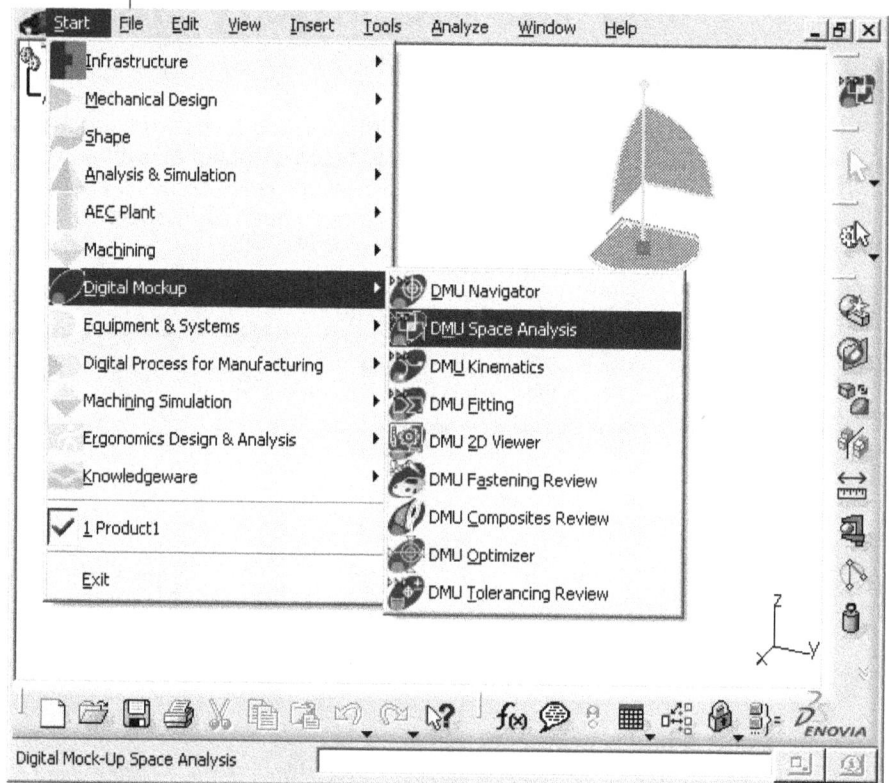

Figure 5–1

5.2 Checking for Clash

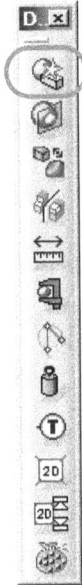

Clash defines three main conditions that can exist between parts and assemblies. These conditions describe how component positions relate to one another, and include the following:

Clearance

Clearance exists when two components have a space between them that is greater than zero, but less than a distance that you specify. Typically, the clearance value is set to a minimum distance that should not be violated within your assembly. For example, you would typically set a clearance value for the offset parting distance of a mold or the distance a fuel line can be from a heat source.

Contact

Contact exists when two parts mate or touch each other. This condition means that no clearance or interference exists between the two parts. For example, the head of a bolt against a water pump or a gasket lying on a machined surface shows contact.

Clash

Clash exists when two components collide or interfere with each other; that is, geometry of one part lies inside the geometry of the other. For example, a fastener whose diameter is too large for a hole, or a press-to-fit insert and a snap clip show a clash.

The Clash tool examines spacing conditions between components. Conducting a clash analysis enables you to do the following:

- Determine how many parts or subassemblies interfere with each other.

- Determine how many are in contact and how many violate a minimum distance criteria.

- Determine where the conditions exist.

- Determine whether conditions are acceptable or not.

- Export results.

General Steps

Use the following general steps to check for clash:

1. Set up the clash analysis.
2. Run the analysis.
3. Review the results.
4. Save the results.

Step 1 - Set up the clash analysis.

Click the [icon] (Clash) icon in the DMU Space Analysis toolbar to begin the clash analysis. The Check Clash dialog box opens, as shown in Figure 5–2.

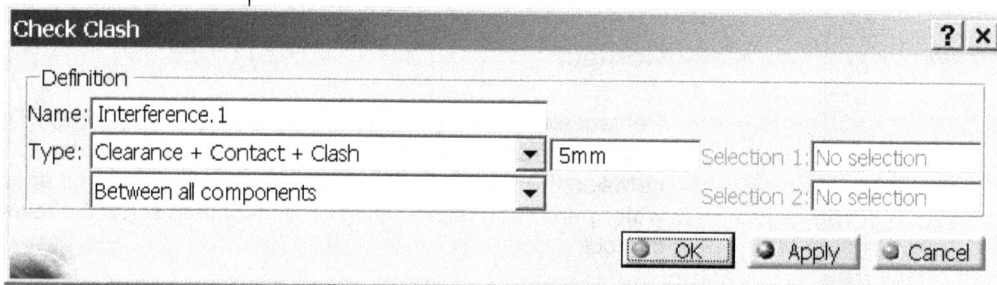

Figure 5–2

Enter a name for the analysis in the Name field. Selecting an appropriate name makes for easy reference in the specification tree or for output to a results file.

Select the type of computation to run in the Type drop-down list. The minimum clearance value can also be set if the type of computation includes clearance, as shown in Figure 5–3.

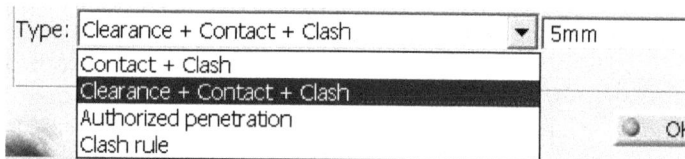

Figure 5–3

The four types of computations available are described as follows:

Computation Type	Description
Contact + Clash	Computes only contact and clash conditions of the selected components.
Clearance + Contact + Clash	Same as Contact + Clash, but adds a clearance calculation to the selected components.
Authorized Penetration	Defines a range within which two parts can interfere but not produce a clash result.
Clash Rule	Uses a Knowledge Rule to calculate clash results.

Select the method of selecting components in the drop-down list below the Type drop-down list, as shown in Figure 5–4.

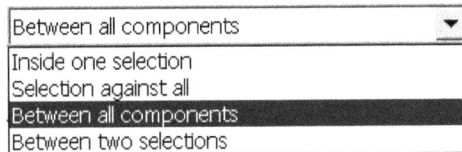

Figure 5–4

Four types of selections are available and provide a brief description. These are described as follows:

Selection Type	Description
Inside one selection	Calculates each part in a subassembly against all other parts in the same subassembly.
Selection against all	Calculates each subassembly against all other subassemblies within the current DMU session.
Between all components	Calculates each part against all other parts in the current DMU session. This is the default setting.
Between two selections	Selects a part or assembly to calculate against another part or assembly. The Selection 1 and Selection 2 fields are available when this option is selected.

Step 2 - Run the analysis.

After setting up the Clash analysis, you can run it by clicking **Apply**. If you click **OK**, it stores the interference calculation to the specification tree and does not display any results.

Step 3 - Review the results.

Once an analysis is run, the Check Clash dialog box expands to display all of the results. The top of the Results section displays the total number of interferences and total number of each type of inference. The Filter drop-down lists can be used to specify which results display. The expanded Check Clash dialog box is shown in Figure 5–5.

Interference Quantities and Filters area

Displayed Results area

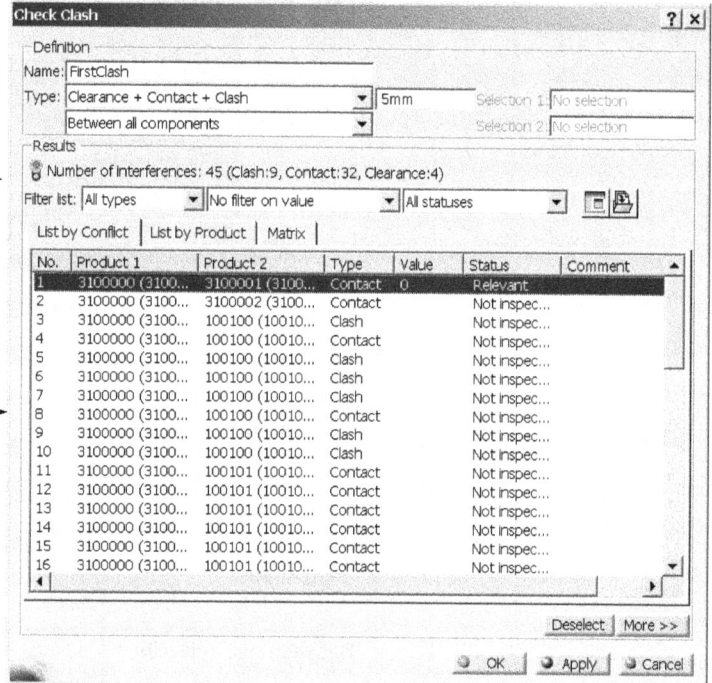

Figure 5–5

Displayed Results Area

You can display the interference results using one of three modes:

- List by Conflict

- List by Product

- Matrix

List by Conflict

The *List by Conflict* tab displays the results in the window by the number of conflicts detected, as shown in Figure 5–6.

List by Conflict	List by Product	Matrix				
No.	Product 1	Product 2	Type	Value	Status	Comment
1	Frame (Frame.1)	Arm (Arm.1)	Contact	0	Irrelevant	Okay
2	Frame (Frame.1)	Arm (Arm.2)	Contact	0	Irrelevant	Okay
3	Frame (Frame.1)	DriveShaft (Drive...	Clash	-0.74	Relevant	
4	Arm (Arm.1)	Mount (Mount.1)	Contact	0	Relevant	
5	Arm (Arm.1)	Hub (Hub.1)	Clearance	2.96	Relevant	Too close!
6	Arm (Arm.2)	Mount (Mount.1)	Clash	-0.62	Relevant	
7	Arm (Arm.2)	Hub (Hub.1)	Clearance	1.48	Relevant	Too close!
8	Mount (Mount.1)	Hub (Hub.1)	Clash		Not inspected	
9	Hub (Hub.1)	Spider (Spider.1)	Contact		Not inspected	
10	Hub (Hub.1)	DriveShaft (Drive...	Clash		Not inspected	
11	Hub (Hub.1)	WheelRim (Wheel...	Clash		Not inspected	
12	Spider (Spider.1)	DriveShaft (Drive...	Clash		Not inspected	
13	DriveShaft (Dri...	Spider (Spider.2)	Clash		Not inspected	

Figure 5–6

Each row lists two components that have conflict, the type of conflict, and the offset distance between the two components. A negative value indicates an interference between the components in question. A positive value indicates a clearance between the two components.

The Status column displays "Not Inspected" until the row is highlighted. To toggle the status between "Irrelevant" and "Relevant", highlight the row and click on the status.

The Comment column enables the reviewer to enter comments about the selected row.

List by Product

The *List by Product* tab displays the results in the window by the product in question. It displays all of the components that conflict with a selected component, as shown in Figure 5–7. The information about each conflict and the Status and Comment columns act the same as when using the *List by Conflict* tab.

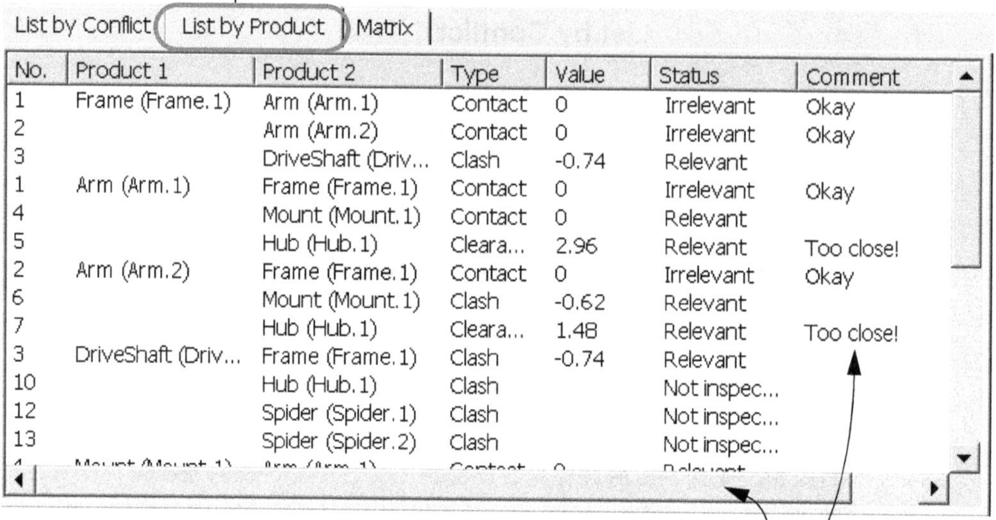

No.	Product 1	Product 2	Type	Value	Status	Comment
1	Frame (Frame.1)	Arm (Arm.1)	Contact	0	Irrelevant	Okay
2		Arm (Arm.2)	Contact	0	Irrelevant	Okay
3		DriveShaft (Driv...	Clash	-0.74	Relevant	
1	Arm (Arm.1)	Frame (Frame.1)	Contact	0	Irrelevant	Okay
4		Mount (Mount.1)	Contact	0	Relevant	
5		Hub (Hub.1)	Cleara...	2.96	Relevant	Too close!
2	Arm (Arm.2)	Frame (Frame.1)	Contact	0	Irrelevant	Okay
6		Mount (Mount.1)	Clash	-0.62	Relevant	
7		Hub (Hub.1)	Cleara...	1.48	Relevant	Too close!
3	DriveShaft (Driv...	Frame (Frame.1)	Clash	-0.74	Relevant	
10		Hub (Hub.1)	Clash		Not inspec...	
12		Spider (Spider.1)	Clash		Not inspec...	
13		Spider (Spider.2)	Clash		Not inspec...	
1	Mount (Mount.1)	Arm (Arm.1)	Contact	0	Relevant	

The Status can be changed and a Comment can be added by selecting in the field.

Figure 5–7

Matrix

The *Matrix* tab displays the results in a graphical chart. The chart displays the conflicts between the two components in question. The conflicts are shown at their chart intersection by shape and color-coded symbols. You can zoom the chart the same way you would a 3D model. The *Matrix* tab is shown in Figure 5–8.

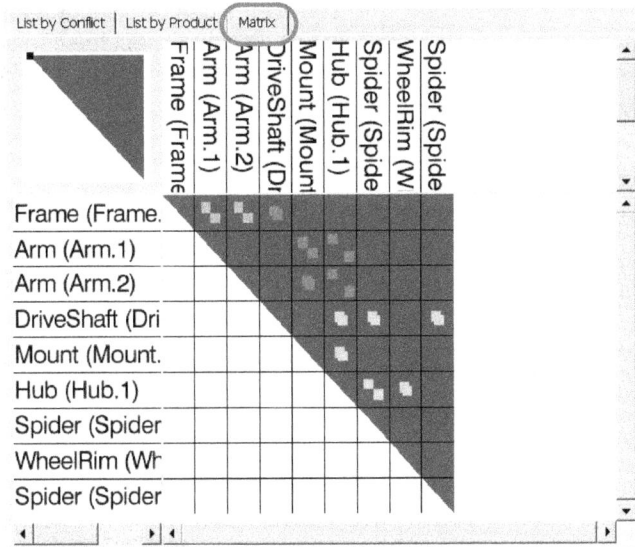

Figure 5–8

The various symbols in the Matrix chart are described as follows:

Symbol/Color	Description
	Displays a Clearance condition.
	Displays a Contact condition.
	Displays a Clash condition.
Yellow symbol	Conflict has not been inspected.
Red symbol	Conflict is inspected and relevant.
Green symbol	Conflict is inspected and irrelevant.

The Status can be changed and a Comment can be added while in this display. Select the conflict symbol, right-click and select an option as shown in Figure 5–9.

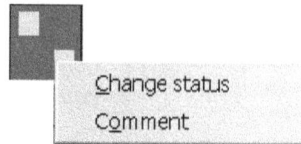

Change status
Comment

Figure 5–9

Preview Window

The Preview window displays the results of the conflict. The window can be resized and placed anywhere on the screen and the results can be graphically manipulated. The Preview window is shown in Figure 5–10, and is activated when a conflict is selected in the Results window.

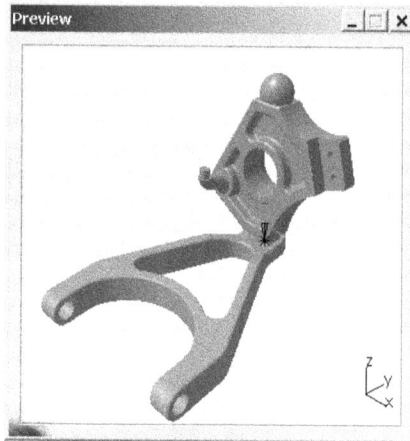

Figure 5–10

Step 4 - Save the results.

The results that are computed can be saved in two ways. They can be saved to the current DMU file within the specification tree or they can be stored to an external file.

To store interference results to the current DMU assembly, click **OK** in the Check Clash dialog box. The results are stored in the **Applications** branch of the tree.

To store the results in an external file, click the  (Export as) icon in the Check Clash dialog box. The results can be saved as: XML, TXT, or model file formats.

The XML file format generates a detailed report that includes graphics and hyperlinks to the various areas of the data. An example is shown in Figure 5–11.

▼Computation Result

Product vs product		Link
		DataBase\Ball_Lever_(3200005.1)_--_Shape_1--++--Pin_Seized_(3200004.1)_--_Shape_1--++--1.xml
		DataBase\Base_(3200000.1)_--_Shape_1--++--Fixutre_Drill_(3200001.1)_--_Shape_1--++--2.xml
		DataBase\Base_(3200000.1)_--_Shape_1--++--Lever_Angle_(3200002.1)_--_Shape_1--++--3.xml
		DataBase\Base_(3200000.1)_--_Shape_1--++--Pin_Pressure_(3200006.1)_--_Shape_1--++--4.xml
		DataBase\Base_(3200000.1)_--_Shape_1--++--Screw_Adjust_(3200008.1)_--_Shape_1--++--5.xml
		DataBase\Base_(3200000.1)_--_Shape_1--++--Thumb_Screw_(3200009.1)_--_Shape_1--++--6.xml

Figure 5–11

5.3 Sectioning a Model

The Sectioning tool enables you to cut sections in one or more components. You can use this tool to perform the following tasks:

- Examine assembly component positions.

- View complex 2D cross-sections.

- Verify the internal design considerations of a part.

- View internal clash conditions.

General Steps

Use the following general steps to section a model:

1. Activate the Sectioning tool.
2. Define the section name and type.
3. Position the cross-section.
4. Define the output of the section.
5. Set the behavior of the section when updating.
6. Save the results.

Step 1 - Activate the Sectioning tool.

The Sectioning tool cuts through all components in an assembly by default. To analyze specific models in the assembly, preselect them for the main window or specification tree using <Ctrl>.

Click the (Sectioning) icon. The Sectioning Definition dialog box opens, as shown in Figure 5–12.

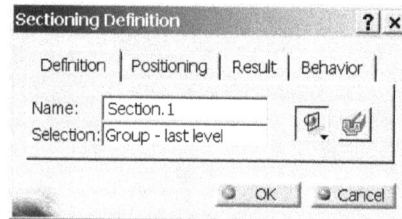

Figure 5–12

A section view is vertically tiled beside the product window, as shown in Figure 5–13.

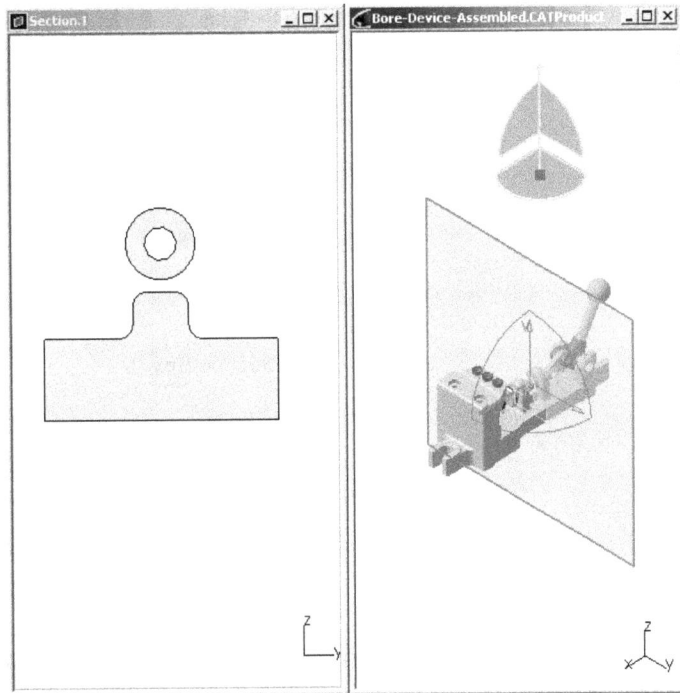

Figure 5–13

Step 2 - Define the section name and type.

Use the *Definition* tab to name the section and determine the section type used, as shown in Figure 5–14.

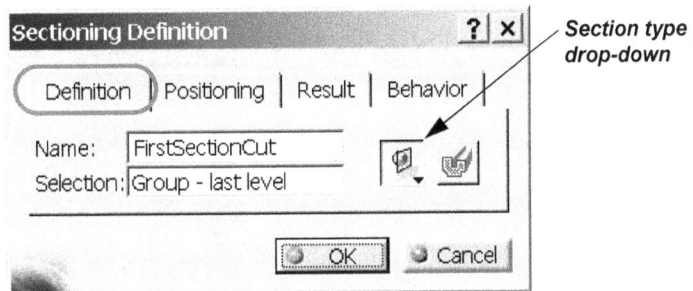

Figure 5–14

The three types of sections that can be created are described as follows:

Selection Type	Description
Section Plane	Uses a single plane to cut the components, and is the default setting.
Section Slice	Uses two parallel planes at a distance apart. This is used to create two offset cross-sections at one time. The master plane drags the slave plane.
Section Box	Uses two parallel planes and a bounding box to cut the components.

Click the icon to create a volume cut. A volume cut visually cuts the selected components, as opposed to only creating a profile of the cross-section (default). This option can be used in combination with any of the section types.

Step 3 - Position the cross-section.

Use the *Positioning* tab to position the section in different ways, as shown in Figure 5–15.

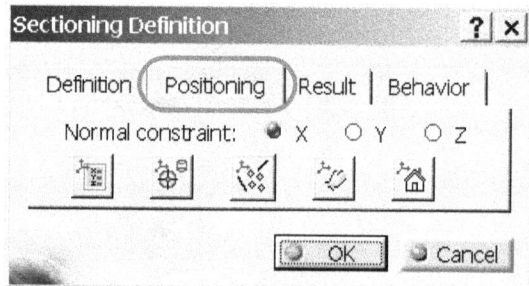

Figure 5–15

The **Normal Constraint** options enable you to determine whether the section plane is normal to the X-, Y- or Z-axis.

The five types of positioning tools available are described as follows:

Positioning Tool		Description
	Edit Position and Dimensions	Defines precise section locations. Can set Origin, Translations, Rotations, and Dimensional sizes of the section.
	Geometrical Target	Quickly positions the section at specific geometrical locations (e.g., cylinders, planes, faces, or edges).
	Positioning by 2/3 Selections	Positions the section at 2 or 3 geometrical references (e.g., axes of two holes/cylinders, or through three points).
	Invert Normal	Inverts the normal direction of the master plane. If used with a Volume Cut, it removes the other side of the cut.
	Reset Position	Quickly positions the section back to the starting location and orientation, but does not resize the section dimensions.

Manual Section Manipulation

You can manually manipulate the section plane, slice, or box using any of the following three methods:

- Dragging: Select the section plane with the left mouse button and drag to translate the plane, as shown in Figure 5–16.

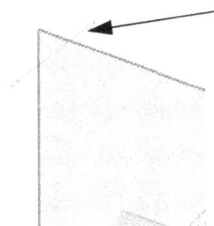

Figure 5–16

- Rotating: Select an arc on the section axis system with the left mouse button and drag to rotate to a new angle, as shown in Figure 5–17.

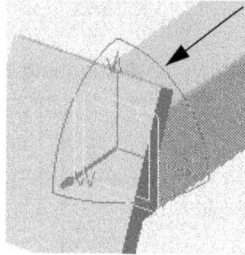

Figure 5–17

- Resizing: Select the sides of the section plane with the left mouse button and drag to change the size of the section, as shown in Figure 5–18.

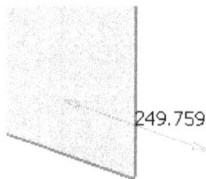

Figure 5–18

Step 4 - Define the output of the section.

The output of the section can be defined using the *Results* tab. It enables you to examine your results and save them for later use, as shown in Figure 5–19.

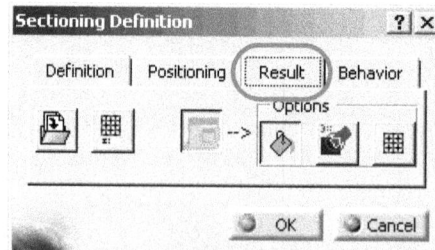

Figure 5–19

The six result information tools available are described as follows:

Result Tool		Description
Export As		Saves the section results to different file formats (e.g., .CATPart, .CATDrawing, model, .dxf, .igs, or .stp).
Edit Grid		Edits the Grid settings, such as location mode (Absolute or Relative), display style (Lines or Crosses), and spacing size.
Results Window		Opens the Results window where you can measure section results. The Results window is open by default and is tiled vertically beside the Product window. When this option is disabled, a Preview window displays. This tool must be activated to perform the following options:
	Section Fill	Toggles the section fill on or off. Useful for measuring section area. The Results Window icon must be activated to use this tool.
	Clash Detection	Circles all areas of clash within the current section. The Results Window and Section Fill icons must be activated to use this tool.
	Grid	Toggles the grid on or off in the Results window. Use the Edit Grid tool to modify the grid. The Results Window icon must be activated to use this tool.

Step 5 - Set the behavior of the section when updating.

The behavior of the section once created can be set using the *Behavior* tab, as shown in Figure 5–20.

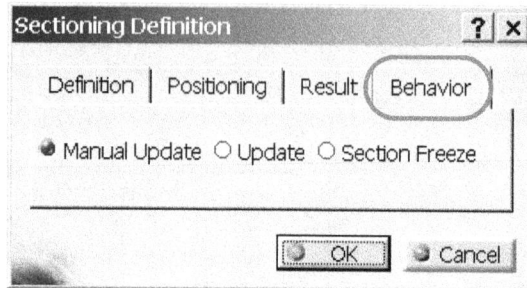

Figure 5–20

You can set the section behavior by selecting one of the following options:

- The **Manual Update** option (default) sets the section results to a manual update.

- The **Update** option sets the section results to an automatic update.

- The **Section Freeze** option freezes the section results while you drag the section plane, until the update mode is changed and the plane is moved again.

Step 6 - Save the results.

You can store section results to the current DMU assembly or to an external file.

Click **OK** in the Sectioning Definition dialog box to store section results to the current DMU assembly. The section is stored in the **Applications** branch of the specification tree.

Click the (Export As) icon in the Sectioning Definition dialog box in the *Result* tab to store the section results to an external file. They can be saved as the following file formats: CATPart, CATDrawing, dxf, dwg, igs, model, stp, or wrl.

Practice 5a

Clash Analysis

Practice Objectives

- Set up a clash analysis.
- Run a clash analysis.
- Interpret the results.
- Store the results.

In this practice, you will be reviewing a product for clash and noting problem areas so the designer can correct the issues.

Task 1 - Open the assembly.

The files for this practice can be found in the FrontWheel directory.

1. Open **FrontWheel.CATProduct**. The assembly displays as shown in Figure 5–21.

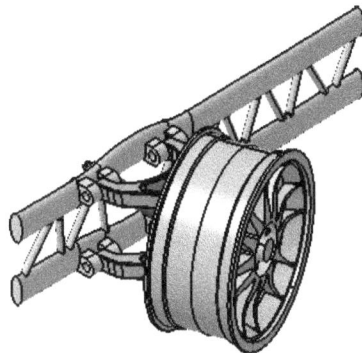

Figure 5–21

Task 2 - Activate the DMU Space Analysis workbench.

1. Ensure that the Space Analysis workbench is active (the workbench icon should be   ).

2. If the Space Analysis workbench is not active, select **Start> Digital Mockup>DMU Space Analysis**. The   (DMU Space Analysis) workbench is now active.

Task 3 - Set up clash analysis.

1. Click the (Clash) icon in the DMU Space Analysis toolbar.

2. Change the *Name* to **FirstClashCheck**.

3. Select **Clearance + Contact + Clash** in the Type drop-down list.

4. Select **Between all components** as the selection set.

5. Set the minimum clearance to **4mm**. The Check Clash dialog box opens, as shown in Figure 5–22.

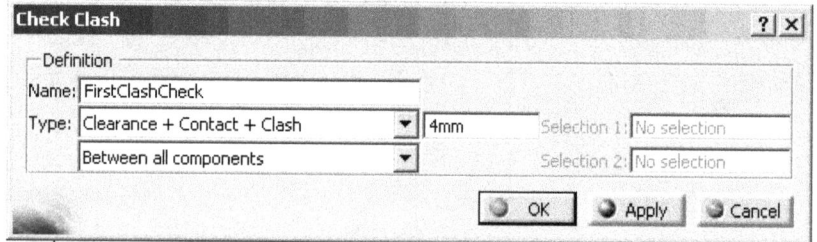

Figure 5–22

6. Click **Apply** in the Check Clash dialog box and begin the clash analysis.

Task 4 - Interpret results.

1. Record the total number of interferences and total number of interferences by type, in the table below. This information displays just below the Results section.

Interference Type	Total Number
All Interferences	
Clash	
Contact	
Clearance	

2. Select the first result in the Check Clash dialog box. It should be a contact result between Frame and Arm.1. These two parts appear in the Preview window, as shown in Figure 5–23.

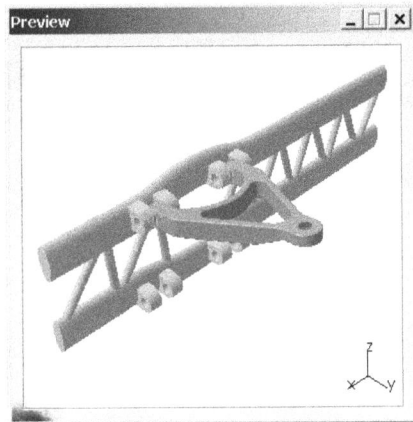

Figure 5–23

3. Pan, zoom, and rotate as required in the Preview window to examine the results of the conflict.

Task 5 - Make comments and change status of a result.

Design Considerations

Once results have been calculated, interpretation of them is essential. Problem areas need to be noted so that they can be corrected before the product goes into production. A minimum clearance of 4mm between the arms and hub is essential for the operation of the assembly. All other components can be in contact with each other but no force fits are noted for this assembly, therefore any clashes need to be noted for correction by the designer.

1. Staying with the first conflict, note that the type of conflict is **Contact**. Since these components are not in violation of the requirements for the assembly, place the cursor in the Comment column at the end of the row for the first conflict. Select this field and enter the comment shown in Figure 5–24.

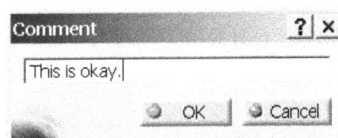

Figure 5–24

2. Under the *Status* column, select **Relevant** to change the conflict status to **Irrelevant**. The window displays as shown in Figure 5–25.

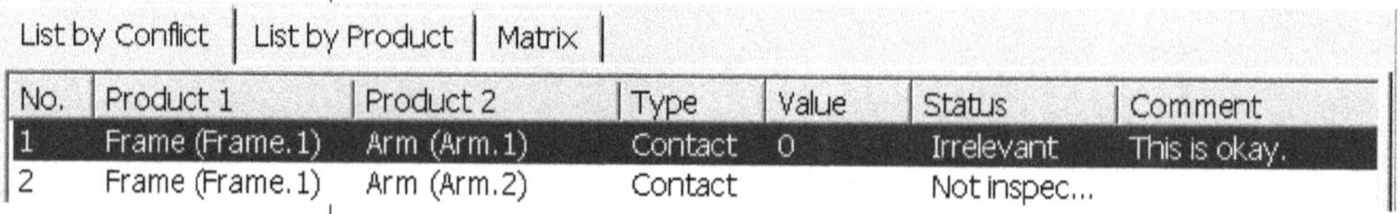

	No.	Product 1	Product 2	Type	Value	Status	Comment
List by Conflict	List by Product	Matrix					
	1	Frame (Frame.1)	Arm (Arm.1)	Contact	0	Irrelevant	This is okay.
	2	Frame (Frame.1)	Arm (Arm.2)	Contact		Not inspec...	

Figure 5–25

Task 6 - Change the Filter lists to sort the results.

1. Select **Contact** in the Filter list drop-down list to change the type of results to display, as shown in Figure 5–26.

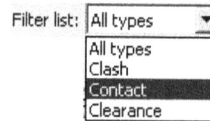

Filter list: All types

All types
Clash
Contact
Clearance

Figure 5–26

Not all of the contact conflicts are between the components of concern (Hub and the Arms).

2. Change the *Status* of all contact conflicts to **Irrelevant**, as shown in Figure 5–27.

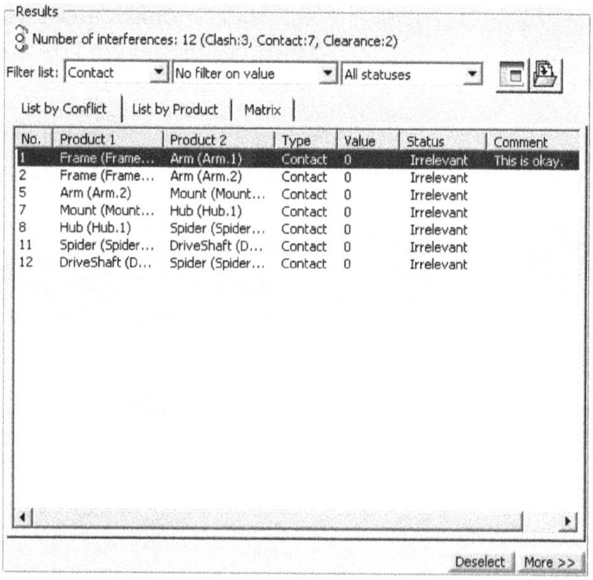

Results

Number of interferences: 12 (Clash:3, Contact:7, Clearance:2)

Filter list: Contact   No filter on value   All statuses

No.	Product 1	Product 2	Type	Value	Status	Comment
1	Frame (Frame...	Arm (Arm.1)	Contact	0	Irrelevant	This is okay.
2	Frame (Frame...	Arm (Arm.2)	Contact	0	Irrelevant	
5	Arm (Arm.2)	Mount (Mount...	Contact	0	Irrelevant	
7	Mount (Mount...	Hub (Hub.1)	Contact	0	Irrelevant	
8	Hub (Hub.1)	Spider (Spider...	Contact	0	Irrelevant	
11	Spider (Spider...	DriveShaft (D...	Contact	0	Irrelevant	
12	DriveShaft (D...	Spider (Spider...	Contact	0	Irrelevant	

List by Conflict   List by Product   Matrix

Deselect   More >>

Figure 5–27

3. Select **Clash** in the Filter list drop-down list to change the type of results to display, as shown in Figure 5–28.

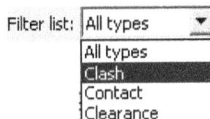

Figure 5–28

4. Select the first clash result in the filtered list and examine it in the Preview window. The parts in question should be the Arm and the Mount.

5. Zoom in on the clash area to examine it. What is the interference amount between the two parts? _____

6. Select the next conflict in the Results window. The parts in question should be the Hub and Driveshaft. Zoom in on the clash area in the Preview window.

Design Considerations

The clash exists between the two components that were constrained in the assembly. To resolve the issue, the constraints must be adjusted.

7. Enter a comment for this clash, as shown in Figure 5–29.

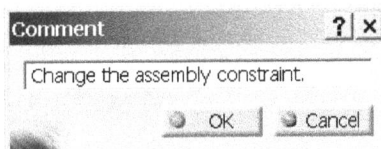

Figure 5–29

8. Review the remaining clash conflict and add a comment to propose a solution for the issue.

Task 7 - Access the Matrix tab and review results.

1. Change the Filter type to **All types**, as shown in Figure 5–30.

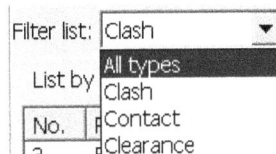

Figure 5–30

2. Select the *Matrix* tab to display the graphical chart results, as shown in Figure 5–31.

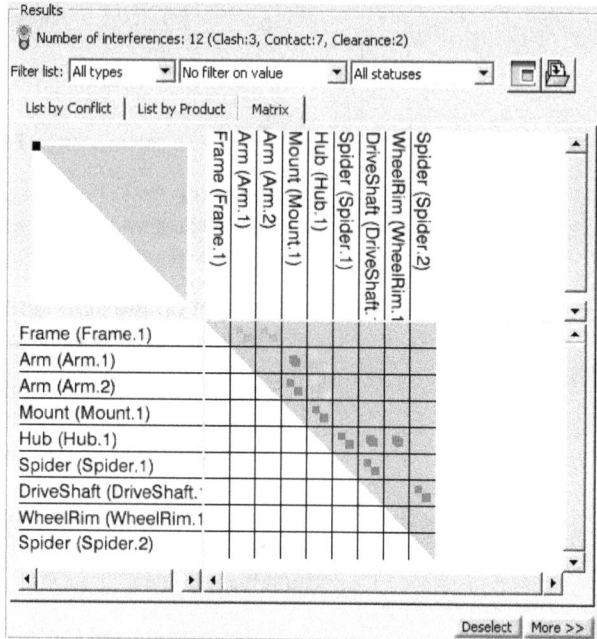

Figure 5–31

3. Select the symbol at the chart intersection of **Hub** and **Arm.1**, as shown in Figure 5–32. The symbol color changes from yellow (Not inspected) to red (Inspected and Relevant).

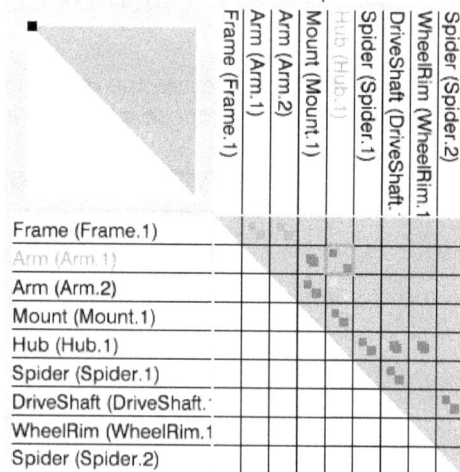

Figure 5–32

4. Review the results of the clash in the preview window. The clearance is not the required 4mm.

5. Right-click on the highlighted conflict and select **Comment**, as shown in Figure 5–33.

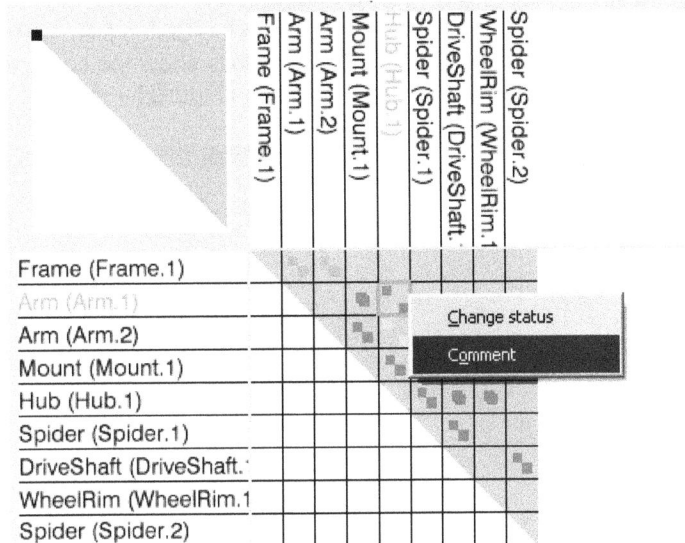

Figure 5–33

6. Enter the comment shown in Figure 5–34.

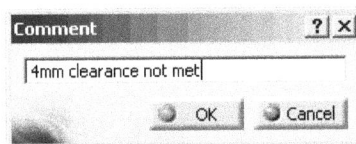

Figure 5–34

7. Inspect the last conflict between the hub and the arm. What type of conflict is it? Is the conflict acceptable? Make notes and change the status of the conflict to coincide with your findings.

Task 8 - Access the List by Conflict tab and change filters again.

1. Select the *List by Conflict* tab to return to the original results list.

2. Change the Status filter to **Relevant** and view the results list. The results show the conflicts that need to be addressed, as shown in Figure 5–35.

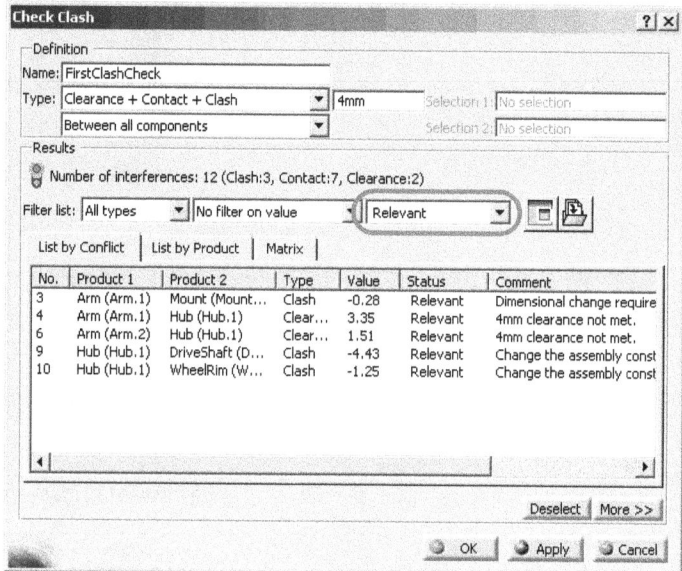

Figure 5–35

Task 9 - Store the Clash results to the DMU file.

1. Click **OK** to store the results to the current DMU file.

Design Considerations

Storing clash analyses is useful for downstream/chronological assessment of a product's development cycle. Interference results are placed in the **Applications>Interferences** node of the specification tree, beneath the clash analysis name. They provide a snapshot of the clearance, contact, and clash conditions of the product assembly at the time of analysis.

2. Expand the **Application>Interference** branch of the specification tree to see the analysis saved with the model as shown in Figure 5–36.

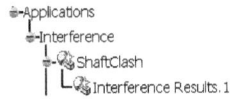

Figure 5–36

3. Save and close the model.

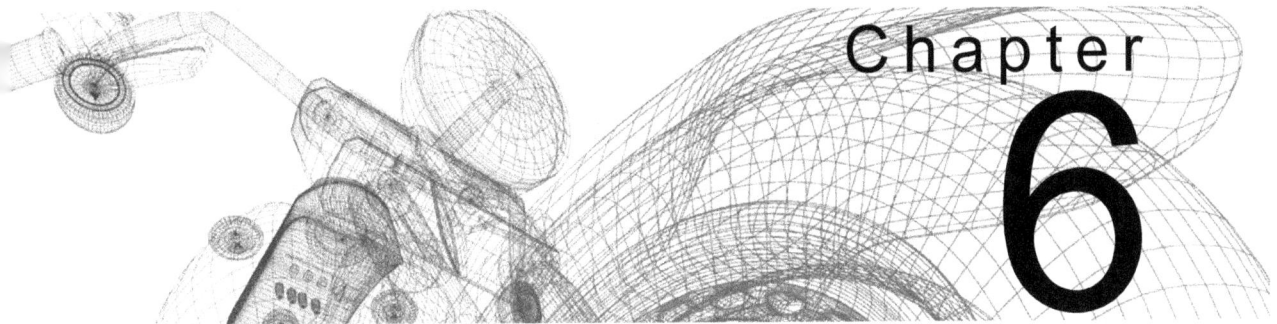

DMU Space Analysis II

This chapter completes the training for the tools in the Space Analysis workbench and focuses on the Distance and Band analysis tool. In addition, the Compare Products and Arc through Three Points tools are introduced.

Learning Objectives in this Chapter

*   Understand the Distance and Band Analysis tool.
*   Understand the Compare Products tool.
*   Learn how to measure an Arc section.

6.1 Distance and Band Analysis Tool

The Distance and Band Analysis tool enables you to measure the minimum X-, Y- or Z-distance between components in a product (distance analysis). Additionally, you can compute and visualize areas of a product that correspond to the minimum and maximum distance as defined by you (band analysis).

General Steps

Use the following general steps to use the Distance and Band Analysis tool:

1. Activate the Distance and Band Analysis tool.
2. Select method for component selection and select components.
3. Select the type of analysis.
4. Run the analysis.
5. Save the results.

Step 1 - Activate the Distance and Band Analysis tool.

Click the [icon] (Distance and Band Analysis) icon. The Edit Distance and Band Analysis dialog box opens, as shown in Figure 6–1. Use the Name field to enter a meaningful name for the analysis.

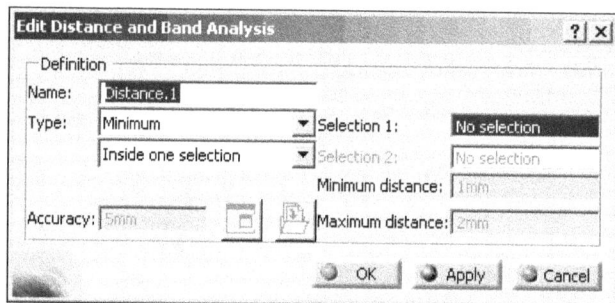

Figure 6–1

Step 2 - Select method for component selection and select components.

Select the selection method in the Type drop-down list, as shown in Figure 6–2.

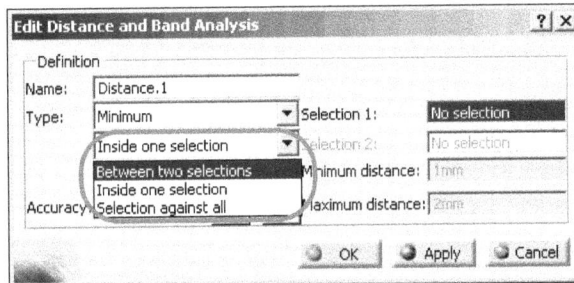

Figure 6–2

The selection methods are described as follows:

Option	Description
Between two sections	Tests each component in the first selection group against all components in the second selection group.
Inside one selection	Tests (default) each selected component against all other selected components.
Selection against all	Tests each selected component against all other components within the assembly.

If you select a component by accident, reselect the component to remove it from the list.

To select component for analysis, select in the appropriate selection field and select the component in the specification tree or directly from the model. You can select as many components for each selection field as required.

Step 3 - Select the type of analysis.

Select the type of analysis to perform in the Type drop-down list. The analyses that you can perform are described as follows:

Option	Description
Minimum	Calculates the minimum distance between selected components.
Along X	Calculates the distance between selected components in the X-direction.
Along Y	Calculates the distance between selected components in the Y-direction.
Along Z	Calculates the distance between selected components in the Z-direction.
Band Analysis	Calculates the area of minimum and maximum distance between selected components.

Step 4 - Run the analysis.

Click **Apply** to run the analysis. The Edit Distance and Band Analysis dialog box expands to display the results, as shown in Figure 6–3. If you click **OK**, it stores the interference calculation to the specification tree and does not display any results.

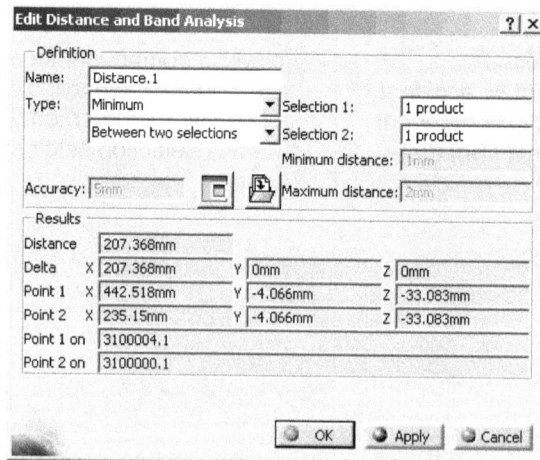

Figure 6–3

The results are also displayed directly on the model and in a Preview window, as shown in Figure 6–4. The Preview window only displays the components that the results correspond to.

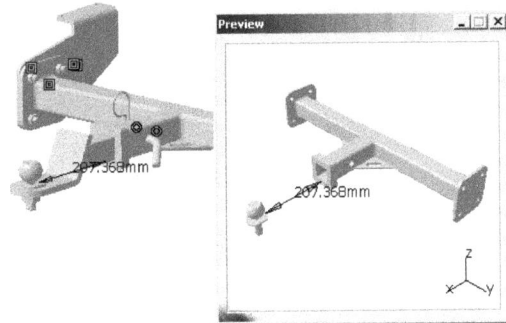

Figure 6–4

Band Analysis

If **Band analysis** is selected, the Minimum and Maximum fields become available. Enter the minimum and maximum values, and click **Apply** to run the analysis. The Edit Distance and Band Analysis dialog box expands to include the analysis results and visualization filters as shown in Figure 6–5.

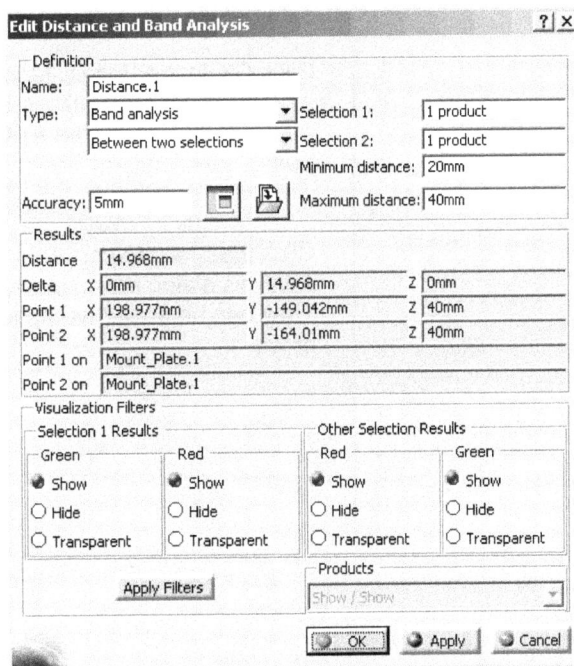

Figure 6–5

The Main and Preview windows display green and red areas on the selected components as shown in Figure 6–6.

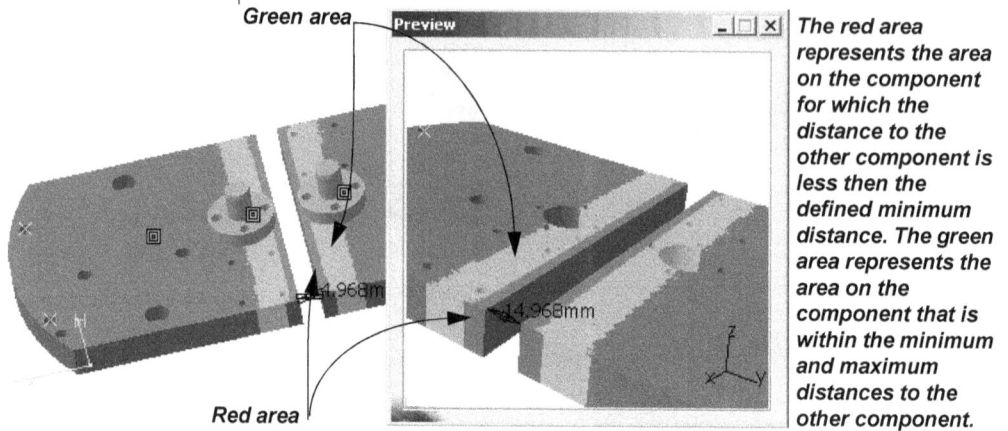

Figure 6–6

Step 5 - Save the results.

Results can be saved to the current DMU assembly or to an external file.

Click **OK** in the Edit Distance and Band Analysis dialog box to store the section results to the current DMU assembly. The results are stored in the **Applications** branch of the specification tree.

Click the (Export As) icon in the Edit Distance and Band Analysis dialog box to store the section results to an external file. They can be saved as the following file formats: model, cgr, xml, or wrl.

6.2 Compare Products Tool

The Compare Products tool detects differences between two parts or products. It is useful for comparing the same product at different stages in a design or for identifying differences in a design after changes are made.

General Steps

Use the following general steps to compare products:

1. Activate the Compare Products tool.
2. Run the comparison.
3. Save the results.

Step 1 - Activate the Compare Products tool.

To compare two parts or products, they must be inserted into the same product document. This can be done using a temporary product file.

Click the ![icon] (Compare Products) icon. The Compare Products dialog box opens, as shown in Figure 6–7. Select the two components you want to compare for the Old version and New version fields.

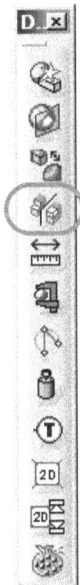

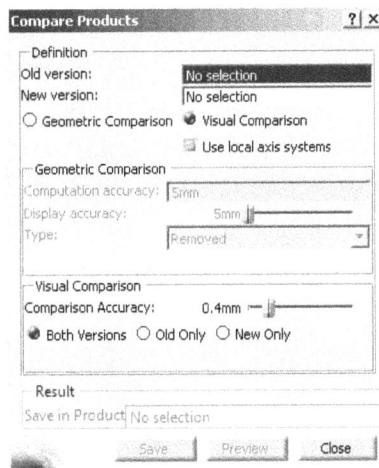

Figure 6–7

Step 2 - Run the comparison.

You can compare the two selections geometrically or visually.

Visual

The **Visual Comparison** option is the default selection. With a visual comparison, the new version is placed over the old version. This method is faster and more precise than a geometric comparison. The differences in the models are indicated by the color.

- Red indicates that the new version contains material not in the old version.

- Yellow indicates material that is common to both the new and old versions.

- Green indicates material that was in the old version and is not in the new version.

The accuracy of the comparison can be increased or decreased. By increasing the accuracy number (i.e., moving the Comparison Accuracy slider to the right), this indicates that the differences between the models must be larger before they are considered different.

Geometric

Select the **Geometric Comparison** option to run a comparison geometrically. The Compare Products dialog box options change, as shown in Figure 6–8.

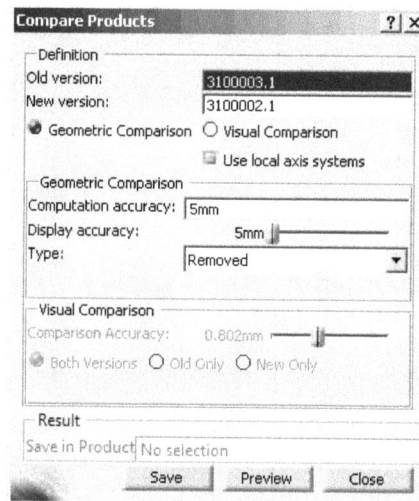

Figure 6–8

The Computation Accuracy slider controls the accuracy of the noted differences. A lower setting results in a slower computation time, but more precise results. Likewise, a higher setting results in a faster computation time, but less precise results. The Display Accuracy slider controls the graphic quality of the results. The Type drop-down list defines what you see. The types are described as follows:

Type	Description
Added	Computes only the material that was added to the new version.
Removed	Computes only the material that was removed from the new version.
Added + Removed	Computes both the material added and removed from the new model. Results display in separate views for clarity. When saved, two separate files are created.
Changed	Computes where material is added and removed from the new model and displays the results in both views. When saved, one file is created.

Click **Preview** to view the comparison. An example of a comparison with **Added + Removed** selected is shown in Figure 6–9.

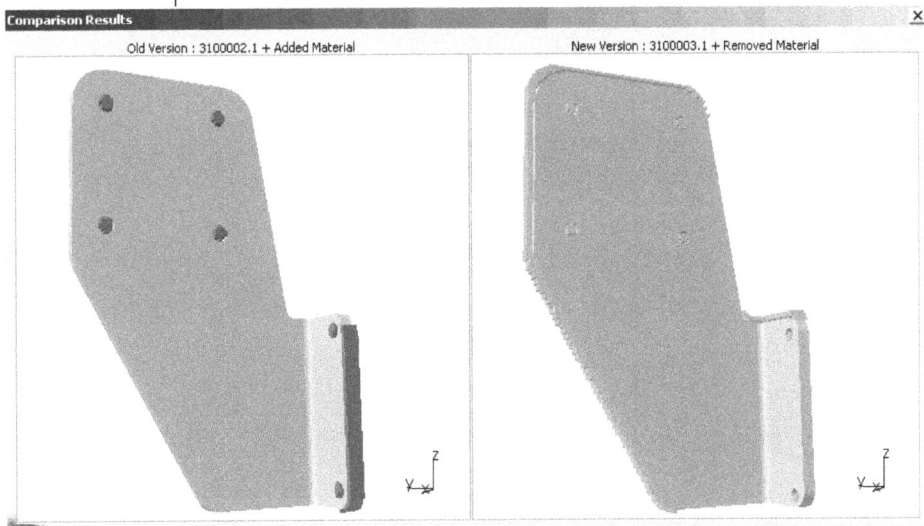

Figure 6–9

Step 3 - Save the results.

You can save the compare product results in any product existing in the active document. The **Save in Product** option enables you select the product in the specification tree in which you want to save the result. When you click **Save** in the Compare Products dialog box, the result gets added to the specification tree under the specified product.

Geometric Comparison results can be saved by clicking **Save**. It can be saved as a .3DMAP, .CGR, .WRL, or .MODEL file. You cannot save a visual comparison.

6.3 Measuring an Arc Section

The Arc Through Three Points tool is used to measure the length, radius, diameter, and angles of an arc. The calculations can be saved as features in the model.

General Steps

Use the following general steps to measure an arc section.

1. Activate the Arc Through Three Points tool.
2. Select points to measure.
3. Save the measurement.

Step 1 - Activate the Arc Through Three Points tool.

Click the $\nwarrow$ (Arc Through Three Points) icon. The Measure Arc Section dialog box opens, as shown in Figure 6–10.

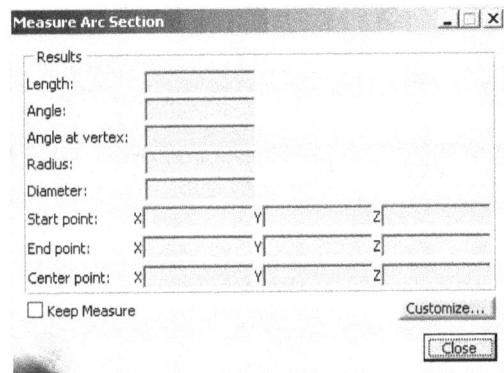

Figure 6–10

Step 2 - Select points to measure.

Select the three points between which to measure the arc. To help you locate the correct points, the system dynamically highlights points as the cursor moves across them.

For example, Figure 6–11 shows the third point selected for an arc measurement. Markers indicate the other two selected points.

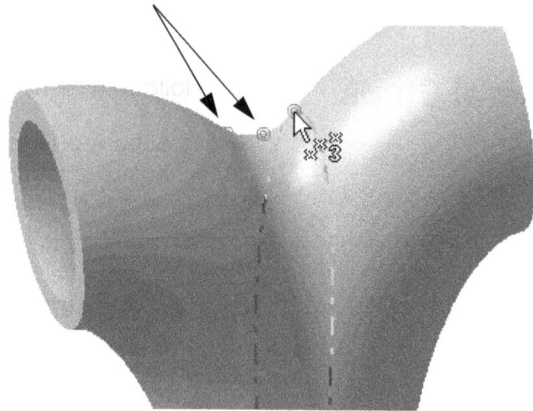

Figure 6–11

Step 3 - Save the measurement.

Once the three points have been selected, an arc is generated that fits between the selected points. The screen displays the three selected points, the arc connecting them, and the calculated center point for the arc. The screen also displays the calculated information on the arc, as shown in Figure 6–12.

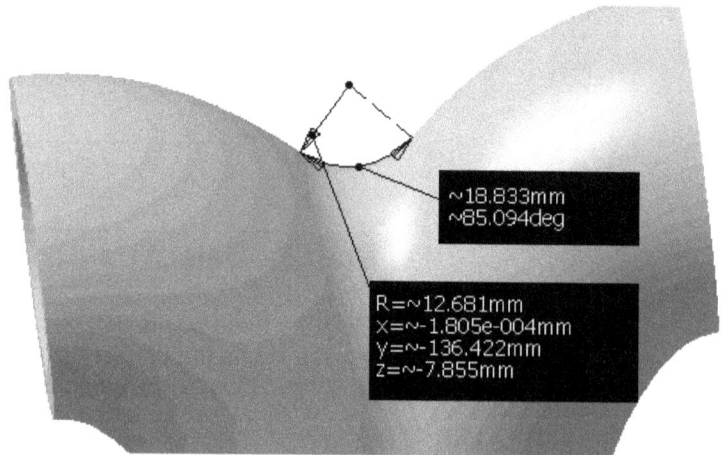

Figure 6–12

The Measure Arc Section dialog box displays all calculated information, as shown in Figure 6–13. To save the information as a feature in the model, select the **Keep Measure** option. The measurement displays in the **Applications** branch of the specification tree.

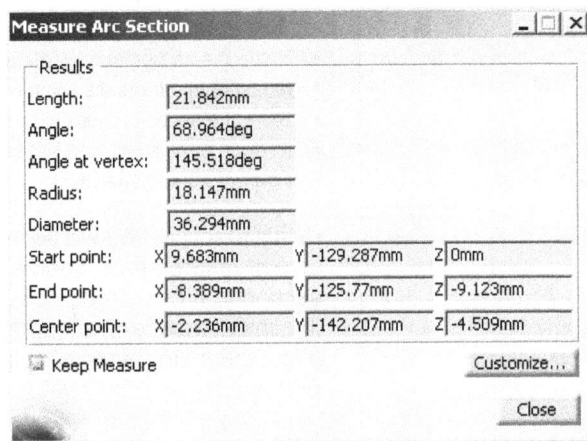

Measure Arc Section			_ □ X
Results			
Length:	21.842mm		
Angle:	68.964deg		
Angle at vertex:	145.518deg		
Radius:	18.147mm		
Diameter:	36.294mm		
Start point:	X 9.683mm	Y -129.287mm	Z 0mm
End point:	X -8.389mm	Y -125.77mm	Z -9.123mm
Center point:	X -2.236mm	Y -142.207mm	Z -4.509mm
☐ Keep Measure			Customize...
			Close

Figure 6–13

Practice 6a

Sectioning and Distance Analysis

Practice Objectives

- Start a sectioning analysis.
- Setup the sectioning parameters.
- Measure in the results window.
- Store the section results to the DMU file.
- Perform a minimum and X-distance analysis.
- Perform a band analysis.

In this practice, you will section a product file in various locations, take measurements, and perform a clash analysis on a particular section that has already been created. You will also check that the link component is long enough in the given configuration for a minimum clearance between the Lever Angle and the Pin Seige.

Task 1 - Open the assembly.

The files for this practice can be found in the BoreDevice directory.

1. Open **SectionBoreDevice.CATProduct**. The assembly displays as shown in Figure 6–14.

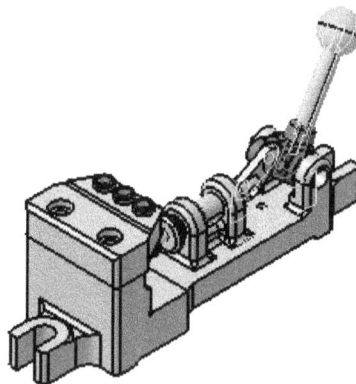

Figure 6–14

Task 2 - Activate the DMU Space Analysis workbench.

1. Ensure that the Space Analysis workbench is active (the workbench icon should be ![icon]).

2. If the Space Analysis workbench is not active, select **Start> Digital Mockup>DMU Space Analysis**. The DMU Space Analysis workbench (![icon]) is now active.

Task 3 - Start the sectioning definition.

1. Click the ![icon] (Sectioning) icon in the DMU Space Analysis toolbar.

2. Change the Name to **FirstSectionCut**. Keep the default settings, as shown in Figure 6–15.

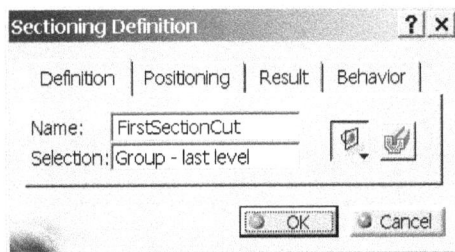

Figure 6–15

Task 4 - Define the positioning settings.

1. Select the *Positioning* tab in the Sectioning Definition dialog box.

2. Change the Normal constraint setting to the **Y-direction**, as shown in Figure 6–16.

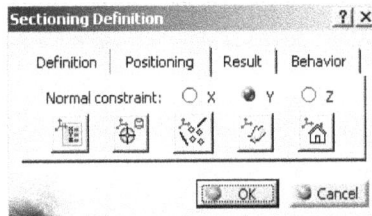

Figure 6–16

3. Select the cutting-plane representation in the display area with the left mouse button and drag it to move the section through the assembly. The section results display dynamically in the FirstSectionCut Preview window.

4. Reset the position by clicking the ⌂ (Reset Position) icon.

5. Change the Normal constraint back to **Y**.

6. Click the (Edit Position And Dimensions) icon to edit the positioning parameters for the plane.

7. Within the Edit Position and Dimensions dialog box, enter the values shown in Figure 6–17.

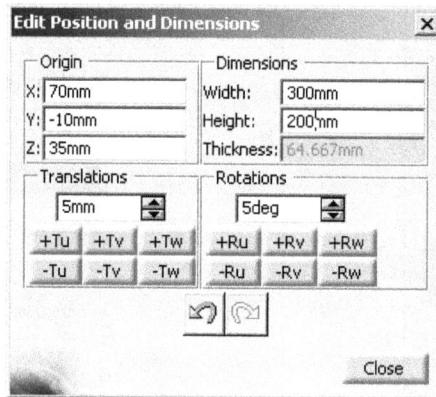

Edit Position and Dimensions

Origin	Dimensions	
X: 70mm	Width:	300mm
Y: -10mm	Height:	200mm
Z: 35mm	Thickness:	64.667mm

Translations: 5mm +Tu +Tv +Tw -Tu -Tv -Tw
Rotations: 5deg +Ru +Rv +Rw -Ru -Rv -Rw

Close

Figure 6–17

8. Click **-TW** twice to translate the plane in 5mm increments for a total of -10mm.

9. Click **-Ru** twice and **+Rv** once to rotate the section plane in 5 degree increments.

The result displays similar to those shown in Figure 6–18. Select **Window>Tile Vertically** to view the section window beside the assembly, as shown in Figure 6–18.

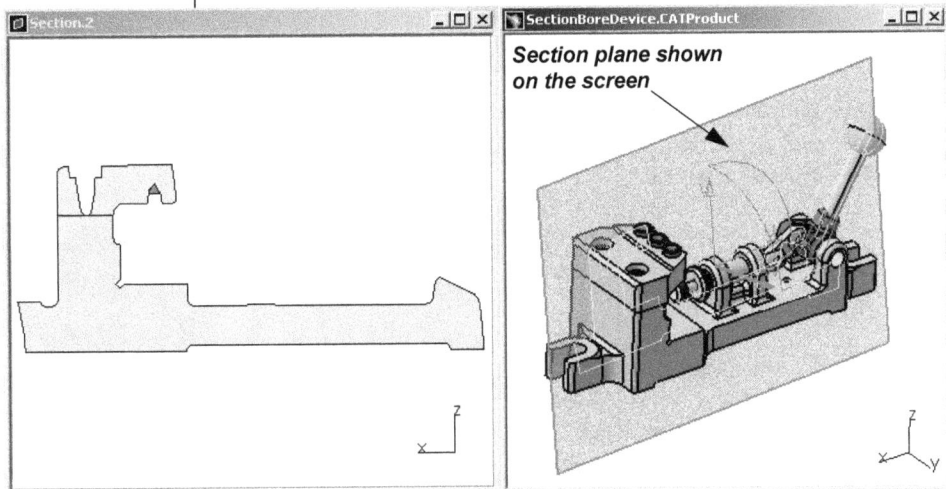

Figure 6–18

10. Click **OK** to save FirstSectionCut to the specification tree. The section analysis is now stored in the current model.

11. Close the FirstSectionCut window and maximize the SectionBoreDevice window.

Task 5 - Create a second sectional cut.

1. Create a second section called **SecondSectionCut**.

2. Click the (Positioning by 2/3 Selections) icon in the *Positioning* tab to position the section through features in the model.

3. Create the section plane that is defined by the axes of the two holes at the top of the Feature Drill component, as shown in Figure 6–19.

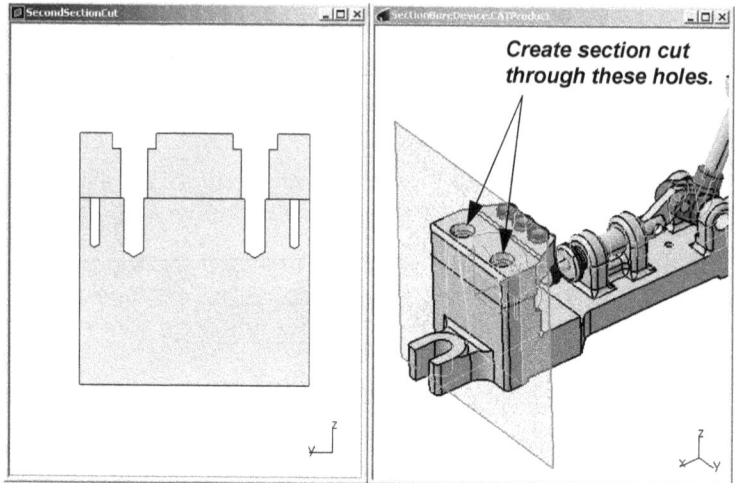

Figure 6–19

Task 6 - Measure the section information in the Results window.

1. Select the *Result* tab in the Sectioning Definition dialog box.

2. Click the (Results Window) icon to remove the Results window and display the Preview window. All of the options in the Section Definition dialog box are grayed out.

3. Click the (Results Window) icon redisplay the Results window.

4. Ensure that the (Section Fill) icon is selected, as shown in Figure 6–20.

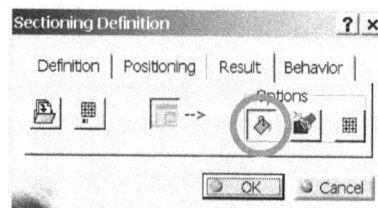

Figure 6–20

5. Without closing the Sectioning Definition dialog box, click the

   (Measure Item) icon in the DMU Space Analysis toolbar

   to perform a measurement. Ensure that the (Measure item) icon is selected in the Measure Item dialog box.

6. Click **Customize** and ensure that the **Area** option is enabled in the Surface column.

7. Within the Results Window (you cannot measure in the Preview window), select the surface of the lower part, as show in Figure 6–21.

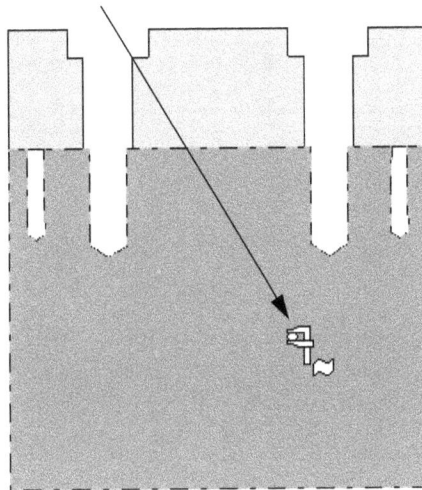

Figure 6–21

8. What is the approximate surface area of the part?

9. Complete the measurement and click **OK** to save SecondSectionCut to the specification tree.

10. Close the Results window and maximize the SectionBoreDevice window.

The (Section Fill) icon must be enabled to retrieve surface area information and to be able to select the Clash tool.

Task 7 - Retrieve a previously stored section.

1. Expand the **Applications>Sections** branch of the specification tree (if not already expanded) by clicking the ✤ symbol for each node.

2. Double-click on **ClashSection** in the specification tree.

3. Click the ![icon] (Clash Detection) icon in the *Result* tab to show all of the clash areas in the Results window, as shown in Figure 6–22.

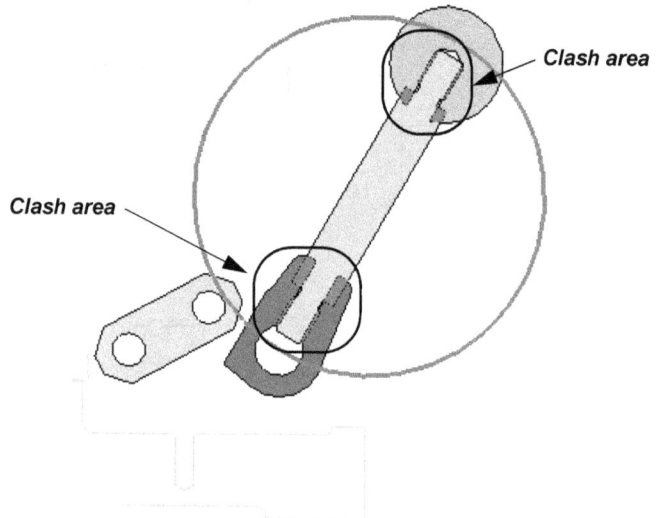

Clash area

Clash area

Figure 6–22

4. Pan and zoom in the Results window to see the clash areas better.

5. Disable the Section Fill tool by clicking the ![icon] (Section Fill) icon. The shaded areas in the Results window now appear in wireframe.

6. Without closing the Sectioning Definition dialog box, click the ![icon] (Measure Between) icon in the DMU Space Analysis toolbar to perform another measurement.

7. Select the **Keep Measure** option in the Measure Between dialog box.

8. Measure the overlap distances between the Lever Angle part (blue) and the Pin Seized part (purple) in the Results window, as shown in Figure 6–23. Pan and zoom the model within the Results window to simplify this process.

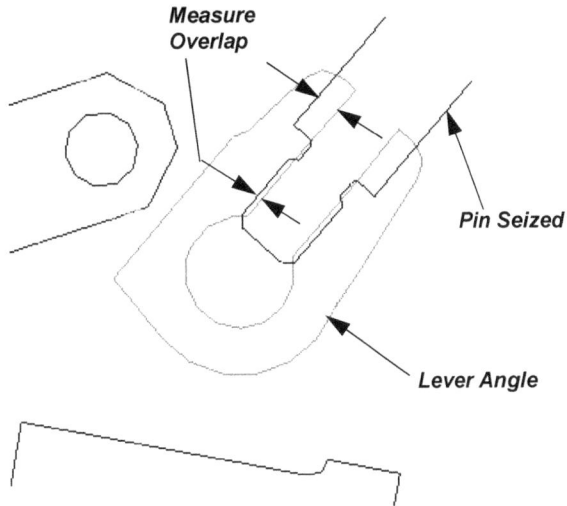

Figure 6–23

9. Click **OK** in the Sectioning Definition dialog box to resave **ClashSection** to the specification tree.

10. Close the Results window and maximize the SectionBoreDevice window.

11. Expand the **ClashSection** branch of the specification tree. The measurements are contained within the section feature, as shown in Figure 6–24.

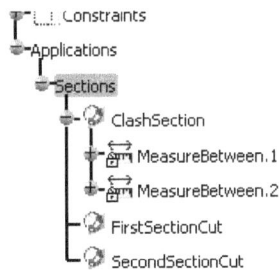

Figure 6–24

Task 8 - Perform Band, Minimum, and X distance analysis.

1. Click the ▨ (Distance and Band Analysis) icon in the DMU Space Analysis toolbar.

2. Change the name of the analysis to **LinkAnalysis**.

3. Select **Band Analysis** and **Between two selections** in the Type drop-down lists.

4. Enter a Minimum distance of **6mm** and a Maximum distance of **8mm**, as shown in Figure 6–25.

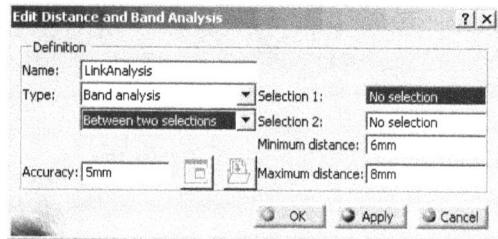

Figure 6–25

5. Select the **Lever Angle** as *Selection 1*.

6. Click in the *Selection 2* field and select the **Pin Pressure** component.

7. Click **Apply** to run the analysis. The results display in a Preview window as shown in Figure 6–26.

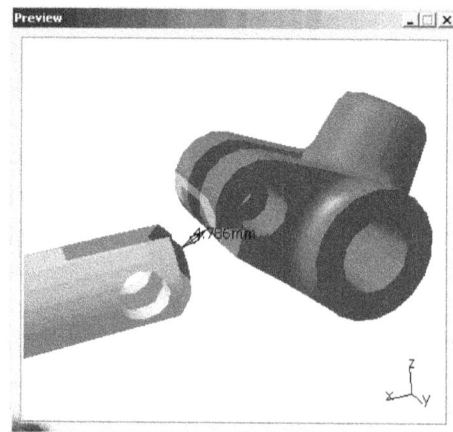

Figure 6–26

8. In the Preview window, review the results. A red area displays. This is the area that is less then the minimum distance required. It indicates that the link needs to be longer if the minimum distance required is to be established. Also displayed in the Preview window is the current straight line (minimum) distance between the two components.

9. Check the minimum distance results obtained from the band analysis by selecting **Minimum** in the Type drop-down list of the Edit Distance and Band dialog box. Rerun the analysis. The results should be the same.

10. Check the X-direction distance between the components by changing the type to **Along X**.

11. Click **OK** to close the dialog box. The LinkAnalysis has been added to the specification tree, as shown in Figure 6–27.

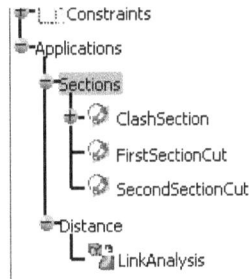

Figure 6–27

12. Save and close the SectionBoreDevice assembly.

Practice 6b

Compare Products

Practice Objectives

- Set up a Compare analysis.
- Run a visual compare.
- Run a geometrical compare.
- Use the Arc Through Three Points tool.

In this practice, you will compare two versions of the same part to check for differences between the revisions. A diffuser vane has been adjusted since its first revision. You will use the compare tool to determine where the changes have occurred. You will also use the Arc Through Three Points tool to determine the different arc lengths between the two revisions.

Task 1 - Create a new Product file.

To compare two files, they must first be inserted into the same product file.

1. Select **File>New** or click the ⬜ (New) icon in the Standard toolbar.

2. Create a new product file.

3. Highlight the product in the specification tree, right-click, and select **Properties**.

4. Change the *Part Number* of the product to **Compare** using the Properties dialog box.

Task 2 - Insert part files to be compared.

The files for this task can be found in the Compare directory.

1. Select the product in the specification tree, right-click and select **Components>Existing Component**.

2. Insert **DiffuserVane_01.CATPart** from the Compare folder. The part is inserted into the assembly, as shown in Figure 6–28.

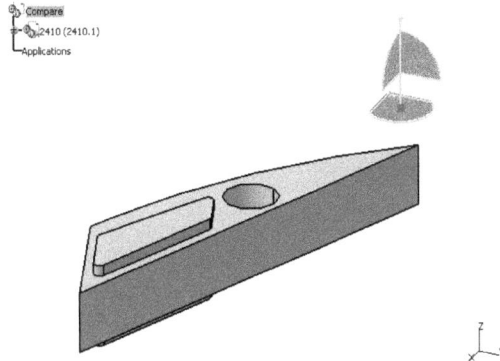

Figure 6–28

3. Select the top-level product in the specification tree and select **Insert>Existing Component**. Insert **DiffuserVane_02.CATPart** into the assembly.

4. Using the compass, move **DiffuserVane_02** so that you can see both parts clearly, as shown in Figure 6–29.

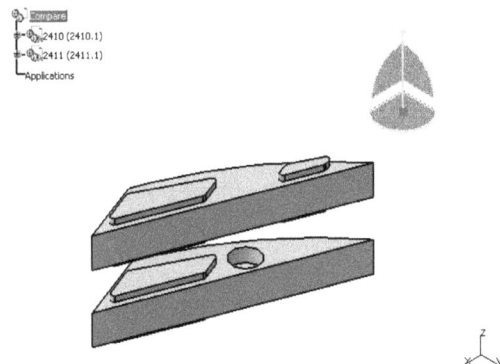

Figure 6–29

Task 3 - Set up a Compare analysis.

1. Activate the Space Analysis workbench (if not already activated).

2. Click the ⌗⌗ (Compare Products) icon.

3. Select **Use local axis systems** in the Compare Products dialog box.

*When the **Use local axis system** option is enabled, the two components are superposed on the origin of the old version part to improve the visualization of the differences between revisions.*

---

4. Select the **2410** component in the specification tree as the old version.

5. Select the **2411** component in the specification tree as the new version. The Compare Products dialog box updates as shown in Figure 6–30.

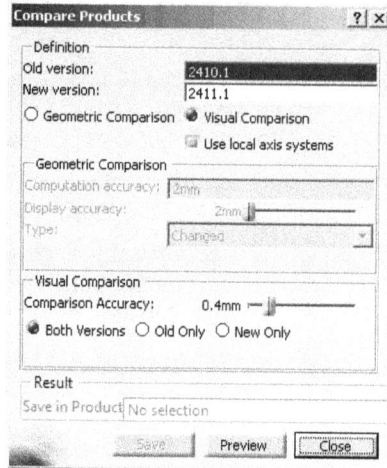

Figure 6–30

Task 4 - Analyze the visual comparison.

1. Once the comparison is set up, the parts move on top of each other and display colors to indicate areas of material removal, addition, and no change.

*You might need to click **Preview** to see the change in accuracy on the screen.*

2. In the Visual Comparison section of the Compare Products dialog box, set the *Comparison Accuracy* slider to **0.02mm**. The differences between the models should become clearer, as shown in Figure 6–31. Rotate and zoom the model to investigate the analysis.

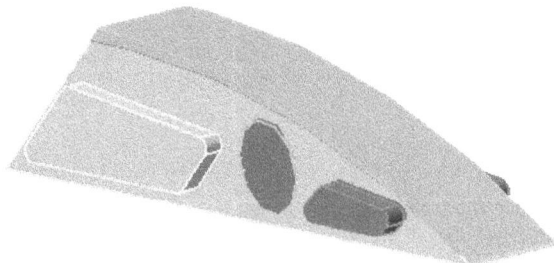

Figure 6–31

3. Set the *Comparison Accuracy* slider to **0.1mm** and click **Preview** to update the model. The visualization displays more yellow because the difference threshold has been increased. At a lower accuracy, the finer differences displayed with a greater comparison accuracy are ignored.

4. Change the **Both Versions** option to **Old Only** and **New Only** and preview each setting. The display changes. By toggling between these options, it should be clear which material has been added to the new revision and which material has been removed.

Task 5 - Run a Geometric Comparison.

1. Select the **Geometric Comparison** option in the Compare Products dialog box. The **Geometric Comparison** options become available, as shown in Figure 6–32.

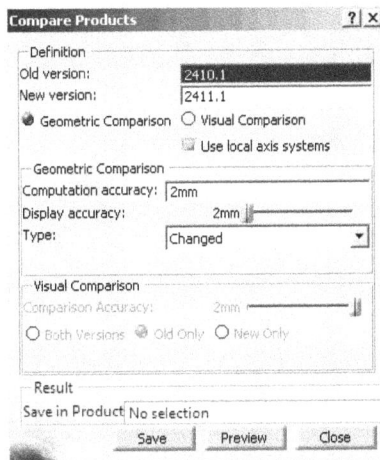

Figure 6–32

2. Select **Changed** in the Type drop-down list. When this option is enabled, material removal and addition data is grouped into a single output file when the results are saved.

3. Click **Preview** to open the Comparison Results window. Note the changes between the models. Because the Type of comparison is **Changed**, it is unclear where the material is added or removed. All that is seen are the areas of change between the models.

4. Change the *Type* to **Added + Removed** and click **Preview**.

5. Material addition and removal is now represented more clearly using different colors. The window on the left displays the old version of the model with red cubes representing additional material that exists in the new version. The window on the right displays the new version, with green cubes indicating areas where material has been removed from the old version.

6. Change the computation accuracy to **1mm** and preview the results. The cubes are smaller and more accurately represent the areas of material removal and addition, as shown in Figure 6–33.

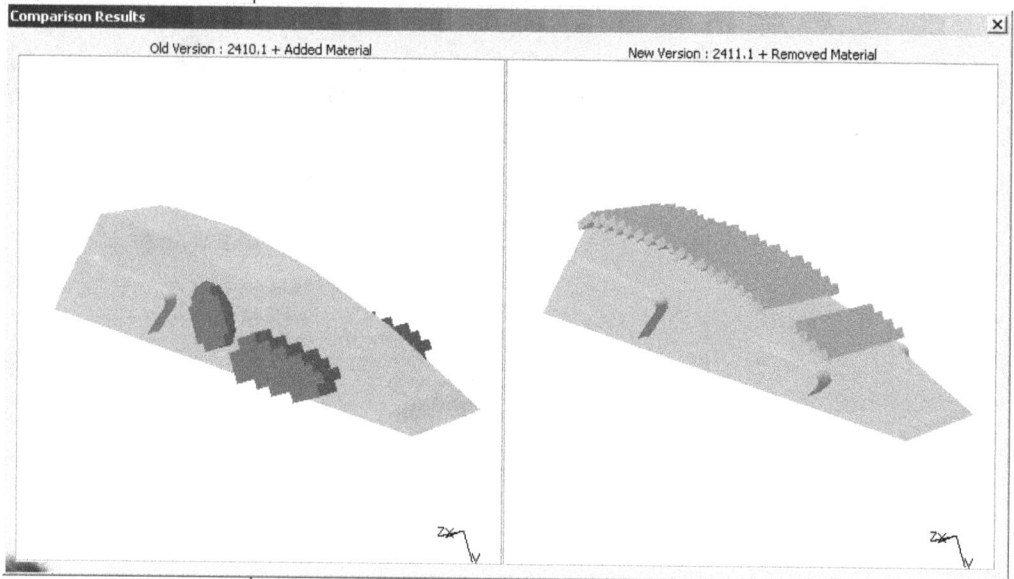

Figure 6–33

7. Close the Comparison Results dialog box.

Task 6 - Save the geometric comparison results.

1. Click **Save** in the Compare Products dialog box. Select a file format to save the file as and enter a filename.

Design Considerations

The results of a compare product analysis can be saved with a .3DMap, .CGR, .WRL, or .MODEL file extension for use with an assortment of CAD/CAM software. Furthermore, these file formats can be inserted into a CATProduct assembly using the **Insert>Existing Component** tool. The material addition and removal data is inserted as a new green or red colored part body. The material representation can be used for a variety of analyses, such as clash and distance and band analysis, to reveal the impact of modifications between revisions.

2. Save the geometric comparison result.

3. Close the Compare Products dialog box.

Task 7 - Measure the arc length.

The Compare Products analysis indicates that the top surface of the new model differs from the old version. You will now use the Arc Through Three Points tool to measure the exact difference in the arc length.

1. Click the 🖉 (Arc Through Three Points) icon.

2. Select the **Keep Measure** option in the Measure Arc Section dialog box, as shown in Figure 6–34.

*To improve the readability of the measure, select **Customize** and clear all options except **Length**.*

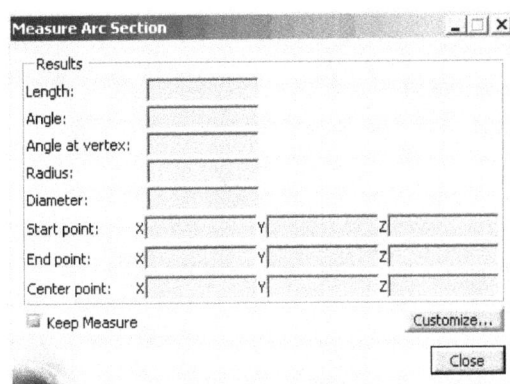

Figure 6–34

Ensure that you are selecting the vertices and the point, and not just the curve.

3. To define the arc, select the vertex at the end of the arc, the point in the middle of the arc, and the vertex at the other end of the arc, as shown in Figure 6–35.

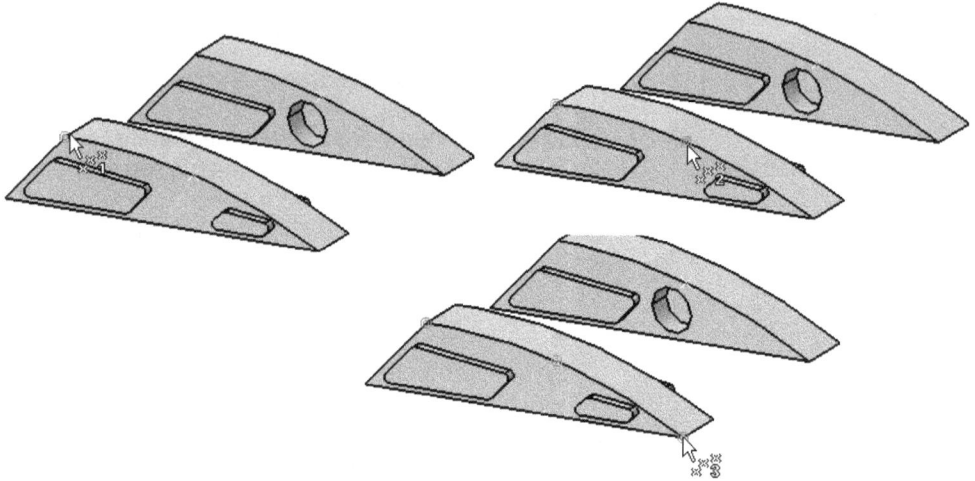

Figure 6–35

4. Repeat Step 3. for the other part, and compare the results, as shown in Figure 6–36.

Your results might differ slightly if you did not select the vertex or point.

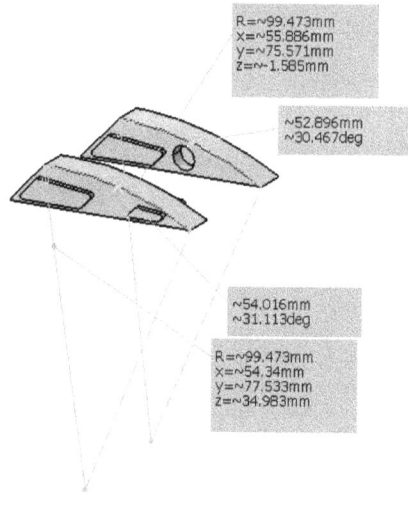

R=~99.473mm
x=~55.886mm
y=~75.571mm
z=~-1.585mm

~52.896mm
~30.467deg

~54.016mm
~31.113deg

R=~99.473mm
x=~54.34mm
y=~77.533mm
z=~34.983mm

Figure 6–36

5. Save and close the document.

Chapter 7

Annotations

Once analysis information has been captured, it can be communicated to designers or manufacturers using model annotations. These annotations enable you to display critical information about the part or assembly directly on the 3D geometry.

Learning Objectives in this Chapter

- Create and manage annotations.
- Create an Annotation View.

7.1 Creating Annotations

You can add annotations to your model using the 3D annotation tool. These notes display with the 3D model and help ensure that important information is included with the model.

General Steps

Use the following general steps to create annotations:

1. Activate the 3D annotation tool.
2. Locate the note.
3. Enter the note.

Step 1 - Activate the 3D annotation tool.

Click the ⓣ (3D Annotation) icon in the DMU Review Creation toolbar and select the object to which to attach a note. The Annotation Text dialog box and the Text Properties toolbar display, as shown in Figure 7–1.

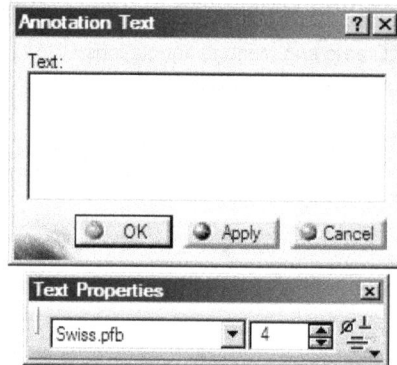

Figure 7–1

Step 2 - Locate the note.

Click **Apply** to preview the note on the screen. The left side of the note is located on the selected point. Move the cursor over the text until the green manipulator displays, as shown in Figure 7–2. Hold the left mouse button to drag the note to a new location on the screen.

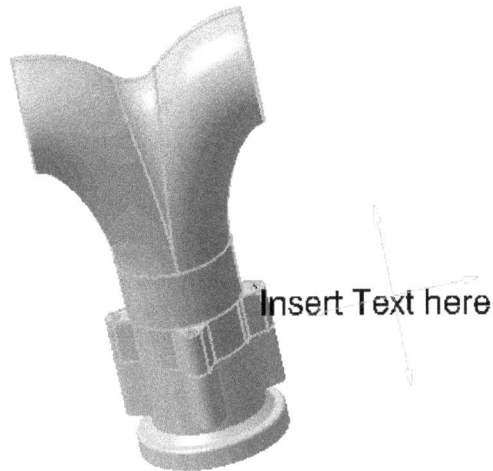

Insert Text here

Figure 7–2

Step 3 - Enter the note.

Enter the note in the Text window. Use the Text Properties toolbar to change the font, style, or size. You can insert symbols using the **Insert Symbol** flyout, as shown in Figure 7–3.

Symbols can be inserted when SymbC format is used.

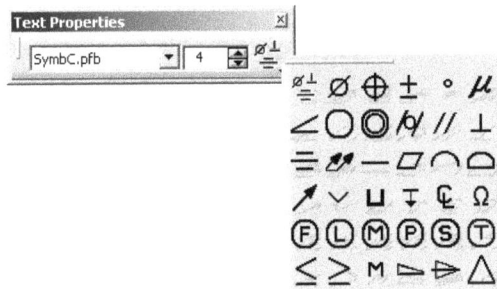

Figure 7–3

Once the note is located correctly, click **OK** to complete it, as shown in Figure 7–4.

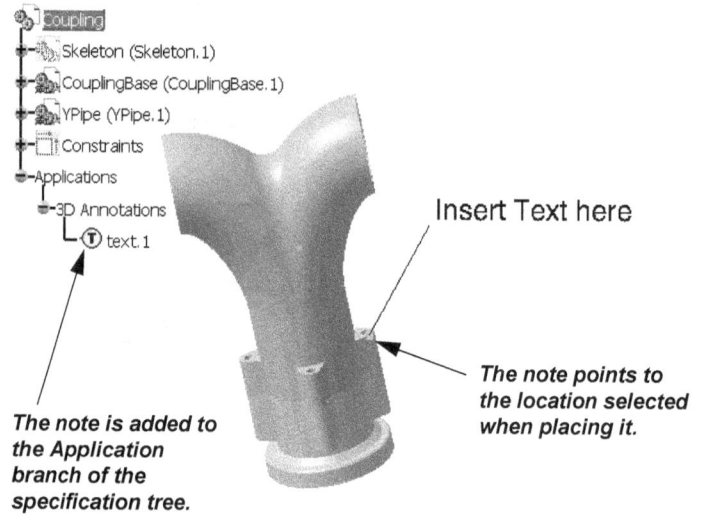

Coupling
Skeleton (Skeleton.1)
CouplingBase (CouplingBase.1)
YPipe (YPipe.1)
Constraints
Applications
3D Annotations
text.1

Insert Text here

The note points to the location selected when placing it.

The note is added to the Application branch of the specification tree.

Figure 7–4

7.2 Managing Annotations

Once annotations are created, you can modify their location, contents, text style, color, and size, and add components to link to the text.

Properties

To access the text properties, right-click on the note in the specification tree or in the model and select **Properties**.

In the *Feature Properties* tab, you can change the name of the note, making it easier to locate it in the specification tree. In the *Text Properties* tab, you can add a border to the text and change its orientation or color as shown in Figure 7–5.

Change the color of the text using Color drop-down list.

Add a border around the note.

Change the orientation of the text.

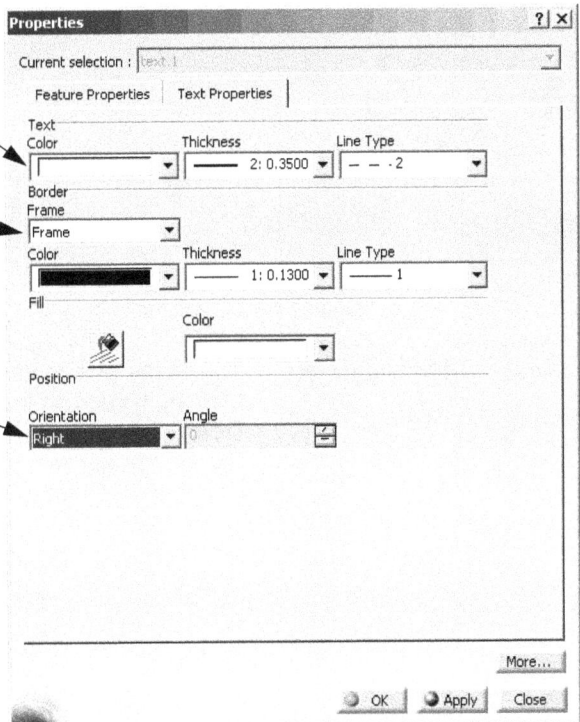

Figure 7–5

Add Link

*The **Remove Link** option is only available when more than one link exists.*

A note can point to more than one component in a model.

How To: Add an Additional Component to the Note

1. Right-click on the note in the specification tree or in the model, and select **Text.x Object>Add Link**, where **Text.x** is the name of the note.
2. Select the location you want the note to point to on the second component. The note then points to both the original component and the new one, as shown in Figure 7–6.
3. Repeat the above steps for any additional components you want the note to point to. To remove a link, right-click on the note and select **Text.x Object>Remove link**.

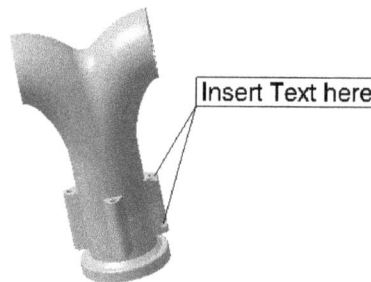

Figure 7–6

Definition

To edit the text contained in the note, including the font style and size, right-click on the note and select **Text.x Object> Definition**. The Annotation Text dialog box and Text Properties toolbar appear with the note contents displayed, as shown in Figure 7–7. Change the text content and style as required.

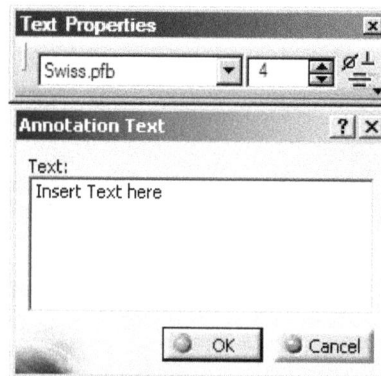

Figure 7–7

7.3 Creating an Annotation View

Annotated views enable you to create 2D simple geometry, complex annotations, import pictures, and create audio to include in a product file. Unlike 3D annotations, which are viewed all the time, Annotated views are only displayed when accessed. Annotated views are 2D, that is, you can pan and zoom an annotated view but you cannot rotate it.

General Steps

Use the following general steps to create an annotated view:

1. Start an Annotated view.
2. Create annotations.
3. Exit the Annotation view.
4. Manage Annotation views.

Step 1 - Start an Annotated view.

To create an Annotated view, orient and zoom the model as

required and click the [2D] (Annotated View) icon. It is important to have the correct orientation before activating the Annotated view, because if you rotate the model when it is active, you exit the Annotated view. You can zoom a model while in the Annotated view. However, each time you access the Annotated view, the zoom defaults to what it was when the Annotated view was first created.

Step 2 - Create annotations.

Use the DMU 2D Marker toolbar to create the required annotations. Figure 7–8 shows the toolbar with a description of each icon.

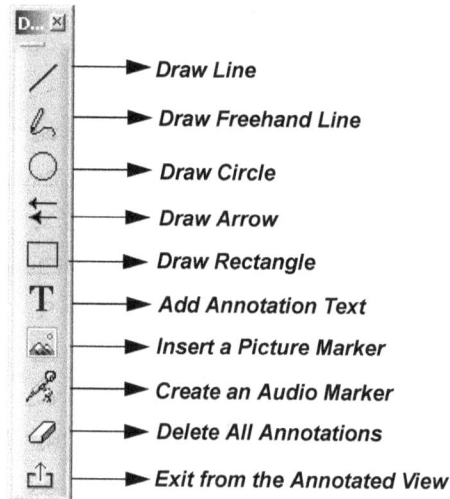

➤ *Draw Line*

➤ *Draw Freehand Line*

➤ *Draw Circle*

➤ *Draw Arrow*

➤ *Draw Rectangle*

➤ *Add Annotation Text*

➤ *Insert a Picture Marker*

➤ *Create an Audio Marker*

➤ *Delete All Annotations*

➤ *Exit from the Annotated View*

Figure 7–8

Geometric Annotation

How To: Create Lines, Freehand lines, Circles, Arrows, and Rectangles

1. Select the appropriate option.
2. Left-click on the screen to start the geometry.
3. Hold the left mouse button and drag the cursor to create the entity.
4. Release the left mouse button to place the geometry.

All Geometric entities can be moved by holding the left mouse button while the cursor is over entity and dragging it to a new location. Right-click on the lines and select **Properties** to modify their color and style.

Annotation Text

How To: Create Annotation Text

1. Click the **T** (Annotated Text) icon.
2. Left-click to place the text.
3. As with 3D Annotation, the Annotation Text dialog box and Text Properties toolbar appear. Enter text and use the Text Properties toolbar as required.
4. Click **OK** to place the note.

Annotation text can be moved by holding the left mouse button while the cursor is over the text and dragging it to a new location. As with 3D Annotation, the text can be modified by double-clicking on the text, or right-clicking and selecting **Marker.x Object>Definition**. Borders can be added and the color and orientation of the text can be changed by right-clicking on the text and selecting **Properties**.

Picture Marker

How To: Insert Images into an Annotation View

1. Click the (Insert a Picture Marker) icon.
2. Select a location on screen to place the image.
3. Select an image in the Select Picture file dialog box. Inserted images can be in .TIFF, .RGB, .JPG, or .BMP formats.
4. Click **Open** to place the image.

The picture can be resized by dragging the manipulators at its corners.

Audio Marker

How To: Attach Audio to an Annotated View

1. Click the (Create an Audio Marker) icon.

2. In the Select Audio File dialog box, navigate to the directory in which to create the .wav file, and save it with a meaningful name.
3. Click **Open** to continue.

4. Select the quality of the audio file in the Audio Attributes dialog box, as shown in Figure 7–9, and click **OK**.

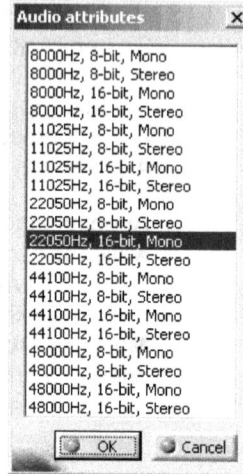

Audio attributes

8000Hz, 8-bit, Mono
8000Hz, 8-bit, Stereo
8000Hz, 16-bit, Mono
8000Hz, 16-bit, Stereo
11025Hz, 8-bit, Mono
11025Hz, 8-bit, Stereo
11025Hz, 16-bit, Mono
11025Hz, 16-bit, Stereo
22050Hz, 8-bit, Mono
22050Hz, 8-bit, Stereo
22050Hz, 16-bit, Mono
22050Hz, 16-bit, Stereo
44100Hz, 8-bit, Mono
44100Hz, 8-bit, Stereo
44100Hz, 16-bit, Mono
44100Hz, 16-bit, Stereo
48000Hz, 8-bit, Mono
48000Hz, 8-bit, Stereo
48000Hz, 16-bit, Mono
48000Hz, 16-bit, Stereo

OK   Cancel

Figure 7–9

5. In the Audio Recorder dialog box, click ● to record the required audio, as shown in Figure 7–10.

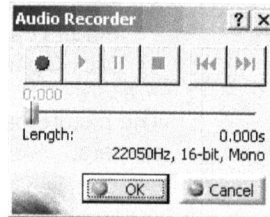

You need a microphone to be connected to the computer to record an audio file.

Audio Recorder   ? ×

● ▶ II ■   I◀◀ ▶▶I

0.000

Length: 0.000s
         22050Hz, 16-bit, Mono

OK   Cancel

Figure 7–10

6. Click **OK** to complete the recording. To replay or edit the audio marker, double-click on Sound in the specification tree, as shown in Figure 7–11.

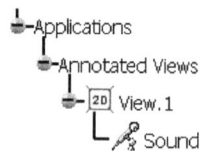

—Applications

—Annotated Views

—[2D] View.1

Sound

Figure 7–11

Step 3 - Exit the Annotation view.

Click the ⬆ (Exit from the Annotated View) icon to save the view. The view is added to the specification tree.

Step 4 - Manage Annotation views.

Any number of annotation views can be created. These 2D views can be located in the specification tree under the **Applications** branch, as shown in Figure 7–12.

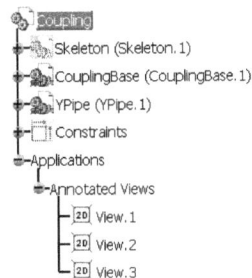

Figure 7–12

You can access the created views to view or edit them, by double-clicking on them in the specification tree. The selected view opens automatically.

You can also access views by clicking the 📑 (Manage Annotated Views) icon. The Annotated Views dialog box opens, as shown in Figure 7–13.

*The View name can be changed by right-clicking and selecting **Properties**.*

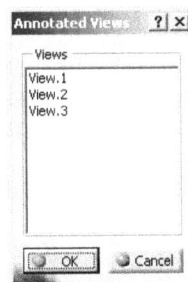

Figure 7–13

Select the required view and click **OK**. The view displays and can be edited.

Practice 7a

Create and Manage 3D Annotations

Practice Objectives

- Create 3D annotations.
- Manage 3D annotations.

In this practice, you will add an annotation to the front wheel assembly to help the designer locate the problem areas so that they can be resolved quickly.

Task 1 - Open the assembly.

1. Open **FrontWheelClash.CATProduct** in the FrontWheel directory. The assembly displays as shown in Figure 7–14.

    If you completed Practice 5a you can also continue with FrontWheel.CATProduct instead.

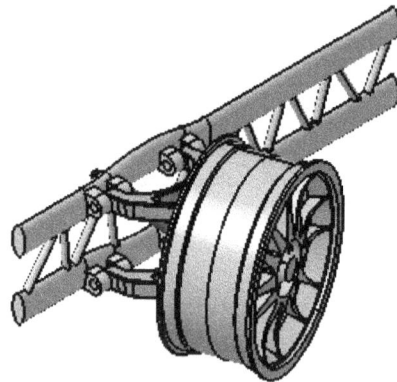

Figure 7–14

2. Ensure that the DMU Navigator workbench is active. To access the workbench, select **Start>Digital Mockup>DMU Navigator**.

Task 2 - Create an annotation.

Annotations must be created to note the areas the designer needs to review. You can remind yourself of the problem areas by reanalyzing your clash results in the **Applications** branch of the specification tree.

1. In the DMU Navigator workbench, click the ⓣ (3D Annotation) icon.

2. Select the top of the ball on the Mount component as shown in Figure 7–15, to place the note.

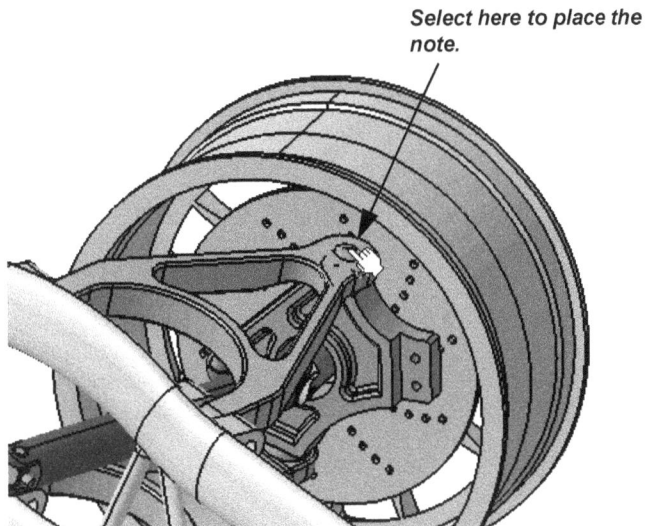

Select here to place the note.

Figure 7–15

3. Enter the text shown in Figure 7–16 using the Annotation Text dialog box.

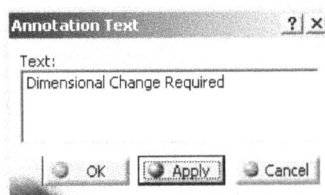

Figure 7–16

4. Click **Apply** to preview the note.

5. Hover the cursor over the note, hold the left mouse button, and drag the note to the location shown in Figure 7–17.

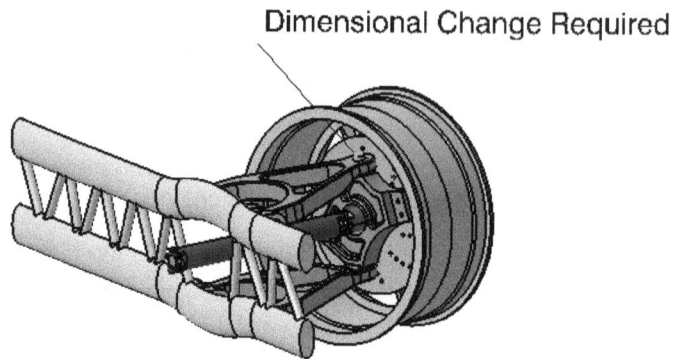

Figure 7–17

6. Click **OK** to complete the text creation.

Task 3 - Create additional annotations.

1. To better view the problem areas, hide the **WheelRim** component by selecting it in the specification tree, right-clicking and selecting **Hide/Show**.

2. Create a second annotation and locate it on the top arm, as shown in Figure 7–18.

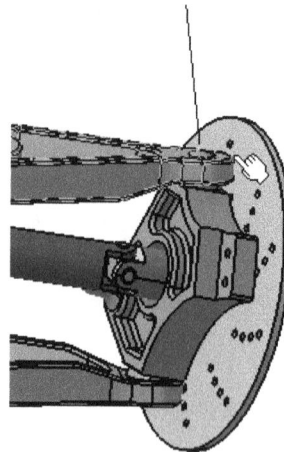

Figure 7–18

3. Enter the note, as shown in Figure 7–19.

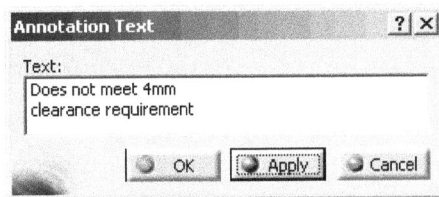

Figure 7–19

4. Preview the note and place it, as shown in Figure 7–20.

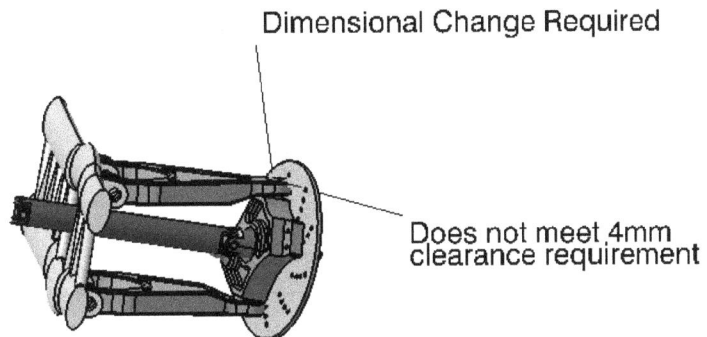

Figure 7–20

5. Click **OK** to complete the text creation.

Task 4 - Add a link to the second note.

1. In the specification tree, right-click on **text.2** and select **Text.2 object>Add link** as shown in Figure 7–21.

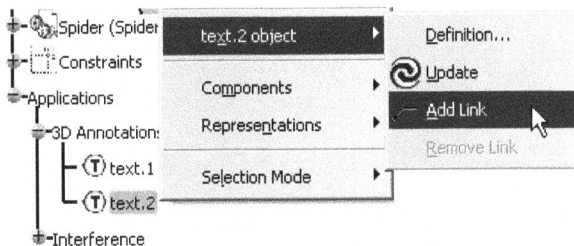

Figure 7–21

2. Select the hub so that a second link is created, as shown in Figure 7–22.

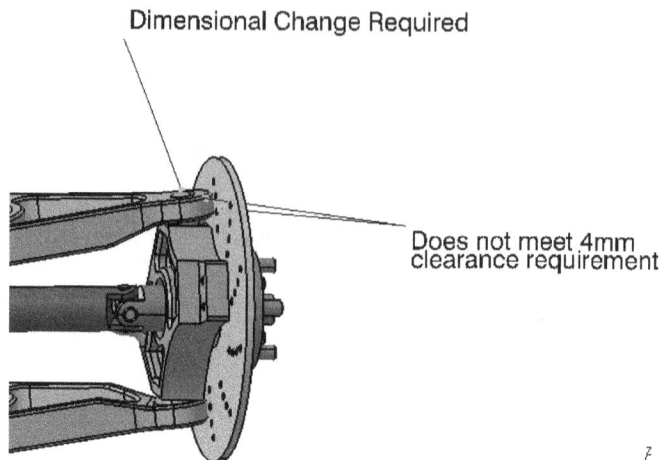

Dimensional Change Required

Does not meet 4mm clearance requirement

Figure 7–22

Task 5 - Complete the notes.

1. Create two more notes to indicate two additional areas the designer needs to look at, as shown in Figure 7–23.

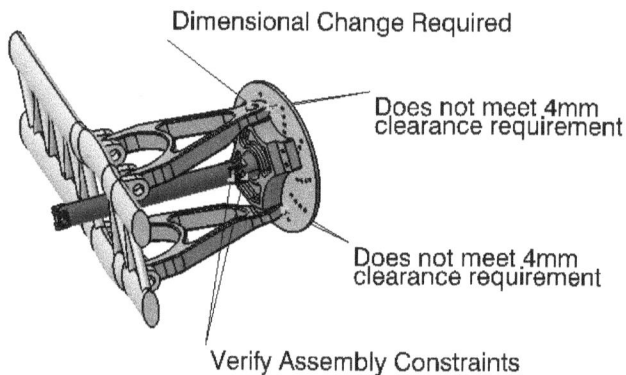

Dimensional Change Required

Does not meet 4mm clearance requirement

Does not meet 4mm clearance requirement

Verify Assembly Constraints

Figure 7–23

2. Manipulate the model to note how the annotations move with the assembly.

3. Save and close the model.

Practice 7b

Annotation Views

Practice Objectives

- Create an annotated view.
- Manage 3D annotations.
- Manage annotated views.

In this practice, you will create annotation views to indicate problems on a bore assembly.

Task 1 - Open the assembly.

The files for this practice can be found in the BoreDevice directory.

1. Open **SectionBoreDevice.CATProduct**. The assembly displays as shown in Figure 7–24.

*If you did not complete Practice 6a, open **BoreDeviceAllSections.CATProduct** instead.*

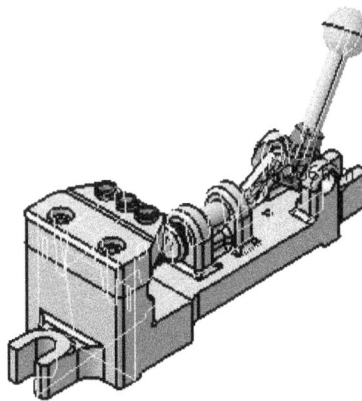

Figure 7–24

2. Ensure that the DMU Navigator workbench is active.

Task 2 - Redefine the ClashSection to Volume Cut.

1. In the **Applications** branch of the specification tree, double-click on **ClashSection** in the **Sections** branch.

2. Resize and rotate the section, as shown in Figure 7–25.

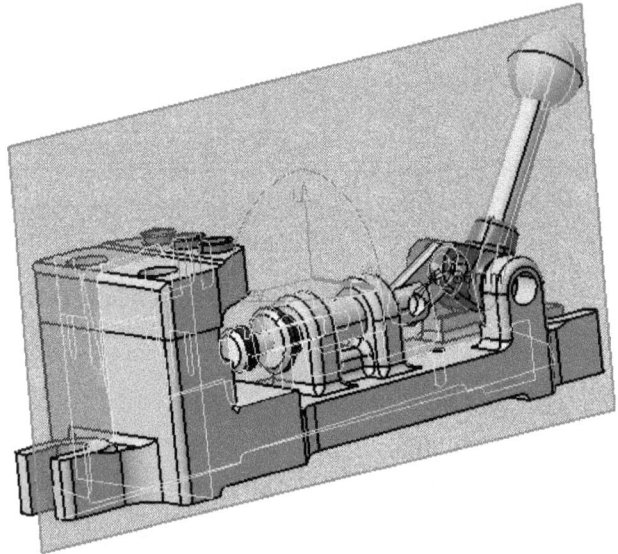

Figure 7–25

3. In the *Definition* tab of the Sectioning Definition dialog box, click [icon], as shown in Figure 7–26.

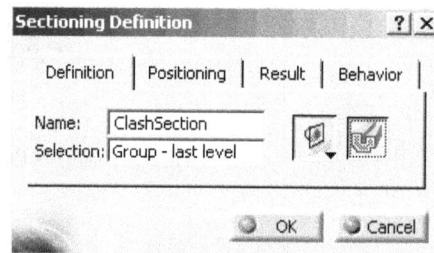

Figure 7–26

4. Click **OK** to close the Sectioning Definition dialog box. Close the Results window and maximize the SectionBoreDevice window. The model displays as shown in Figure 7–27.

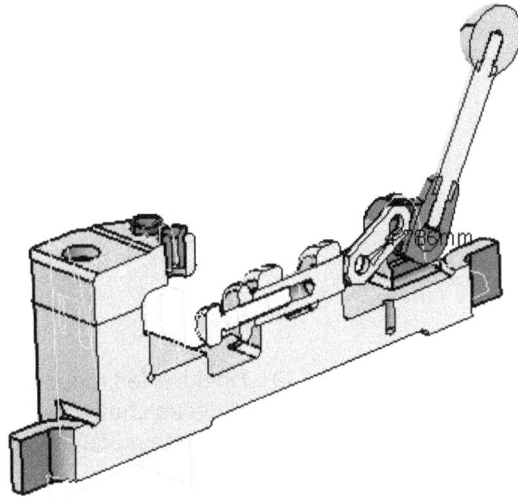

Figure 7–27

Task 3 - Set up an Annotated View.

Before the Annotated view can be accessed, you must ensure that the model is oriented correctly. Once in the view, the model cannot be rotated.

1. In the **Quick View** flyout, click the (Right View) icon.

2. Click the (Annotated View) icon in the DMU Review Creation toolbar. The DMU 2D Marker toolbar displays, as shown in Figure 7–28.

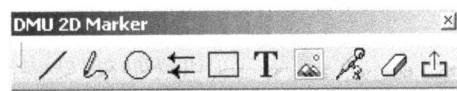

Figure 7–28

Task 4 - Create a circle.

This annotation view notes the interference detected inside the ClashSection.

1. Click the ⭕ (Draw Circle) icon. Locate the cursor as shown in Figure 7–29, to locate the center of the circle.

Figure 7–29

2. Hold the left mouse button and drag outward to create the circle as shown in Figure 7–30. Release the left mouse button to place the circle.

Figure 7–30

Task 5 - Create an arrow.

1. Create the arrow as shown in Figure 7–31 by clicking the

   ⇇ (Draw Arrow) icon. Start the arrow by holding the left mouse button. Drag the cursor to the location you want the arrow to point to. Release the left mouse button to place the arrow.

Hold the left mouse button here to begin creating the arrow.

Release the left mouse button here to place the arrow.

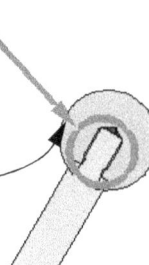

Figure 7–31

Task 6 - Add text.

1. Click the **T** (Text) icon.

2. Click above the start of the arrow to place the text.

3. Enter the text as shown in Figure 7–32.

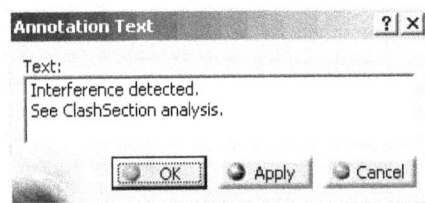

Figure 7–32

4. In the Text Properties toolbar, change the size of the text to **6** as shown in Figure 7–33.

Figure 7–33

5. Click **OK** to place the text.

6. Left-click on the text and, while holding the left mouse button, drag the text to the location shown in Figure 7–34, if required.

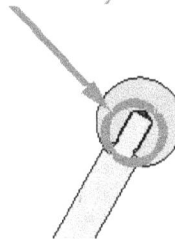

Figure 7–34

Task 7 - Create a freehand line and arrow to note other interferences.

1. Click the ⟋ (Draw Freehand Line) icon.

2. Place the cursor, as shown in Figure 7–35. This is the location where the freehand line starts.

3. Hold the left mouse button and begin to move the cursor to indicate the location of the line. The line should look approximately like Figure 7–35.

Place the cursor here to locate the start point of the line

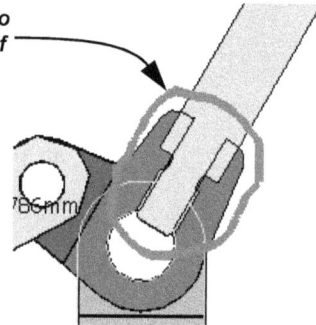

Figure 7–35

4. Release the left mouse button to complete the freehand line.

5. Create a second arrow to point the text to the new freehand line, as shown in Figure 7–36.

Interference detected.
See ClashSection analysis.

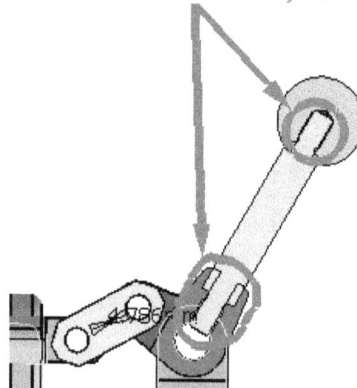

Figure 7–36

Task 8 - Change properties on annotation.

1. Hold <Ctrl> and select the two arrows.

2. Right-click and select **Properties**.

3. Change the color of the arrows to **white** and the line thickness to **3** as shown in Figure 7–37.

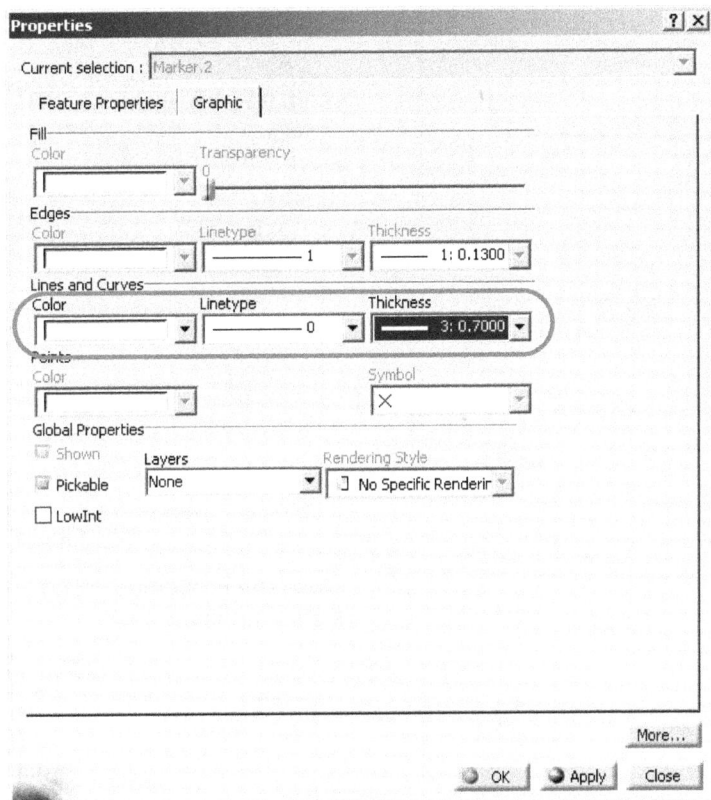

Figure 7–37

4. Click **OK** to close the Properties dialog box and update the arrows.

5. Hold <Ctrl> and select the circle and the freehand line. Right-click and select **Properties**.

6. Change the Linetype to **3** and the Thickness to **4**, as shown in Figure 7–38.

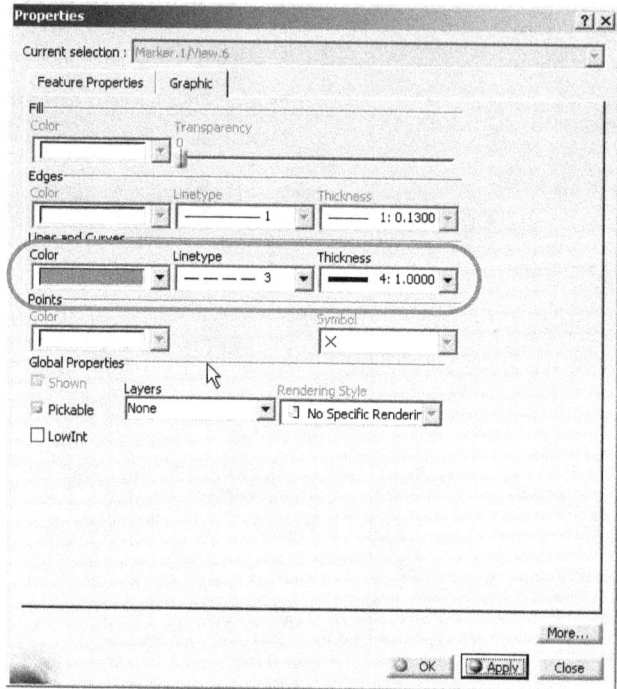

Figure 7–38

7. Close the Properties dialog box. The annotations update, as shown in Figure 7–39.

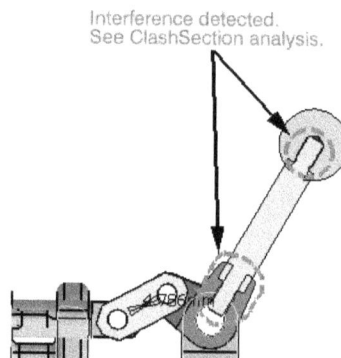

Figure 7–39

8. Click the ⬆ (Exits from the Annotated View) icon to exit the Annotated view. All of the annotations that were just created disappear.

Task 9 - Create an Annotated view for Band Analysis results.

When the band analysis was run for this model it detected that the minimum distance was not obtained. In this task, you will create another annotated view to note this to the designer.

1. Click the ⬒ (Left View) icon in the **Quick View** flyout.

2. Click the 🔲 (Annotated View) icon to create a second annotated view.

3. Create a rectangle around the link, as shown in Figure 7–40.

Left-click here to start the rectangle.

Release the left mouse button here to complete the rectangle.

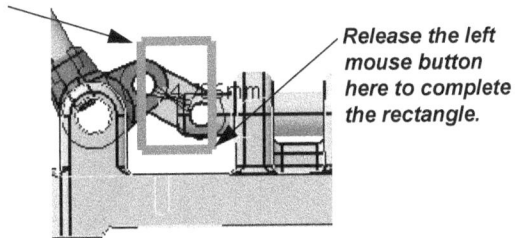

Figure 7–40

4. Create an arrow and text as shown in Figure 7–41.

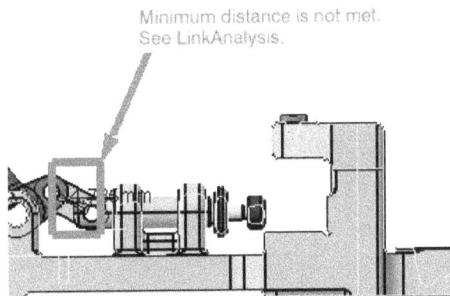

Figure 7–41

Task 10 - Manage annotations.

Leave the rest of the properties at their defaults.

1. Using the Properties dialog box, change the properties of the annotations to:

   Rectangle:

   - *Linetype:* **3**
   - *Thickness:* **3**

   Arrow:

   - *Color:* **White**
   - *Thickness:* **2**

   Text:

   - Add a Frame using the default thickness, color, and linetype.

   The Annotated view displays as shown in Figure 7–42.

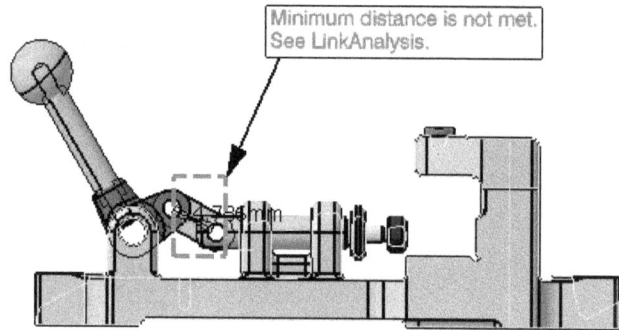

Figure 7–42

2. Exit the Annotated view.

Task 11 - Rename Annotated Views.

*The **Annotated views** branch is in the **Applications** branch of the specification tree.*

1. In the **Annotated views** branch of the specification tree, right-click on **View.1** and select **Properties**.

2. Change the name of the view to **Interference Comments**.

3. Change the name of *View.2* to **Band Analysis Comments** using the technique used to change the name of **View.1**. The specification tree displays as shown in Figure 7–43.

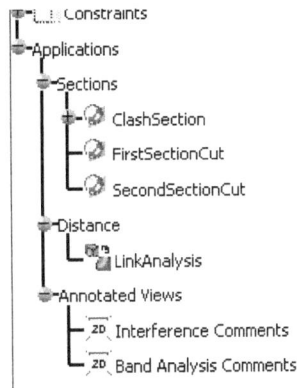

Figure 7–43

Task 12 - Manage Annotated Views.

1. Click the ⬛ (Manage Annotated Views) icon in the DMU Navigator Tools toolbar.

2. In the Annotated Views dialog box, select **Interference Comments** and click **OK**. The Interference View displays in the same orientation and zoom that it was created in. The DMU 2D Marker toolbar displays again, enabling you to edit the view.

3. Exit the Interference View.

4. In the specification tree, double-click on the **Band Analysis Comments** view. The View displays along with the DMU 2D Marker toolbar.

5. Exit the View.

6. Save and close the file.

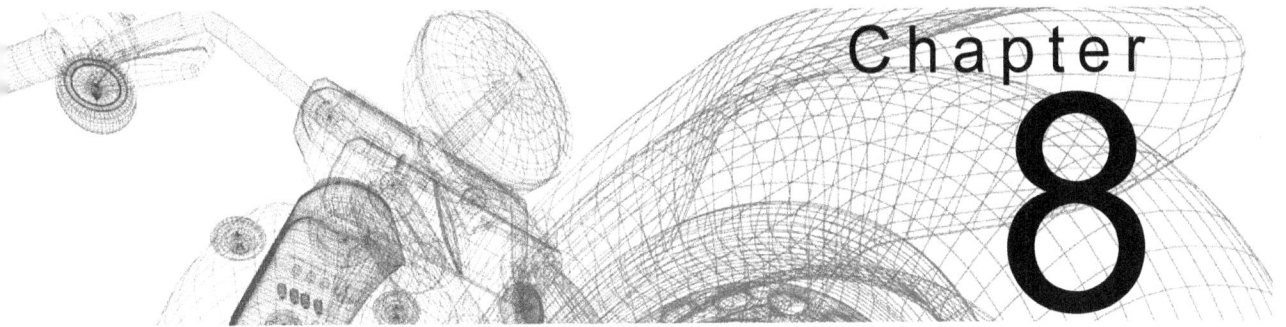

Image Capture

Model images might be required to communicate information about the design to other people. These images can be attached to an e-mail or inserted into product documentation. This chapter also discusses methods of printing images directly from ENOVIA DMU.

Learning Objectives in this Chapter

- Capture model images.
- Learn how to print images.

8.1 Capturing Images

CATIA enables you to capture images from the screen in raster or vector formats. These images can be saved to an album, printed, or copied to a clipboard for use in other applications.

General Steps

Use the following general steps to capture an image:

1. Activate the Capture tool.
2. Define image properties.
3. Capture the image.
4. Define the output of the image.

Step 1 - Activate the Capture tool.

Select **Tools>Image>Capture**. The Capture dialog box opens, as shown in Figure 8–1.

Figure 8–1

Step 2 - Define image properties.

Images can be taken in pixel or vector formats. A pixel image, often called a raster image, consists of squares of color (pixels). When you zoom into a pixel image, you can see each individual pixel. Pixel formats are resolution-dependent; meaning that the higher the resolution of the image, the better the quality when

increasing its size. To create a pixel image, click the (Pixel Mode) icon in the Capture dialog box.

The previous icon

selected (or) is the icon selected by default the next time you open the Capture dialog box.

Vector images are comprised of mathematical instructions on how to create the image. It is divided into objects, each of which is stored in the file with information about its position in the image, color, size, etc. Vector images are resolution-independent, enabling it to be resized without losing

detail. To create a vector image, click the (Vector Mode) icon in the Capture dialog box.

Additional options can be set to control the output of the image.

Click the ⬚ (Options) icon to open the Capture Options dialog box.

General Tab

The *General* tab shown in Figure 8–2 controls options relevant to both types of image output (pixel and vector).

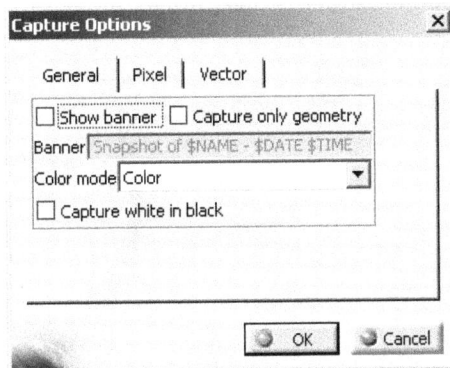

Figure 8–2

Banner

Select the **Show Banner** option to display a banner at the bottom of the image. By default, this banner displays the name of the model and the date and time when the shot was taken, as shown in Figure 8–3. Use the Banner field to modify the information output in the banner.

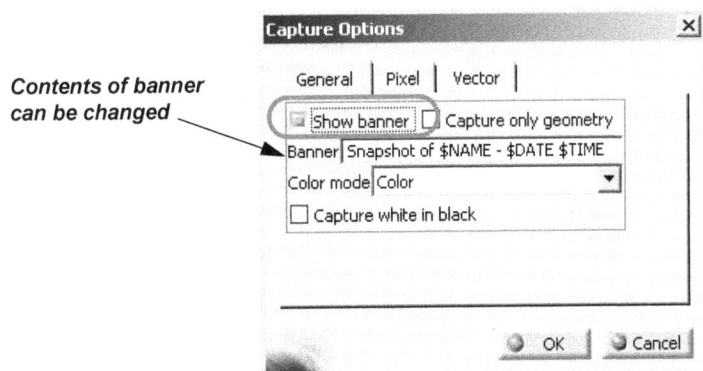

Figure 8–3

Capture Only Geometry

Select the **Capture Only Geometry** option to capture the geometry of the model without the background information, such as the specification tree and compass. For example, the image on the left of Figure 8–4 is taken without having the option selected and the image on the right is taken with the option selected. The **Capture Only Geometry** option cannot be used with vector images.

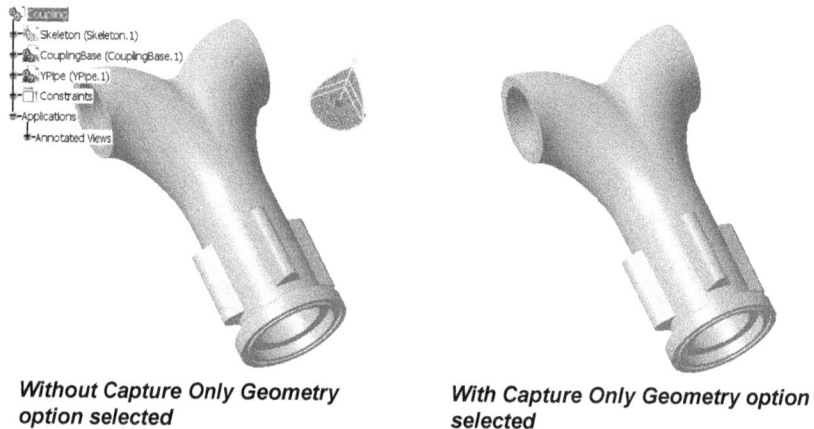

Without Capture Only Geometry option selected

With Capture Only Geometry option selected

Figure 8–4

Color Mode

Use the Color mode drop-down list to select the appropriate output color, as shown in Figure 8–5. By default, images are output in color, but can be changed to Greyscale or Monochrome.

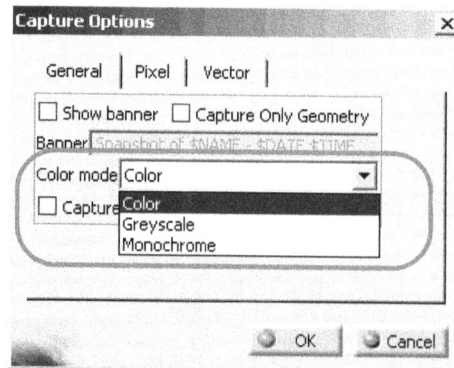

Figure 8–5

Capture White Pixels as Black

Select the **Capture White Pixels as Black** option to change all of the white elements on the screen to black in the image. This is useful if you are creating the image on a white background.

Pixel Tab

Select the *Pixel* tab, as shown in Figure 8–6, to customize options specific to pixel images. The options in this tab are described in the table below.

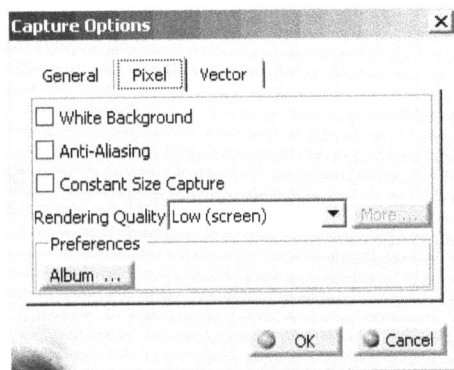

Figure 8–6

Option	Description
White Background	CATIA background color is replaced with white in the image.
Anti-Aliasing	Modifies the appearance of lines to make jagged edges look smoother.
Constant Size Capture	Captures images to a scale of 1:1, no matter the resolution.
Rendering Quality	Sets the quality of the output image. Quality can be set to: • Low (screen) - quality matches the screen resolution. • Medium • Highest • Custom - Image pixel and print size can be customized by clicking **More**.
Album	Defines preferences for storing the images captured to an album.

Vector Tab

Select the *Vector* tab, as shown in Figure 8–7, to customize options specific to vector images. The options in the *Vector* tab are described in the table below.

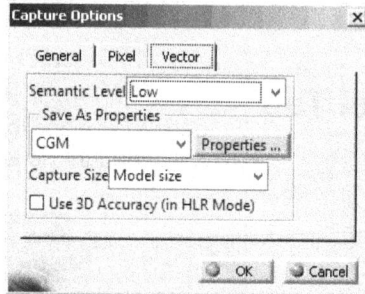

Figure 8–7

Option	Description
Semantic Level	Selects the Rendering mode, which can be: • Discretized • Low • Polyline • Polyline and Conic • Polyline and Spline
Save As Properties	Formats image can be saved as: • CGM • Generic PostScript • Generic HP-GL2 RTL Use **Properties** to customize the format properties.
Capture Size	The image of the model can be saved as: • Model size • Display size
Use 3D Accuracy (in HLR Mode)	Use 3D Accuracy when the display is in HLR Mode.

Step 3 - Capture the image.

You can capture only a selected section of the screen or the entire screen. To capture the entire screen area, click the

(Screen Mode) icon in the Capture dialog box. To capture

only a section of the screen, click the (Select Mode) icon to activate the Selection mode. Click on the screen to open the selection box. While holding the left mouse button, drag the cursor to create the selection area. Release the left mouse button to complete the selection box, as shown in Figure 8–8.

Selection box can be resized by dragging the border of the box.

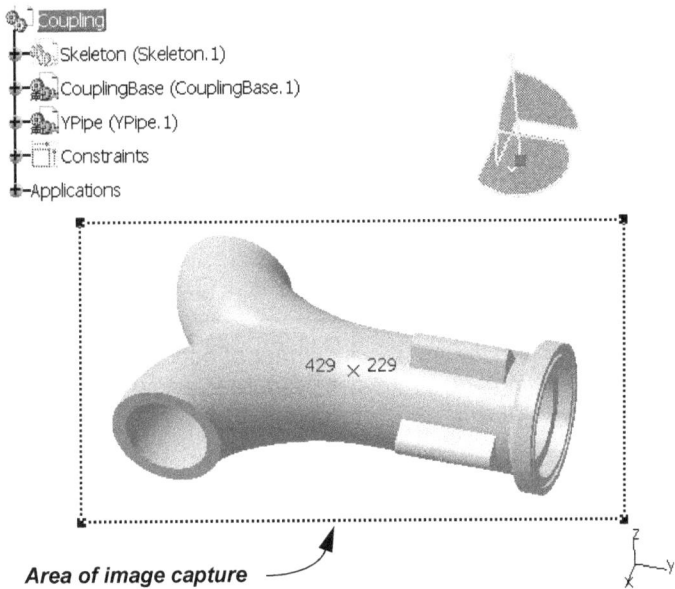

Coupling
Skeleton (Skeleton.1)
CouplingBase (CouplingBase.1)
YPipe (YPipe.1)
Constraints
Applications

429 × 229

Area of image capture

Figure 8–8

To capture the image, click the ▣ (Capture) icon. The Capture Preview dialog box opens, showing the image taken as shown in Figure 8–9.

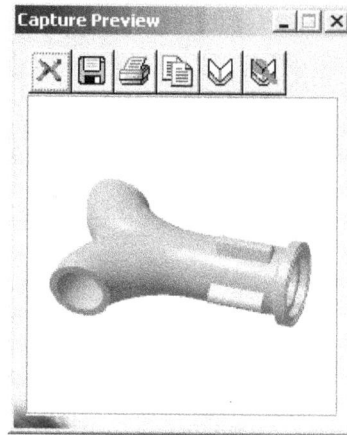

Figure 8–9

Step 4 - Define the output of the image.

You can also open the album by selecting Tools>Image>Album.

A number of options are available for the output of the image in the Capture Preview dialog box. These options are described as follows:

Icon	Option	Description
✕	Cancel	Cancels the capture and closes the preview window.
💾	Save As	Saves the capture to the hard drive.
🖨	Print	Opens the Print dialog box to print the image.
📋	Copy	Copies the image to the clipboard where it can be pasted into another Windows application.
⌄	Album	Stores the image in the album.
⌄	Open Album	Opens the album.

Album

The album is used to store images, which are stored on your system in the folder defined by the CATTemp environment variable. You can open the album from the Capture Preview window by clicking the (Open Album) icon. The Album dialog box opens, as shown in Figure 8–10. The options that are available in the dialog box and in the shortcut menu are described in the table below.

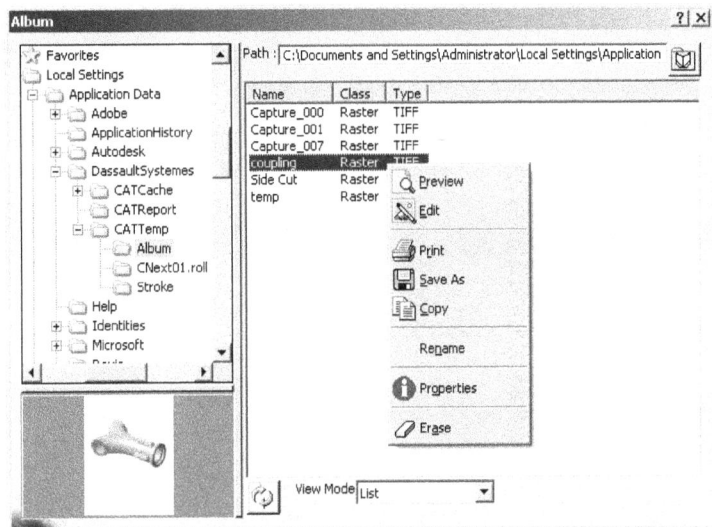

Figure 8–10

Icon	Description
	Changes the file path to the album folder.
	Refreshes the list of files stored in the current Album folder.
	Saves the selected image under another name or in another format.
	Opens the Print dialog box to print the image.
	Opens the selected image in the Print Preview dialog box. Use <Ctrl> to select more then one image to print preview at a time. All images are placed on the same sheet for printing.
	Copies the image to the clipboard where it can be pasted into another windows application.

	Removes the selected image from the album.
	Opens the Image Information Panel for the selected image.
	Opens the Image Editor panel to modify the image. Not available for vector images.
Rename	Enables you to rename the image.

8.2 Printing Images

Once you have completed and saved your image(s), you can print them.

General Steps

Use the following general steps to print a document:

1. Activate the Print tool.
2. Select the printer.
3. Configure the layout.
4. Print the document.

Step 1 - Activate the Print tool.

Select **File>Print** to open the Print dialog box shown in Figure 8–11.

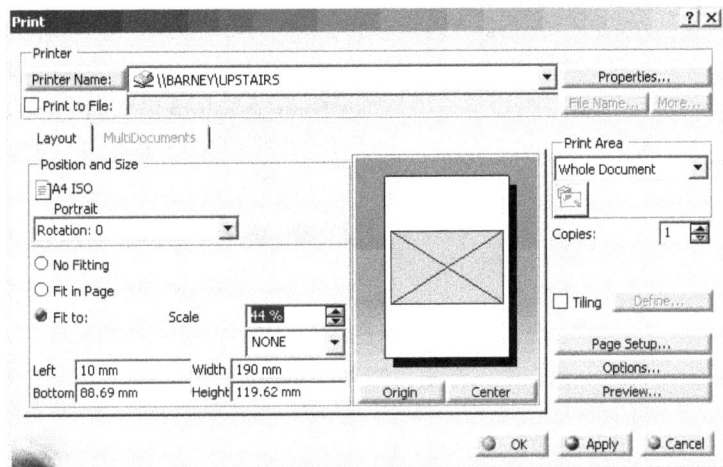

Figure 8–11

Step 2 - Select the printer.

Images can be sent to any printer set up in Windows, or saved to a .PRN file.

Printer

To print to a printer, select it in the Printer drop-down list. If required, the properties of the printer can be modified by clicking **Properties**.

File

Prints can be saved to a .PRN file by selecting the **Print To File** option. Click **File Name** to create a print file to which to save the document. Using the Print to File dialog box, navigate to the directory to which you want to save the print, and enter a name for the print in the *File Name* field, as shown in Figure 8–12.

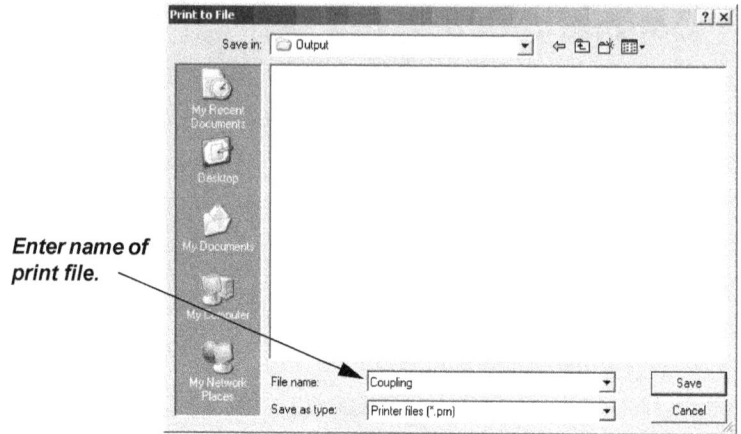

Enter name of print file.

Figure 8–12

Click **Save** to return to the Print dialog box. The Print to File field is populated with the path and filename, as shown in Figure 8–13.

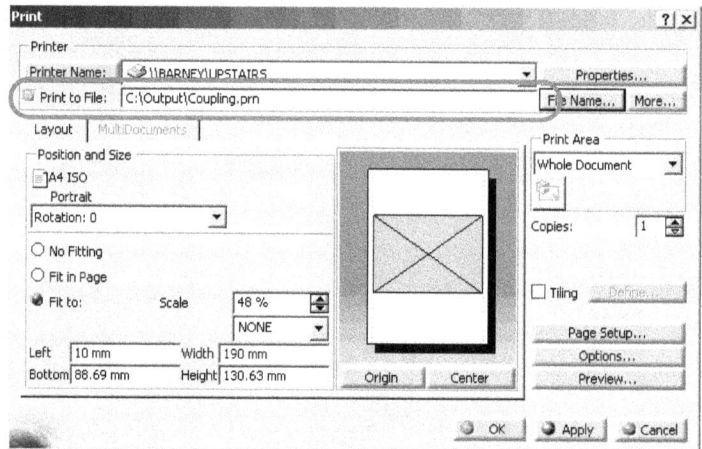

Figure 8–13

Step 3 - Configure the layout.

The layout of the print can be customized to suit your requirements.

Position and Size

The preview window of the Print dialog box indicates how the print displays on the page. If the current position is not correct, you can change it using a number of options.

Documents can be rotated on the sheet using the Rotation drop-down list. To change the scale of the document, use the fitting options **Fit in Page** and **Fit to**.

The **Fit in Page** option scales the document to fit the page based on the selected rotation and also centers the document on the page.

Fitting can be customized by selecting **Fit to**, as shown in Figure 8–14. This option enables you to customize the scale of the document and its location on the page.

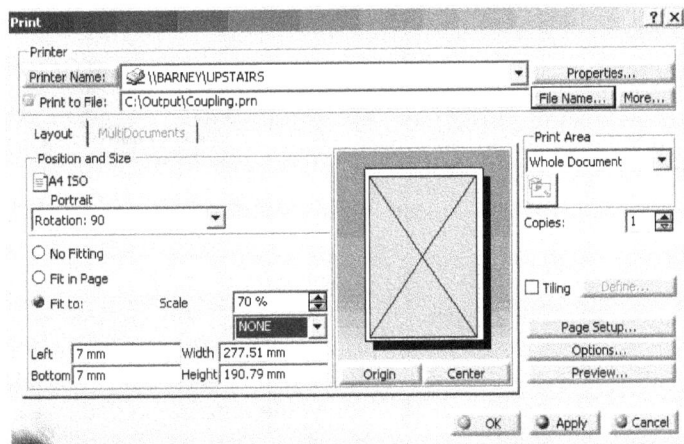

Figure 8–14

The position of the document can also be changed from the center of the page to the origin by clicking **Origin**. An example of both origin and center position is shown in Figure 8–15.

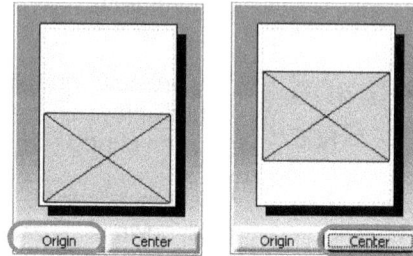

Figure 8–15

You might need to change the paper size to fit the document.

Select the **No Fitting** option to scale the document to a 1:1 scale. Click **Page Setup** to select a new page size, as shown in Figure 8–16.

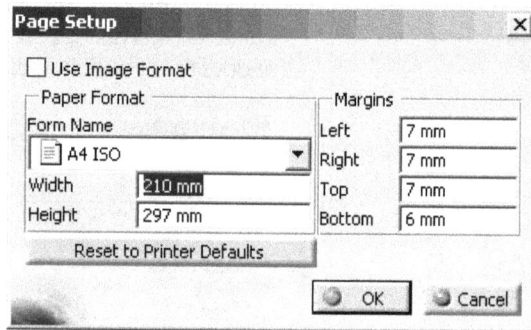

Figure 8–16

Print Area

By default, the **Whole Document** option is selected in the Print Area section. The **Display** option enables you to change what displays on the screen. The **Selection** option enables you to define the area of the document that you want to print. To define the print area, click the 🖺 icon, left-click in the document to start the box and while holding the left mouse button, drag the cursor. Release the left mouse button to finish, as shown in Figure 8–17.

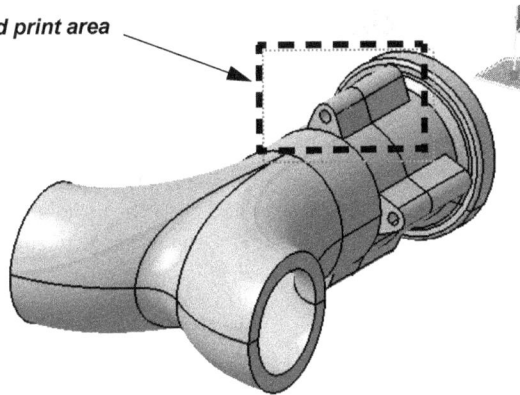

Defined print area

Figure 8–17

Options

Additional options for the print can be configured by clicking **Options** to open the Options dialog box, as shown in Figure 8–18. Using this dialog box, you can adjust the image's color output, add banners and company logos, and customize its quality.

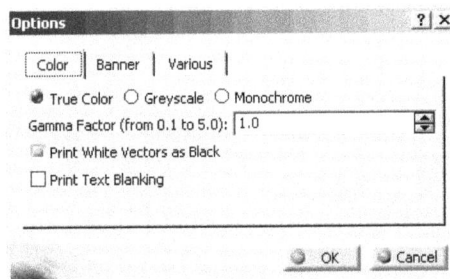

Figure 8–18

Step 4 - Print the document.

Click **OK** to print the image. It is printed to the selected printer with the customized settings.

Quick Print

Documents can also be printed using the **Quick Print** option. With this option, the document is sent to the default printer, using the default settings. To **Quick Print** a document, click the

(Quick Print) icon in the Standard toolbar.

Practice 8a

Capturing Images

Practice Objectives

- Set up an image capture.
- Capture an image.
- Save an image to an album.
- Copy an image to other documents.

In this practice, you will take screen shots of annotation views, which will be used to document your findings. You will save these images to the album and import them into other documents.

Task 1 - Open the assembly.

The files for this practice can be found in the BoreDevice directory.

1. Open **SectionBoreDevice**. The assembly displays as shown in Figure 8–19.

    If you did not finish *Practice 7b*, open **BoreDeviceComplete. CATProduct**.

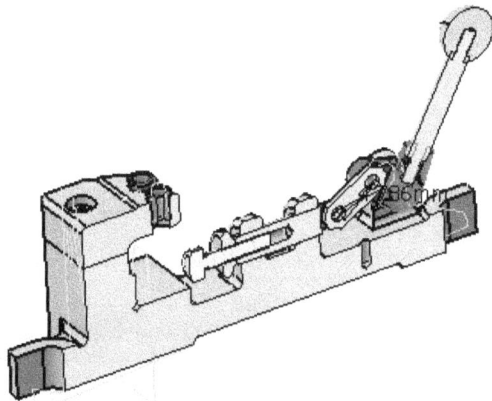

Figure 8–19

2. Ensure that the DMU Navigator workbench is active.

Task 2 - Capture an image.

1. Select **Tools>Image>Capture** to open the Capture dialog box.

2. Click the ![icon] (Pixel Mode) icon to set the capture to Pixel mode.

3. Click the ![icon] (Manage Annotated Views) icon in the DMU Review Navigation toolbar, and select the **Interference Comments** view.

4. Click the ![icon] (Capture) icon to capture the image. A snapshot of the screen is taken and displayed in the Capture Preview window, as shown in Figure 8–20.

Your preview might not look exactly like the preview shown.

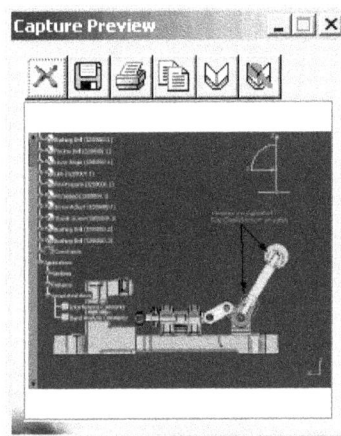

Figure 8–20

This image does not meet the requirements. The background should not have a color, and the compass and specification tree should not be in the view.

5. Click the ![icon] (Cancel) icon to cancel the image capture.

Task 3 - Change the options for the image.

1. Click the ⬛ (Options) icon to change the configuration of the capture.

2. In the *General* tab, select the **Capture Only Geometry** option to ensure that the specification tree and compass do not appear in the image. Select the **Capture White in black** option to ensure that any white geometry displays when the background is changed to white.

3. Select the **White Background** option in the *Pixel* tab.

4. Click **OK** to return to the Capture dialog box.

5. Click the ⬤ (Capture) icon to recapture the image. The Preview Window displays the new capture, as shown in Figure 8–21.

Figure 8–21

Task 4 - Save the image.

1. Click 💾 (Save As) in the Capture Preview window to save the file.

2. Enter **Interference Comments** in the *File Name* field and save the file to the BoreDevice directory. Leave the file format as **Windows Bitmap**.

3. Click **Save** to save the file to the hard drive.

4. In the Capture Preview window, click the ⌄ (Album) icon to save the image to the album.

5. Click the ✕ (Cancel) icon to exit the preview window and return to the Capture dialog box.

Task 5 - Create another image.

1. Click the ⊞ (Manage Annotated Views) icon in the DMU Review Navigation toolbar and select the **Band Analysis Comments** view.

2. Click the ● (Capture) icon to capture the image and the Capture Preview windows displays as shown in Figure 8–22.

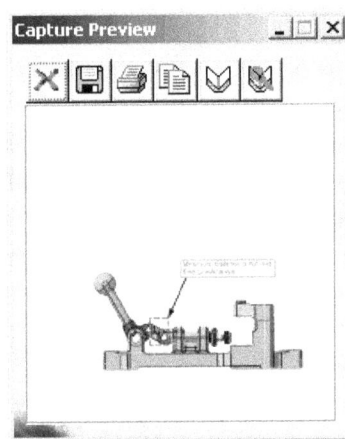

Figure 8–22

In this capture, only the area around the rectangle, including the text, is required.

3. Click the ✕ (Cancel) icon to cancel the capture.

Task 6 - Select the area for capture.

1. In the Capture dialog box, click the ![icon] icon to select the area to be captured.

2. Left-click in the top left corner of the box and drag the cursor to the bottom right of the box. Release the left mouse button to create the selection box, as shown in Figure 8–23.

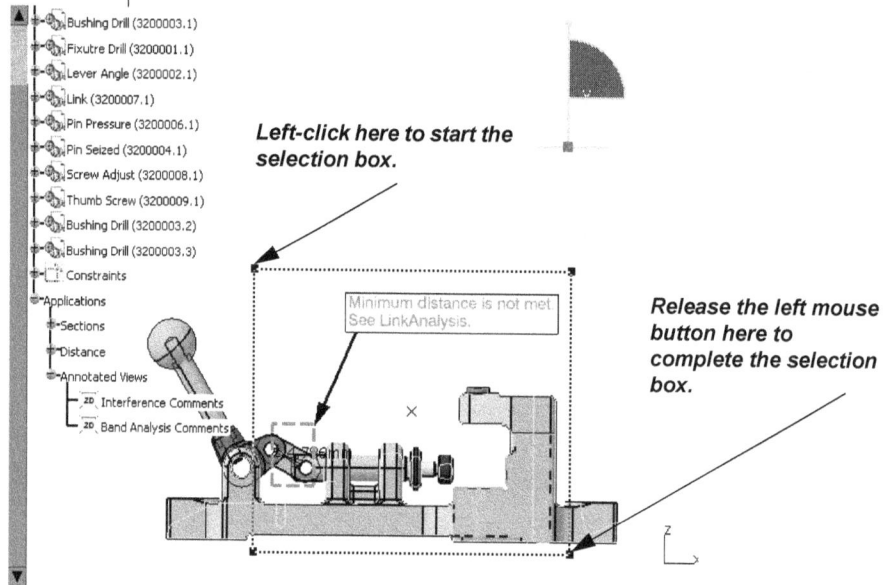

Left-click here to start the selection box.

Release the left mouse button here to complete the selection box.

Figure 8–23

3. Click the ![icon] (Capture) icon to capture the image. The Capture Preview window displays the results, as shown in Figure 8–24.

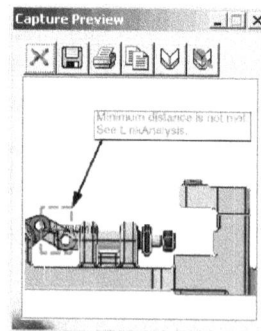

Figure 8–24

Task 7 - Copy an image and save it to an album.

1. Click the 📋 (Copy) icon to copy the image to the clipboard.

2. Open Windows Paint by selecting **Start>Run...** in Windows.

3. Enter **mspaint** in the Open field of the Run dialog box, as shown in Figure 8–25.

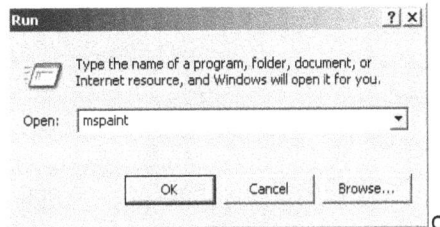

Figure 8–25

4. Click **OK** and the MS Paint application opens.

5. Select **Edit>Paste** in the Paint application. The copied image displays as shown in Figure 8–26. This technique can be used to copy images to most Windows applications.

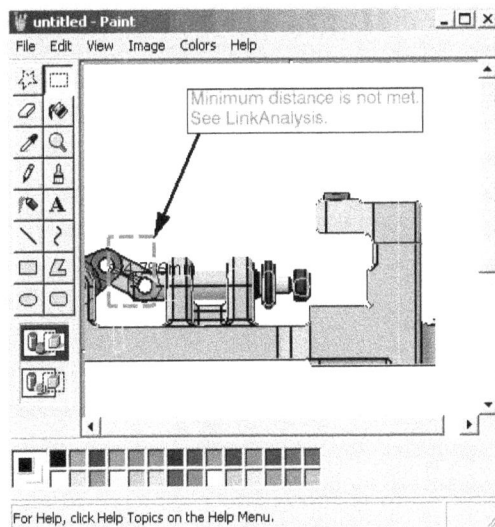

Figure 8–26

6. Close the Paint application. Do not save the image.

7. Click the ⬙ (Album) icon in the Capture Preview Window to save the image to the album.

8. Cancel the Preview to return to the Capture dialog box.

Task 8 - Take a capture in Vector mode.

1. Click the ◩ (Vector Mode) icon to change to Vector mode.

2. Leave the selection area the same and click the

   ⬤ (Capture) icon to capture the image. Note the difference between the outputs of Vector and Pixel modes.

3. Save the Vector image to the album. Do not exit the Capture Preview window.

Task 9 - View the album.

1. Click the ⬙ icon in the Capture Preview dialog box. If you have closed the Capture Preview dialog box, select **Tools> Image>Album**. The Album dialog box opens, as shown in Figure 8–27.

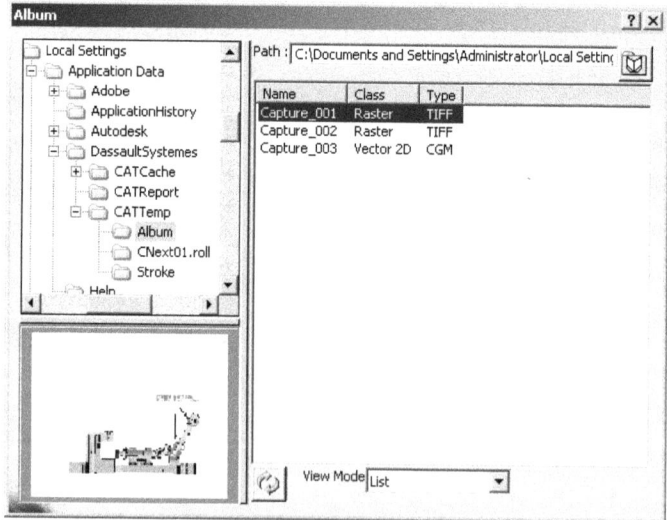

Figure 8–27

© 2018, ASCENT - Center for Technical Knowledge®

2. Right-click on the first image in the album and click the
   (Properties) icon. View the information obtained from the
   Properties dialog box. It enables you to determine information
   such as the size, type, and location of the captured files.

3. Click **OK** to close the dialog box.

4. Right-click on the Vector image in the Album. The (Edit)
   icon is grayed out. Vector images cannot be edited from the
   Image Editor.

5. Right-click the Vector image and click the (Erase) icon.

6. Click **Yes** to confirm the erase, and the Vector image is
   removed from the album. Removing an image from the album
   also removes it from the hard drive.

7. Click ⊠ to close the Album dialog box.

8. Close the file.

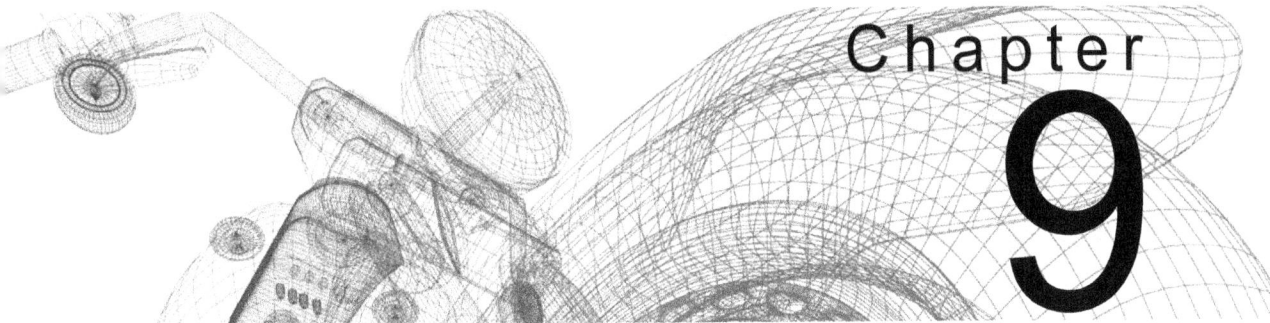

Chapter 9

Advanced Viewing Tools

This chapter introduces tools to help you to visualize a model. You can set viewpoints from different angles, add visualization effects (such as lighting) or see the details of a model under the magnification tool.

Learning Objectives in this Chapter

- Create Viewpoints to create snapshots of the model.
- Use additional visualization effects to create more realistic viewing.
- Use the Magnification tool to zoom in on details in the model using a separate window.

9.1 Creating Viewpoints

Viewpoints are snapshots of the model at various orientations and zooms. They are used to help point out areas on the model of particular interest. You can create Temporary, Standard, and Saved viewpoints:

General Steps

Use the following general steps to create a viewpoint.

1. Orient the model.
2. Save the viewpoint.
3. Edit the viewpoint.

Step 1 - Orient the model.

Models can be oriented using Examine mode, Fly mode, or Walk mode. They can also be oriented using the Viewpoint palette or using Look At mode.

Viewpoint Palette

The Viewpoint palette can be used to create exact views and to quickly orient to standard viewpoints. The palette enables you to fine-tune the orientation of the model. To access the Viewpoint palette, select **View>Viewpoint Palette**. The dialog box opens, as shown in Figure 9–1.

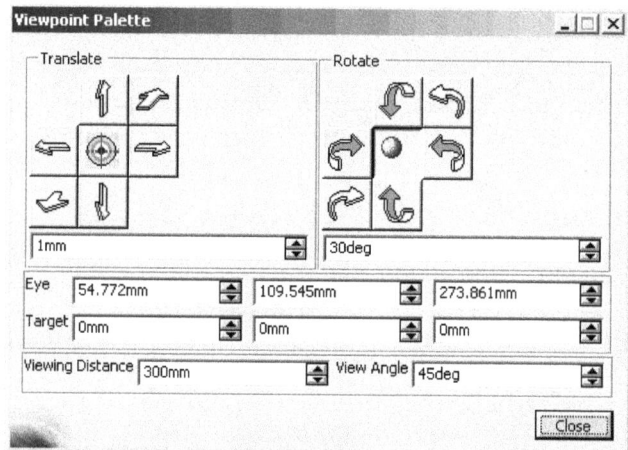

Figure 9–1

Use the Eye and Target fields to locate the coordinates of the position you are looking from (the eye) and what you are looking at (the target). You can use the Viewing Distance field to indicate the straight line distance between the eye and the target, and use the View Angle field to change the field of view, as shown in Figure 9–2.

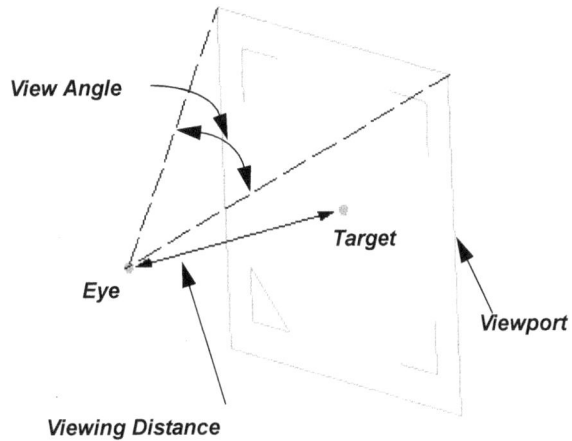

Figure 9–2

Translate

Use the **Translate** options to move, pan, and zoom the viewport in increments, as shown in Figure 9–3. When the middle icon is selected, use the translation icons to switch between the standard views (i.e, Front, Back, Left, Right, and Isometric).

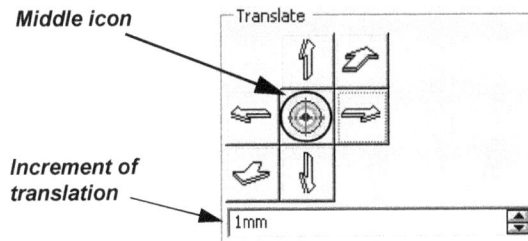

Figure 9–3

Rotate

Rotation can be defined from the eye or the target, depending on whether the middle icon is selected. If the middle icon is selected, as shown on the left side of Figure 9–4, the target remains stationary and the eye rotates. If the middle icon is not selected, as shown on the right side of Figure 9–4, the eye remains stationary and the target rotates.

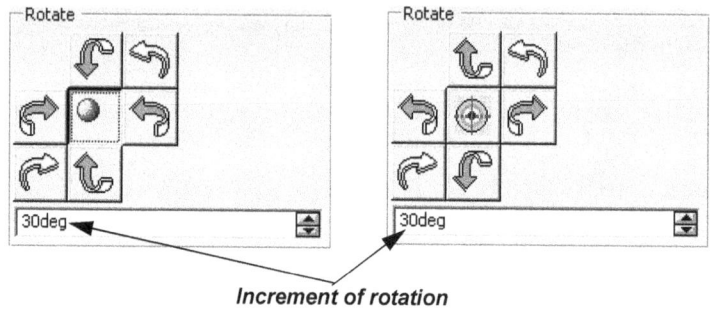

Increment of rotation

Figure 9–4

Look At Mode

The Look At tool is used to view a close-up area of a model.

How To: Use Look At

1. Click the ⊕ (Look At) icon in the DMU Viewing toolbar or select **View>Modify>Look At** in the menu bar.
2. Hold the left mouse button on an object in the model to center the viewport.
3. While holding the left mouse button, drag the cursor to display the viewport, as shown in Figure 9–5. The viewport grows larger when you drag in the same direction.

Figure 9–5

4. Change the direction while you are dragging the cursor to locate your eye point. The rectangular viewport changes to a pyramid shape as shown in Figure 9–6. The top vertex of the pyramid represents the eye point. Move the cursor to indicate the position of the eye point.

Figure 9–6

5. While still holding the left mouse button, press the middle mouse button to adjust the size of the viewport. Release the middle mouse button to return to defining the eye point.
6. Once you are satisfied with the size of the viewport and location of the eye point, release the left mouse button. The targeted area displays as shown in Figure 9–7.

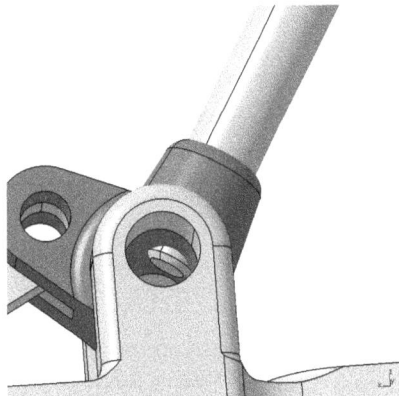

Figure 9–7

Step 2 - Save the viewpoint.

Once the model is in the correct orientation and zoom, you can save the viewpoint. To save a view, select **View>Named Views** and the Named Views dialog box opens. Click **Add** to create a new view. Its default name is Camera x, where x is the number of saved views, as shown in Figure 9–8. You can change this name or keep the default name. Click **OK** to save the new view.

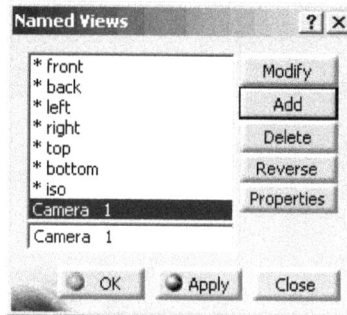

Figure 9–8

To access the saved views, return to the Named Views dialog box, select **View>Named Views**, select the view, and click **OK**.

Temporary Saved Viewpoints

Each time the model is reoriented, ENOVIA DMU creates a temporary saved view. When in Walk or Fly modes, a temporary viewpoint is saved each time the navigation pauses. You can view the temporary viewpoints by clicking the ⟨⟨ (Previous View) and ⟩⟩ (Next View) icons in the DMU Viewing toolbar. If you want to keep a temporary viewpoint, save it using the Named Views dialog box.

Step 3 - Edit the viewpoint.

Saved viewpoints are located in the **Cameras** branch of the specification tree, as shown in Figure 9–9. They can be edited directly on the model, or using the Camera window.

```
            ⊥
           ═── Applications
                │
               ═── Cameras
                     │
                     ├── Camera  1
                     │
                     ├── Camera  2
                     │
                     └── Camera  3
```

Figure 9–9

Rotate and zoom out on the model to see the viewport correctly.

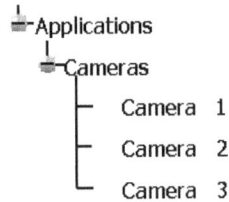

To edit a viewpoint, double-click on the saved viewpoint in the **Cameras** branch of the specification tree. The model is oriented to the selected viewpoint and the viewport, eye, and target display.

To move the viewport, drag the compass to the center of the viewport. The compass snaps onto the viewport, as shown in Figure 9–10. Use the compass to manipulate the view the same way you would manipulate a component.

To rotate the eye or target, drag the target point to a new location. To zoom the eye or target, select the line with the left mouse button and drag it to a new location, as shown in Figure 9–10.

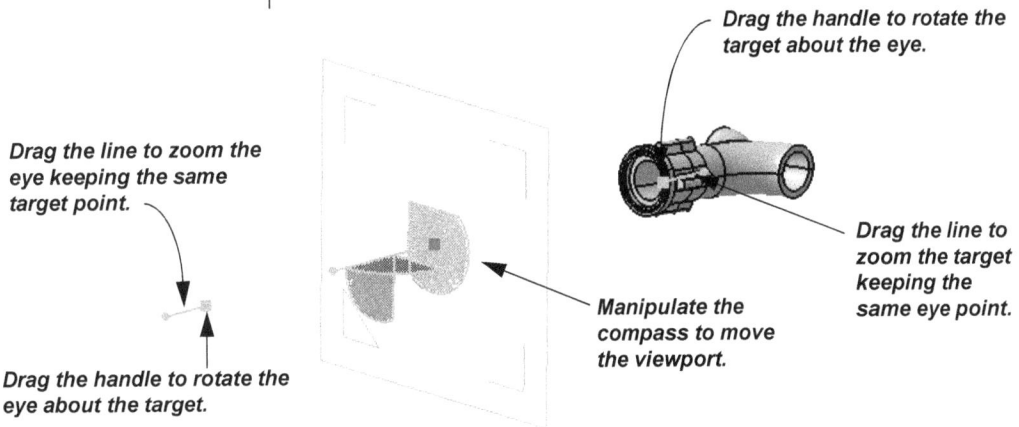

Drag the handle to rotate the target about the eye.

Drag the line to zoom the eye keeping the same target point.

Drag the line to zoom the target keeping the same eye point.

Manipulate the compass to move the viewport.

Drag the handle to rotate the eye about the target.

Figure 9–10

Once the view is correct, left-click anywhere on the screen to exit the viewpoint.

Camera Window

Saved viewpoints can also be opened in a separate window to view or edit them. To access a Camera window, select **Window> Camera Window>Camera.x** and select the appropriate camera, as shown in Figure 9–11.

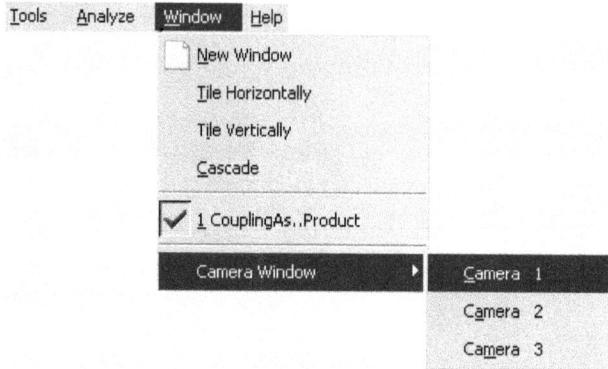

Figure 9–11

Another window opens containing the viewpoint. To edit the viewpoint, reorient the model using any technique (mouse buttons, Walk or Fly mode, Look At, Viewpoint palette, compass, etc.). The view is automatically saved with the new orientation.

To exit the Camera window, click the ⊠ (Close) icon.

9.2 Visualization Effects

Additional visualization effects can be applied to your model, such as adding depth, a floor, and changing the lighting. Using these options, you can create more realistic viewing.

Depth

Depth effects enable you to clip the geometry between two planes, enabling you to see what is inside the model. This is useful to show important internal information in your model.

How To: Use Depth Effects

1. Click the ⬜ (Depth Effects) icon in the DMU Viewing toolbar or select **View>Depth Effect** in the menu bar.
2. By default, no depth effects are set. The Depth Effect dialog box, when it is first opened, is shown in Figure 9–12. The orange circle in the center represents the model and the cutting planes are outside the model, indicating that it is not being cut. Clear the **Fixed** options for the far and near limits to change the location of the cutting planes.

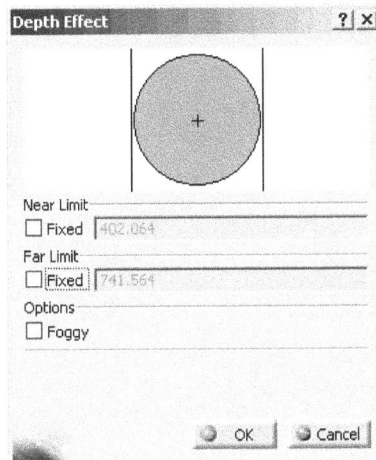

Figure 9–12

3. Set the near and far limits and the cutting planes move in the dialog box, as shown in Figure 9–13.

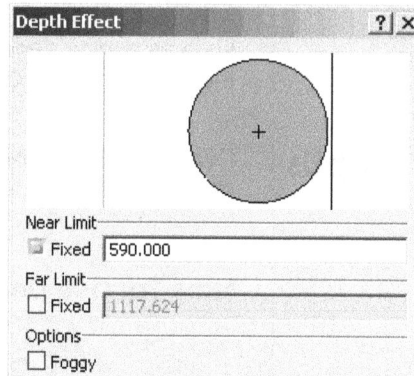

Figure 9–13

4. Zoom in and out on the model to cross it through the planes. As the model passes near the cutting plane, it is cut to show only what is behind the plane, as shown in Figure 9–14. If the **Fixed** option is used in the Far Limit section, the geometry is removed from the display as it passes the far plane.

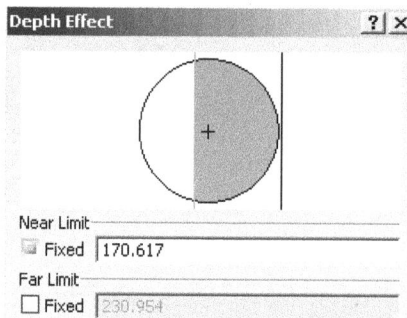

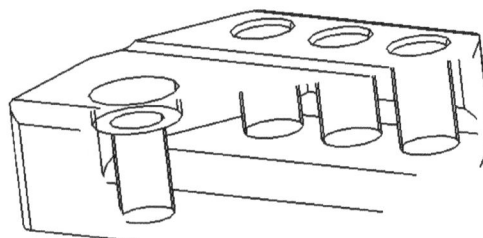

Figure 9–14

5. Use the **Foggy** option to show more depth perception. The further away you move from the cutting plane, the lighter the model displays, as shown in Figure 9–15.

Figure 9–15

6. Depth effects are always on, even when the dialog box is closed. To disable the depth effects, clear the **Fixed** and **Foggy** options.

Lighting

You can change the default lighting source for the model. The light source, brightness, and direction can be changed to help better visualize the model.

How To: Change the Default Lighting

1. Click the (Lighting) icon in the DMU Viewing toolbar, or select **View>Lighting** in the menu bar. The Light Sources dialog box opens to the default settings.
2. Select the type of light. Various options are listed as follows:

Option	Description
	No light source.
	One light source.
	Two light sources.
	Neon lights.

3. For the **One Light Source** and **Two Light Source** options, locate the direction of the light source. Use the left mouse button to drag the handles, as shown in Figure 9–16, and locate the direction of the light source. As you move the handle, the light source dynamically updates in the model.

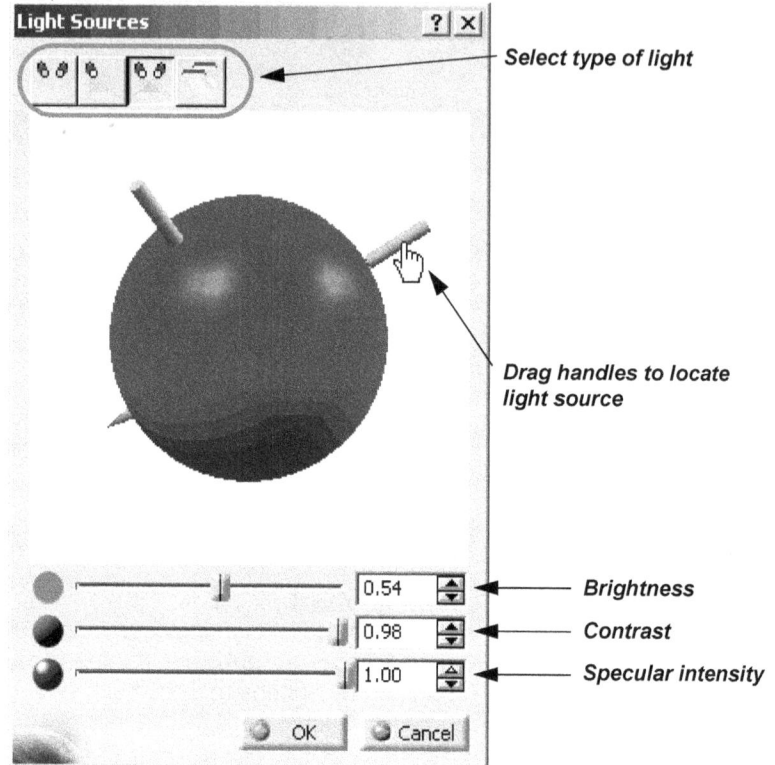

Figure 9–16

4. Use the sliders at the bottom of the dialog box to change the brightness, contrast, and specular intensity of the light.
5. Click **OK** to confirm the lighting changes.

Ground

Ground is used to help orient your model. It is a horizontal plane that is placed in the model to denote ground level. By default, ground is created parallel or tangent to the bottom point of the model.

How To: View the Ground Level

1. Click the ![icon] (Horizontal Ground) icon or select **View> Ground** in the menu bar. A plane is inserted into your document, as shown in Figure 9–17.

Figure 9–17

2. Move the horizontal ground up and down by selecting the grid with the left mouse button and dragging it to a new location.

This option also gives the impression that you are tilting or banking with respect to the selected axes when in Fly mode.

3. You can change the location of the ground to another axis. Select **Tools>Options>General>Display**, and select the *Navigation* tab. In the Navigation section, select the **Gravitational effects during navigation** option and select the appropriate axis to act as the ground, as shown in Figure 9–18.

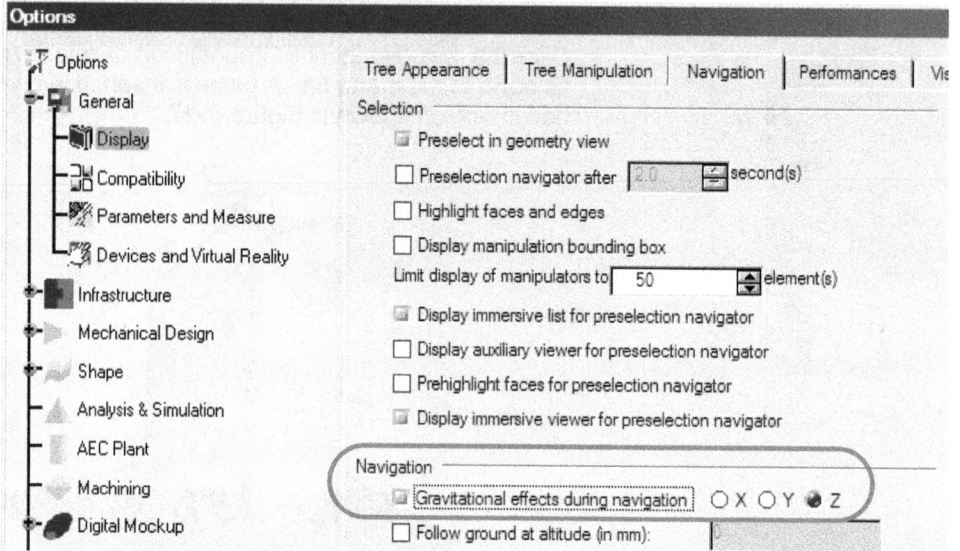

Options

Options
  General
    Display
    Compatibility
    Parameters and Measure
    Devices and Virtual Reality
  Infrastructure
  Mechanical Design
  Shape
  Analysis & Simulation
  AEC Plant
  Machining
  Digital Mockup

Tree Appearance | Tree Manipulation | Navigation | Performances | Vie

Selection
- Preselect in geometry view
- Preselection navigator after [2.0] second(s)
- Highlight faces and edges
- Display manipulation bounding box
- Limit display of manipulators to [50] element(s)
- Display immersive list for preselection navigator
- Display auxiliary viewer for preselection navigator
- Prehighlight faces for preselection navigator
- Display immersive viewer for preselection navigator

Navigation
- Gravitational effects during navigation ○ X ○ Y ● Z
- Follow ground at altitude (in mm): [0]

Figure 9–18

4. Ground can remain on display while performing other tasks.

Toggle off the Ground display by clicking the ![icon] (Horizontal Ground) icon again.

9.3 Magnification Tool

The **Magnification** option enables you to zoom in on details in the model using a separate window. The model itself remains at the same magnification. This is useful to quickly magnify a section without having to reorient the whole model.

General Steps

Use the following general steps to magnify:

1. Activate the Magnification tool.
2. Manipulate the Magnifier window.
3. Exit the Magnifier window.

Step 1 - Activate the Magnification tool.

Click the ⊘ (Magnifier) icon. The Magnifier window opens as shown in Figure 9–19.

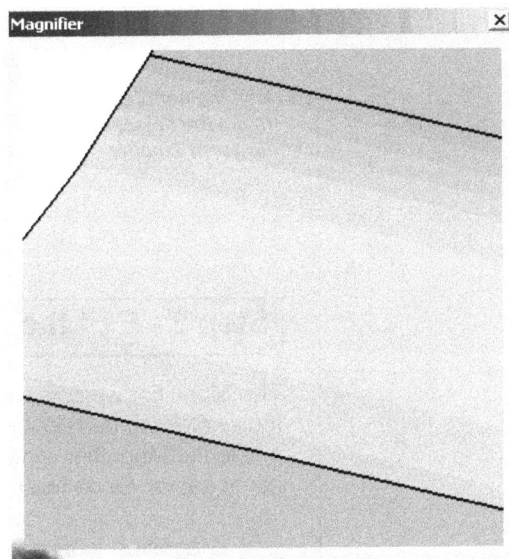

Figure 9–19

Step 2 - Manipulate the Magnifier window.

The area being magnified is defined by a selection area, as shown in Figure 9–20. The area of magnification can be moved by holding the left mouse button on the "+" symbol in the center of the box and dragging it to a new location. The Magnifier window dynamically updates. The Selection area can be increased or decreased by holding the left mouse button on one of the handles at the corners of the box and dragging the box inward or outward.

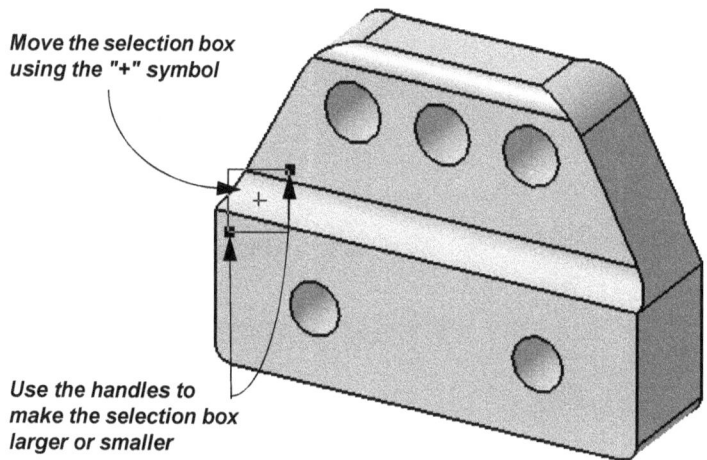

Move the selection box using the "+" symbol

Use the handles to make the selection box larger or smaller

Figure 9–20

Step 3 - Exit the Magnifier window.

The Magnifier window can remain open while working with other tools. You can use options such as measurement tools directly inside the Magnifier window, making measurements of small items easier. Once finished with the Magnifier window, click the

(Magnifier) icon again or click the (Close) icon to close the window.

Practice 9a | Advanced Viewing

Practice Objectives

- Orient a model using the viewport palette.
- Save custom views.
- Use the Look At tool to define a view.
- Use the Magnification viewing tool.

In this practice, you will use DMU viewing tools to closely examine a product model. These views will be saved with the model and appear in the specification tree for quick access.

Task 1 - Open the assembly.

The files for this practice can be found in the CVJoint directory.

1. Open **CVJoint.CATProduct**. The product displays as shown in Figure 9–21.

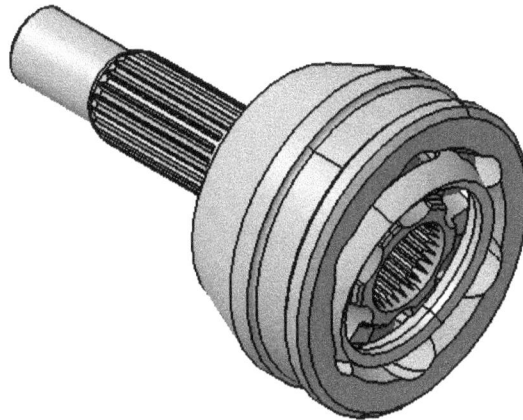

Figure 9–21

2. Ensure that the DMU Navigator workbench ( ) is active.

3. Ensure that the DMU Viewing toolbar is shown. Move it to a floating position, as shown in Figure 9–22.

Figure 9–22

Task 2 - Use the viewpoint palette.

1. Select **View>Viewpoint Palette** in the menu bar. The Viewpoint Palette displays as shown in Figure 9–23.

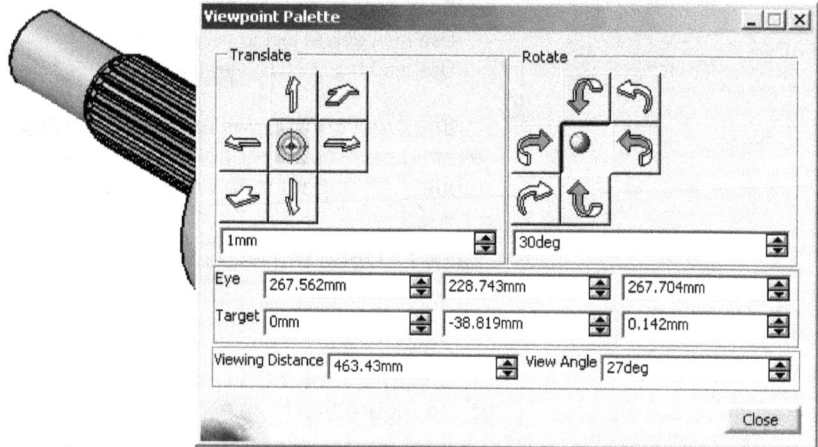

Figure 9–23

2. Enter **100mm** as the incremental translational value, as shown in Figure 9–24.

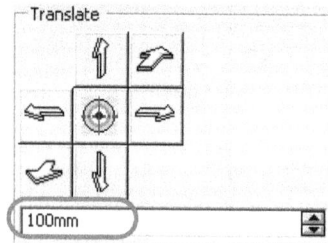

Figure 9–24

3. Click the ⇨ icon once to move the model 100mm to the left.

4. Enter **500** in the *Viewing Distance* field, as shown in Figure 9–25.

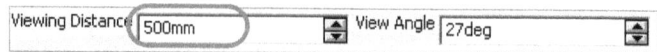

Figure 9–25

5. Press <Enter>. The model displays further away.

6. Change the *Viewing Distance* value to **300**. Press <Enter>. The model displays closer.

7. Use the icons found in the Rotate section of the Viewpoint Palette, as shown in Figure 9–26, to achieve a view similar to the one shown in Figure 9–27.

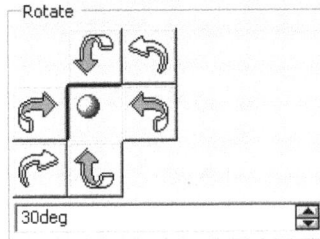

Figure 9–26

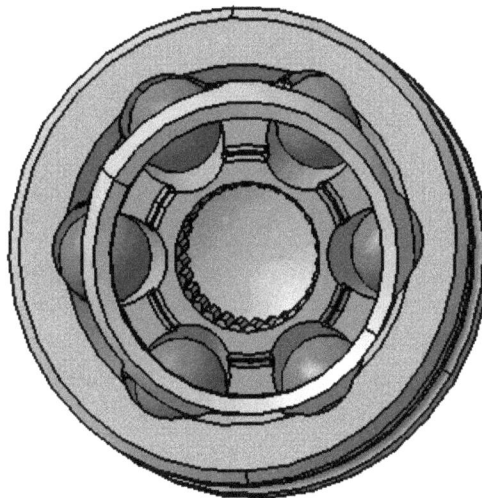

Figure 9–27

8. Click **Close**.

Task 3 - Save the view.

1. Select **View>Named Views** in the menu bar. The Named Views dialog box opens, as shown in Figure 9–28.

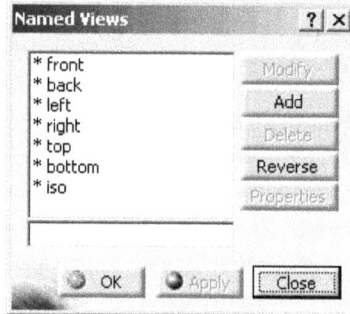

Figure 9–28

2. Click **Add**. **Camera 1** is added to the Named Views list, as shown in Figure 9–29.

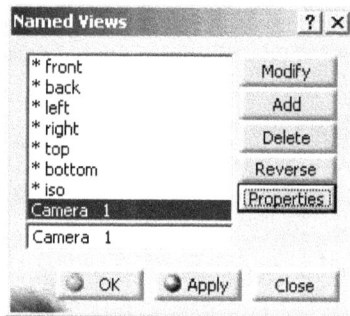

Figure 9–29

3. Click **OK**.

4. Click the ▱ (Isometric View) icon. The model is oriented to the standard isometric view.

Task 4 - Recall a saved view.

1. Select **View>Named Views.**

2. Select **Camera 1** and click **Apply**, as shown in Figure 9–30. The model orients to the saved view.

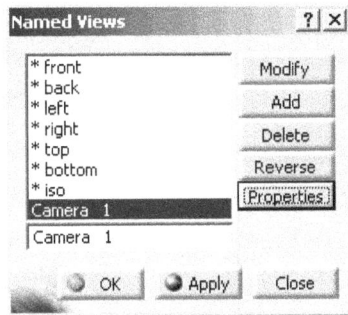

Figure 9–30

3. Close the Named Views dialog box and click the

   ⬜ (Isometric View) icon.

Task 5 - Create a view point.

1. Click the ⊕ (Look At) icon in the DMU Viewing toolbar.

2. Hold the left mouse button at the location shown in Figure 9–31 and drag the cursor until a viewport displays. Do not release the left mouse button.

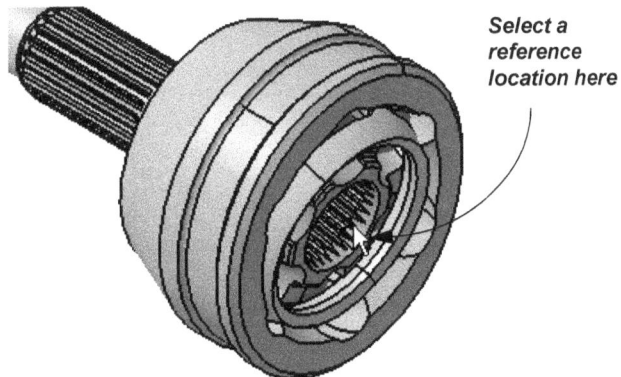

Select a reference location here

Figure 9–31

3. While holding the left mouse button, drag the cursor in a different direction to locate the eye point, as shown in Figure 9–32.

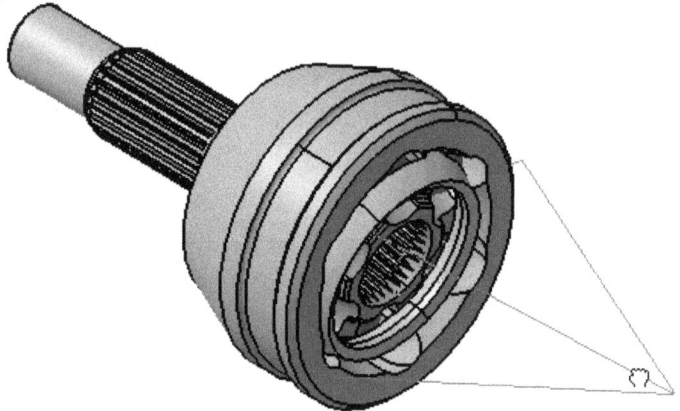

Figure 9–32

4. Save this view as **Camera 2**.

5. Click the ⬜ (Isometric View) icon and fit the model to the window.

6. Use the ⊕ icon to create another view. Select a reference location, as shown in Figure 9–33 and drag the cursor to the location, as shown in Figure 9–34.

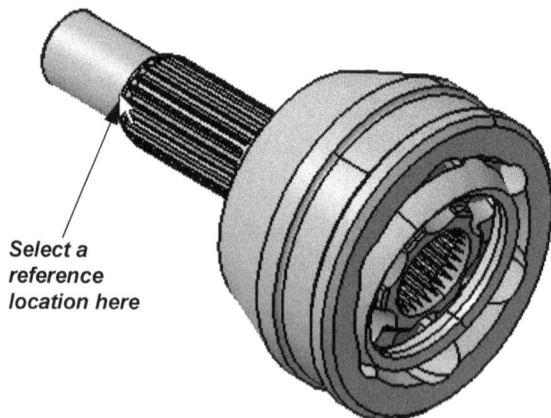

Select a reference location here

Figure 9–33

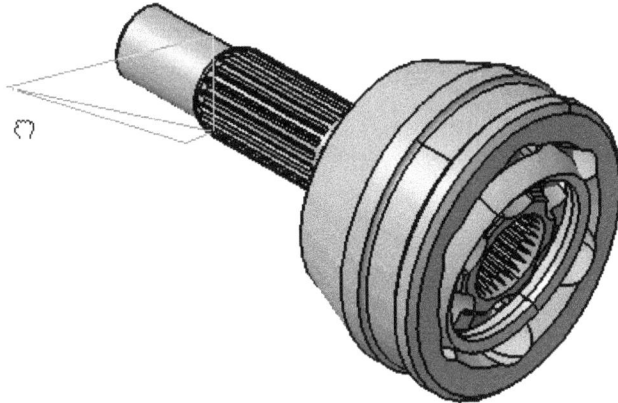

Figure 9–34

7. Save this view as **Camera 3**.

8. Expand the **Applications** node of the specification tree, as shown in Figure 9–35, to view the list of saved camera views.

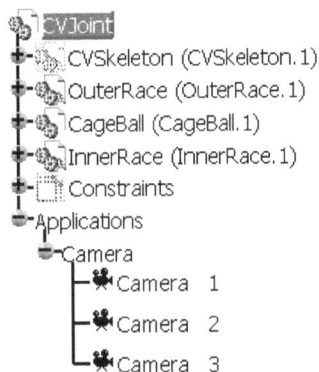

Figure 9–35

9. Activate **Camera 1** by double-clicking on the entry in the specification tree.

10. Return to the isometric view.

Task 6 - Use the magnification tool.

1. Click the [Magnifier icon] (Magnifier) icon in the DMU Viewing toolbar.

2. Zoom and rotate the model to view the geometry in the Magnifier window, as shown in Figure 9–36.

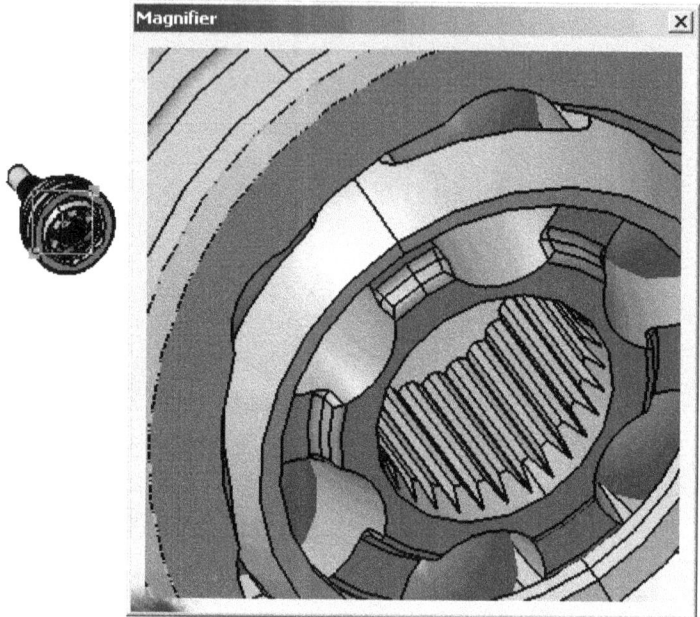

Figure 9–36

3. Click the [Magnifier icon] icon to exit Magnifier View mode.

4. Save the file and keep it open. It is used in the next practice.

Practice 9b

Viewing Effects

Practice Objectives

- Set depth effect.
- Set lighting options.
- Add horizontal ground effects.

In this practice, you will look at the internal features of a model using the depth tool. Additionally, a model can be viewed under different light sources. You will also be introduced to the ground tool.

Task 1 - Fit the assembly in the window.

The files for this practice can be found in the CVJoint directory.

*If you did not complete Practice 9a, open **CVJoint_exercise_9a_completed.CATProduct**.*

1. Open **CVJoint.CATProduct**.

2. Click the ⬜ (Isometric view) icon.

3. Click the ⬕ (Fit All In) icon.

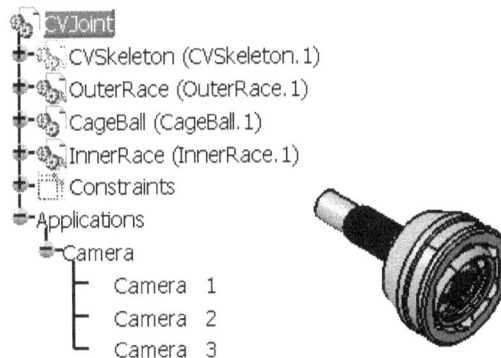

Figure 9–37

The model displays far away due to the saved view frames that have been saved with the model, and hence, are part of the view as shown in Figure 9–37.

4. Hide the saved views by selecting **Camera** in the specification tree, right-clicking and selecting **Hide/Show** as shown in Figure 9–38.

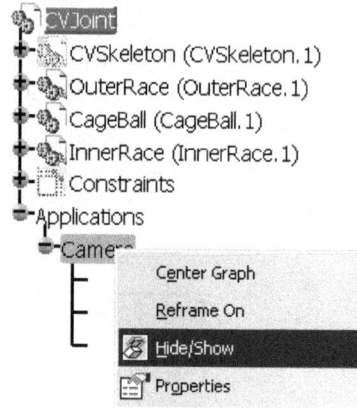

Figure 9–38

5. Click the ⊹ (Fit All In) icon.

Task 2 - Use the depth effects.

1. Click the (Depth Effects) icon in the DMU Viewing toolbar. The Depth Effect dialog box opens, as shown in Figure 9–39

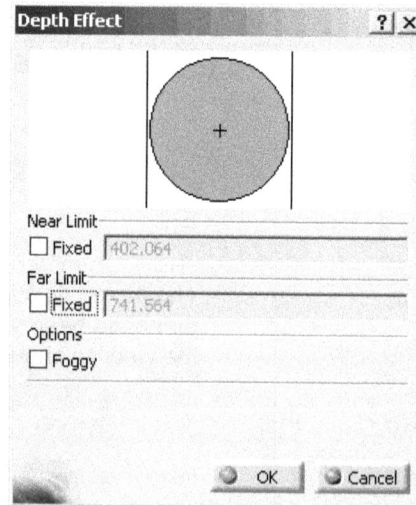

Figure 9–39

2. Select the near limit from the window of the Depth Effect dialog box, as shown in Figure 9–40.

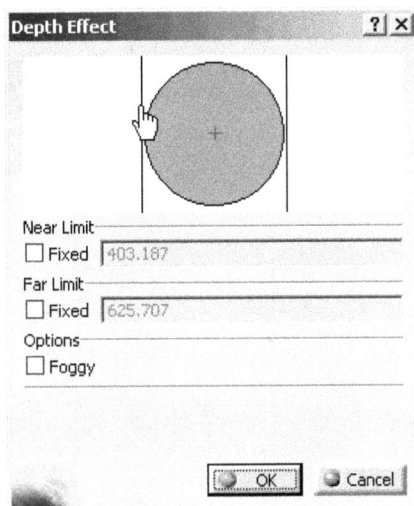

Figure 9–40

3. Drag the near limit to the approximate location shown in Figure 9–41.

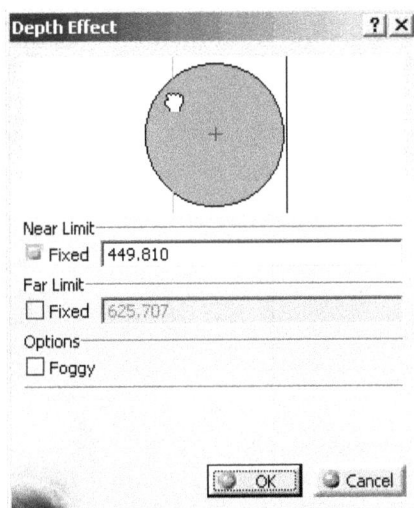

Figure 9–41

4. Zoom in and zoom out to see the effect of the depth effect setting, as shown in Figure 9–42.

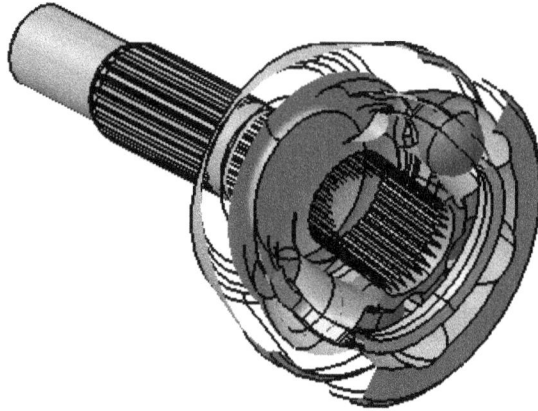

Figure 9–42

5. Make the following changes as shown in Figure 9–43:

- Select **Near Limit**, set value to **450**
- Select **Far Limit**, set value to **700**
- *Options:* **Foggy**

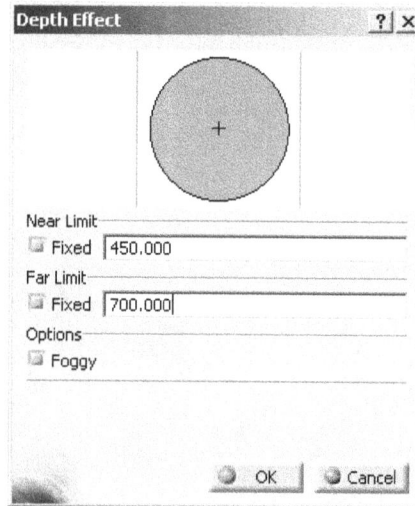

Figure 9–43

6. Zoom in and out to see the effect, as shown in Figure 9–44.

Far limit is foggy

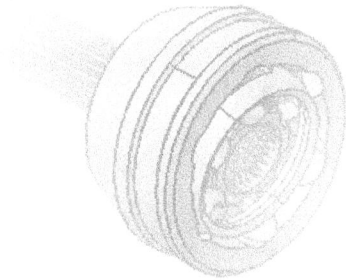

Near limit is a cutting plane

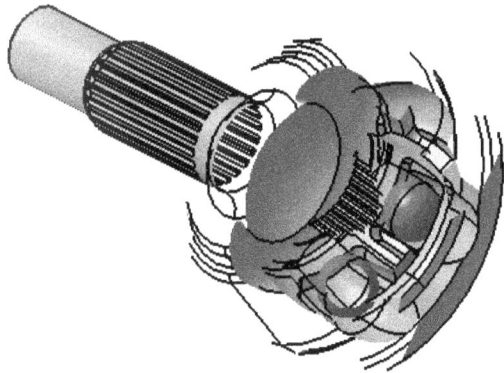

Figure 9–44

7. Click **OK**. The depth effects are still applied.

8. Click the ⬚ (Depth Effects) icon, clear all three options, and click **OK**.

Task 3 - Add ground effect.

1. Click the ⬚ (Horizontal ground) icon. Ground is added to the model display as shown in Figure 9–45.

Figure 9–45

Task 4 - Make changes to the light source.

1. Click the [icon] (Lighting) icon. The Light Sources dialog box opens, as shown in Figure 9–46.

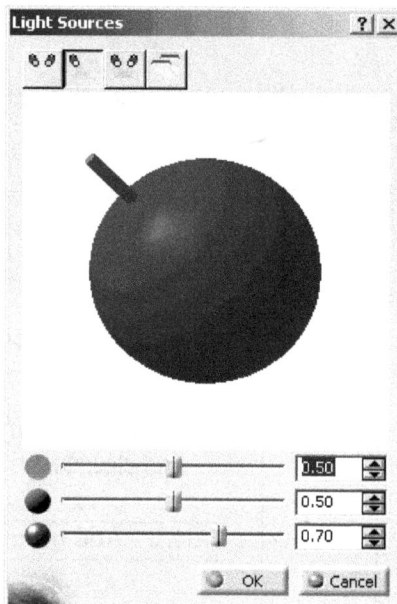

Figure 9–46

2. Click the [icon] (Neon Light) icon.

3. Zoom in, zoom out, and rotate to see the effect.

4. Click the ⊙ (Single Light) icon. Rotate the direction of light within the Light Sources dialog box, as shown in Figure 9–47.

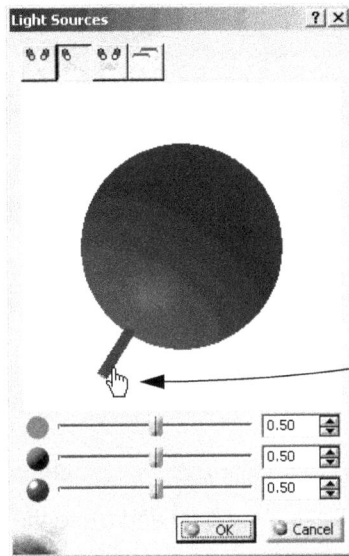

Drag the direction of the light using the cursor.

Figure 9–47

5. Experiment with various directions using the ⊙⊙ (Two Lights) icon, as shown in Figure 9–48.

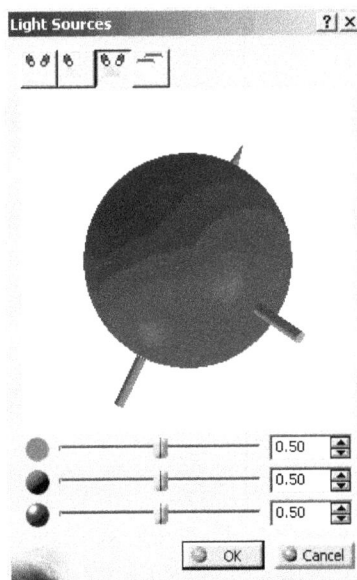

Figure 9–48

6. Click **OK**. The model displays as shown in Figure 9–49.

Figure 9–49

7. Save the model and close the file.

10

DMU Data Navigation

This chapter introduces tools to help you investigate a model. They enable you to quickly locate specific elements within a large assembly. The Search and Spatial Query tools output results according to search criteria that you specify. You can then record the search results in a published report, to be used in presentations or as reference material.

Learning Objectives in this Chapter

- Perform a search to locate specific elements.
- Run a Spatial Query to select elements inside or outside a certain zone or in proximity of a selected element.
- Create a Published Report of your review for use by others.

10.1 Performing a Search

In complex models with a large number of components, locating specific elements within the model can become difficult. The Search tool can be used in these cases to quickly locate elements in the specification tree.

General Steps

Use the following general steps to define a search.

1. Activate the Search tool.
2. Define the properties of the search.
3. Run the search.
4. Save the search to use later.

Step 1 - Performing a Search

To perform a search, select **Edit>Search**, or press <Ctrl> and <F>. The Search dialog box opens, as shown in Figure 10–1.

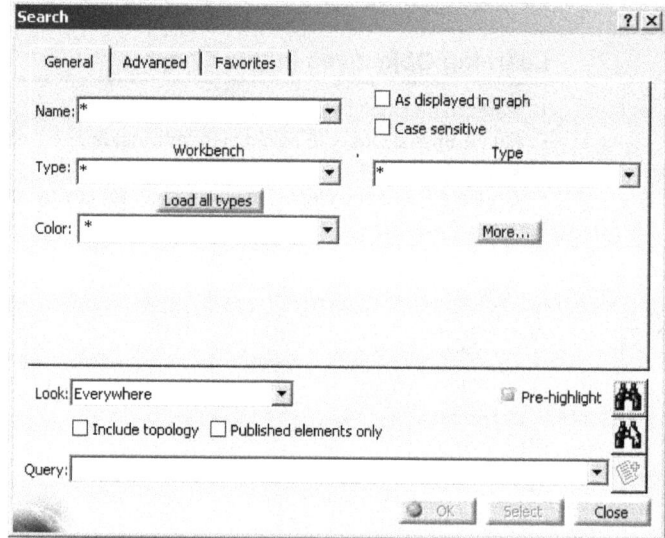

Figure 10–1

Step 2 - Define the properties of the search.

Enter the name of the element you are searching for in the Name field. An asterisk (*) can be used as a wildcard if you are unsure of the full name of the element. For example, Figure 10–2 shows a search for an element with the word Drill in it. The asterisk before and after the word indicate that characters might exist before or after the word Drill.

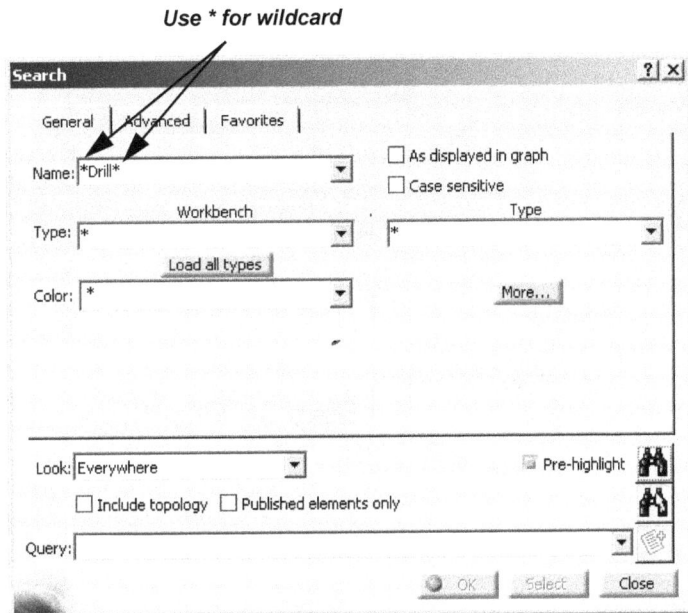

Figure 10–2

You can also define a search using the Workbench, Type, or Color drop-down lists. They help narrow the search by only looking for elements created in a certain workbench, a certain type, or a certain color. For example, Figure 10–3 shows a search for any component that has Steel assigned as its material.

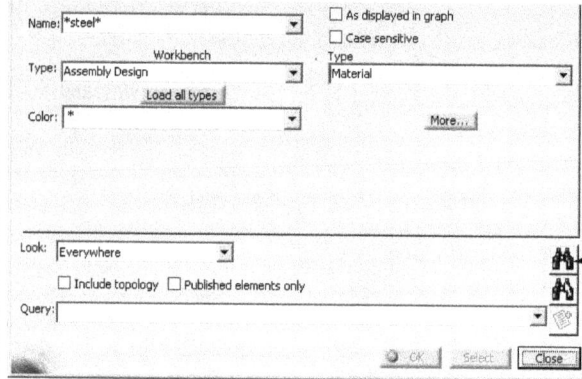

Select this icon to run the search.

Figure 10–3

Step 3 - Run the search.

To run the search, click the ⚲ icon. The dialog box expands to show the results, as shown in Figure 10–4.

You do not need to close the Search dialog box to perform other operations.

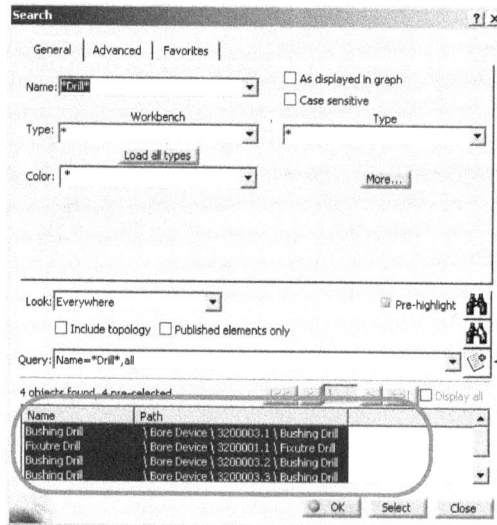

Select this icon to save the search.

Figure 10–4

To select a search result, highlight the element in the results window and click **Select**. The element highlights in the specification tree. Multiple results can be selected by pressing <Ctrl> while selecting the elements.

Step 4 - Save the search to use later.

Results of a search can also be saved for use later by clicking the ⬚ icon. Select the *Favorites* tab to access a saved search, as shown in Figure 10–5.

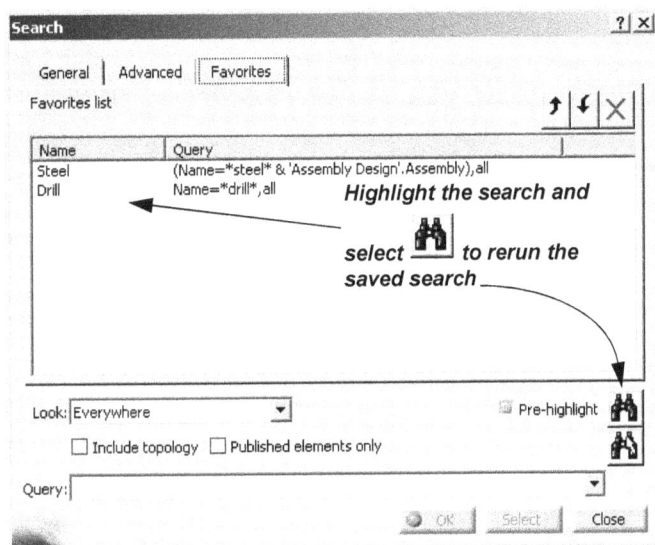

Figure 10–5

10.2 Running a Spatial Query

Like searches, spatial queries are used to quickly select elements within an assembly. Spatial queries select elements inside or outside a certain zone or in proximity of a selected element. They can be used to manage elements within the assembly, such as helping to simplify the assembly you are working with for clarity or faster update times.

Spatial queries are not based on the visual representation of your model but instead each component is reduced to cubes. Adjusting the accuracy of the query decreases or increases the size of the cubes that combine to create the components thereby making the computation more or less accurate.

General Steps

Use the following general steps to run a spatial query.

1. Activate the Spatial Query tool.
2. Define the properties of the query.
3. Run the Query.

Step 1 - Activate the Spatial Query tool.

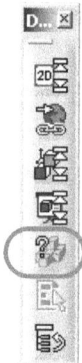

To start a spatial query, click the (Spatial Query) icon in the DMU Review Navigation toolbar.

Step 2 - Define the properties of the query.

You can create two types of spatial queries:

• Proximity

• Zone

Proximity

Proximity Queries select components close to or away from the selected component(s). In the *Proximity Query* tab, select the component(s) to be the reference for the query. The Clearance field defines the area around the reference component(s) within which any product inside or outside that area is selected.

When running a Proximity Query, the distance between components is not calculated based on the visual model; instead, each component is divided into cubes. The size of the cubes can be changed using the Accuracy field. A smaller value in the Accuracy field results in smaller cubes, which means they reflect the component more accurately. As a result, it is possible to have a clearance of 0mm and still have the query calculate parts within the area around the component.

For example, Figure 10–6 shows two components that are 38.36mm apart. The clearance was set to 0mm and the accuracy was set to 20mm. Although the parts are not touching, the results indicate that they are because of the accuracy of the settings.

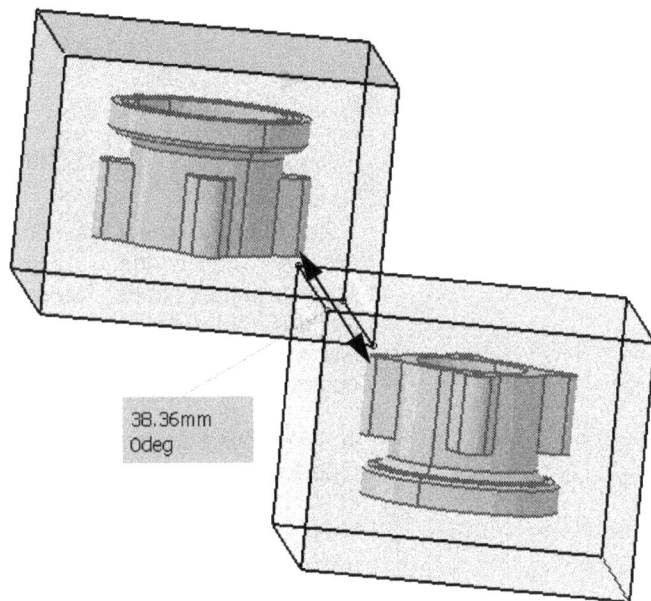

38.36mm
0deg

Figure 10–6

You can run the query to select products within the clearance area (including or not including the reference component(s)), or outside the clearance area, as shown in Figure 10–7.

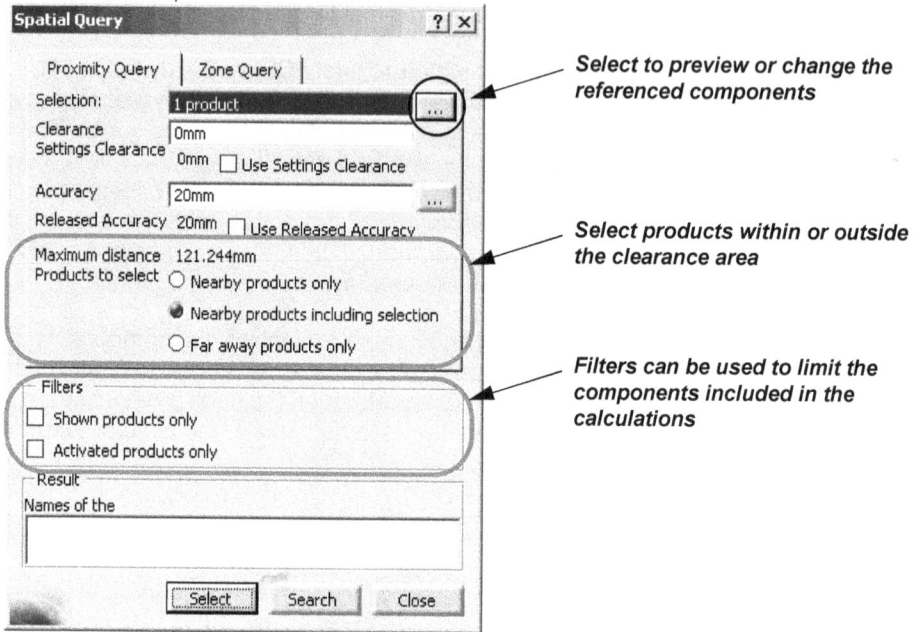

Select to preview or change the referenced components

Select products within or outside the clearance area

Filters can be used to limit the components included in the calculations

Figure 10–7

Zone

A Zone Query uses a bounding box to indicate the reference area. As with Proximity Queries, the components are represented as cubes. The size of the cubes depends on the accuracy of the calculation. The greater the number in the Accuracy field, the greater the size of the cubes representing the components.

To run a Zone Query, select the *Zone Query* tab in the Spatial Query dialog box. A bounding box displays on the model, as shown in Figure 10–8. The edges of the bounding box can be used to translate and resize it. Use the dashed lines of the box to translate and the solid lines to resize.

*Use the dash lines to
translate the box.*

*Use the solid lines to
resize the box.*

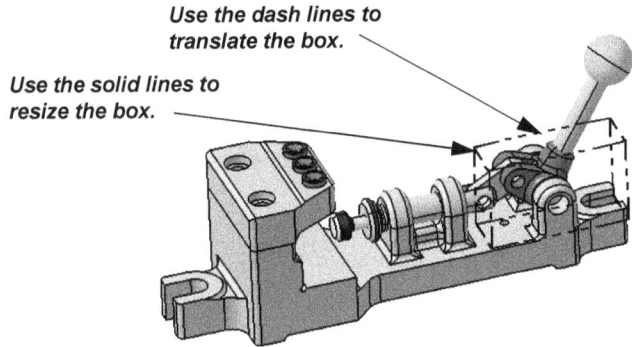

Figure 10–8

You can control the results of the Zone Query using the options
in the Products to select the section, as shown in Figure 10–9.
You can select just the products that are included in the
bounding box, or products that are completely and partially
included in the bounding box.

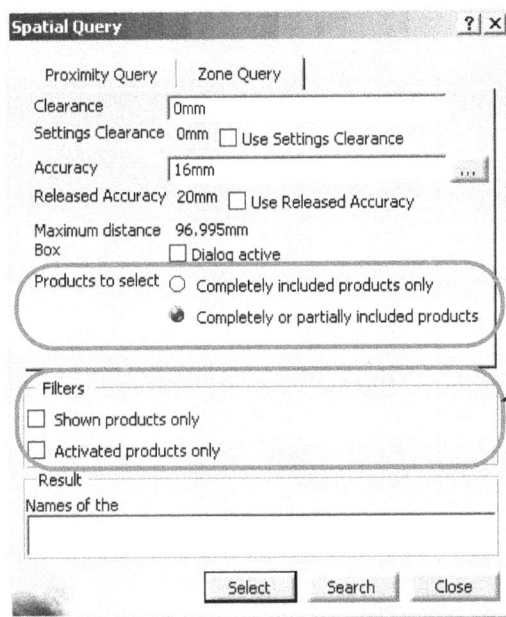

*Filters can be
used to limit the
components
that are
included in the
calculations.*

Figure 10–9

Step 3 - Run the Query.

Once the query has been defined, click **Search** to calculate the results. The results display in the Result window of the dialog box, as shown in Figure 10–10.

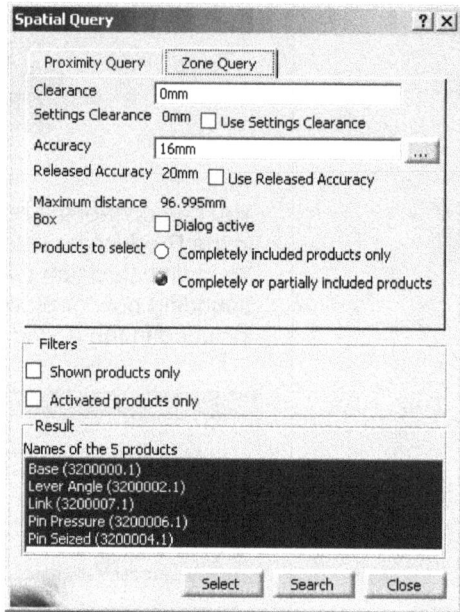

Figure 10–10

By default, all results are highlighted. To select only a certain result, select it in the Result window. Press <Ctrl> to select multiple results. Once the results are highlighted, click **Select**. The selected results are also highlighted in the specification tree. Actions can then be applied to the highlighted items as a group. For example, you can hide all of the selected items to simplify the display.

Cache

Each time you run a query, the approximated cube components are temporarily stored in the systems cache. To free cache space, click **...** beside the Accuracy field, as shown in Figure 10–11.

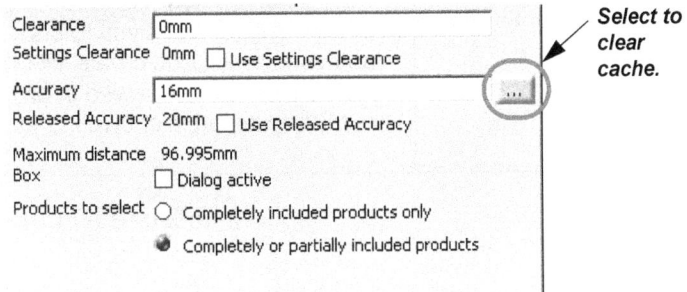

Figure 10–11

The Cache Management and Accuracy dialog box opens, as shown in Figure 10–12. It displays the current amount of cache used to store the cubed versions of the components. To clear the cache, click **Free total cache**.

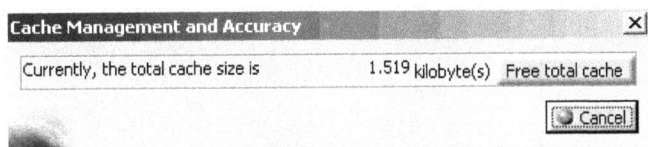

Figure 10–12

10.3 Creating a Published Report

Publishing creates HTML reports of your review for use by others. This enables you to create snapshots, report clashes, add comments, and create VRML links to selected components. HTML files can be viewed in any web browser. An example of a published report is shown in Figure 10–13.

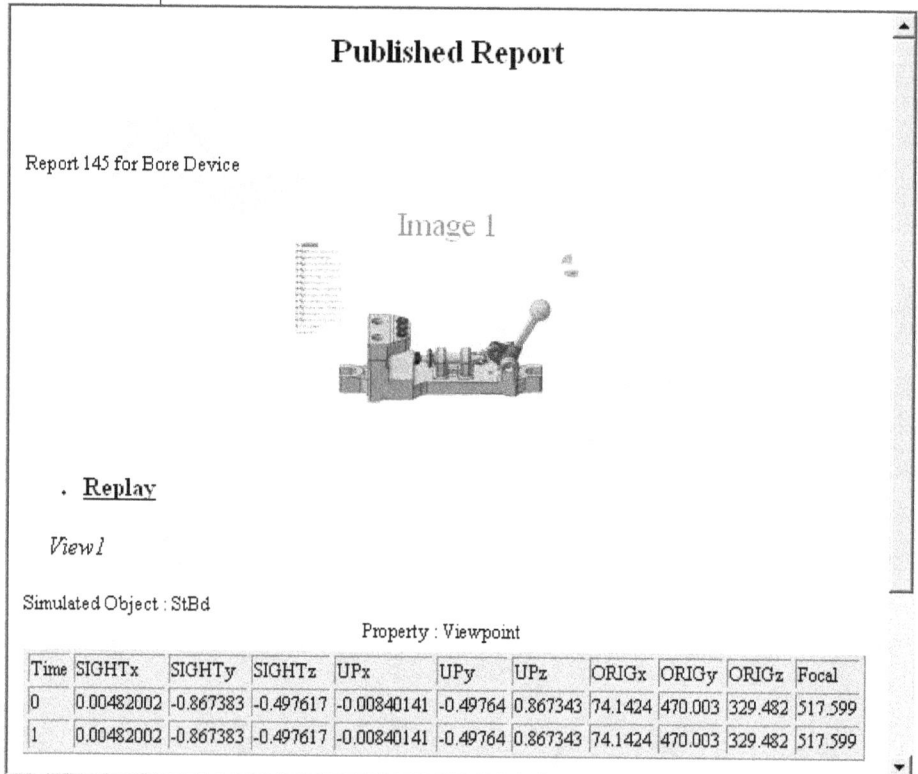

Published Report

Report 145 for Bore Device

Image 1

. **Replay**

View1

Simulated Object : StBd

Property : Viewpoint

Time	SIGHTx	SIGHTy	SIGHTz	UPx	UPy	UPz	ORIGx	ORIGy	ORIGz	Focal
0	0.00482002	-0.867383	-0.497617	-0.00840141	-0.49764	0.867343	74.1424	470.003	329.482	517.599
1	0.00482002	-0.867383	-0.497617	-0.00840141	-0.49764	0.867343	74.1424	470.003	329.482	517.599

Figure 10–13

Cache

Each time you run a query, the approximated cube components are temporarily stored in the systems cache. To free cache space, click **...** beside the Accuracy field, as shown in Figure 10–11.

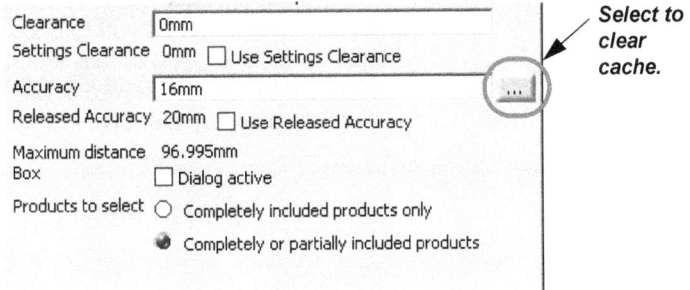

Select to clear cache.

Figure 10–11

The Cache Management and Accuracy dialog box opens, as shown in Figure 10–12. It displays the current amount of cache used to store the cubed versions of the components. To clear the cache, click **Free total cache**.

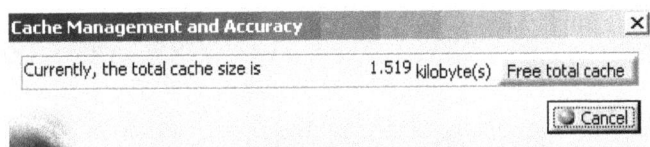

Figure 10–12

10.3 Creating a Published Report

Publishing creates HTML reports of your review for use by others. This enables you to create snapshots, report clashes, add comments, and create VRML links to selected components. HTML files can be viewed in any web browser. An example of a published report is shown in Figure 10–13.

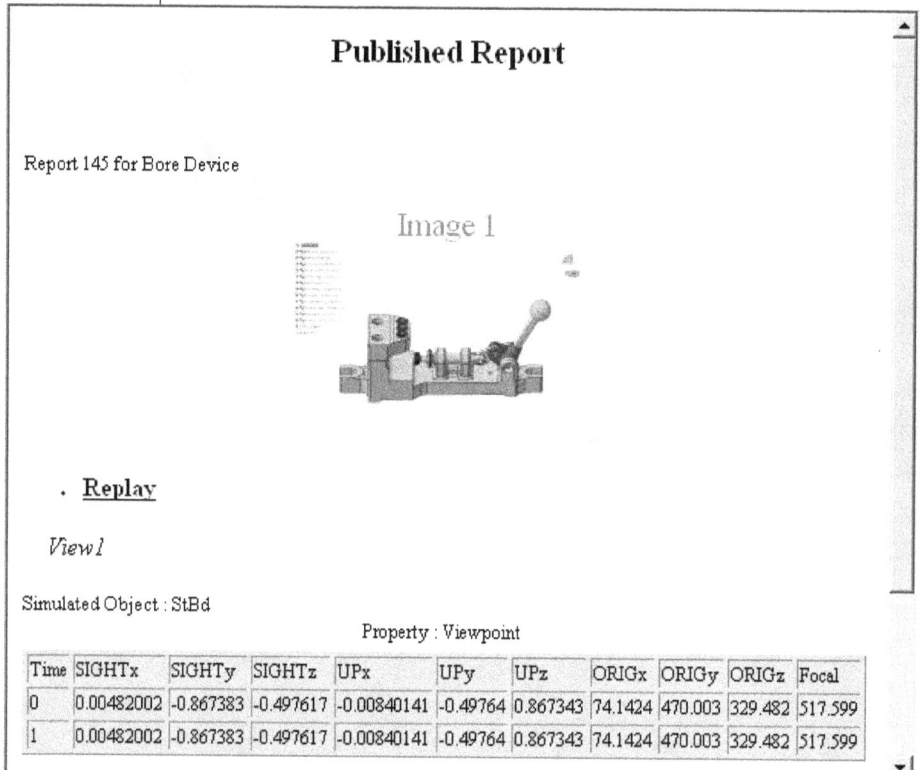

Figure 10–13

General Steps

Use the following general steps to create a published report of your results.

1. Activate the Publishing tool.
2. Select the elements to include in the report.
3. Save the published report.

Step 1 - Activate the Publishing tool.

To begin publishing, select **Tools>Publish>Start Publish**. The Save As dialog box opens. Enter a meaningful name in the *File Name* field and identify the path in which to save the file. Click **Save** to create an HTML file. The Publishing Tools toolbar displays as shown in Figure 10–14.

Figure 10–14

Step 2 - Select the elements to include in the report.

Inside the report, you can take snapshots of your model, publish findings, enter comments, and create VRML links to selected components.

Snapshots

Including images of your results is a good way to illustrate your findings. Snapshots can be used to create an image of the information inside the ENOVIA window. Any information displayed in the window, (including the model, annotation, specification tree, compass, etc.) displays in the snapshot. To use a snapshot, place the elements on the screen in the required positions and click the (Snapshot) icon. The image is added to the HTML file.

A snapshot created of a model with a section cut is shown in Figure 10–15. The image can be enlarged in the HTML viewer by clicking on it.

If the compass and specification tree are seen in the window, they are included in the snapshot. To control the display, use the options in the View drop-down list.

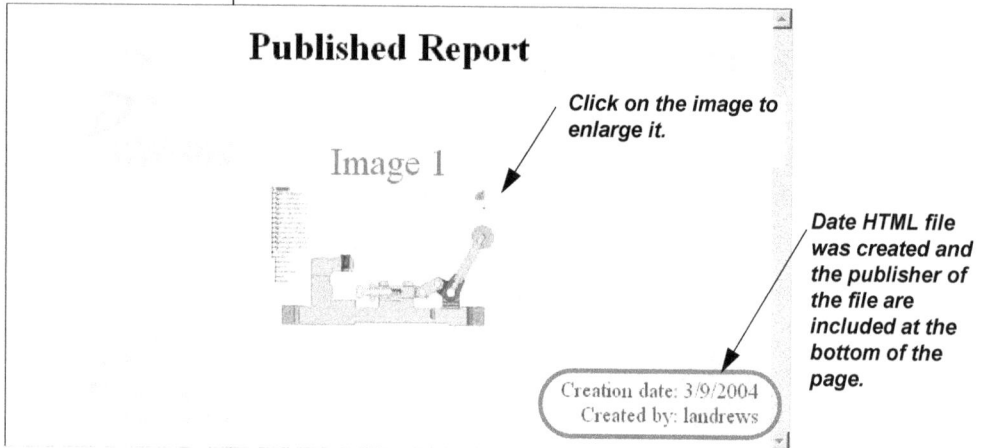

Figure 10–15

Feature Publish

Results of clash calculations, Hyperlinks, Simulations, and Replays can be published to the report. To add results to the report, click the 𝒫 (Feature Publish) icon and select the feature to publish. Published results are placed at the end of the HTML page.

Text

Comments can be added to the report to clarify information. To enter a comment, click the **T** (Text) icon and enter the comment in the Publish Text dialog box. If the text is created after an image is added, the text displays below the image. If the text is created first and then the image is added, the text displays above the image.

VRML

Components can be added to the report as VRML files. A VRML file enables you to orient and view 3D geometry inside a web browser without the need to use or install an ENOVIA license. A VRML plug-in is required and can typically be downloaded from the internet for free.

These VRML files can be viewed by clicking on the link in the report. To create a link to a VRML file select the component(s) to which to create the link and click the ▣ (VRML) icon. A link to the created file is added to the HTML file where it was created.

Step 3 - Save the published report.

Once all of the required elements have been added to the report, click the ▨ (Stop Publish) icon. The HTML file is created and saved to the specified directory. An example of a published report is shown in Figure 10–16.

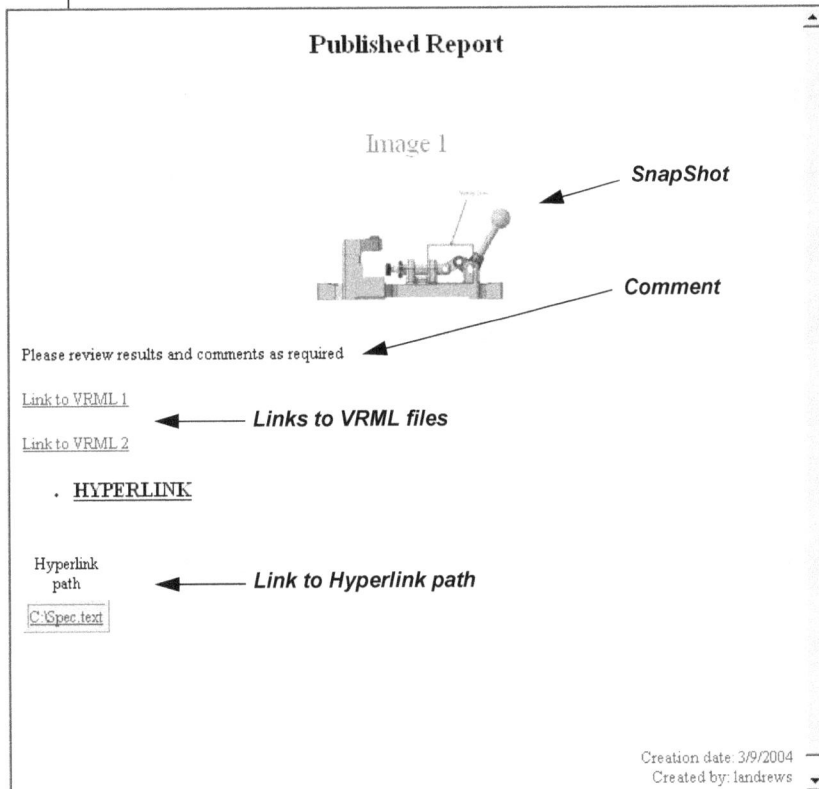

Published Report

Image 1

SnapShot

Comment

Please review results and comments as required

Link to VRML 1

Link to VRML 2

Links to VRML files

. **HYPERLINK**

Hyperlink
path

C:\Spec.text

Link to Hyperlink path

Creation date: 3/9/2004
Created by: landrews

Figure 10–16

Practice 10a | Locate Data

Practice Objectives

- Search for parts.
- Select components using Spatial Queries.

In this practice, you will open an existing assembly and select components using the Search Spatial Query techniques available in ENOVIA.

Task 1 - Open the assembly.

The files for this practice can be found in the HydraulicCylinder directory.

1. Open **HydraulicCylinder.CATProduct**. The assembly displays as shown in Figure 10–17.

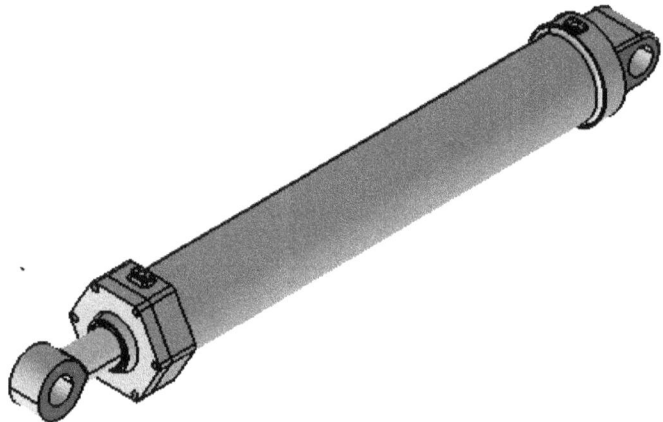

Figure 10–17

2. Select **Edit>Search**. The Search dialog box opens, as shown in Figure 10–18.

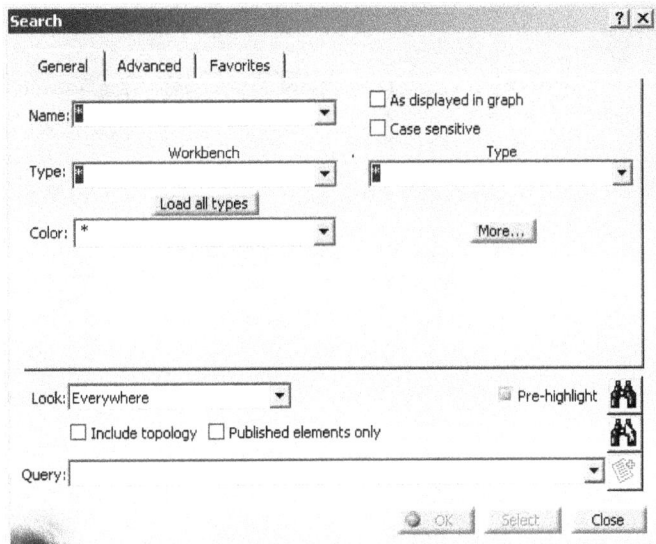

Figure 10–18

3. Specify the following, as shown in Figure 10–19:

   - *Name:* enter ***ring***
   - *Look:* **From HydraulicCylinder to bottom**

Use the drop-down arrow in the Look drop-down list to make your selection.

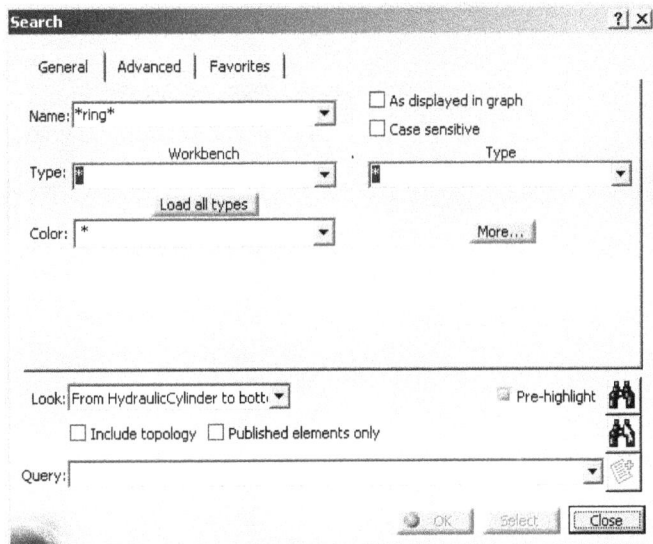

Figure 10–19

4. Click the 🔍 icon in the Search dialog box to run the query. The system reports that four objects have been found matching the search criteria, as shown in Figure 10–20.

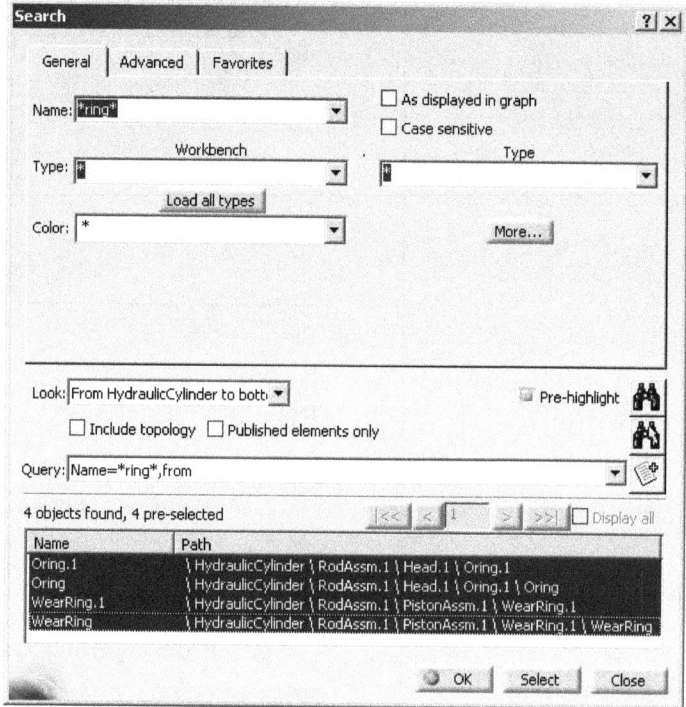

Figure 10–20

5. Find **WearRing.1** in the specification tree by selecting it in the list, right-clicking and selecting **Center Graph**, as shown in Figure 10–21.

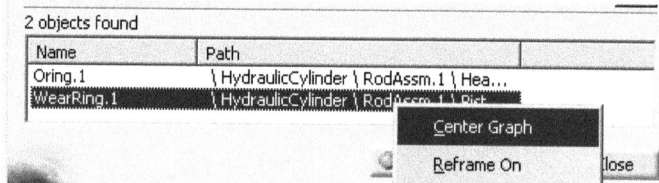

Figure 10–21

6. The specification tree expands to the assembly level containing the selected object, as shown in Figure 10–22, and highlights it.

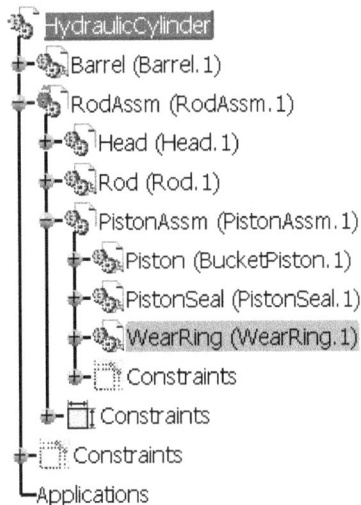

Figure 10–22

7. Use the search tool to locate the following items in the specification tree:

   • **RodWiper.CATPart**
   • **PistonSeal.CATPart**

8. Close the Search dialog box.

Task 2 - Select components using the spatial search tool.

---

1. Ensure that the DMU Review Navigation toolbar displays, as shown in Figure 10–23.

Figure 10–23

2. Click the (Spatial Query) icon. The Spatial Query dialog box opens.

3. Select the *Zone Query* tab, as shown in Figure 10–24.

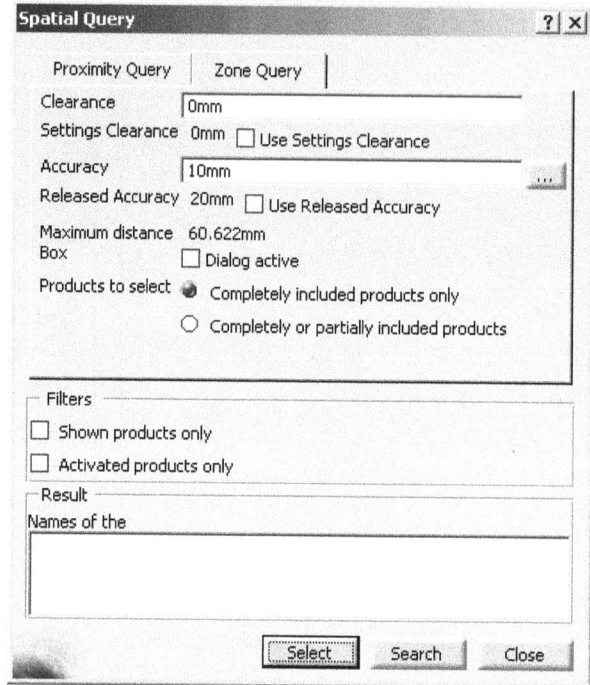

Figure 10–24

4. Select the solid line of the bounding box as shown in Figure 10–25.

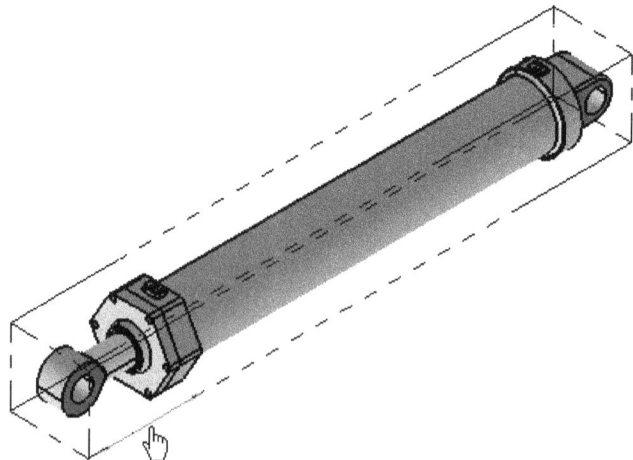

Figure 10–25

5. Drag it to the location shown in Figure 10–26.

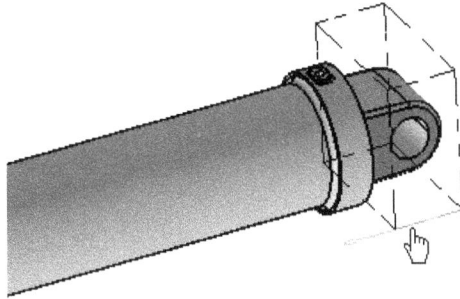

Figure 10–26

6. Make the following selections in the Spatial Query dialog box, as shown in Figure 10–27:

- *Clearance:* **0mm**
- *Accuracy:* **10mm**
- Select **Completely or partially included products**.

Figure 10–27

7. Click **Search**. The result should include the Barrel part, as shown in Figure 10–28.

Figure 10–28

8. Click **Select**.

9. Click the [icon] (Hide/Show) icon. The barrel part is now hidden, as shown in Figure 10–29.

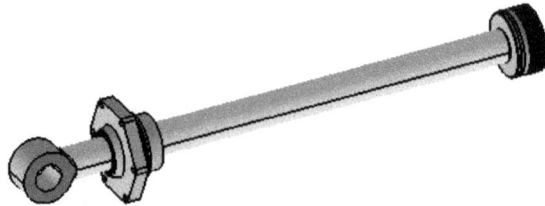

Figure 10–29

10. Perform a second spatial query using a bounding box as shown in Figure 10–30.

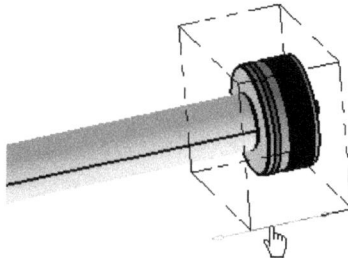

Figure 10–30

11. Select the **Completely included products only** option. The result should include the three products shown in Figure 10–31.

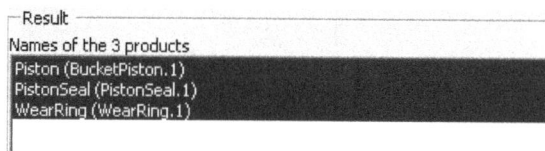

Result

Names of the 3 products

Piston (BucketPiston.1)
PistonSeal (PistonSeal.1)
WearRing (WearRing.1)

Figure 10–31

12. Select the results and hide them. The product should appear as shown in Figure 10–32.

Figure 10–32

13. Perform another spatial query. This time use the *Proximity Query* tab.

14. Select the following as shown in Figure 10–33:

   - *Selection:* **Rod (Rod.1)**
   - *Accuracy:* **10mm**
   - Select **Far away products only**.

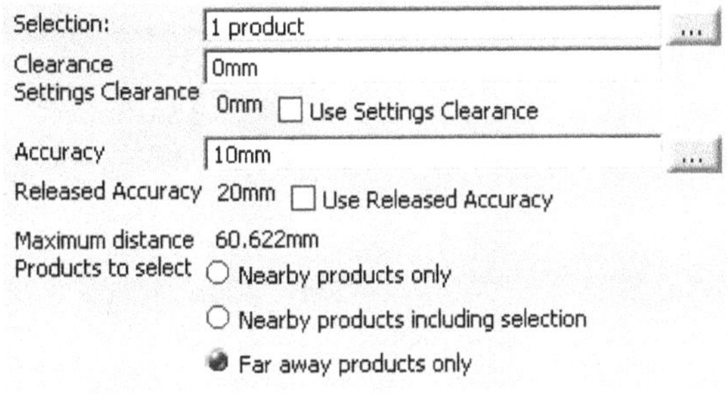

Figure 10–33

15. Click the [...] icon beside the Selection field. The Input window verifies your selection as shown in Figure 10–34.

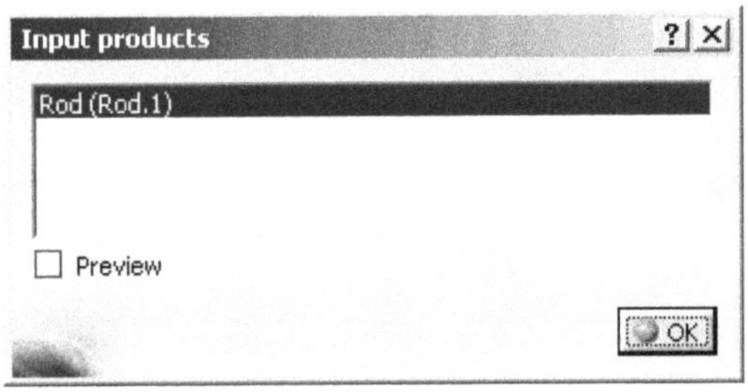

Figure 10–34

16. Click **OK**.

17. Click **Search**. The search results appear as shown in Figure 10–35.

Figure 10–35

18. Click **Select**.

19. Click the [icon] icon. The product displays as shown in Figure 10–36.

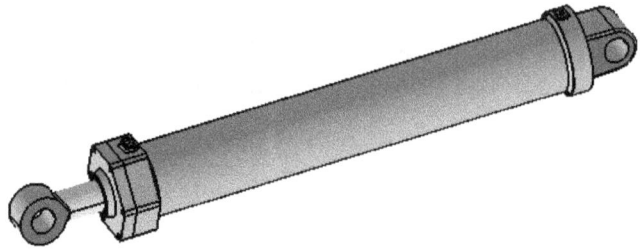

Figure 10–36

20. Save the file.

Practice 10b	# Publish a Report

Practice Objectives

- Publish an HTML report.
- Create a snap shot for the report.
- Create text for the report.

HTML reports can be published for viewing by others. In this practice you will add comments and publish a report.

Task 1 - Publish a report.

The files for this practice can be found in the HydraulicCylinder directory.

1. Open **HydraulicCylinder.CATProduct**.

2. Select **Tools>Publish>Start Publish**.

3. Enter **CylinderReport** in the *File name* field.

4. Ensure that the *html file is saved in the *HydraulicCylinder* directory, as shown in Figure 10–37.

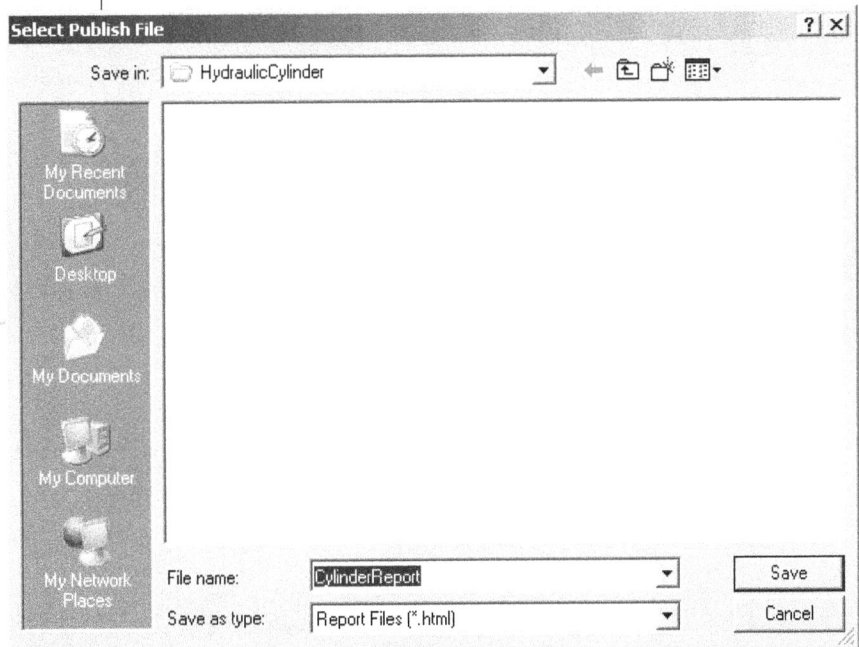

Figure 10–37

5. Click **Save**. The Publishing Tools toolbar displays as shown in Figure 10–38.

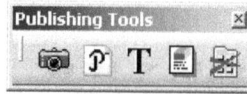

Figure 10–38

6. Click the (Front View) icon, as shown in Figure 10–39.

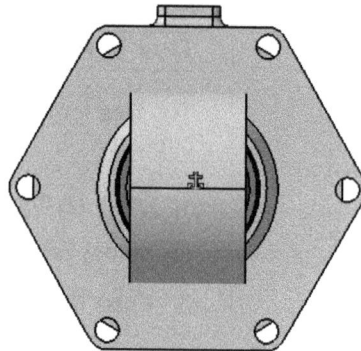

Figure 10–39

7. Click the (Snapshot) icon. You do not see any changes, however, the system has taken a snapshot of the screen.

8. Click the (Text) icon and enter the following text as shown in Figure 10–40:

   • Source grade 8 bolts for the head

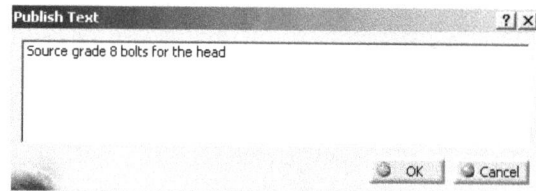

Figure 10–40

9. Click **OK**.

10. Click the (Stop Publish) icon.

Task 2 - Open the report.

1. Use Windows Explorer to browse to the *C:\DMU_Navigator_ and_SpaceAnalysis_Class_Files\HydraulicCylinder* directory and open **CylinderReport.html**, as shown in Figure 10–41.

Name ↑
- Barrel.CATPart
- Corp.gif
- CylinderReport.html
- CylinderReport_image1.jpg
- CylinderReport_imageSmall1.jpg
- Gland.CATPart
- Head.CATProduct
- HydraulicCylinder.CATProduct
- Oring.CATPart
- Piston.CATPart
- Piston.CATProduct
- PistonSeal.CATPart
- Rod.CATPart
- RodAssm.CATProduct
- RodSeal.CATPart
- RodWiper.CATPart
- WearRing.CATPart

Figure 10–41

The report displays as shown in Figure 10–42.

Published Report

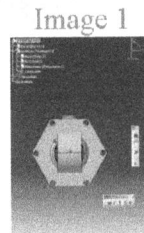

Image 1

Source grade 8 bolts for the head

Creation date: 07/22/2004
Created by: rsamra

Figure 10–42

2. Close the HTML viewer.

3. Save and close the model.

Chapter 11

Geometry Creation

Creating reference geometry (such as axis systems, points, lines, and planes) is sometimes required while investigating a model. They can be used to help take measurements, position components in an assembly, or better illustrate the orientation of the model when creating reports or capturing images.

Learning Objectives in this Chapter

- Create an Axis System.
- Create Points, Lines, and Planes.
- Create Datum elements.

11.1 Creating an Axis System

Axis systems are useful for better illustrating the orientation of a model, as a reference when moving components, or as a reference when creating additional reference geometry. They are also useful in other DMU workbenches, such as Kinematics.

General Steps

Use the following general steps to create an axis system:

1. Activate the Axis system tool.
2. Select a component in which to create the axis system.
3. Constrain the axis system.
4. Complete axis system creation.

Step 1 - Activate the Axis system tool.

To create an axis system, click the ⚓ (Axis System) icon in the DMU Geometry Creation toolbar.

Step 2 - Select a component in which to create the axis system.

Features cannot be created directly inside the product file; they must be created inside a part. The axis system can be created within an existing part or you can create a new part. In the Geometry Creation dialog box, select where you would like to create the feature. The Geometry Creation box (as shown in Figure 11–1) indicates that the feature is to be created in a new component in the top-level product file. Click **OK** to begin axis system creation.

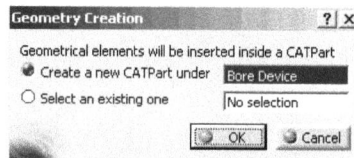

Geometry Creation ? X

Geometrical elements will be inserted inside a CATPart

⦿ Create a new CATPart under   Bore Device

◯ Select an existing one   No selection

OK   Cancel

Figure 11–1

Step 3 - Constrain the axis system.

In the Axis System Definition dialog box, select an option from the Axis system type drop-down list, as shown in Figure 11–2.

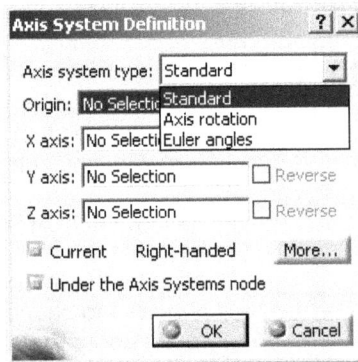

Figure 11–2

Standard

To create a Standard axis system, select a point to act as the origin for the system. The point can be the vertex of existing geometry, or a point feature. You can create a point to act as the origin on the fly by right-clicking on the Origin field and selecting **Create Point**, as shown in Figure 11–3.

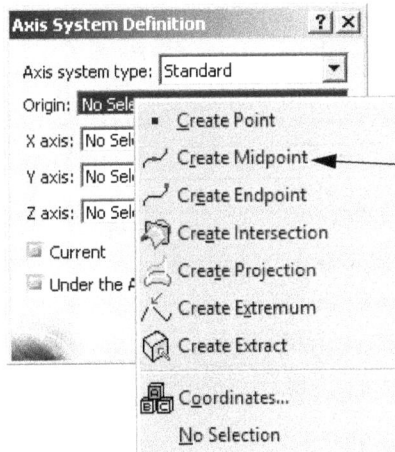

You can also create the origin at the midpoint or endpoint of a 2D element, such as the edge of a surface.

Figure 11–3

By default, the X-, Y-, and Z-axis are aligned to the X-, Y-, and Z-coordinates of the compass. Select in the field of the axis you want to define and select an edge on the model to indicate the axis orientation. To reverse the direction of an axis, select the **Reverse** option. Only two of the three axes need to be defined; the third is forced by the right hand rule.

Axis Rotation

An Axis Rotation system rotates two axes about a fixed axis to create the system. To create an axis rotation system, select a vertex or point on the model to act as the origin. As with standard systems, you can also create the origin point on the fly.

Axis Rotation systems require that only one axis be defined. Select in the field of the axis you want to define and select an edge on the model to indicate axis orientation. If required, select **Reverse** to change the direction of the axis. The other two axes rotate about the selected axis. In the Reference field select an element to act as the base from which the angle is measured. Figure 11–4 shows two axis systems. The axis system of the left side was created using Standard. The axis system on the right side uses a reference in the same orientation for its Z-axis as the Standard, with the other two axes rotated by 50 degrees.

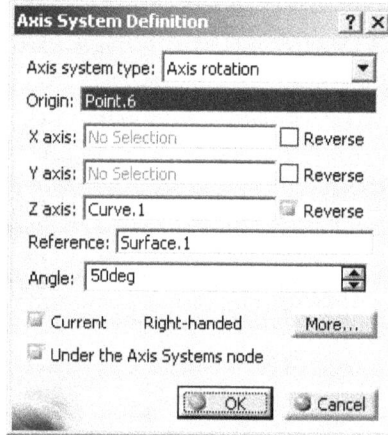

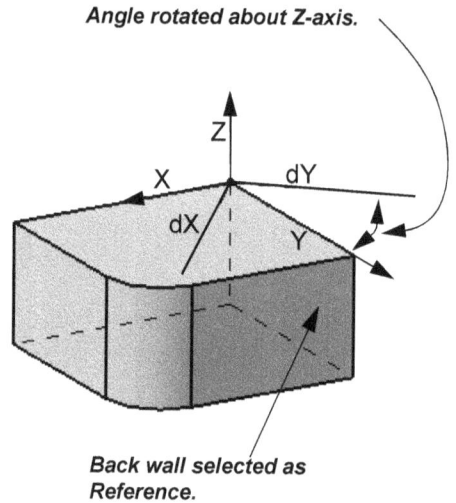

Angle rotated about Z-axis.

Back wall selected as Reference.

Figure 11–4

Euler Angles

Euler Angles rotate about the standard axis system in three directions as shown in Figure 11–5.

- Angle 1 rotates the axis system about the Z-axis.

- Angle 2 rotates the axis system about the X-axis after Angle 1 has been applied.

- Angle 3 rotates the axis system about the Z-axis after Angles 1 and 2 have been applied.

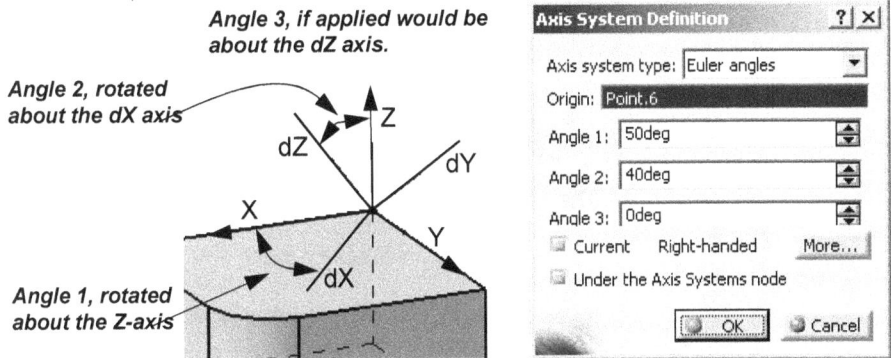

Figure 11–5

Step 4 - Complete axis system creation.

Click **OK** to finish creating the axis. The axis is created within the selected part, in the **Axis System** branch of the specification tree, as shown in Figure 11–6.

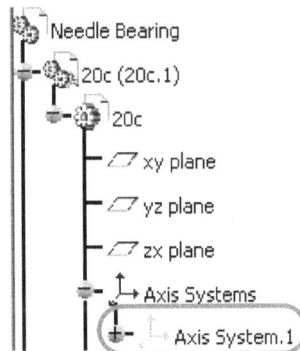

Figure 11–6

11.2 Creating Points

Points are 3D markers in a model. They can be used to build geometry, make measurements, or as location markers when creating reports.

General Steps

Use the following general steps to create points:

1. Access the Point creation tool.
2. Select references to create the point.
3. Complete point creation.

Step 1 - Access the Point creation tool.

To create a point, click the ▪ (Point) icon in the DMU Geometry Creation toolbar.

Features cannot be created directly inside the product file; they must be created inside a part. The point can be created within an existing part or in a new part. In the Geometry Creation dialog box, select where you want to create the feature. The dialog box, indicating that the feature is to be created in an existing part called Locator_Points, is shown in Figure 11–7.

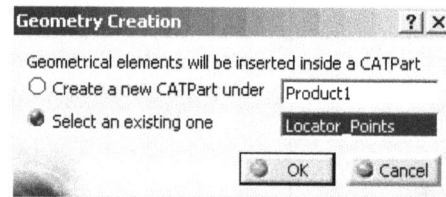

Figure 11–7

Click **OK** to begin point creation.

Step 2 - Select references to create the point.

In the Point Definition dialog box select the type of point to create, as shown in Figure 11–8. Depending on the point creation type, the references required to create the point differs. The methods used to create a point are described in the table below.

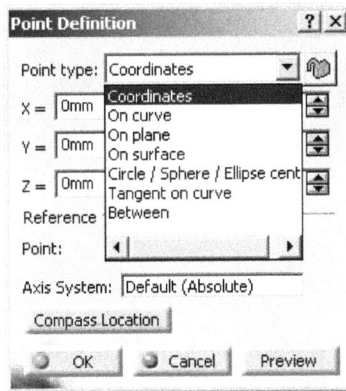

Figure 11–8

Point Type		Description
Coordinates		Enter the X, Y, and Z distances from an existing reference point or the origin of the part.
Point at X=0, Y=0 and Z=0 *Point at X=0, Y=2, Z=1*
		You can define the reference for the point using the following options:
	Point	The point's coordinates are measured from the selected point. By default, the coordinates are measured from the origin of the current local axis system.
	Axis System	The direction of the point's X, Y, and Z coordinates are changed with respect to the selected axis system.
	Compass Location	If the compass is located on geometry, the X, Y, and Z coordinates of the point can be set based on the compass location.

On Curve		Select an edge of a solid feature, a segment of a sketch, or a line for the point to be located on.
		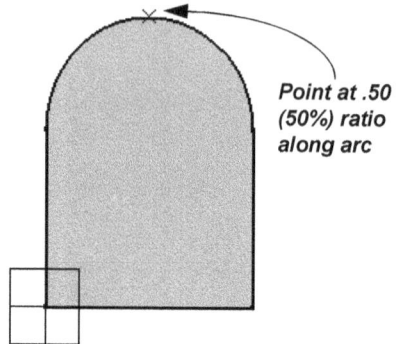 Point at .50 (50%) ratio along arc
		You can define the location of the point along the edge using the following options:
	Ratio	Percentage along curve.
	Geodesic Distance	Distance measured along the curve.
	Euclidean Distance	Absolute distance from a reference.
		The **Repeat object after OK** option enables you to specify additional points spaced at an incremental distance. Also, there is an option to create planes through the points that are normal to the curve.
On Plane		Select the location for the point on a planar surface and specify the horizontal and vertical distances for the point. By default, the distances are relative to the origin of the part. Optionally, another reference point can be selected.
		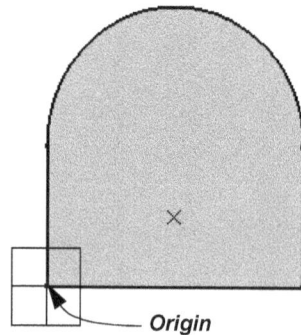 Origin

On Surface	Select the location for the point on a curved surface. By default, the point is created at the center of the surface. You can locate the point on the surface using one of the following: • An edge • The surface normal of a plane • Points X, Y, and Z values using the shortcut menu 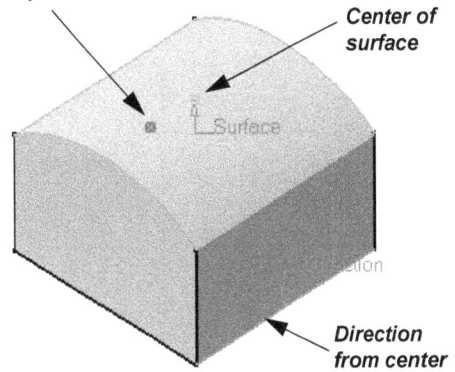
Circle / Sphere / Ellipse Center	Locate a point at the center of a circle, sphere, arc, or ellipse. 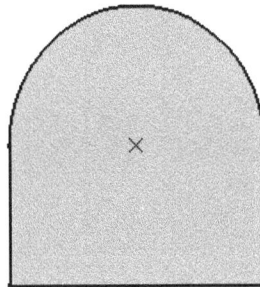

Tangent on Curve	Select a planar curve and a direction line. A point is placed at each tangent location relative to the direction line. 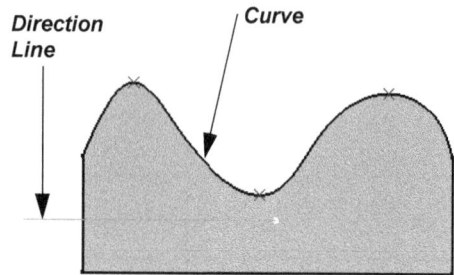
Between	Select two points and enter the ratio of the distance from the first point to the new point. You can use the **Reverse Direction** option to specify the distance from the second point to the new point. If the ratio is greater than one, the point is located on a virtual line extended beyond the two points. 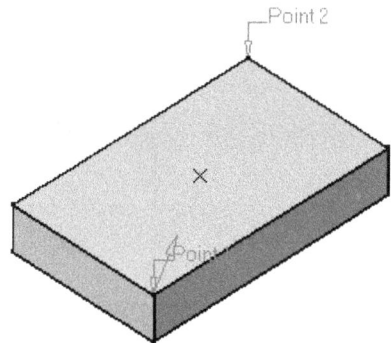

Step 3 - Complete point creation.

Once the point has been defined, click **OK** to create it. The point is added to the selected part under the **Geometrical Set** branch of the specification tree, as shown in Figure 11–9.

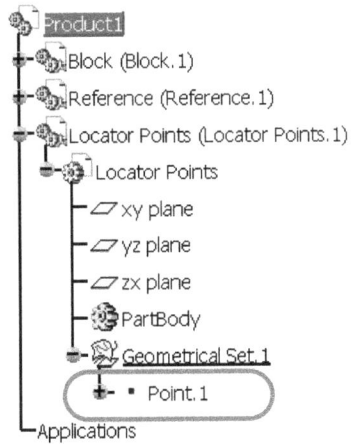

Figure 11–9

11.3 Creating Lines

Lines can be used to align and orient a model during assembly. Axis systems can also be oriented with respect to orthogonal lines in the model.

General Steps

Use the following general steps to create a line:

1. Access the Line creation tool.
2. Select references to create the line.
3. Complete the line creation.

Step 1 - Access the Line creation tool.

To create a line, click the ╱ (Line) icon in the DMU Geometry Creation toolbar.

Features cannot be created directly inside the product file, they must be created inside a part. The line can be created within an existing part or in a new part. In the Geometry Creation dialog box select where you want to create the feature. The Geometry Creation dialog box, shown in Figure 11–10, indicates that the feature is to be created in a new part.

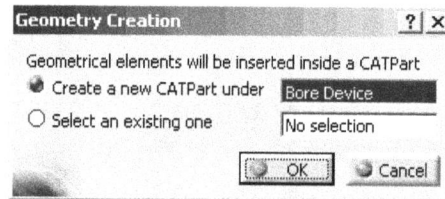

Figure 11–10

Click **OK** to begin the line creation.

Step 2 - Select references to create the line.

In the Line Definition dialog box, select the type of line to create, as shown in Figure 11–11. The references required to create the line differ depending on the line creation type.

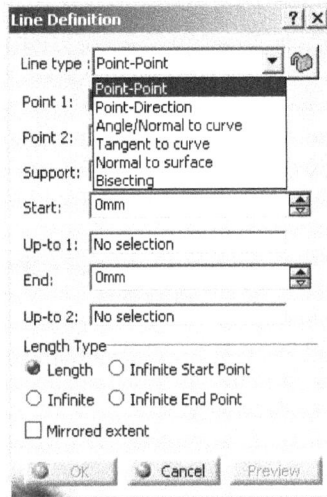

Figure 11–11

The methods used to create a line are described as follows:

Method	Description
Point-to-Point	Select two points or vertices for the line to connect between. By default, a straight line between the two points is created. If required, you can select a support surface for the line to follow.

You can enter the distance for the start and end points of the line to extend beyond the two points.

Point - Direction	Select a starting point and an edge, line, or plane to define the line direction. Enter the length of the line.

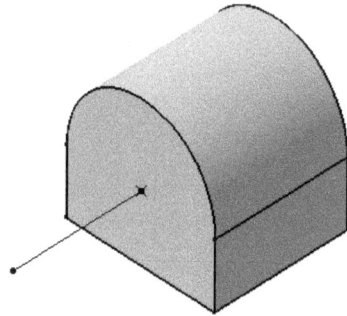

Angle/Normal to curve	Select the start point for the line and a line or edge to measure the angle relative to. Select a plane that has both the point and the line, and enter the angle.

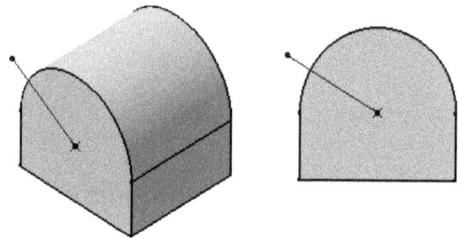

The **Repeat object after OK** option enables you to create a number of additional lines spaced at the same angle. They are not related to each other after they are created.

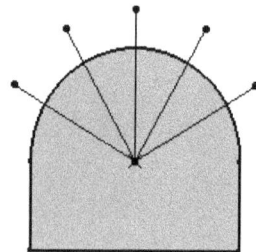

Tangent to curve	Select an edge for the line to be tangent to and a point for for the start of the line. Enter the line length. 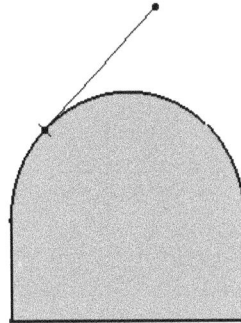
Normal to surface	Select a surface for the line to be perpendicular to and a starting point. Enter the length of the line. *Point* 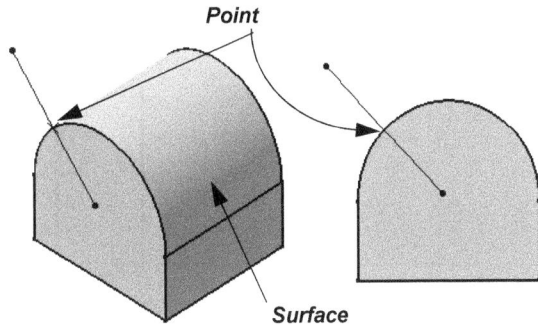 *Surface* The **Mirror Extent** option constructs the line equally on each side of the point.
Bisecting	Select two lines or edges and a new line is created that bisects them. If there is more than one solution, you can select the location for the bisecting line. 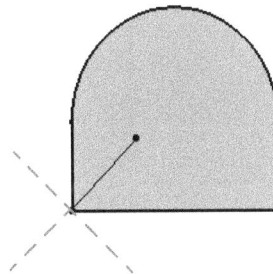

Step 3 - Complete the line creation.

Once the line has been defined, click **OK** to complete the feature. The line is added to a new part under the **Geometrical Set** branch of the specification tree, as shown in Figure 11–12.

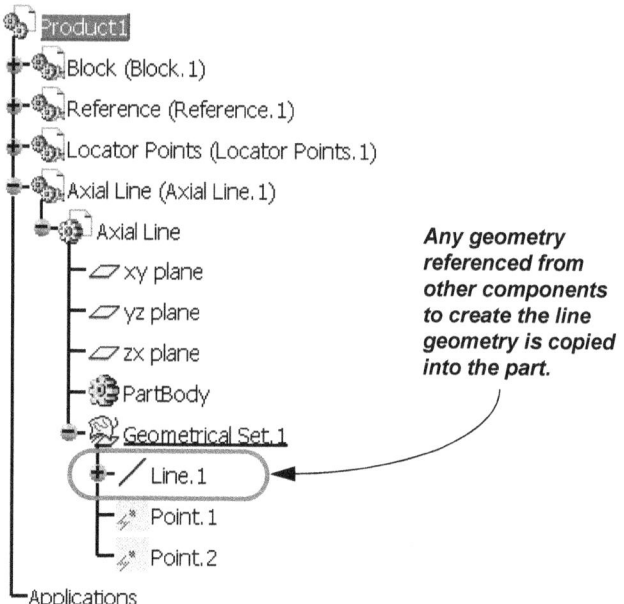

Product1
- Block (Block.1)
- Reference (Reference.1)
- Locator Points (Locator Points.1)
- Axial Line (Axial Line.1)
  - Axial Line
    - xy plane
    - yz plane
    - zx plane
    - PartBody
    - Geometrical Set.1
      - Line.1
      - Point.1
      - Point.2
- Applications

Any geometry referenced from other components to create the line geometry is copied into the part.

Figure 11–12

11.4 Creating Planes

Planes can be used to snap models to existing geometry or to set the position and orientation of a model.

General Steps

Use the following general steps to create a plane:

1. Access the Plane creation tool.
2. Select references to create the plane.
3. Complete the plane creation.

Step 1 - Access the Plane creation tool.

To create a plane, click the ◇ (Plane) icon in the DMU Geometry Creation toolbar.

Features cannot be created directly inside the product file, they must be created inside a part. As with other geometric features, the plane can be created within an existing part or in a new part. In the Geometry Creation dialog box select where you want to create the feature. Click **OK** to begin the plane creation.

Step 2 - Select references to create the plane.

In the Plane Definition dialog box select the type of plane to create, as shown in Figure 11–13. The references required to create the plane differ depending on the Plane creation type. The most common methods used to create a plane are described in the table below.

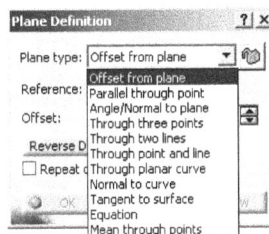

Figure 11–13

Method	Description
Tangent to surface	Select a point for the plane to pass through and a surface to which the plane is tangent. *Tangent to this surface*
Offset from plane	Select a planar face on the model or a reference plane and enter the offset distance. *Offset from this plane*
Normal to a curve	Select a line, edge, or sketch segment for the plane to be perpendicular to and a point for the plane to pass through. *Plane is normal to this edge*
Parallel through point	Select a planar face on the model, or a reference plane for the plane to be parallel to, and select a point for the plane to pass through. *Parallel to this face*

Angle/Normal to plane	Select a line, edge or axis for the plane to pass through and a planar reference for the angle to be measured relative to.

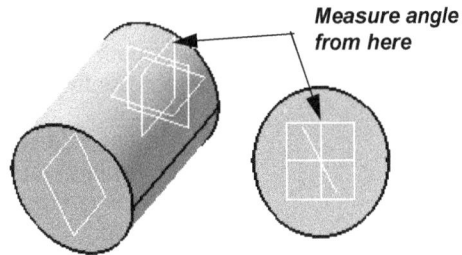

Measure angle from here

Implicit Axis Selection

By default cylindrical features do not display their axis. To reference the axis of a cylindrical feature, hold <Shift> with the cursor over the feature. The axis displays and you can select it, as shown in Figure 11–14. This is useful for creating a plane that is at an angle to a planar reference and passes through the axis.

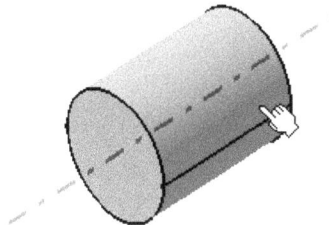

Figure 11–14

Step 3 - Complete the plane creation.

Once the plane has been defined, click **OK** to complete the feature. The plane is added to the specified part under the **Geometrical Set** branch of the specification tree.

11.5 Creating Datum Elements

In some cases, you might be required to break the associativity between elements of your model. Datum elements are axis system, point, line, and plane elements that are not modifiable or associative to the reference geometry used to create them.

Datum elements are not associative, which means that you are not able to modify the parameters used to create them. If any referenced geometry is modified, the datum element does not update.

To create a datum element, click the [icon] (Create Datum) icon in the DMU Geometry Creation toolbar and create the required geometry. The datum element displays with an icon in the specification tree, as shown in Figure 11–15.

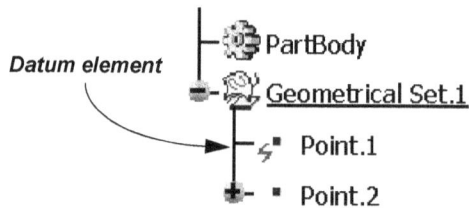

Datum element

PartBody

Geometrical Set.1

Point.1

Point.2

Figure 11–15

Practice 11a

Geometry Creation I

Practice Objectives

- Create a reference point.
- Create a reference line.
- Create a reference plane.
- Create an axis system.

In this practice, you will create a new, temporary assembly so that you can view the relative positions between components, take measurements, and run analyses. To do this, the positions of the components must be defined within the product. This is accomplished by creating a new part file and adding reference elements (points, lines, planes, and axis systems) using the DMU Geometry Creation toolbar.

Upon completion of this practice, you will have created an assembly that displays as shown in Figure 11–16.

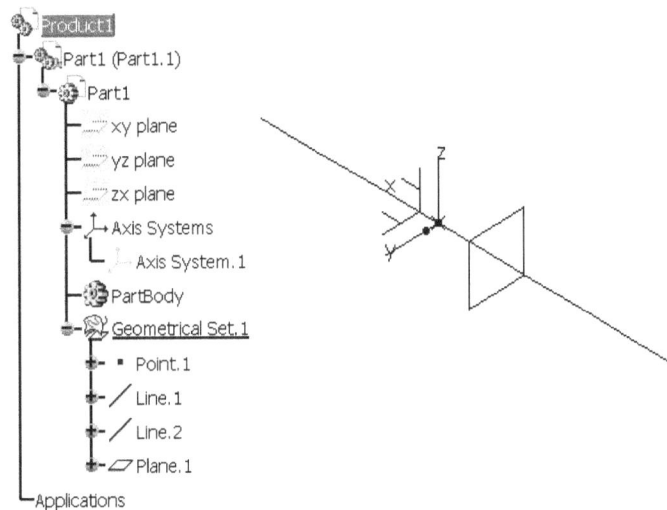

Figure 11–16

Task 1 - Create a temporary Product file for analysis.

1. Select **File>New>Product**.

2. Ensure that the DMU Navigator workbench ( ) is active.

Task 2 - Create a reference point.

*By Default, the DMU Geometry Creation toolbar is not displayed. If you do not see the toolbar, select **View> Toolbars** and ensure the DMU Geometry Creation toolbar is active.*

1. Click the ▣ (Point) icon in the DMU Geometry Creation toolbar.

2. The Geometry Creation dialog box opens, as shown in Figure 11–17. You must define a part or product for the reference geometry to be created in. Since currently there are no parts in this assembly, the **Select an existing one** option is not available. Click **OK** to create the reference point in a new part file that the system creates.

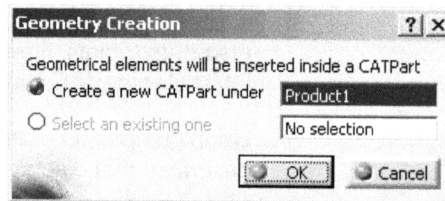

Figure 11–17

The system creates a part file called Part1. The Point Definition dialog box opens, as shown in Figure 11–18, enabling you to define the references to locate the reference point.

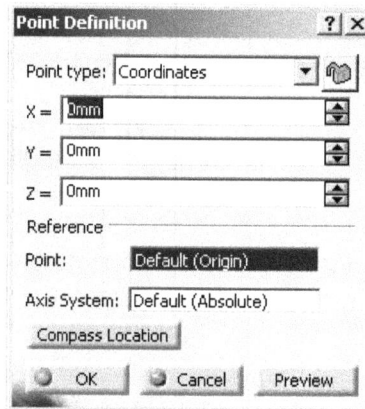

Figure 11–18

3. Click **OK** to accept the default location of the point. It is located at the origin of the three reference planes on the newly created part.

Task 3 - Create a reference line.

1. Click the [Line icon] (Line) icon in the DMU Geometry Creation toolbar. The Geometry Creation dialog box opens, as shown in Figure 11–19.

2. Select the **Select an existing one** option and select Part1 in the specification tree so that the reference line is created in Part1.

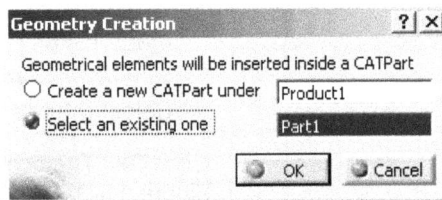

Figure 11–19

3. Click **OK**. Define the line using the following parameters:

   - *Line type:* **Point - Direction**
   - *Point:* **Point.1**
   - *Direction:* **yz plane**
   - *Start:* **0**
   - *End:* **20**

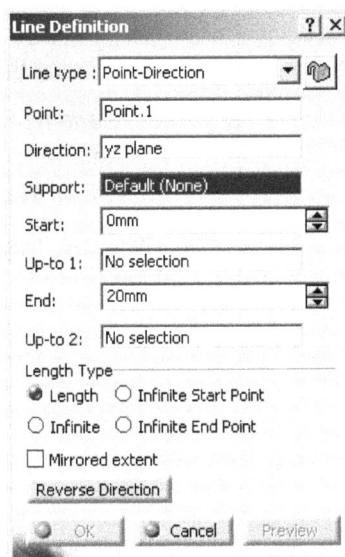

Figure 11–20

4. Click **OK**. The completed line displays as shown in Figure 11–21.

Figure 11–21

5. Create a second line in Part1 using the following parameters:

   - *Line type:* **Point - Direction**
   - *Point:* **Point.1**
   - *Direction:* **zx plane**
   - Select **Infinite**.

6. Click **OK**. The completed line displays as shown in Figure 11–22.

Figure 11–22

Task 4 - Create a reference plane.

1. Click the (Plane) icon. Define the reference plane in Part1 using the following parameters:

   - *Plane type:* **Offset from plane**
   - *Reference:* **zx plane**
   - *Offset:* **100**

2. Click **OK**. The reference plane displays as shown in Figure 11–23.

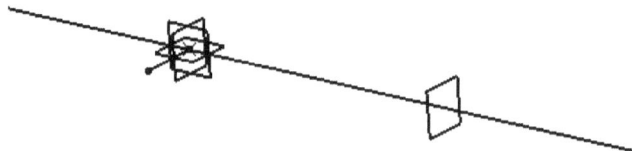

Figure 11–23

Task 5 - Manage the display of reference elements.

*Hold <Ctrl> to multi-select. To hide elements, right-click and select **Hide/Show**.*

1. Select the three default part reference planes (xy plane, yz plane, zx plane) in the specification tree and hide them. The default reference planes have been hidden to provide a clear view of the axis system that you create in the next task.

Task 6 - Create an axis system.

In this task, you will create an axis system whose z-axis lies on the y-axis of the part axis system.

1. Click the ⊿ (Axis System) icon in the DMU Geometry Creation toolbar. Define the axis system in Part1 as follows:

    *   *Axis system type:* **Euler angles**
    *   *Origin:* **Point.1**
    *   *Angle 2:* **90**

    The Axis System Definition dialog box opens, as shown in Figure 11–24.

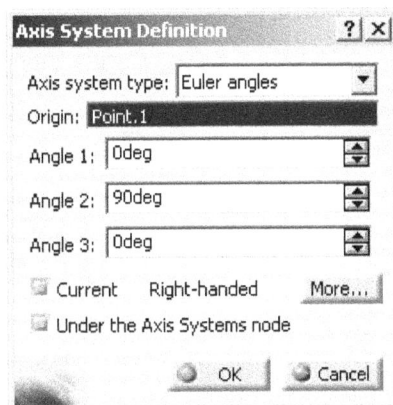

Figure 11–24

2. Click **OK** to complete the definition of the axis system. The reference elements appear as shown in Figure 11–25.

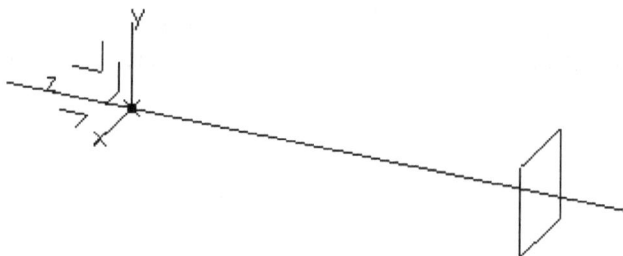

Figure 11–25

3. Save the product file to the top-level directory containing the class files using Save Management. Enter **Temp.CATProduct** as the name of the product file and **Skel.CATPart** as the part filename.

Design Considerations

The product is now ready for component assembly. The geometry created in **Skel.CATPart** can be used to position new components in the temporary assembly so that accurate clash, section, and distance analyses can be performed.

4. Close the window.

Practice 11b | Geometry Creation II

Practice Objective

- Take measurements from an assembly using reference elements.

In this practice, you will use the creation of reference elements in DMU Navigator to assist in taking measurements from an assembly. The creation of points, lines, and planes is not always required to generate a required measurement. However, it will simplify the measurement process.

Two measurements are required from the assembly:

- Vertical distance from the center of the ball bearing to the top of the outer race.

- Radial distance from the center of the ball bearing to the center of the shaft.

Task 1 - Open the assembly.

The files for this practice can be found in the CVJoint directory.

1. Open **CVJoint.CATProduct**. The assembly displays as shown in Figure 11–26.

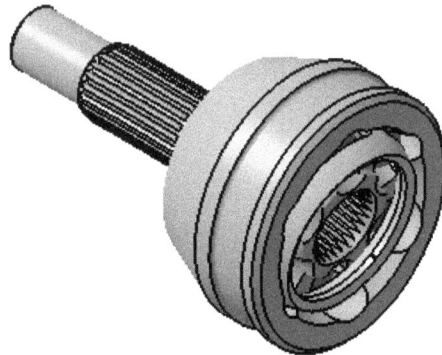

Figure 11–26

2. Hide the following components:

- **InnerRace**
- **Cage** (from the **CageBall** subassembly)

3. Orient the model as shown in Figure 11–27.

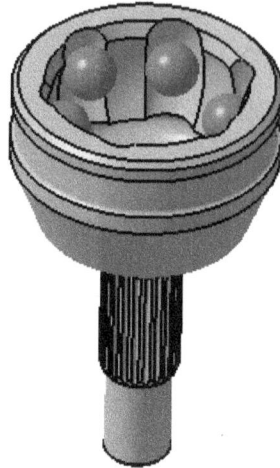

Figure 11–27

Task 2 - Create a reference point.

To take the first measurement, the center of the ball bearing must be located using a reference point.

1. Select on the surface of one of the ball bearings as shown in Figure 11–28.

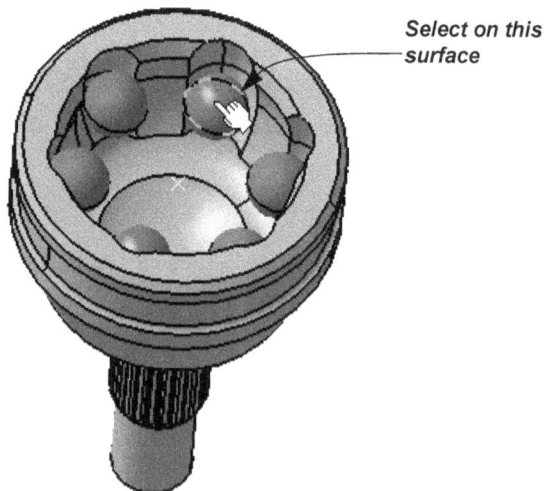

Select on this surface

Figure 11–28

2. Click the ⬛ (Point) icon. Since the BallBearing component has been preselected, the Geometry Creation dialog box opens, as shown in Figure 11–29.

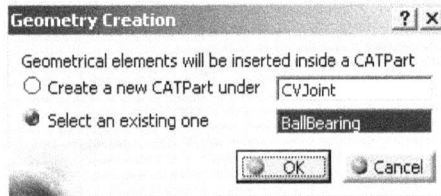

Geometry Creation   ? ✕

Geometrical elements will be inserted inside a CATPart

○ Create a new CATPart under   CVJoint

◉ Select an existing one   BallBearing

                        ◉ OK   ◉ Cancel

Figure 11–29

3. Click **OK** to create the point in the BallBearing part. The Point Definition dialog box opens. Since a surface was selected, the default Point type is set to On surface.

4. Select **Circle / Sphere /Ellipse center** in the Point type drop-down list.

5. Click **OK**. The model displays as shown in Figure 11–30.

Figure 11–30

Design Considerations

A reference point is created in each of the BallBearing components. The point is created in the part model, which is the same model that has been assembled into the product six times. Therefore, the point is reflected in each assembly instance.

Task 3 - Create a reference plane.

The creation of a reference plane is useful to break the components of a measurement and ensure that you are getting the required value. In this case, the vertical distance is required, so a horizontal reference plane is constructed.

1. Select one of the points you just created, and click the

    [plane icon] (Plane) icon.

2. Create the plane in the BallBearing. Define the reference plane using the following parameters:

    *   *Plane type:* **Parallel through point**
    *   *Reference:* Select the face shown in Figure 11–31.
    *   *Point:* **Point.2**

Preselected point

Select this face

Figure 11–31

3. Complete the feature. A reference plane is created in each instance of the BallBearing component and are not all of the planes are at the same orientation, as shown in Figure 11–32. Why is this?

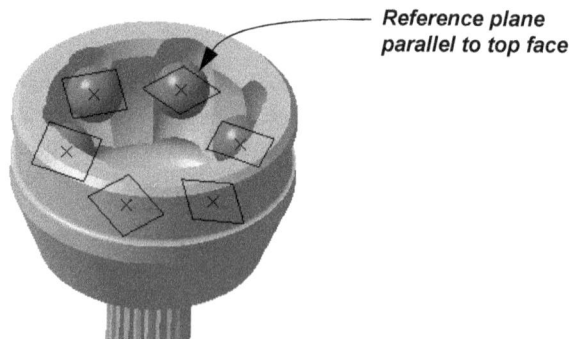

Reference plane parallel to top face

Figure 11–32

Task 4 - Measure the distance.

1. Measure the distance between the top face of the OuterRace and the parallel reference plane just created. The minimum distance is 12.793 mm, as shown in Figure 11–33. Ensure that the measured angle is 0° indicating that the parallel plane was selected.

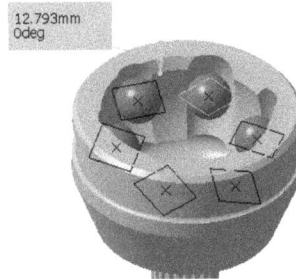

12.793mm
0deg

Figure 11–33

2. Select the **Keep measure** option and complete the feature.

Task 5 - Create a reference line.

1. Preselect a reference point and click the [/] (Line) icon.

2. Create the line in the BallBearing. Define the reference line using the following parameters:

   - *Line type:* **Point-Direction**
   - *Point:* **Point.2**
   - *Direction:* Select the face shown in Figure 11–34.
   - *Start:* **20**
   - *End:* **0**

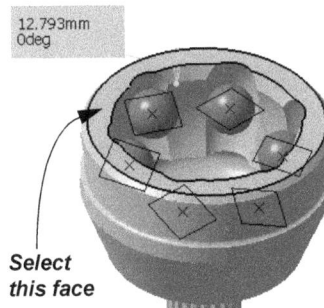

12.793mm
0deg

Select this face

Figure 11–34

3. If required, click **Reverse Direction** to orient the lines as shown in Figure 11–35 and complete the feature. Remember the point selected to create the line. At this point the line is parallel with the axis of the OuterRace.

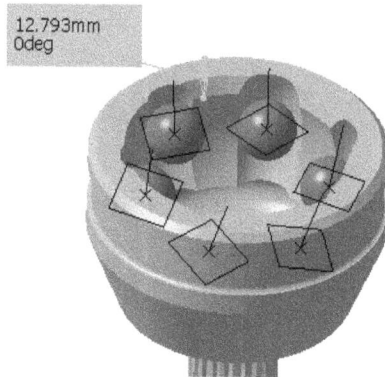

12.793mm
0deg

Figure 11–35

Task 6 - Measure the radial distance.

1. Measure the distance from the point to the axis of the OuterRace. The distance is 25.324mm as shown in Figure 11–36.

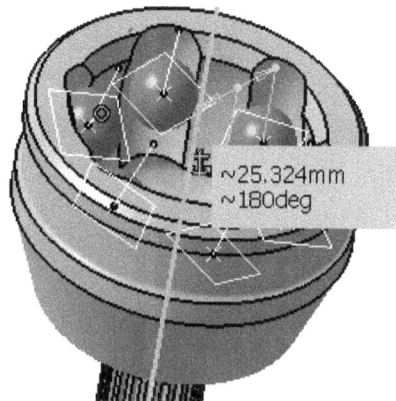

~25.324mm
~180deg

Figure 11–36

Task 7 - Control the display of the reference elements.

1. Expand one of the instances of the BallBearing component in the specification tree so that the contents of the geometrical set display, as shown in Figure 11–37.

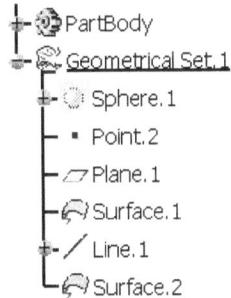

Figure 11–37

2. Hide the geometrical set and measurements (if kept). The model displays as shown in Figure 11–38.

Figure 11–38

3. Save the assembly and close the window.

Moving Components

While many products analyzed in DMU are already fully constrained using the CAD application they were created in, it is sometimes necessary to move components to better visualize information.

Learning Objectives in this Chapter

- Learn how to translate and rotate components.
- Move a component by selecting two geometric elements.
- Perform a Symmetry Operation.
- Learn how to reset a component's position.

12.1 Moving Components

In this section, you learn how to translate and rotate components using the Translation and Rotation operations.

Movement of a component using the Translation or Rotation tool depends on the **Relative Move** option, as shown in Figure 12–1.

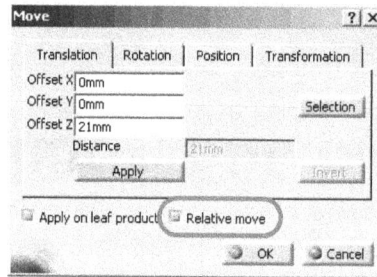

Figure 12–1

If this option is selected, the move is performed with respect to the parent component of the selected object. If the option is not selected, the movement is based on the root product's origin, as shown in Figure 12–2.

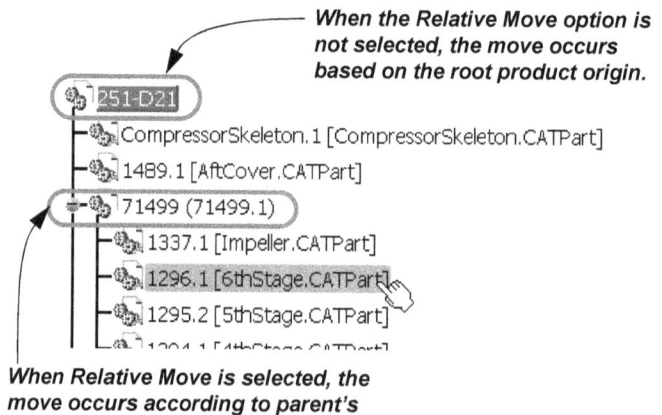

When the Relative Move option is not selected, the move occurs based on the root product origin.

When Relative Move is selected, the move occurs according to parent's

Figure 12–2

General Steps

Use the following general steps to move a component:

1. Activate the Move tool.
2. Define the movement method.
3. Complete the move.

Step 1 - Activate the Move tool.

Select the component(s) to be moved. Use <Ctrl> to select more then one component at once. Click the  (Translation or Rotation) icon in the toolbar. The compass moves to the origin of the product and the Move dialog box opens, as shown in Figure 12–3.

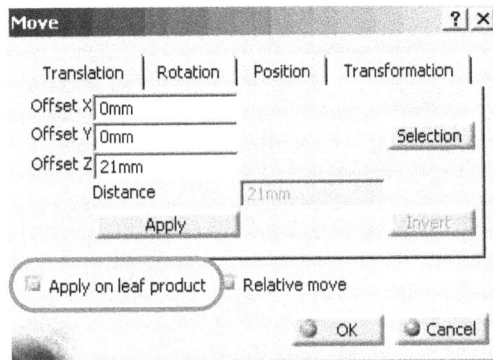

Figure 12–3

The object to be moved depends on whether or not the **Apply on leaf product** option is selected, as shown in Figure 12–3. If it is selected, only the selected component moves. If it is not selected, the movement is applied to the first branch level of the selected component, as shown in Figure 12–4.

The **Apply on leaf product** option only applies if the selected component is part of a subassembly.

If the Apply on leaf product option is not selected, the entire subassembly to which the selected component belongs moves.

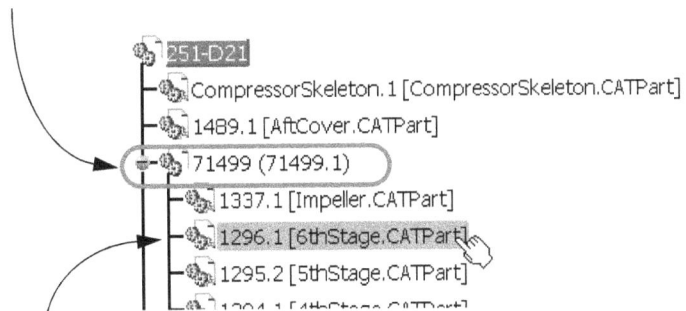

If the Apply on leaf product option is selected, only the selected component moves.

Figure 12–4

Step 2 - Define the movement method.

Component(s) can be moved using four different methods:

- Translation

- Rotation

- Position

- Transformation

All movements are based on the current location of the component. For example, you can translate a component, and then rotate it from its translated position.

Translation

Select the *Translation* tab to move the selected component in the X-, Y-, or Z-direction. If the exact offset distance in each direction is known, enter the coordinates using the Offset fields. If the exact measurements are not known, click **Selection** and select two geometric elements. The system calculates the direction vector and distance between the two features. For example, the holes on component 1, shown in Figure 12–5, need to be aligned with the holes on the base component. To accomplish this, click **Selection** and select the hole axes of both components to align them.

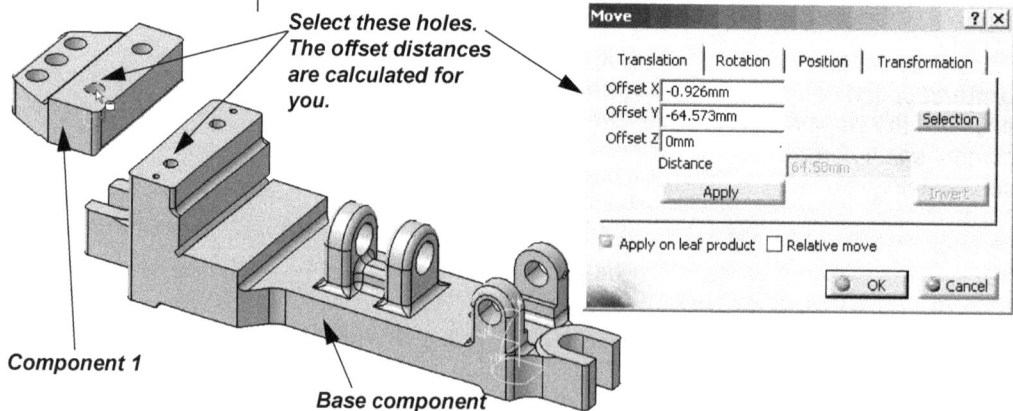

Select these holes. The offset distances are calculated for you.

Component 1

Base component

Figure 12–5

Click **Apply** to preview the move, as shown in Figure 12–6. You can apply as many translations, rotations, positions, and transformations as required until the component is in the correct location.

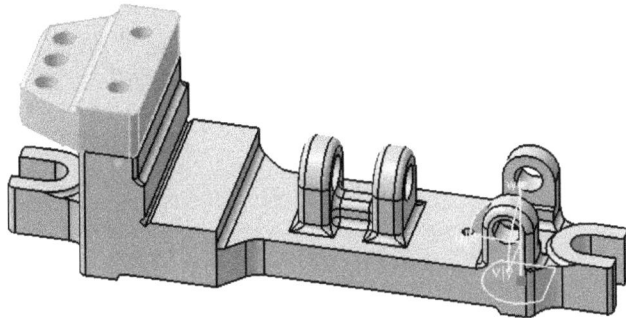

Figure 12–6

Rotation

Select the *Rotation* tab to rotate the selected component(s) about the X-, Y-, or Z-axis. They can also be rotated about a selected reference by clicking **Selection** and selecting the feature to rotate about. Enter the angle of rotation and click **Apply** to view the move.

For example, the component in Figure 12–6 needs to be rotated 180 degrees. Since no elements occur in the correct location for the rotation, a line is created to rotate about, as shown in Figure 12–7. This line can be hidden once the movement is complete. The placement could have also been done without extra features. However, more translations would have been required to place the component correctly.

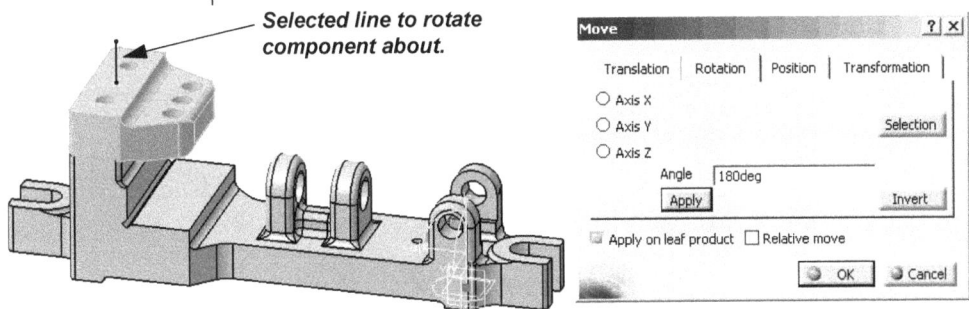

Selected line to rotate component about.

Figure 12–7

Position

Select the *Position* tab to set the absolute position of the components. The selected components are translated and rotated based on the origin. Use the X-, Y- and Z-fields to translate the selected object, where **0mm** is the origin of the move, based on the **Relative Move** option. Use RotX, RotY, and RotZ to angle the selected component about the corresponding origin axis. Figure 12–8 shows the Move dialog box with the *Position* tab selected.

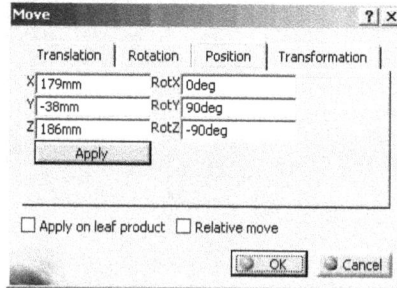

Figure 12–8

Transformation

Select the *Transformation* tab to specify increments for both translation and rotation. The selected components are translated and rotated based on their current location. Figure 12–9 shows the Move dialog box with the *Transformation* tab selected.

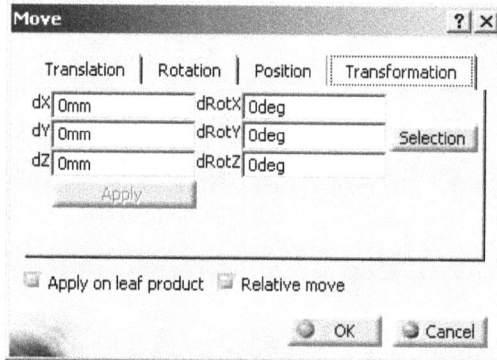

Figure 12–9

Step 3 - Complete the move.

Once you are satisfied with the position of the component, click **OK** to confirm the move.

12.2 Snap Components

The Snap tool enables you to move a component by selecting two geometric elements. The first element indicates the component that is used to connect to the second element. The movement of the first component depends on which elements are selected. For example, selecting a point or vertex on one component and then a point or vertex on a another component makes the two points coincident.

General Steps

Use the following general steps to snap components.

1. Activate the Snap tool.
2. Select the geometric elements to snap.
3. Invert the move, if required.
4. Deactivate the Snap tool.

Step 1 - Activate the Snap tool.

To move components using the snap tool, click the  (Cumulative Snap) icon in the DMU Move toolbar. The Cumulative Snap dialog box opens, as shown in Figure 12–10. The options are grayed out until a move is applied.

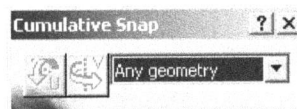

Figure 12–10

Step 2 - Select the geometric elements to snap.

Select a geometric element on the component you want to move. The first element selected indicates the component to be moved. Then select a geometric element to which to snap the first element. The first component is moved so that the references snap together.

Lines (including axes), points, vertices, planes and planer surfaces, and axis systems, can all be used as geometric references for snapping. For example, the axis of Component 1, shown in Figure 12–11, is selected to snap to the axis of another component.

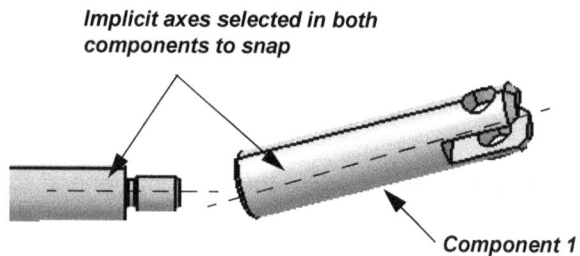

Implicit axes selected in both components to snap

Component 1

Figure 12–11

Once the two elements have been selected, the first component is snapped into place, as shown in Figure 12–12.

Figure 12–12

Step 3 - Invert the move, if required.

Use the Cumulative Snap dialog box to change the orientation of the selected components. Click the (Invert the snap direction by U axis rotation) icon to mirror the results. Figure 12–13 shows what would happen to Figure 12–12 if Snap by Symmetry was applied.

Figure 12–13

Click the (Invert the snap direction by V axis rotation) icon to mirror and rotate the component. Figure 12–14 shows what would happen to Figure 12–12 if **Invert Snap by Rotation** was applied.

Figure 12–14

Step 4 - Deactivate the Snap tool.

Additional snap operations can be used to continue placing the selected component. Once the component is in the correct

location, click the (Cumulative Snap) icon in the DMU Move toolbar to close the Snap tool.

12.3 Perform a Symmetry Operation

Symmetry features transform an existing component in an assembly with respect to a symmetry plane. Depending on the settings of the symmetry feature, a new model is created or the source model is transformed. If a new model is created, it can be retrieved as a separate model and used in other assemblies.

General Steps

Use the following general steps to transform an existing component in an assembly:

1. Activate the Symmetry operation.
2. Select the symmetry plane.
3. Select the model to transform.
4. Define the symmetry conditions.

Step 1 - Activate the Symmetry operation.

Click the [icon] (Symmetry) icon in the DMU Move toolbar. The Assembly Symmetry Wizard dialog box opens, as shown in Figure 12–15.

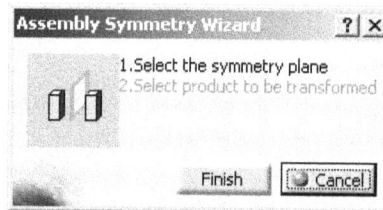

Figure 12–15

Step 2 - Select the symmetry plane.

Select a planar reference on the model to define the symmetry plane. This reference can be a model face, planar surface feature, or reference plane.

Once the symmetry plane has been selected, the Assembly Symmetry Wizard dialog box updates as shown in Figure 12–16.

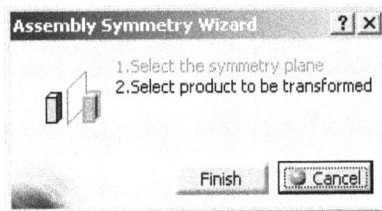

Figure 12–16

Step 3 - Select the model to transform.

The model to be transformed can be a part model or a subassembly; however, only one component can be selected per symmetry operation. Once the model is selected, a preview of the transformed component displays and the Assembly Symmetry Wizard dialog box expands to show additional options, as shown in Figure 12–17.

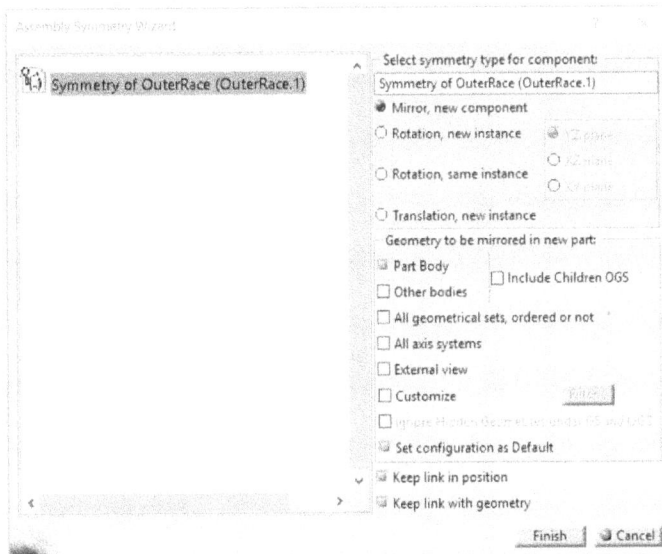

Symmetry plane

Figure 12–17

Step 4 - Define the symmetry conditions.

Define the symmetry conditions by selecting one of the options shown in Figure 12–18.

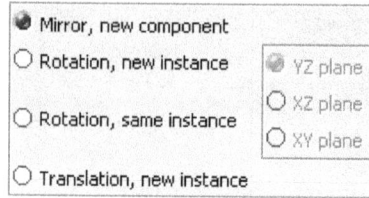

Figure 12–18

Mirror, new component

This option creates a new model that contains a mirror image of the source component. Figure 12–19 shows an example of a left wing created using this option.

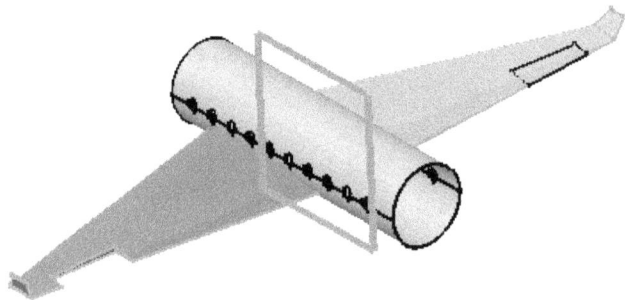

Figure 12–19

The **Mirror, new component** option creates a new component in the specification tree. Additionally, the **Rotation, new instance** and **Translation, new instance** options create new instances in the specification tree. The Assembly Symmetry Result dialog box reports the number of new components or instances created as a result of the symmetry operation as shown in Figure 12–20.

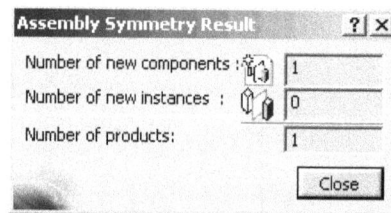

Figure 12–20

Rotation, new instance

This option creates a rotated symmetrical component.
Figure 12–21 shows the left wing mirrored and rotated about an axis. The axis is defined where the symmetry plane and selected reference plane (in this case the XZ plane) intersect.

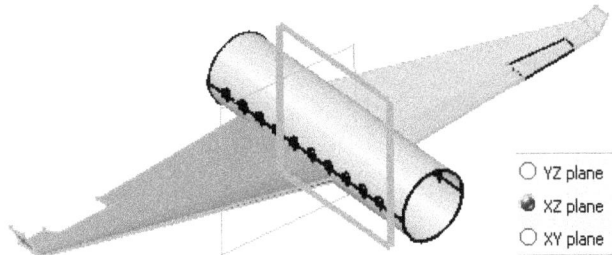

Figure 12–21

In Figure 12–22 the XY plane defines the rotational axis.

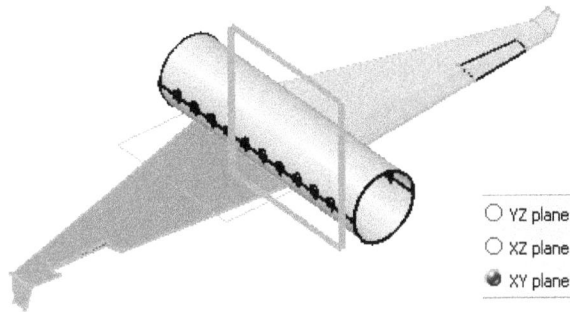

Figure 12–22

Rotation, same instance

This option mirrors and rotates the selected component, as shown in Figure 12–23.

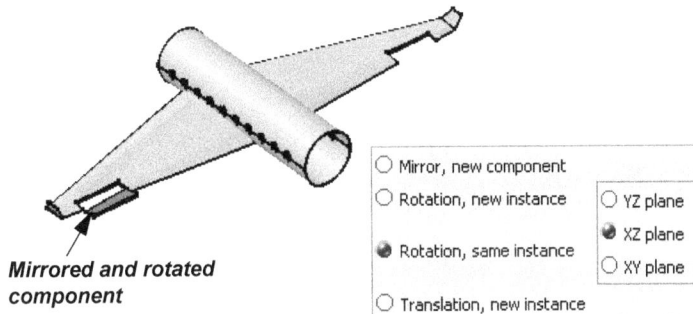

Mirrored and rotated component

Figure 12–23

The Assembly Symmetry Result dialog box reports that no new components or instances have been created, shown in Figure 12–24.

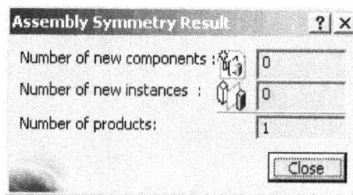

Figure 12–24

Translation, new instance

Dimensions cannot be specified for the translation operation.

This option changes the orientation of components, as shown in Figure 12–25.

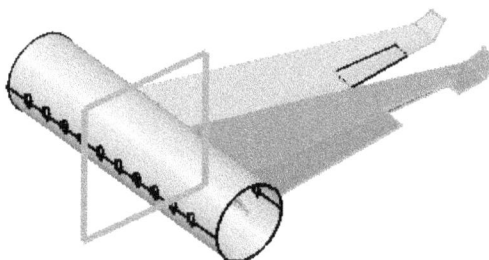

Figure 12–25

The **Keep link in position** option updates the symmetry result with positional changes to the source model.

The **Keep link with geometry** option updates the symmetry result with geometrical changes made to the source model. This link can be isolated. An example is shown in Figure 12–26.

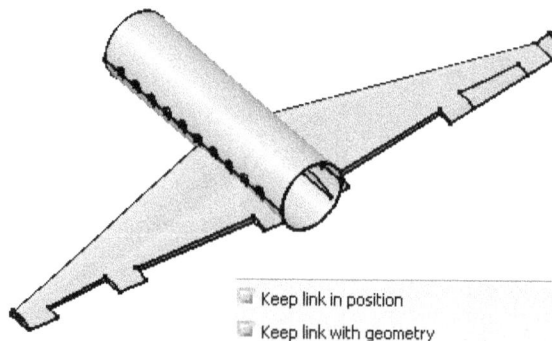

Figure 12–26

12.4 Reset Position

Moving components can often be required to correctly view details in an assembly or create exploded scenes. These movements are often temporary and can quickly be reset using the Reset Position tool. Resetting components relocates them to their initial position. Initial position depends on the documents as described below.

Document Type	Initial Position
Existing	Reset to the position when the document was opened.
Inserted	Reset to the position when the document was inserted.
New	Reset to the position when the document was created.

To reset the position of all components in an assembly, click the

(Reset Position) icon in the DMU Move toolbar. All components in the assembly are reset to their initial position. To reset only selected components, select them first and then click the (Reset Position) icon.

Changing Initial Position

The initial position of a component can be changed from the default position. To change the initial position, locate the component(s) in the correct location, select the component(s), and click the (Store Current Position) icon. To change the initial position of all components in the assembly, click the

(Store Current Position) icon without highlighting any components.

Practice 12a | Moving Components I

Practice Objectives

- Move components using the Rotation, Translation and Position options.
- Snap components together.

In this practice, you will use transformation features to translate and rotate a component to create an assembly.

Task 1 - Create a Product file.

1. Select **File>New** or click the ⬜ (New) icon in the Standard toolbar.

2. The New dialog box opens, as shown in Figure 12–27. Select **Product** and click **OK**. The new product opens.

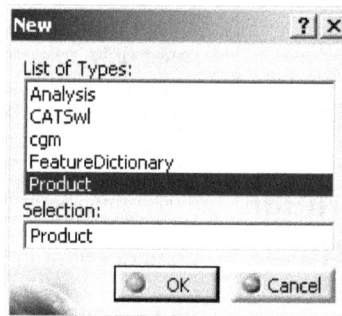

Figure 12–27

Task 2 - Insert components.

1. Select **Product1** in the specification tree, right-click and select **Components>Existing Component**.

2. Browse to the FrontWheel directory and open **Frame.CATPart**. The model displays as shown in Figure 12–28.

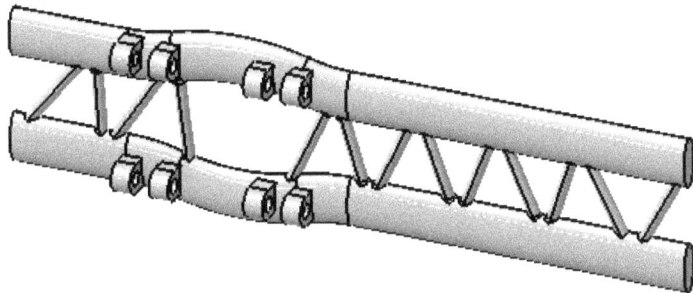

Figure 12–28

3. Select **Product1** in the specification tree, right-click and select **Components>Existing Component**.

4. Open **Arm.CATPart**. The model displays as shown in Figure 12–29.

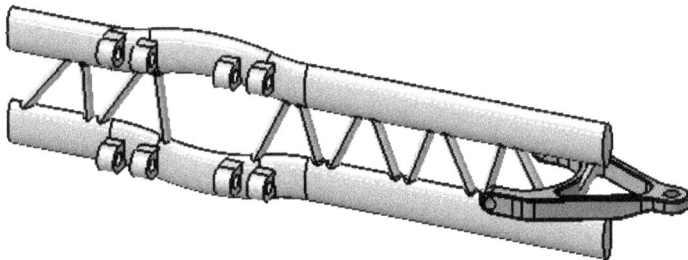

Figure 12–29

Task 3 - Rotate the model.

1. Select **Arm** in the specification tree and click the

   ![icon] (Translation or Rotation) icon.

2. The Move dialog box opens. Select the *Rotation* tab as shown in Figure 12–30.

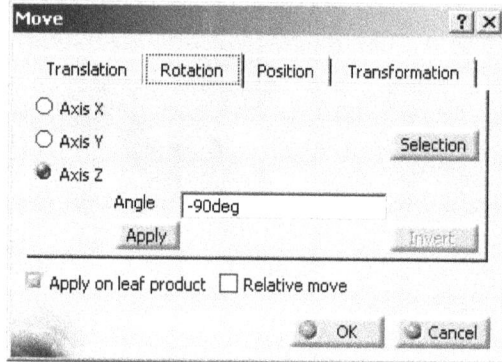

Figure 12–30

3. Select **Axis Z** and enter **-90deg** in the *Angle* field.

4. Click **Apply** and **OK**. The Arm rotates as shown in Figure 12–31.

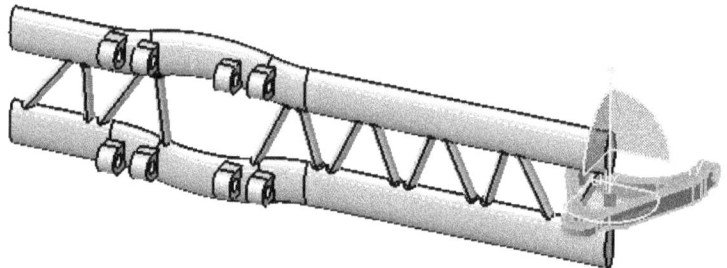

Figure 12–31

Task 4 - Snap the axes of the two components together.

1. Select the arm component and click the ![Cumulative Snap icon] (Cumulative Snap) icon.

2. Zoom in on the arm and select the axis of the hole, as shown in Figure 12–32.

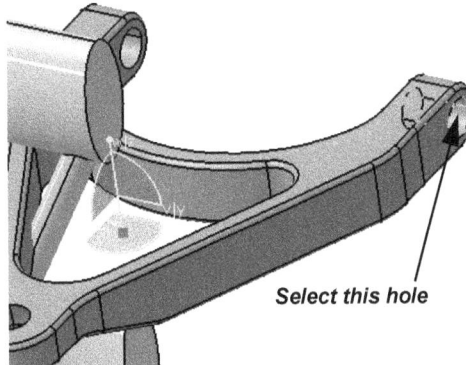

Select this hole

Figure 12–32

3. Select the hole on the frame, as shown in Figure 12–33.

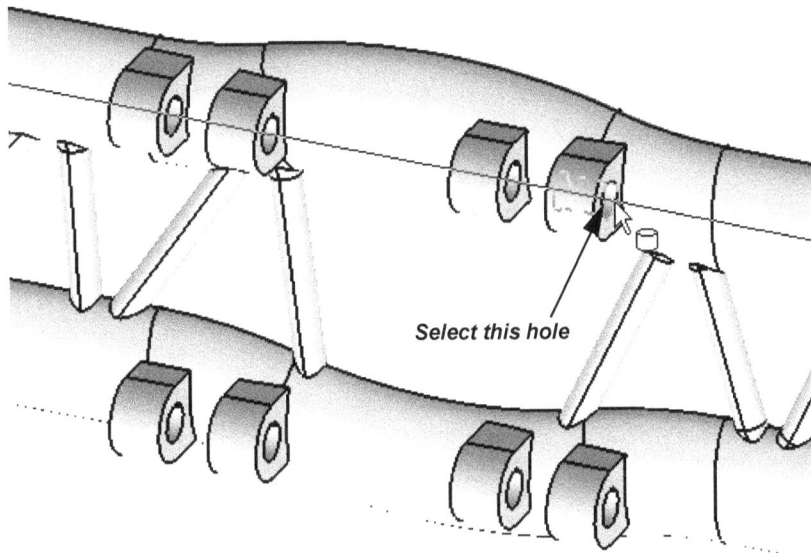

Select this hole

Figure 12–33

The model displays as shown in Figure 12–34. The axis of the holes on the arm and frame are aligned.

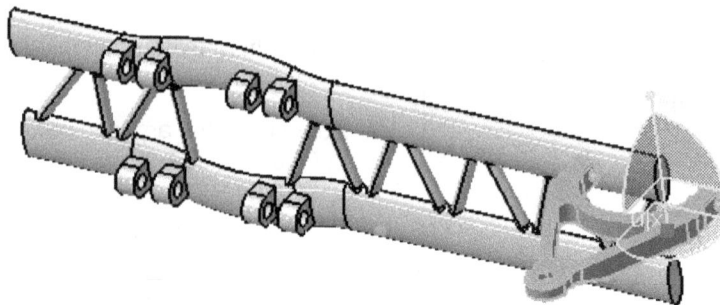

Figure 12–34

4. Click the (Cumulative Snap) icon to close the Cumulative Snap dialog box.

5. Click the (Measure Between) icon. Measure the distance between the faces as shown in Figure 12–35.

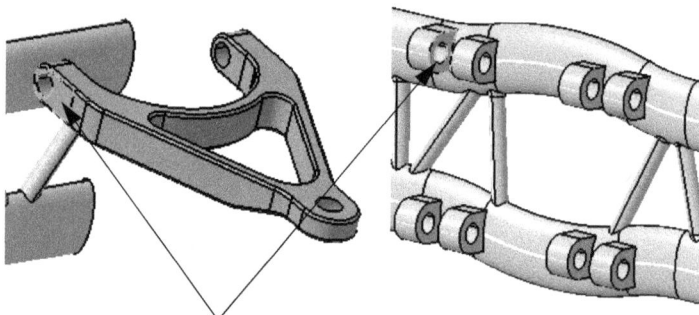

Select these two faces

Figure 12–35

6. The faces should be 635mm apart. Select the **Keep measure** option in the Measure Between dialog box and click **OK**.

7. Select Arm in the specification tree and click the

   (Translation or Rotation) icon. Select the *Position* tab. The Move dialog box opens, as shown in Figure 12–36.

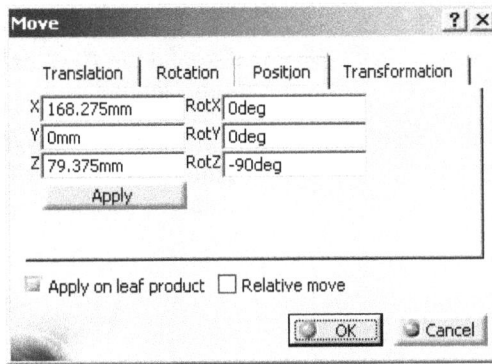

Figure 12–36

8. The arm needs to translate 635mm to fit correctly in the frame. Enter **-635mm** in the *Y* field.

9. Click **Apply** and **OK**. The model displays as shown in Figure 12–37.

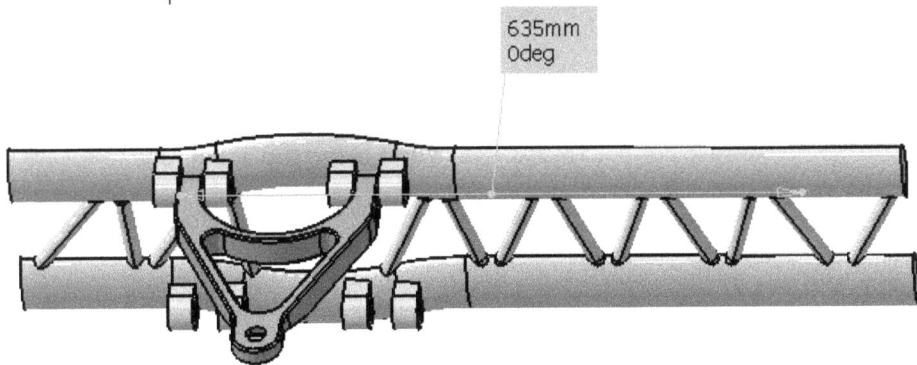

Figure 12–37

Task 5 - (Optional) Update the measurement.

Although the arm is now contacting the frame, the measurement is still indicating a distance of 635mm. In this task, you will update the measurement.

1. Expand the **Applications>Measure** branch in the specification tree.

2. Right-click on **MeasureBetween.1** and select **MeasureBetween.1 object>Measure Update**. The model displays as shown in Figure 12–38.

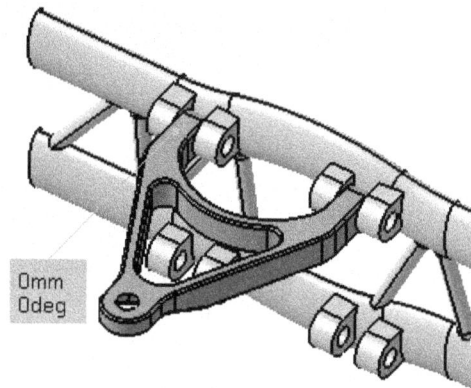

Figure 12–38

Task 6 - Save and close the assembly.

1. Save the assembly as **FrontWheel-2.CATProduct** in the FrontWheel directory.

2. Select **File>Close**.

Practice 12b	# Moving Components II

Practice Objectives

- Snap components.
- Mirror an existing component.

In this practice, you will use a skeleton model to align and duplicate components in the assembly.

Task 1 - Insert a component.

If you completed **Temp.CATProduct** in the previous Geometry Creation practice, you can continue to use this model. If you did not complete this practice, the files can be found in the ReferenceElementsComplete directory.

1. Open **Temp.CATProduct**.

2. Select Product1 in the specification tree, right-click and select **Components>Existing Component**. Browse the DirectionalControlValve directory and select **EndCap.CATPart** as the component to insert. The model displays as shown in Figure 12–39.

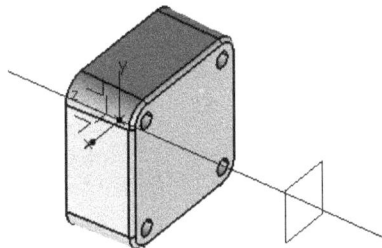

Figure 12–39

3. Rotate the model to the view, as shown in Figure 12–40.

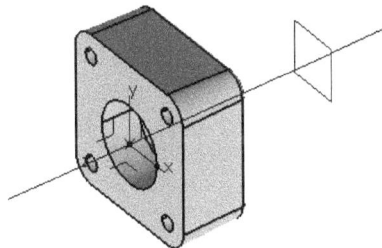

Figure 12–40

Task 2 - Translate the component.

1. Select **EndCap** in the specification tree and click the

   (Translation or Rotation) icon. The Move dialog box opens, as shown in Figure 12–41.

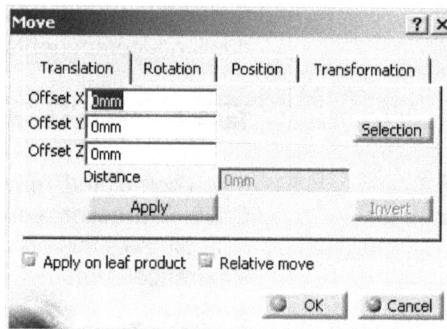

Figure 12–41

2. Click **Selection**.

3. Select the planar face of EndCap, as shown in Figure 12–42.

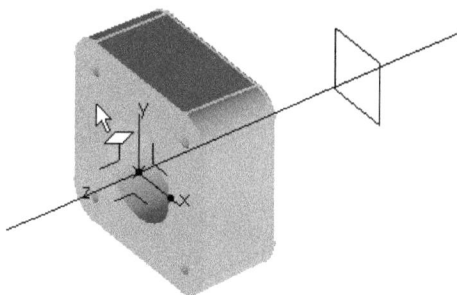

Figure 12–42

4. Select the reference plane from **Part1.** The Move dialog box updates with the offset dimension of 100mm in the y-direction.

5. Click **Apply**. The EndCap component moves to the reference plane, as shown in Figure 12–43.

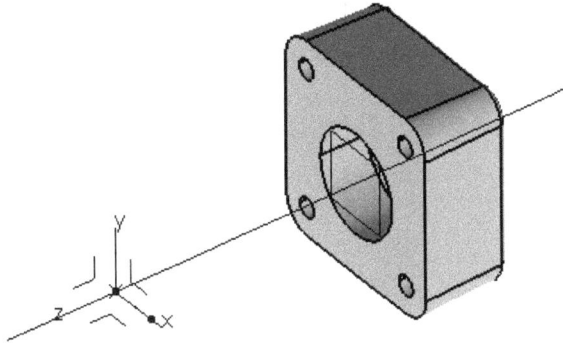

Figure 12–43

6. Click **OK** to complete the translation.

Task 3 - Create a symmetrical component.

1. Show the zx plane of **Part1**. The plane displays as shown in Figure 12–44.

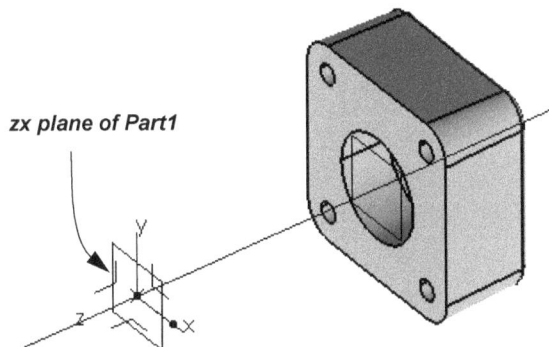

zx plane of Part1

Figure 12–44

2. Click the [icon] (Symmetry) icon. The Assembly Symmetry Wizard dialog box opens, as shown in Figure 12–45.

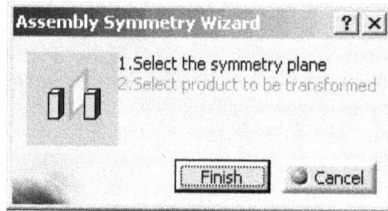

Figure 12–45

3. Define the symmetry as follows:

  • *Symmetry plane:* **zx plane**
  • *Product to be transformed:* **EndCap**

  The Assembly Symmetry Wizard dialog box opens, as shown in Figure 12–46. It can be used to rotate the component and create a new instance or component.

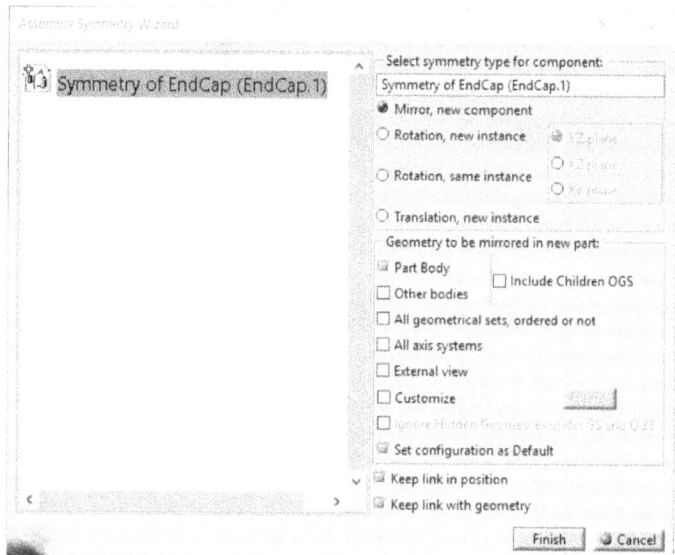

Figure 12–46

4. Accept the default options and complete the operation by clicking **Finish**. The Assembly Symmetry Result dialog box opens (as shown in Figure 12–47), indicating that one new component has been created.

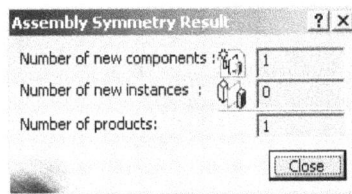

Assembly Symmetry Result

Number of new components : 1
Number of new instances : 0
Number of products: 1

Close

Figure 12–47

5. Click **Close** in the Assembly Symmetry Result dialog box. The assembly displays as shown in Figure 12–48 and the name of the new component displays in the specification tree.

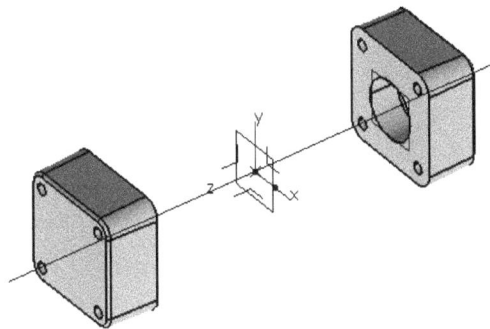

Figure 12–48

Task 4 - Save and close the assembly.

1. Right-click on **Symmetry of End Cap** in the specification tree and select **Properties**.

2. Make the following changes in the *Product* tab:

   • *Instance Name:* **LeftEndCap.1**
   • *Part Number:* **LeftEndCap**

3. Use Save Management to save the assembly and the new part is automatically saved.

4. Select **File>Close**.

Cache Management

The cache system enables you to load a complete top-level assembly into the viewer using a CGR representation. This management system greatly reduces file retrieval time, view manipulation, and update time.

Learning Objectives in this Chapter

- Learn how to work with the cache system.
- Run in Visualization Mode when working with large product files.

13.1 Working with the Cache System

The cache system enables you to load a complete top-level assembly into the viewer using a CGR representation. This management system greatly reduces file retrieval time, view manipulation, and update time.

When the **Work with the cache system** option is selected, the system converts all of the solid geometry of the assembly into tessellated (or faceted) surfaces, which results in a simplified representation of the geometry.

Design Mode

By default, all parts and products are created and manipulated in Design mode. When working in Design mode, components carry the full geometric weight of the solids they represent. The specification tree of a product in Design mode is shown in Figure 13–1. The specification tree reports the part number and instance number for each part. Each part is expandable and lists the features of that part.

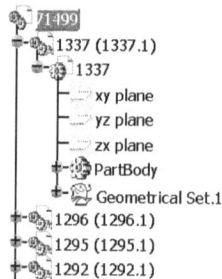

Figure 13–1

Visualization Mode

When a product file is retrieved with the **Work with the cache system** option selected, all components are in Visualization mode. The specification tree of a product in Visualization mode is shown in Figure 13–2. The component instances are listed along with the name of the part or product file and it cannot be expanded to list features.

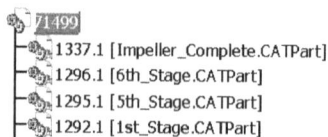

Figure 13–2

CGR File

When working with the cache system, the system displays a representation of the solid geometry. The first time a component is retrieved when working with the cache system, the system writes the geometry representation to a specified directory with a CGR extension.

The Design mode part and product names are shown in Figure 13–3.

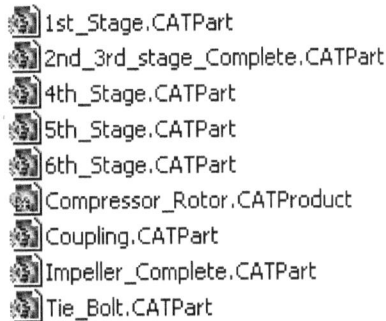

1st_Stage.CATPart
2nd_3rd_stage_Complete.CATPart
4th_Stage.CATPart
5th_Stage.CATPart
6th_Stage.CATPart
Compressor_Rotor.CATProduct
Coupling.CATPart
Impeller_Complete.CATPart
Tie_Bolt.CATPart

Figure 13–3

The same part files that have been written to a.cgr directory as a result of activating and working with the **Cache System** option, are shown in Figure 13–4. The *.cgr file extension and the date code preceding it.

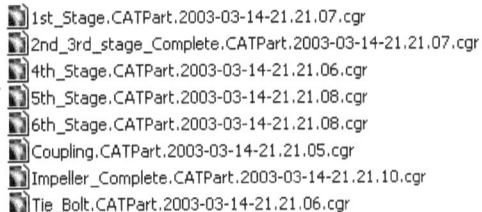

1st_Stage.CATPart.2003-03-14-21.21.07.cgr
2nd_3rd_stage_Complete.CATPart.2003-03-14-21.21.07.cgr
4th_Stage.CATPart.2003-03-14-21.21.06.cgr
5th_Stage.CATPart.2003-03-14-21.21.08.cgr
6th_Stage.CATPart.2003-03-14-21.21.08.cgr
Coupling.CATPart.2003-03-14-21.21.05.cgr
Impeller_Complete.CATPart.2003-03-14-21.21.10.cgr
Tie_Bolt.CATPart.2003-03-14-21.21.06.cgr

Figure 13–4

13.2 Run in Visualization Mode

When working with very large product files it is beneficial to run in Visualization mode. By doing so the time to load, reorient, or make a change to a large product file can be greatly reduced compared to Design mode.

General Steps

Use the following general steps to run in Visualization mode:

1. Activate the cache system.
2. (Optional) Set cache options.
3. Exit and restart ENOVIA.
4. Open a product file for viewing.

Step 1 - Activate the cache system.

Select **Tools>Options>Infrastructure>Product Structure**. Select the *Cache Management* tab and enable the **Work with the cache system** option to activate the cache system, as shown in Figure 13–5.

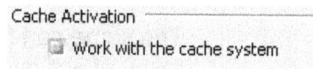

Cache Activation
☑ Work with the cache system

Figure 13–5

A dialog box opens, indicating that the system must be restarted before the cache management setting takes effect as shown in Figure 13–6.

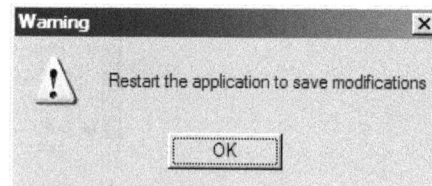

Warning ✕

⚠ Restart the application to save modifications

OK

Figure 13–6

Step 2 - (Optional) Set cache options.

Local Cache

The local cache directory path specifies the file path to a directory on your system where the *.cgr files are stored. The first time a component is retrieved, it is tessellated, and the corresponding *.cgr file is computed and written to the local cache directory. The next time the component is loaded using cache management, the system searches for the corresponding *.cgr file from the local cache directory and loads it.

For Windows 2000, the system default local cache directory is *C:\Documents and Settings\<user name>\Local Settings\Application Data\DassaultSystemes\CATCache.* (Windows XP).

Click the 🗎 icon beside the Path to the local cache field to browse to the required directory, as shown in Figure 13–7. The file path only needs to be set once; however, it must be set again if the directory changes.

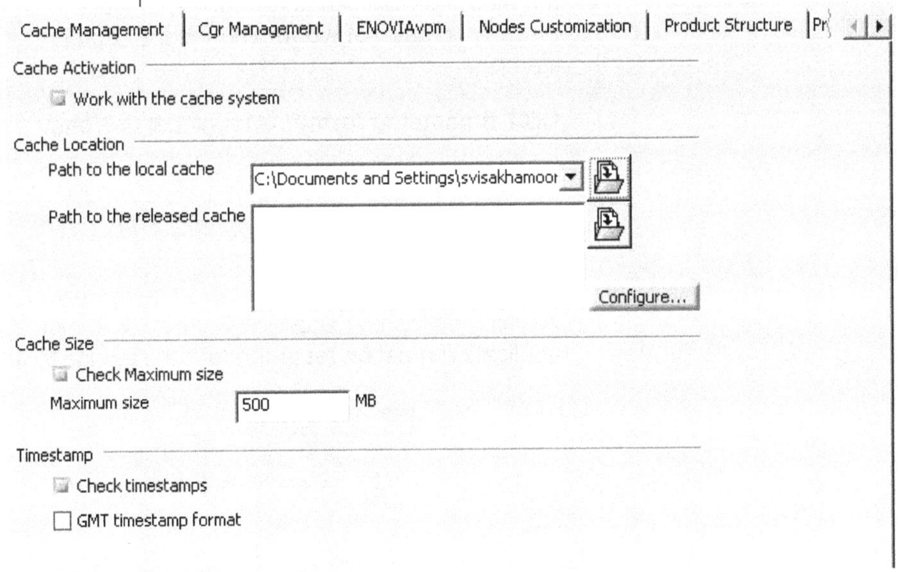

Figure 13–7

Released Cache

A file path and search order can be specified for released cache. Released cache is a read-only cache directory that can be located anywhere on a network. Multiple released cache directories can be specified. Click the ![icon] icon beside the Path to the released cache field to browse to the required directory.

*Click **Configure** to configure the search order.*

If a *.cgr file is required for loading but cannot be found in the local cache directory, the system searches the released cache directories in the specified search order. If the *.cgr file is not found, the system creates one in the local cache directory. Typically a system administrator manages released cache directories.

Cache Size

The default size of the writable cache is 500 MB. If the value is exceeded the system automatically deletes *.cgr files on a first-in first-out basis.

Time Stamp

If the **Check timestamps** option is enabled, the system saves the *.cgr file with a time stamp. This verifies that no modifications have been made to the model since the creation of the *.cgr file. If a model is modified, the *.cgr file is overwritten with the latest tessellated geometry data and the file contains an updated time stamp.

GMT timestamp format is for global use only.

Step 3 - Exit and restart ENOVIA.

Click **OK** to confirm the changes. The system displays the Warning dialog box shown in Figure 13–8, indicating that the application must be restarted for the settings to take effect.

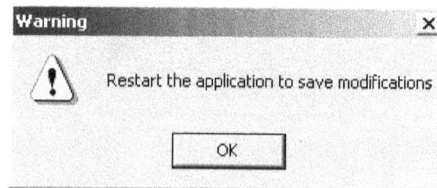

Figure 13–8

Step 4 - Open a product file for viewing.

Restart ENOVIA and open a product file. The system loads all
*.cgr files into the viewer. Selected components can be changed
to Design mode by right-clicking on the component in the
specification tree, and selecting **Representations>Design
mode**, as shown in Figure 13–9.

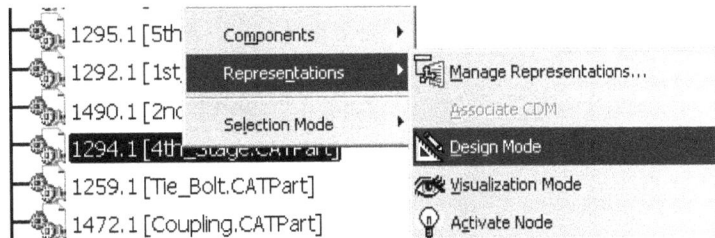

Figure 13–9

Note the following restrictions:

*   If the **Work with the cache system** option is selected,
    components can be toggled between Visualization mode and
    Design mode.

*   If the **Work with the cache system** option is not selected,
    components cannot be switched from Design mode to
    Visualization mode even if its *.cgr file exists in the local
    cache.

*   Mass properties can be calculated from a component that is
    in Visualization mode.

*   ENOVIA must be restarted for the **Work with the cache
    system** option to take effect.

Practice 13a | Working with Cache

Practice Objectives

- Work with the cache system.
- Switch between Visualization and Design modes.

In this practice, you will work with the cache system and toggle between the Visualization and Design modes to make changes to a part.

Task 1 - Open the assembly.

The files for this practice can be found in the DriveShaft directory.

1. Open **DriveShaft.CATProduct** from the DriveShaft folder. The assembly displays as shown in Figure 13–10.

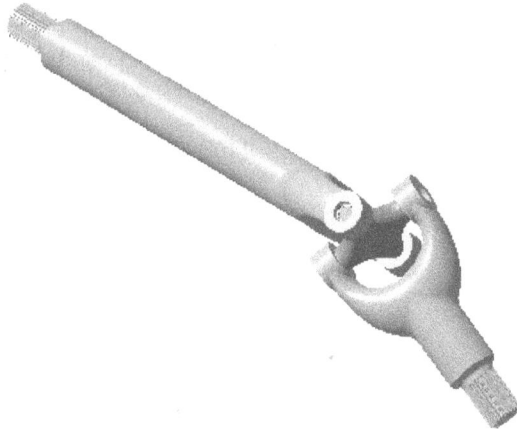

Figure 13–10

2. Spin the model and note the length of time the system requires to process the geometry.

3. Close the model without saving.

Task 2 - Activate the cache system.

1. Select **Tools>Options>Infrastructure>Product Structure** and select the *Cache Management* tab, as shown in Figure 13–11.

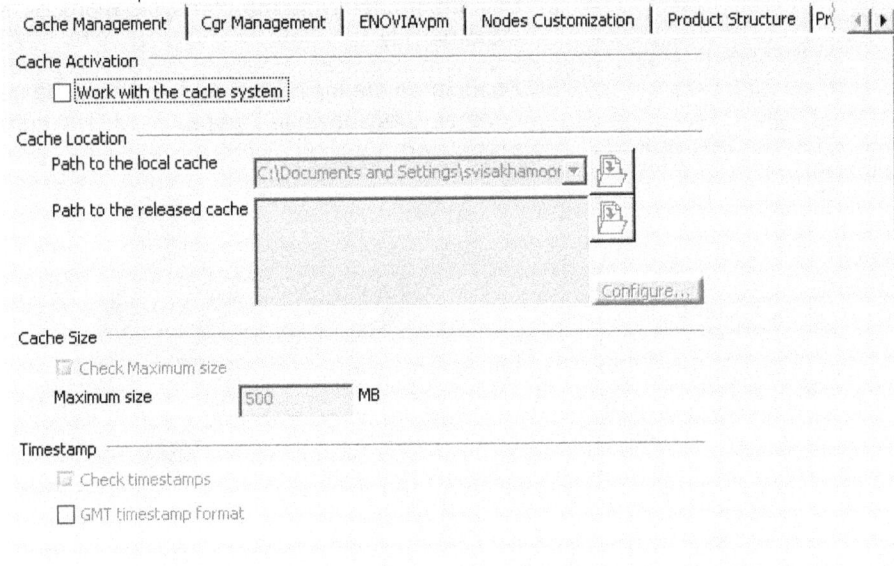

Figure 13–11

2. Select the **Work with the cache system** option, as shown in Figure 13–12.

Figure 13–12

3. A warning displays indicating that the system must be restarted. Click **OK**.

4. Click **OK**.

5. Exit and restart ENOVIA.

Task 3 - Open another assembly.

1. Open **DriveShaft.CATProduct** from the DriveShaft directory. A Progress window displays indicating that CGR files are being generated.

2. Spin the model. Note that the system processes the display more quickly.

3. Zoom in on the InputShaft part and hold the cursor over the geometry, as shown in Figure 13–13. The surfaces are tessellated.

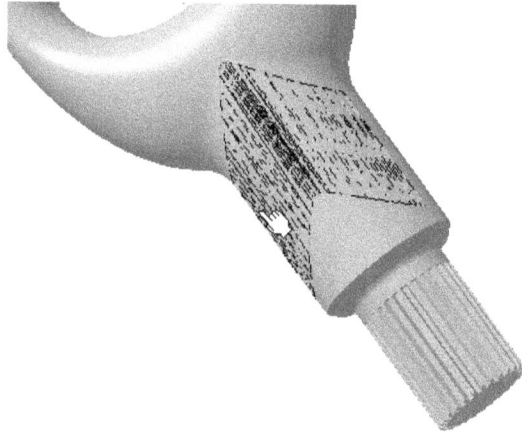

Figure 13–13

4. View the specification tree to see that it is not possible to expand it to the part body level, as shown in Figure 13–14.

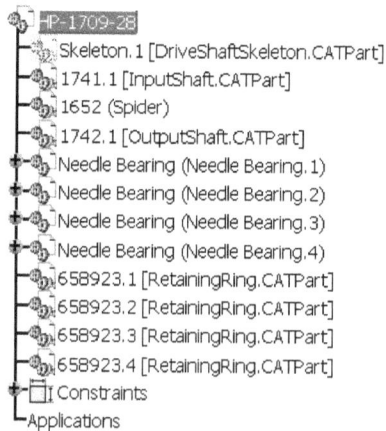

Figure 13–14

Task 4 - Switch component to Design mode.

In this task, you will make changes to a component. Components can only be modified while in Design mode.

1. Right-click on part **1741.1** in the specification tree and select **Representations>Design mode**, as shown in Figure 13–15.

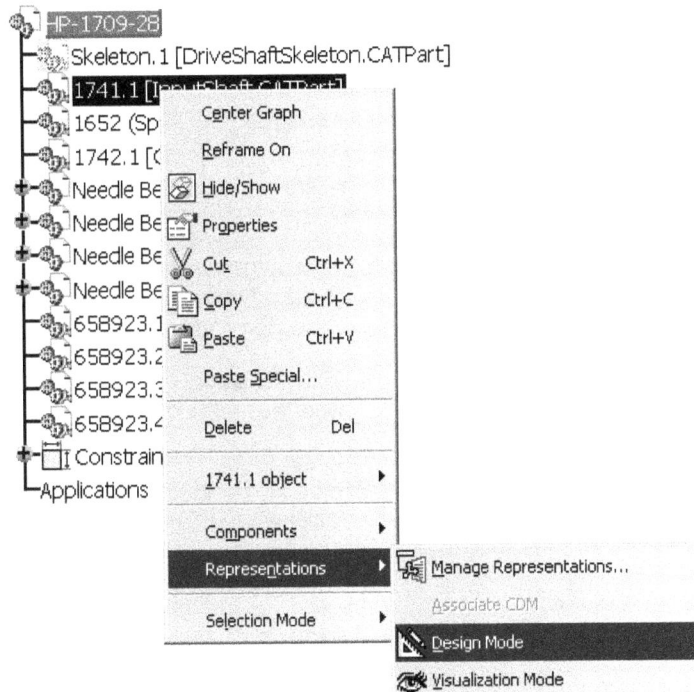

Figure 13–15

2. Part 1741 is now in Design mode, as shown in Figure 13–16.

3. Expand the **1741** node in the specification tree to access and make changes to its features.

4. Right-click on the PartBody for 1741 and select **Properties**, as shown in Figure 13–16.

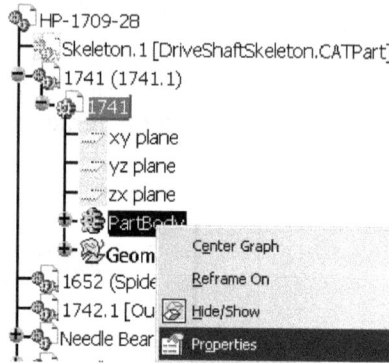

Figure 13–16

5. Select the *Graphics* tab, and change the properties of the PartBody by changing the color to green in the Color drop-down list.

6. Use **Save Management** to save **DriveShaft.CATProduct** and **InputShaft.CATPart**.

7. Change part **1741.1** back to **Visualization** mode. Right-click on it and select **Representations>Visualization Mode**. The **1741** branch collapses and the CGR version of the model is placed back into the assembly, as shown in Figure 13–17.

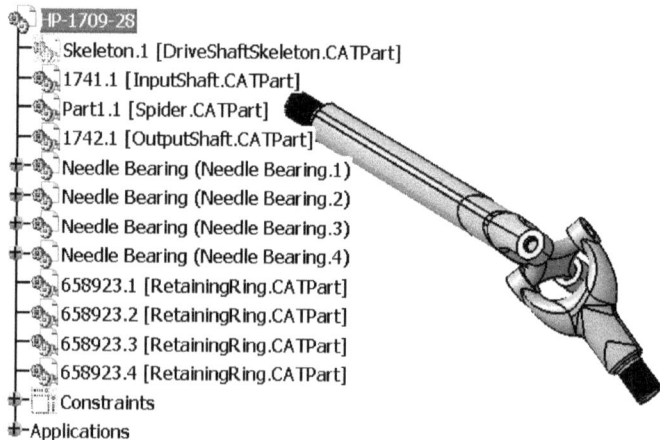

Figure 13–17

8. Select **Tools>Options>Infrastructure>Product Structure** and select the *Cache Management* tab.

9. Clear the **Work with the cache system** option.

10. Close the window without saving.

11. Restart CATIA.

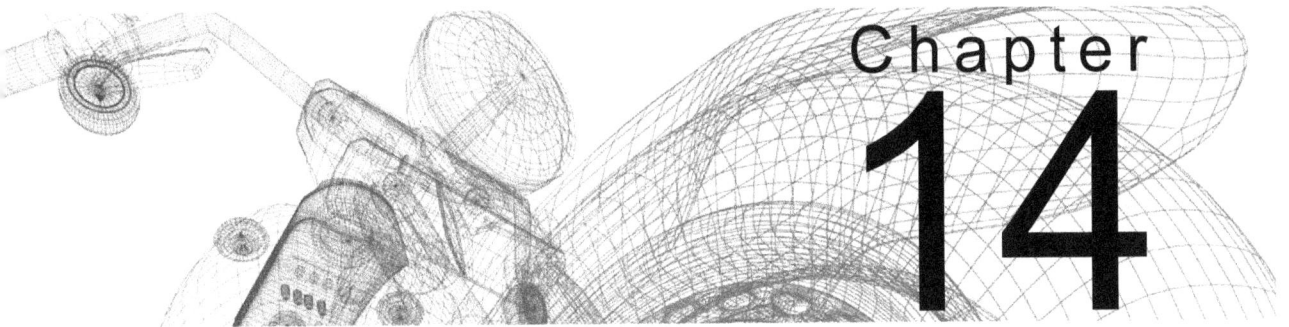

Managing the Assembly

As product models become larger, visualizing and manipulating the model becomes more complex. ENOVIA provides a number of tools that help reduce the complexity of the product model and enable you to work more efficiently with large amounts of data.

Learning Objectives in this Chapter

- Create a group of components for easier selection.
- Use product management techniques to increases your efficiency in working in the DMU Navigator workbench.
- Create Scenes to save the various view setting configurations of your product model for reuse.

14.1 Creating a Group

Several components within a model can be grouped together for easy selection. Grouping enables you to perform operations, such as hide/show or modifying the properties, on several components simultaneously. Groups are saved with the assembly so that they do not need to be recreated each time it is opened.

General Steps

Use the following general steps to create a group:

1. Select components to group.
2. Group components.
3. Select a group.

Step 1 - Select components to group.

Select the components to group in the Main window or specification tree. To select multiple components, press and hold <Ctrl> while making the selection. Selecting components can also be performed using the Search and Spatial Query tools.

Step 2 - Group components.

To group the selected components, click the ![icon] (Group) icon in the DMU Review Creation toolbar. The Edit Group dialog box opens, as shown in Figure 14–1. A Preview window also opens, showing the selected components.

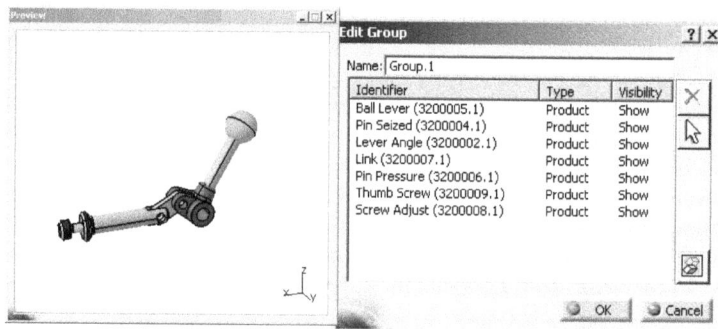

Figure 14–1

Give the group a meaningful name in the Name field. If an undesired component has been included in the group, select it in the specification tree to remove it from the group. To add an additional component to the group, select it from the model or specification tree.

Once you are satisfied with the group of products, click **OK** to finalize the group. A **Group** branch is added under the **Applications** branch of the specification tree, as shown in Figure 14–2.

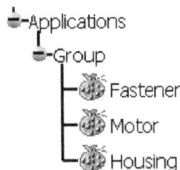

Figure 14–2

Step 3 - Select a group.

To use the group, right-click on it in the specification tree and select **Group.x Object>Select Content**, as shown in Figure 14–3. All components within the group are highlighted. You can then perform operations on the entire group. For example, you can hide the grouped components by clicking the

 (Hide/show) icon.

To edit the group, select **Group.x Object>Definition**, as shown in Figure 14–3, to reopen the Edit Group dialog box.

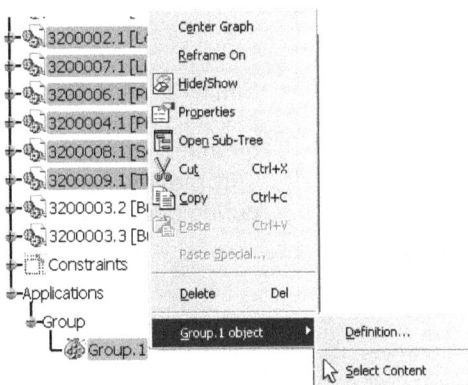

Figure 14–3

14.2 Product Management

Using product management techniques increases your efficiency in working in the DMU Navigator workbench. The techniques enable you to control and simplify your display, which decreases retrieval and refresh times for the product.

Use the following techniques to reduce the update and retrieval times of your assembly and simplify your display:

- Hide/Show

- Activate/Deactivate

- Load/Unload

Hide/Show

The display of components in an assembly can be toggled on and off quickly by right-clicking on the component and selecting **Hide/Show**, or selecting **View>Hide/Show>Hide/Show** in the menu bar.

The Hide/Show operation simplifies your display. The settings for a Hide/Show operation are saved with the product model. The hidden or shown status of a component is indicated by the components symbol in the specification tree, as shown in Figure 14–4.

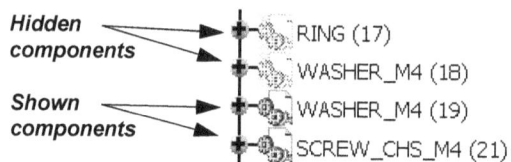

Figure 14–4

Activate/ Deactivate

Similar to Hide/Show, Activate/Deactivate simplifies the display of components in the product. If you deactivate a component, its geometry is also removed from consideration by the assembly. This means that the component is not calculated by the system during update, which decreases update time.

To toggle the activation status, right-click on a component, and select **Representation**. The four options available are described as follows:

Option	Description
Activate Node	Activates the selected part model in the product.
Deactivate Node	Deactivates the selected part model in the product.
Activate Terminal Node	Activates the selected product model (subassembly or top-level assembly).
Deactivate Terminal Node	Deactivates the selected product model (subassembly or top-level assembly).

The settings for an Activate/Deactivate operation are not saved with the product model. Regardless of prior settings, when a product is opened all components are activated. The activated or deactivated status of a node or terminal node is indicated by the components symbol in the specification tree, as shown in Figure 14–5.

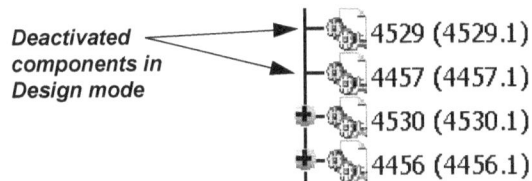

Deactivated components in Design mode

- 4529 (4529.1)
- 4457 (4457.1)
- 4530 (4530.1)
- 4456 (4456.1)

Figure 14–5

A method for handling complex assemblies upon loading is by toggling on an option to avoid loading default shapes when opening a product. This enables you to select the components you want to activate from the specification tree after the file has been opened.

To set this option select **Tools>Options>Infrastructure> Product Structure** and select the *Product Visualization* tab. Select the **Do not activate default shapes on open** option, as shown in Figure 14–6.

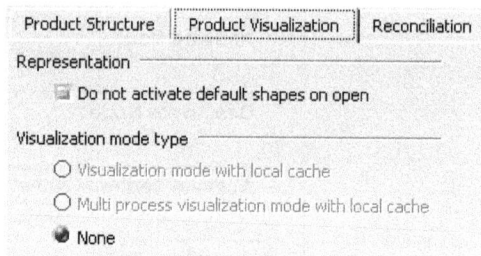

| Product Structure | Product Visualization | Reconciliation |

Representation ————————————————————

☐ Do not activate default shapes on open

Visualization mode type ——————————————

○ Visualization mode with local cache

○ Multi process visualization mode with local cache

⦿ None

Figure 14–6

Load/Unload

Load/Unload enables you to remove or restore components from the product. Right-click on the component and select **Components>Unload** to remove it or select **Load** to restore it.

When unloading a component, it is completely removed from memory. Additionally, if the component is assembled more than once, all instances of it are unloaded from the assembly since the model is removed from memory.

Unloaded components display with a unique symbol in the specification tree, as shown in Figure 14–7

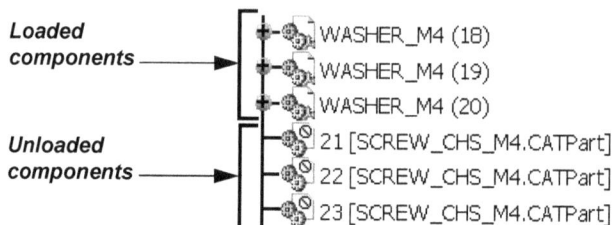

Loaded components ————▶ WASHER_M4 (18)
WASHER_M4 (19)
WASHER_M4 (20)

Unloaded components ————▶ 21 [SCREW_CHS_M4.CATPart]
22 [SCREW_CHS_M4.CATPart]
23 [SCREW_CHS_M4.CATPart]

Figure 14–7

The settings for a Load/Unload operation are not saved with the product model. By default, all components are loaded when a product is opened. It is possible to configure the system to not load any of the components of an assembly. Select **Tools> Options>General**, and select the *General* tab. Clear the **Load referenced documents** option, as shown in Figure 14–8.

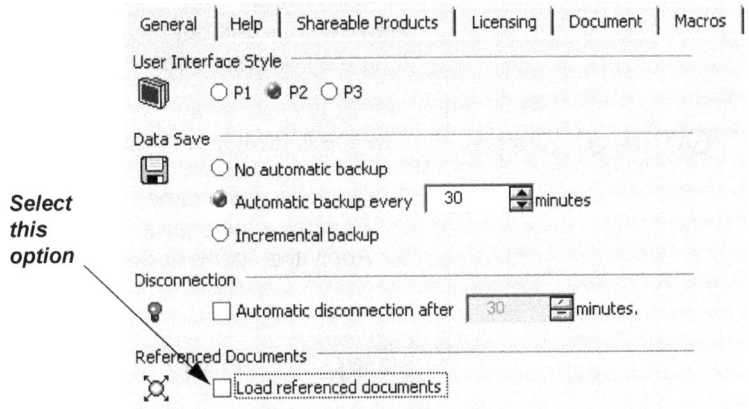

Select this option

| General | Help | Shareable Products | Licensing | Document | Macros |

User Interface Style

○ P1 ● P2 ○ P3

Data Save

○ No automatic backup
● Automatic backup every 30 ⬍ minutes
○ Incremental backup

Disconnection

☐ Automatic disconnection after 30 ⬍ minutes.

Referenced Documents

☐ Load referenced documents

Figure 14–8

With this option disabled, the assembly model loads more quickly. No model geometry displays, but the specification tree lists all of the components of the assembly. You can then individually load only the components of the assembly that you require using the specification tree.

Summary

The Load/Show/Hide operations are summarized in the table below to help you decide which technique best suits your assembly.

Option	Settings saved with model	Removed from memory
Hide/Show	Yes	No
Activate/Deactivate	No	No (visible in drawing)
Load/Unload	No	Yes (not visible in assembly or drawings)

14.3 Creating Scenes

Exploded views and the load/show/hide operations enable you to work with a simplified version of your model. However, the operations must be performed on the fly. Scenes enable you to save the various view setting configurations of your product model for reuse. You can quickly switch between scenes and view settings without having to manually configure them each time they are required.

General Steps

Use the following general steps to configure and save a view:

1. Create a new scene.
2. Configure the scene.
3. Apply the scene to the product.

Step 1 - Create a new scene.

Click the  (Enhanced Scene) icon in the DMU Review Creation toolbar. The Enhanced Scene dialog box opens, as shown in Figure 14–9.

Figure 14–9

Clear the **Automatic naming** option and enter a name for the scene. Click **OK**.

Once the scene is created, the background color changes to indicate that the Scene window is active. The name of the scene is added to the specification tree.

Step 2 - Configure the scene.

You can configure the following settings using scenes:

- Hide/Show components

- Activate/Deactivate components

- Snap two components for placement

- Define explode positions

- Save viewpoints

The Search and Publish functions available in the Navigator workbench are also available in the Scene workbench.

By default, when the scene is applied, it displays in the orientation that it was first defined in. To define a new viewpoint, orient the model into the required viewpoint and click the

(Save Viewpoint) icon in the Enhanced Scenes toolbar.

Explode

Exploded views enable you to visualize a group of constrained components separately.

To explode an assembly, click the (Explode) icon in the Enhanced Scenes toolbar. The Explode dialog box opens, as shown in Figure 14–10.

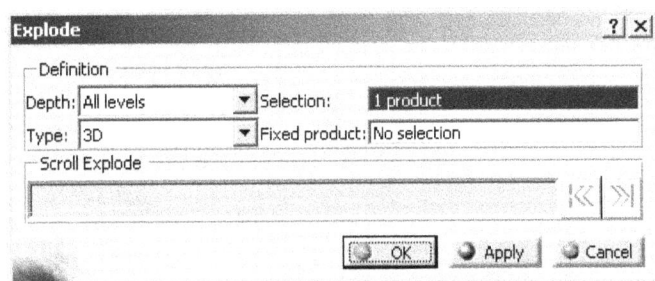

Figure 14–10

The options for the Explode dialog box are described as follows:

Option		Description
Depth		Determines which components in the assembly are exploded.
	All levels	Explodes all levels of the assembly.
	First level	Explodes all first-level components of the assembly. In this case, subassembly components are not exploded.
Type		Determines the exploded placement of the components.
	3D	Places components in a 3D arrangement with respect to the position of the unexploded assembly.
	2D	Explodes components to positions within the 2D plane of the current view. Use named views to determine the 2D explode plane.
	Constrained	Explodes components with respect to the constraints used to contextually place them in the assembly.
Selection		Specifies the product to explode. The active assembly is automatically selected. If multiple levels of the assembly are selected, the assembly explodes in stages.
Fixed Product		Select one component to remain fixed during the explode. If the depth is set to **All levels**, you can select a part. If the depth is set to **First level**, you can select a subassembly.

The components in a 3D explode can be positioned anywhere in 3D space, while the components of the 2D explode can only move within a 2D plane. This plane is always parallel to the screen and is therefore specified by orienting the model. The difference between 3D and 2D explode types is shown in Figure 14–11.

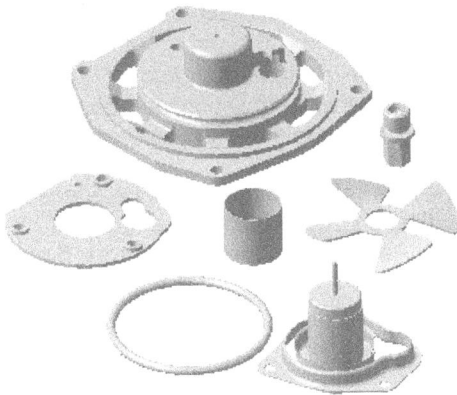

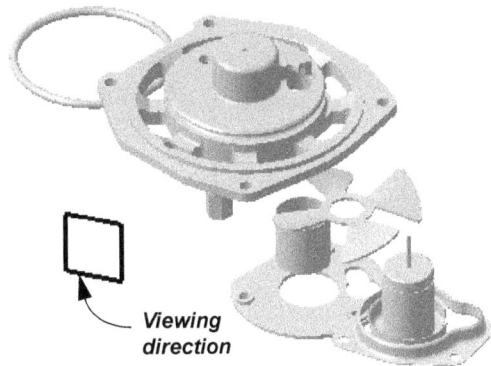

Viewing direction

Type set to 3D   *Type set to 2D*

Figure 14–11

Once the model is exploded, the positions of individual components can be moved using the compass. You can then position the components to display how the assembly is put together. An example is shown in Figure 14–12.

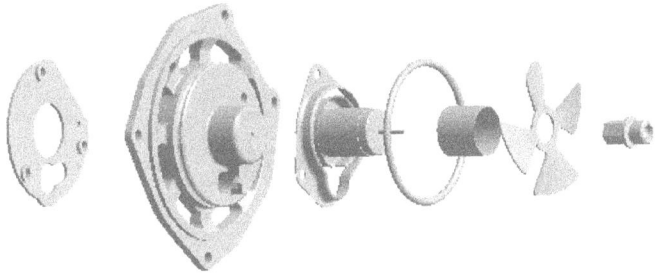

Figure 14–12

To reset the components back to the constraint positions, select the assembly in the specification tree and click to reset the

(Selected Products) icon in the Select toolbar. Individual components can also be reset by selecting them and applying the **Reset** command.

Step 3 - Apply the scene to the product.

There are two ways to work with a scene of a product. You can edit the scene and work with the assembly configuration directly in the scene editor. You can also apply the scene to the product.

To apply the scene to the assembly model, select the scene in Applications in the specification tree. Right-click and select ***object>Apply Scene on Assembly>Apply the Entire Scene**, as shown in Figure 14–13.

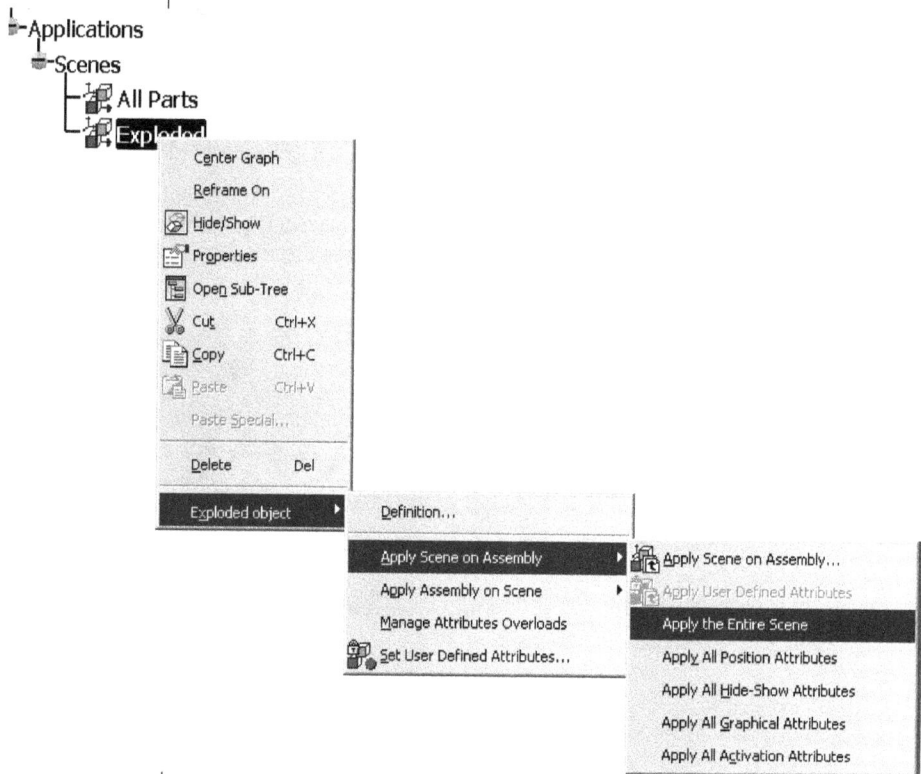

Applications
Scenes
All Parts
Exploded

	Center Graph	
	Reframe On	
	Hide/Show	
	Properties	
	Open Sub-Tree	
	Cut	Ctrl+X
	Copy	Ctrl+C
	Paste	Ctrl+V
	Paste Special...	
	Delete	Del

Exploded object ▶ Definition...

Apply Scene on Assembly ▶ Apply Scene on Assembly...
Apply Assembly on Scene ▶ Apply User Defined Attributes
Manage Attributes Overloads Apply the Entire Scene
Set User Defined Attributes... Apply All Position Attributes
Apply All Hide-Show Attributes
Apply All Graphical Attributes
Apply All Activation Attributes

Figure 14–13

No default scene exists for an assembly. Once you have applied a scene with specific view settings, the only way to return to the original settings is to create an additional scene. Therefore, it is recommended that you create a scene with no configurations before creating any additional scenes. This scene can then be used as the default to restore the assembly to its original configuration.

Practice 14a	# Creating Groups

Practice Objective

• Create a group.

In this practice, you will create two groups in an assembly model. The groups will facilitate the selection of multiple models when performing operations such as hide/show or changing properties.

Task 1 - Open the assembly.

The files for this practice can be found in the Fan directory.

1. Open **Fan.CATProduct**. The assembly displays as shown in Figure 14–14.

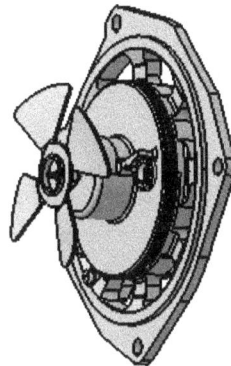

Figure 14–14

2. Investigate the structure of the assembly. The model consists of 17 components, all at the top level. The components can be categorized into three groups: fasteners, fan motor, and housing.

Task 2 - Create a group for the housing components.

During the use of this model, you will need to view the internal components of the fan assembly. In this task, you will create a group that contains the housing components. This will enable you to change the properties and hide/show these components quickly.

1. Click the icon in the DMU Review Creation toolbar. The Edit Group dialog box opens, as shown in Figure 14–15. A Preview window also displays displaying the components that have been added to the group.

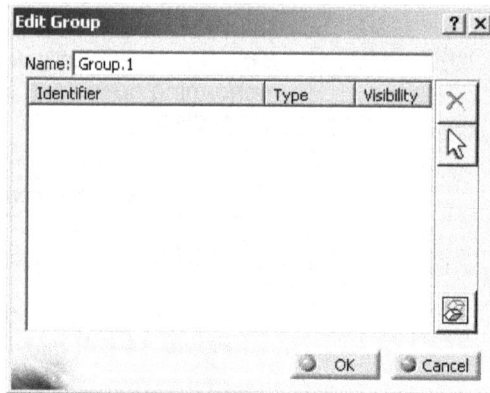

Figure 14–15

2. Enter **Housing** in the Name field.

3. Select the following four components in the specification tree:

   - **yoke**
   - **fan_contact_cylinder**
   - **plunger_contact**
   - **ring**

   The Edit Group dialog box and Preview window appear as shown in Figure 14–16.

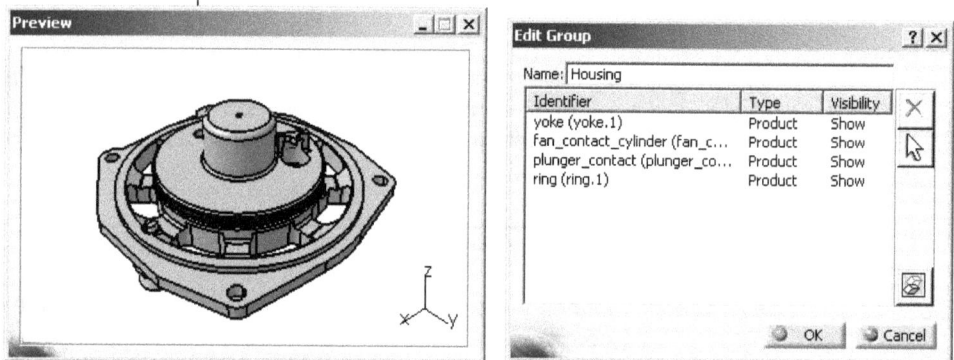

Figure 14–16

4. Click **OK** to complete the creation of the group.

5. Expand the **Applications** and **Group** branches of the specification tree. A new Housing group has been added, as shown in Figure 14–17.

Figure 14–17

Task 3 - Hide the housing group.

1. Select the Housing entry in the **Applications** branch of the specification tree. When selected, the four models belonging to the group are highlighted automatically.

2. Click the [icon] (Hide/Show) icon to hide the group. The model displays as shown in Figure 14–18.

Figure 14–18

Task 4 - Create a fastener group using a search.

Small components, such as screws and washers, increase the visual complexity and update times of a large product. In this task, you will create a group to facilitate the selection of the fasteners in the fan product. The components to be added to the group are selected using the Search tool.

1. Select **Edit>Search**. The Search dialog box opens.

2. Enter **screw*** in the Name field and click the [icon] icon. The system locates three components.

3. Click **Select** and **OK**.

4. To add these components to a group, click the ![icon] icon. The Edit Group dialog box and Preview window appear as shown in Figure 14–19.

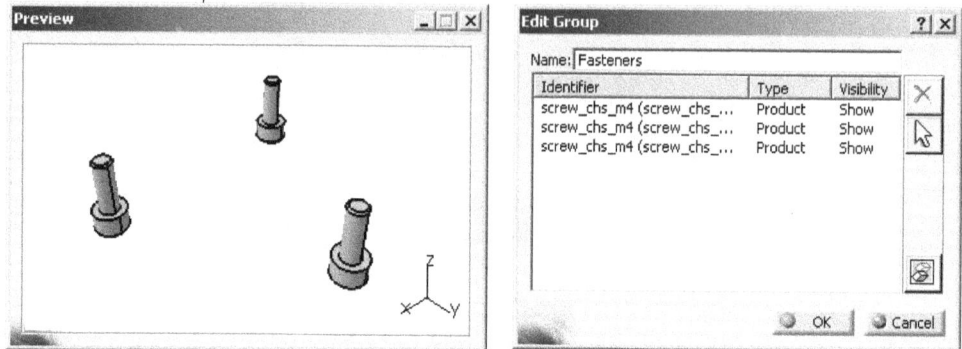

Figure 14–19

5. Name the group **Fasteners** and click **OK**. The group is added to the **Applications** branch of the specification tree.

Task 5 - Edit the group and add additional components.

A group can also be edited by double-clicking on it in the specification tree.

1. Right-click on the **Fasteners** group in the specification tree and select **Fasteners object>Definition**. The Edit Group dialog box opens.

2. Another search is performed to locate the additional components. Leave the Edit Group dialog box open and select **Edit>Search**.

3. Perform a search that locates all of the models that start with the word washer. The search results appear as shown in Figure 14–20.

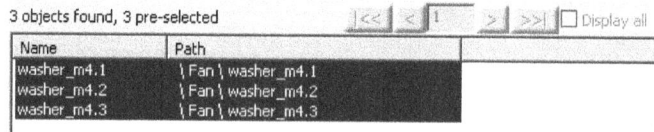

Figure 14–20

4. Click **Select**. The components are automatically added to the Edit Group dialog box. Do not close the Search dialog box until you have completed the Group.

5. The Edit Group dialog box and Preview window appear as shown in Figure 14–21. Click **OK** to close the Edit Group dialog box.

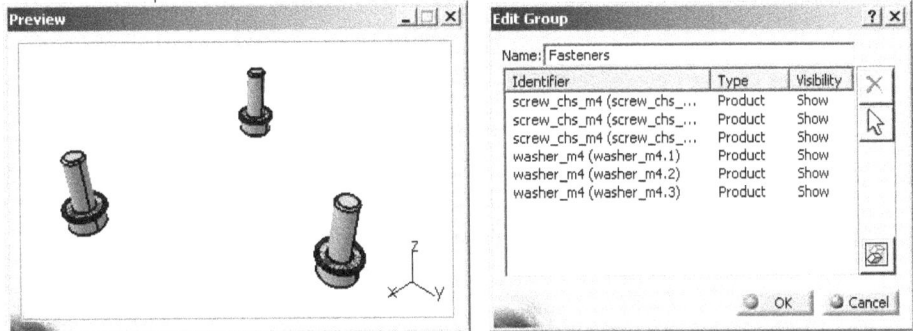

Figure 14–21

6. Click **OK** to close the Search dialog box.

7. Using the Fasteners group, hide the screw and washer components. The model displays as shown in Figure 14–22.

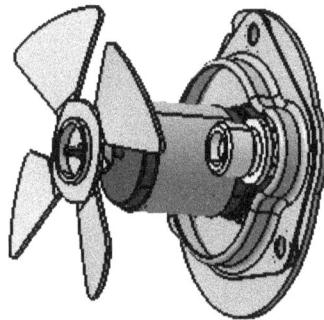

Figure 14–22

Task 6 - Show the housing group and change the properties.

In this task, you will show the housing group and then modify its properties to visualize the assembly more clearly.

1. Show the Housing group.

2. Right-click on **Housing** in the specification tree and select **Properties**.

3. Select the *Graphic* tab and set the following properties:

   - *Color:* **Cyan**
   - *Linetype:* **6**
   - *Thickness:* **1**
   - *Transparency:* **80**

   The assembly displays as shown in Figure 14–23.

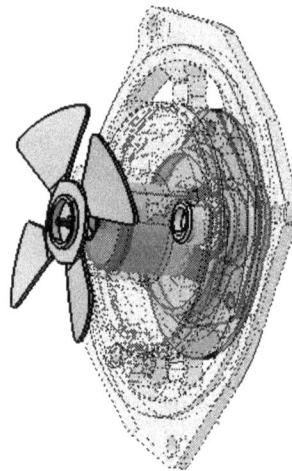

Figure 14–23

4. Show the Fasteners group.

5. Save the assembly and close the window.

Creating Scenes I

Practice Objectives

- Create a scene.
- Apply a scene to an assembly.

In this practice, you will create various scenes and apply them to the assembly to facilitate assembly of additional components.

Task 1 - Create a scene.

If you completed the last practice, you can also continue using the same model.

1. Open **Fan_b.CATProduct** from the Fan directory. The assembly displays as shown in Figure 14–24.

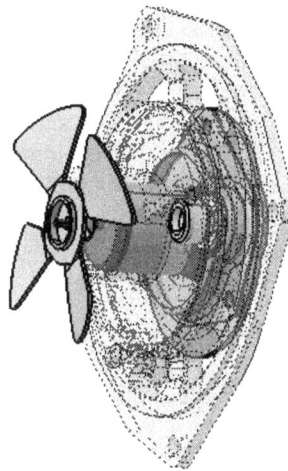

Figure 14–24

2. Click the ⊞ (Enhanced Scene) icon.

3. Clear the **Automatic naming** option.

4. Enter **All Parts** as the name, as shown in Figure 14–25.

Figure 14–25

5. Click **OK**.

6. The system activates the Scene window. Select **Do not display this message again** in the Warning dialog box and close it.

7. Since this is a scene of all parts, no changes are required.

Click the (Exit Scene) icon to exit the Scene window. The scene name is added to the **Scenes** node under **Applications** in the specification tree, as shown in Figure 14–26.

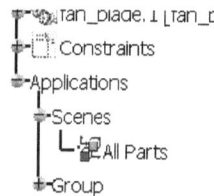

Figure 14–26

8. Create a scene named **Exploded**, as shown in Figure 14–27.

Figure 14–27

9. In the Scene window, click the [icon] (Explode) icon.

10. Select **First level** from the Depth drop-down list, as shown in Figure 14–28.

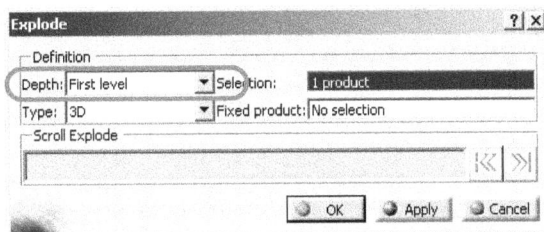

Figure 14–28

11. Click **OK** in the Explode dialog box. The updated scene displays as shown in Figure 14–29.

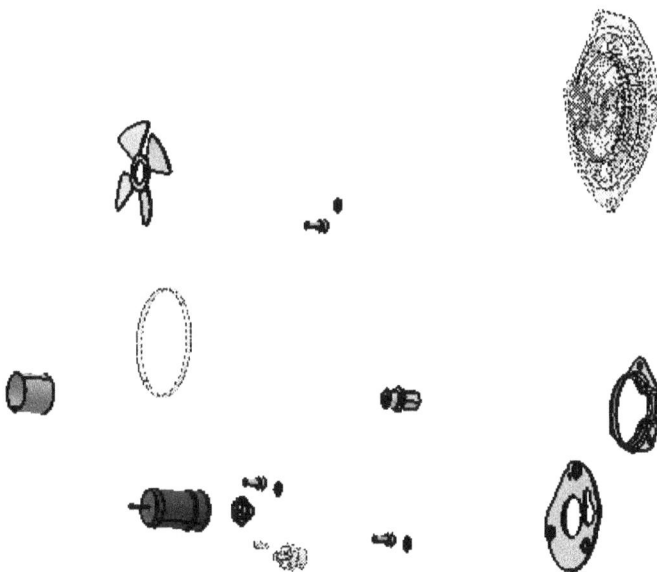

Figure 14–29

12. Click the [icon] (Exit Scene) icon to exit the Scene window.

Task 2 - Apply a scene to the assembly.

1. Right-click on the **Exploded** scene and select **Exploded object>Apply Scene on Assembly>Apply the Entire Scene**, as shown in Figure 14–30.

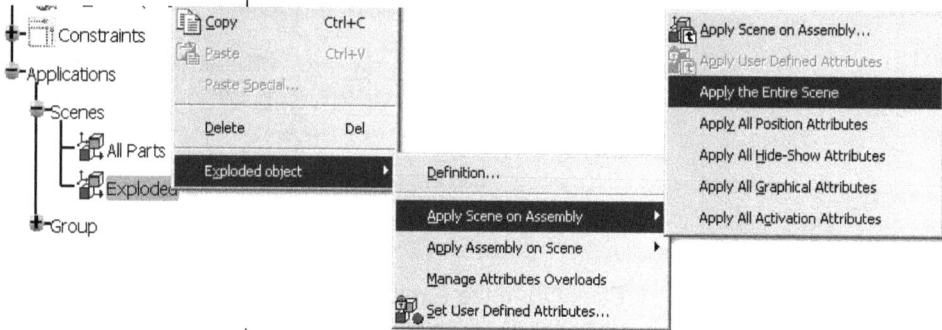

Figure 14–30

2. Click (Reset Positions) to unexplode the assembly. You

   might need to click the icon twice to get all of the components to return to their original positions.

Task 3 - Create a scene.

1. Create a scene named **Yoke Removed**, as shown in Figure 14–31.

Figure 14–31

2. Once in the Scene window, right-click on the yoke component and select **Representations>Deactivate Node**, as shown in Figure 14–32.

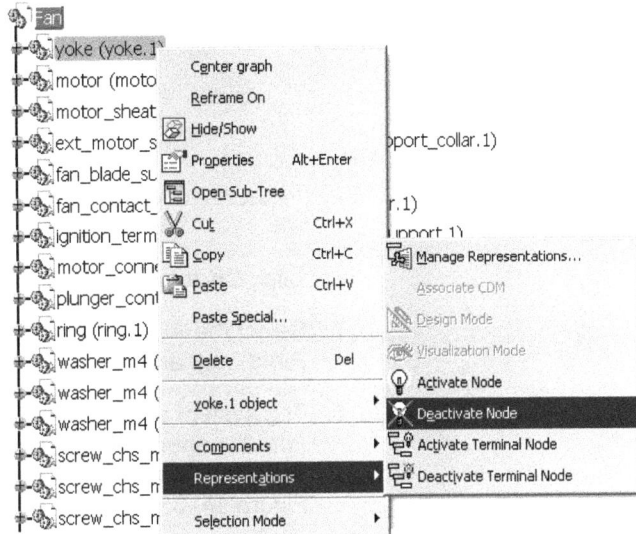

Figure 14–32

3. Click the ⬆ (Exit Scene) icon to exit the Scene window.

4. Apply the **Yoke Removed** scene to the assembly. The assembly displays as shown in Figure 14–33.

Figure 14–33

5. Apply the All Parts scene to the assembly. The system gives an error shown in Figure 14–34. Since there is no difference between this scene and the main assembly, it cannot be applied this way.

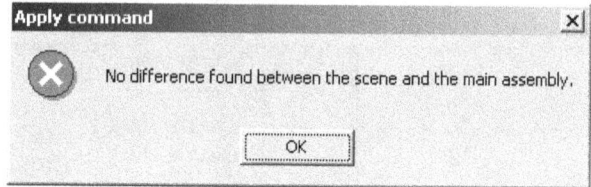

Figure 14–34

6. Click **OK** to close the Apply command window.

7. Select the All Parts scene from the specification tree. Right-click and select **All Parts.object>Definition**.

8. The system activates the scene window. Right-click on **Fan** from the specification tree select **Representations>Activate Terminal Node**. The assembly displays as shown in Figure 14–35.

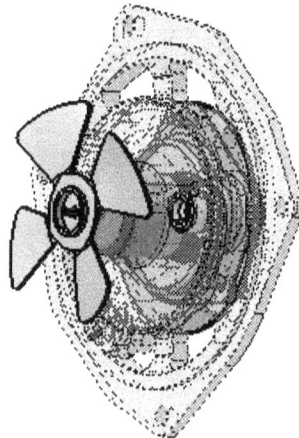

Figure 14–35

9. Click the [icon] (Exit Scene) icon to exit the Scene window.

10. Apply the All Parts scene to the assembly.

11. Close the file without saving.

Generic Animation

This chapter introduces various techniques of creating animations. Tools are available to record your movements as you rotate or translate the model. Additional tools enable you to change the colors of features in a model and use a number of tracks to create sequences to compose the animation. The animation can also be configured to detect clashes between components.

Learning Objectives in this Chapter

- Learn how to record tracks for animations.
- Change the Color and Visibility of selected objects.
- Combine tracks, visibility, and color actions to create sequences.
- Learn how to set Automatic Clash Detection.
- Understand how to record viewpoints.

15.1 Recording Tracks

A track is the route traveled when moving an object. Objects can include: Products, Shuttles, Section Planes, Cameras, and Lights. Tracks define the position of an assembly at predefined time intervals. They can be used to create an animation of your assembly to better report information. In more advanced DMU applications animations can be used to simulate motion.

General Steps

Creating tracks requires the DMU Fitting (FIT) license.

Use the following general steps to record a track:

1. Define the type of track.
2. Select an object to modify.
3. Create additional shots of the object.
4. Preview the track.
5. (Optional) Modify or delete shots.
6. Finalize the track.

Step 1 - Define the type of track.

In the DMU Generic Animation toolbar, click the ▦ (Track) icon. The Track dialog box opens, as shown in Figure 15–1.

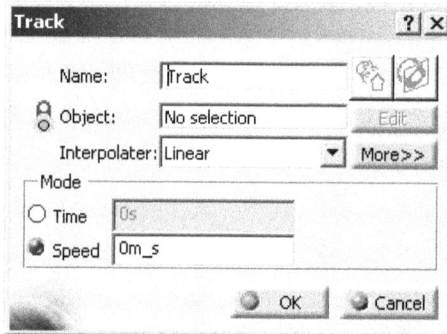

Figure 15–1

Select the type of trajectory in the Interpolater drop-down list. The trajectory types are described as follows:

Type	Description	Illustration
Linear	Straight connection between shots. Default option for products, shuttles, and section planes.	
Spline	Trajectory between shots is smooth. Default option for cameras and lights.	
Composite Spline	Minimizes the impact of positional changes over the trajectory.	

Step 2 - Select an object to modify.

Tracks can record the movement of products, lights, cameras, shuttles, or section planes. Select the object to modify in the specification tree. The Track dialog box updates to display specific options for that object. A snapshot is taken of the selected object in its default position to create shot 1.

For example, if a camera is selected, the compass snaps to the eye of the camera and a snapshot is taken in the default viewpoint, as shown in Figure 15–2.

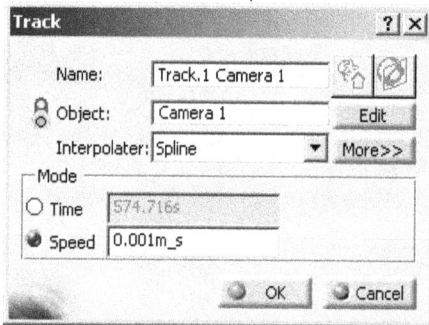

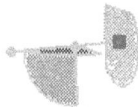

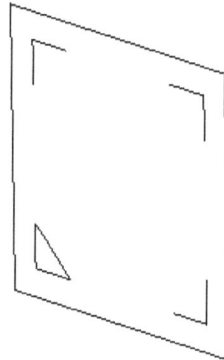

Figure 15–2

Step 3 - Create additional shots of the object.

Manipulate the object using the compass or Manipulation toolbar, as shown in Figure 15–3.

Figure 15–3

When the object is in the correct location, click the (Record) icon in the Recorder toolbar. A second shot is taken (shot 2). The Player toolbar advances 1 shot, as shown in Figure 15–4, and the time of the track increases.

Use the drop-down to toggle between time and shot.

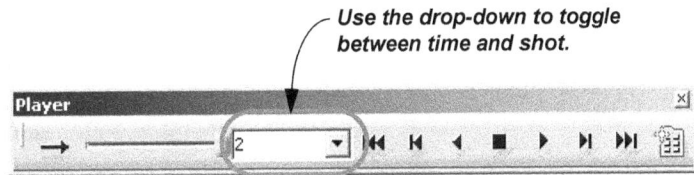

Figure 15–4

Continue to manipulate the camera and recording shots. The trajectory of the track displays on the model, For example, in Figure 15–5, the camera has been moved to create 4 shots, and a spline trajectory has been created linking them.

Points where shots were taken.

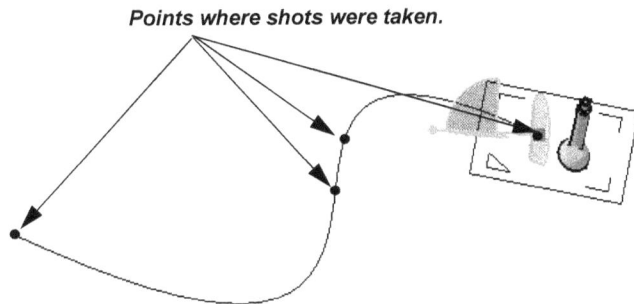

Figure 15–5

Step 4 - Preview the track.

Once all shots have been taken, review the track using the Player toolbar, as shown in Figure 15–6.

Figure 15–6

Icons in the toolbar act like VCR buttons, click ⏮ to rewind the track to the first shot. Click ▶ to play the track or click ⏭ to manually move through each step of the track.

Step 5 - (Optional) Modify or delete shots.

When reviewing the track, you might decide one of the shots is not required. If you need to remove a shot, go to the shot that is not required using the Player toolbar and click the ▦ (Delete) icon in the Record toolbar. If one of the shots is incorrect, navigate to it using the Player toolbar, make changes to the object, and click the ▦ (Modify) icon in the Record toolbar. The shot updates to the new position.

Step 6 - Finalize the track.

Once you are satisfied with the track, click **OK** in the Track dialog box. The Track is added to the specification tree, as shown in Figure 15–7. The trajectory of the track is also displayed on the screen. Use the **Hide/Show** option on the track to hide the trajectory from display.

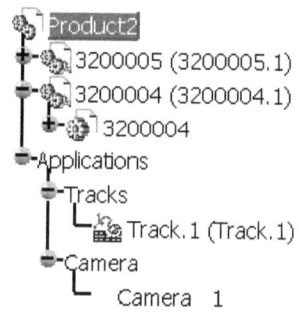

Product2
3200005 (3200005.1)
3200004 (3200004.1)
3200004
Applications
Tracks
Track.1 (Track.1)
Camera
Camera 1

Figure 15–7

If you want to edit a track again, double-click on it in the specification tree.

The model is in the configuration of the last displayed shot in the track. To return to the default configuration of the model, rewind the track to the beginning. If the track was used to change the placement of components the ▦ (Reset Position) icon in the DMU Move toolbar can also be used. To play back a track, select it in the specification tree and click the ▦ (Play a Simulation) icon in the DMU Generic Animation toolbar. Use the icons on the player to play back the track.

15.2 Color and Visibility Actions

Two additional special tracks are available to change the color or visibility of a selected object. These actions can be used to help point out areas of a product of particular importance when creating the animation.

Color Action

Color action can be used to change the color or transparency of a selected object over a time interval.

How To: Create a Color Action

1. Click the ![icon] (Color Action) icon.
2. Select the object in the specification tree. The Color Action dialog box opens, as shown in Figure 15–8.

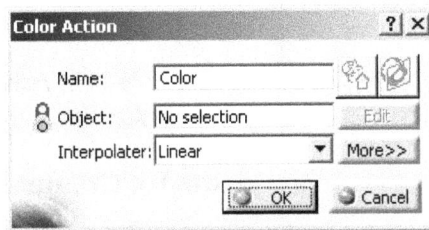

Figure 15–8

3. Click **Edit** in the Color Action dialog box.
4. Select the *Graphic* tab in the Properties dialog box, as shown in Figure 15–9, and change the graphic qualities of the selected object.

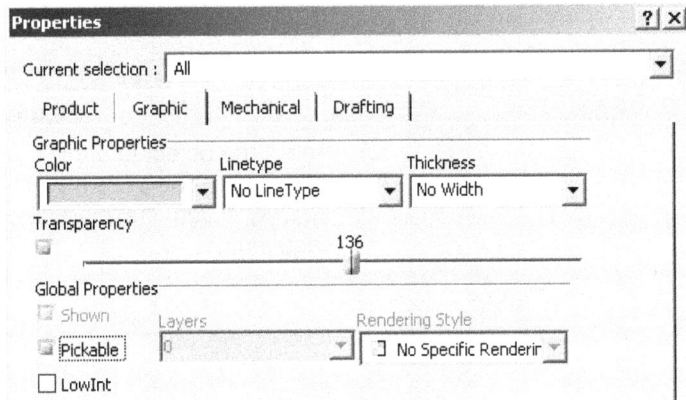

Figure 15–9

5. Click **OK** to close the Properties dialog box.

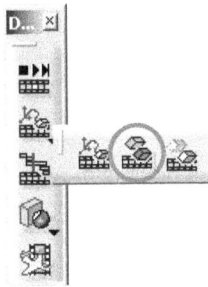

6. Click the ▦ (Record) icon in the Recorder toolbar to take a shot of the new graphic properties.
7. Repeat steps to change the graphic qualities again and take additional shots as required.
8. Preview the track using the Player toolbar.
9. Modify or delete any shots using the same technique as used in Step 5: of the Create Track procedure.
10. Click **OK** to complete the track. The color action is added to the specification tree, as shown in Figure 15–10.

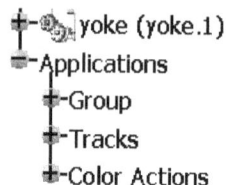

yoke (yoke.1)
Applications
Group
Tracks
Color Actions

Figure 15–10

Visibility Action

Use the Visibility Action tool to hide or show objects in an assembly.

How To: Create a Visibility Action

1. Click the ▦ (Visibility Action) icon.
2. Select **Visibility** in the Edit Visibility Action dialog box, as shown in Figure 15–11.

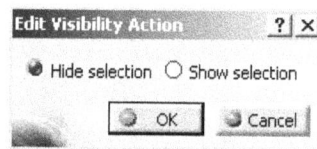

Edit Visibility Action   ? ×
● Hide selection ○ Show selection
OK   Cancel

Figure 15–11

3. Select the object to apply visibility to.
4. Click **OK** to complete the action. You cannot preview a visibility action, these are seen when the action is applied to a sequence.

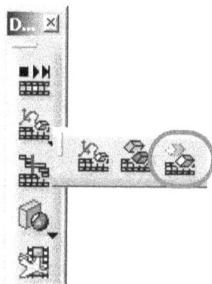

15.3 Creating Sequences

Tracks, visibility, and color actions can be combined to create sequences. Sequences are a series of actions used to create a simulation.

General Steps

Use the following general steps to create a sequence:

1. Open the Sequence dialog box.
2. Add actions to the sequence.
3. Reorder actions as required.
4. Modify durations, if required.
5. Preview and complete the sequence.
6. Play back the sequence.

Step 1 - Open the Sequence dialog box.

To begin creating a sequence, click the ⬛ (Edit Sequence) icon in the DMU Generic Animations toolbar. The Edit Sequence dialog box opens, as shown in Figure 15–12. All of the created actions display in the window on the left side of the box.

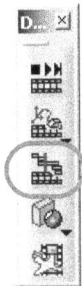

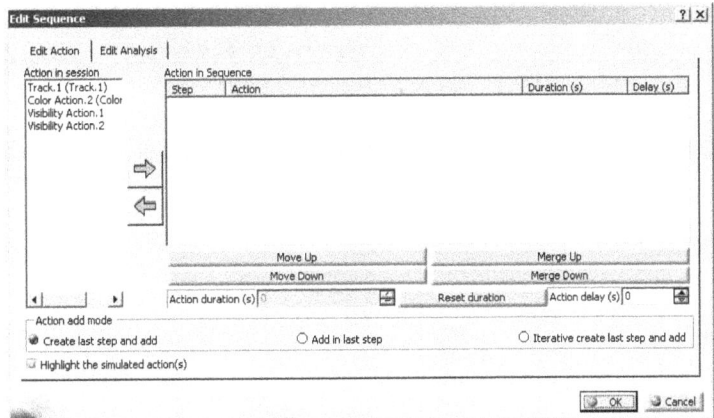

Figure 15–12

Step 2 - Add actions to the sequence.

Move the actions required in the sequence to the right side window by clicking the ⇨ icon. The right side window of the Edit sequence dialog box updates, as shown in Figure 15–13.

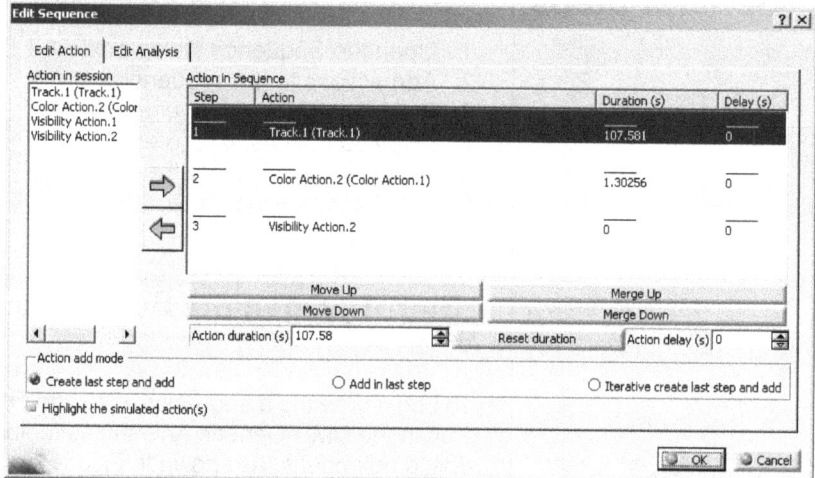

Figure 15–13

Step 3 - Reorder actions as required.

By default, the actions take place right after each other in the order in which they were added to the sequence. Actions can be changed to run at the same time and to be reordered. The options used to change the sequence are described as follows:

Option	Description
Move Up	Move the selected action up in the sequence.
Move Down	Move the selected action down in the sequence.
Merge Up	Make the selected action occur at the same time as the action above it in the sequence.
Merge Down	Make the selected action occur at the same time as the action below it in the sequence.

For example, action 1 and 2 added in Figure 15–13, need to occur at the same time followed by action 3. By highlighting action 2 and clicking **Merge Up**, the Sequence updates as shown in Figure 15–14.

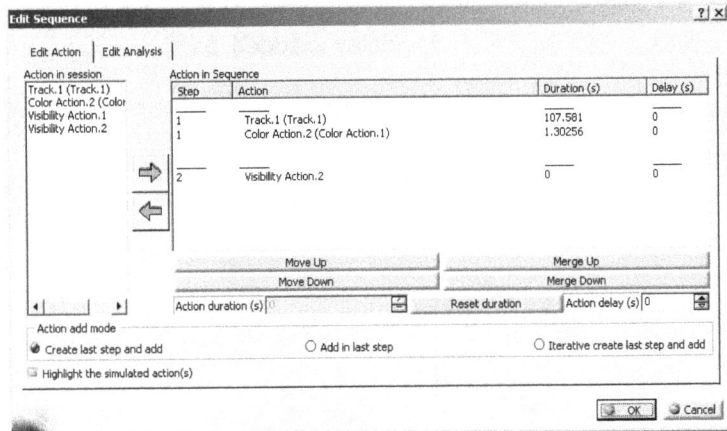

Figure 15–14

Step 4 - Modify durations, if required.

Times for each action in the sequence can be changed from their default by highlighting the action in the window and changing the time in the Action Duration field. In Figure 15–14, actions 1 and 2 have different durations associated with them. Since they are supposed to run for the same amount of time, the duration of one or both can be set so that they match, as shown in Figure 15–15.

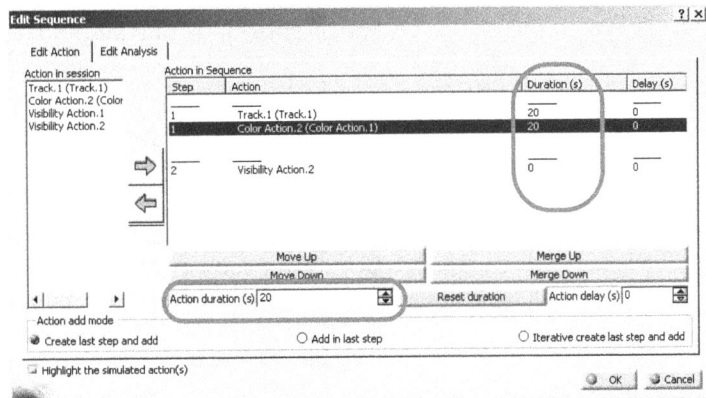

Figure 15–15

A delay can be added at the end of any step in the sequence by highlighting an action in the step and entering a delay in the Action Delay field. The next step in the sequence does not start until after the delay time has completed. For example, to add a 5 second delay before the visibility changes from our previous example, the Color action is highlighted in Step 1 and a 5 second delay is added, as shown in Figure 15–16.

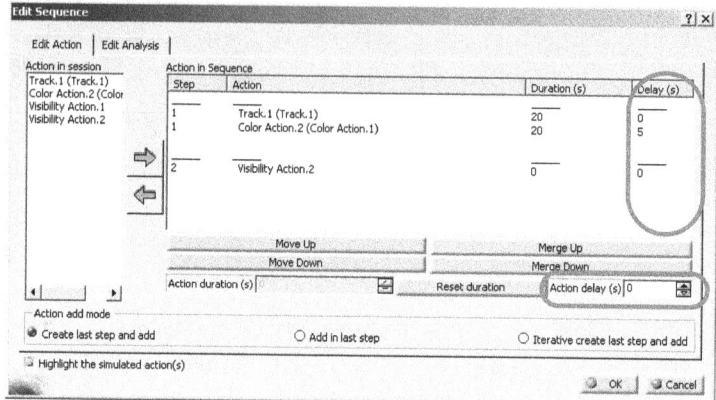

Figure 15–16

Step 5 - Preview and complete the sequence.

Use the Player toolbar to preview the created sequence and make changes to the sequences as required. Once the sequence is correct click **OK** to complete the operation. The sequence is added to the specification tree. To edit a sequence again once it has been created, double-click on it in the specification tree, and the Edit Sequence dialog box opens.

Step 6 - Play back the sequence.

Sequences can be played back by clicking the ▣▶▶ (Play a Simulation) icon in the DMU Generic Animation toolbar. Select the sequence to play in the specification tree and use the icons in the player to run the sequence. The Play a Simulation tool can also be used to play back tracks, color actions, and replays.

15.4 Automatic Clash Detection

When components are moved in a track or simulation, clashes can automatically be detected. This is useful when analyzing how components interact with each other over a range of motions. The DMU Kinematics workbench enables you to setup linkages to move components and test the flexibility of the model over a range of positions. The different clash detection options are described as follows:

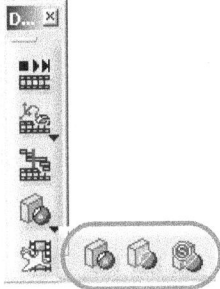

Option	Description
	Clash Detection Off: This is the default option and clash is not detected.
	Clash Detection On: Any clash between the selected object and another highlights as the component moves.
	Clash Detection Stop: When a clash is detected between the moving component and another the animation stops. Use the player to continue the animation.

In large assemblies, running with Clash detection on can slow down the computer. It is recommended that you do not to toggle on Clash detection until after the first step, since the first step is in default position and a static clash analysis can check for issues in this position. If a detected interference needs further investigation stop the animation at that point and use the Clash analysis tool in the Space Analysis workbench.

15.5 Recording Viewpoints

Navigating through a model can be recorded using the Record Viewpoint Animation tool. This is commonly used to record fly and walk-throughs and can also be used to record viewpoint changes using any method. Recorded viewpoints are called replays.

General Steps

Use the following general steps to record a viewpoint:

1. Set up the replay.
2. Record movements.
3. Save the replay.

Step 1 - Set up the replay.

Click the (Record Viewpoint Animation) icon in the DMU Generic Animation toolbar. The Viewpoint Animation Recorder toolbar displays as shown in Figure 15–17.

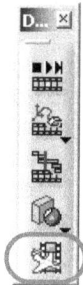

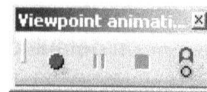

Figure 15–17

Click the (Recording) icon and give the replay a meaningful name using the Resulting Replay dialog box, as shown in Figure 15–18. Click **OK** to begin recording.

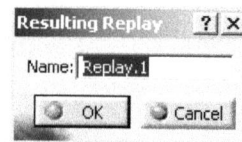

Figure 15–18

Step 2 - Record movements.

Move the model required using any of the orientation techniques (e.g., Standard and Save Viewpoints, Walk through, Fly through, Look At, Viewpoint palette). Use the ❚❚ (Pause) icon to pause the recording. While the recording is paused changes in model orientation are not recorded. Click the ● (Recording) icon to resume recording.

Step 3 - Save the replay.

Once the sequence is complete, click the ■ (Stop) icon to complete the replay. Click the ● (Recording) icon again to create another replay. If no more replays are required, click the 🗇 (Record Viewpoint Animation) icon in the DMU Generic Animation toolbar to toggle off the Record viewpoint tool.

To play back a replay, select it in the specification tree and click the ▪▶▶ (Play a Simulation) icon in the DMU Generic Animation toolbar. Use the icons on the player to run the replay.

Replays cannot be edited.

Practice 15a | # Creating Animations

Practice Objective

- Create an animation.

In this practice, you will use an existing assembly to create a simple animation. You will also use the Track and Color action tools to create the animation.

Task 1 - Open the assembly.

The files for this practice can be found in the Fan directory.

1. Open **Fan.CATProduct**. The assembly displays as shown in Figure 15–19. Ensure that the DMU Navigator workbench is active. If you did not complete *Practice 14a*, open **Fan_bCompleted.CATProduct**.

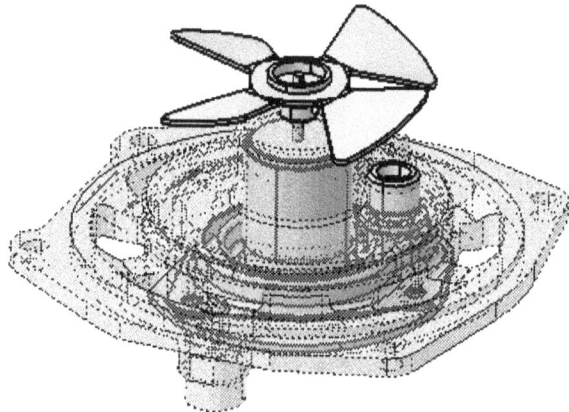

Figure 15–19

Task 2 - Record a Track.

1. Click the ![track icon] (Track) icon in the DMU Generic Animation toolbar. The Track dialog box opens, as shown in Figure 15–20.

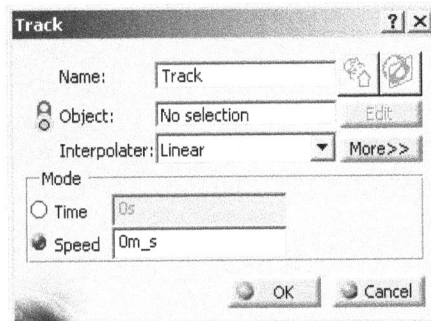

Figure 15–20

2. Select fan_blade in the specification tree as the object to track. Figure 15–21 shows the Update dialog box and the compass as it snaps to the model.

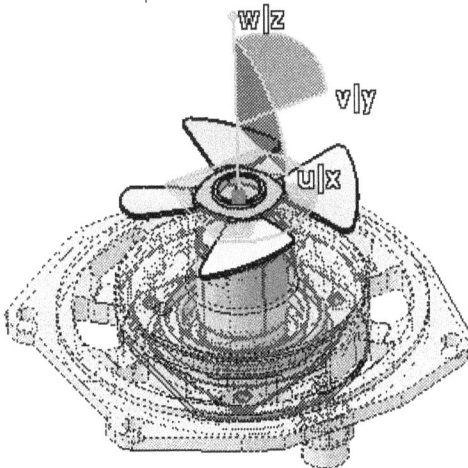

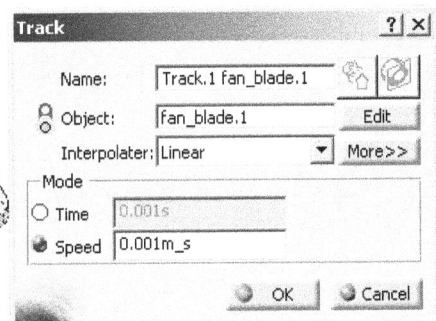

Figure 15–21

3. Move the cursor over the red dot on the compass until the move handles appear. Right-click over the red dot and select **Edit** as shown in Figure 15–22.

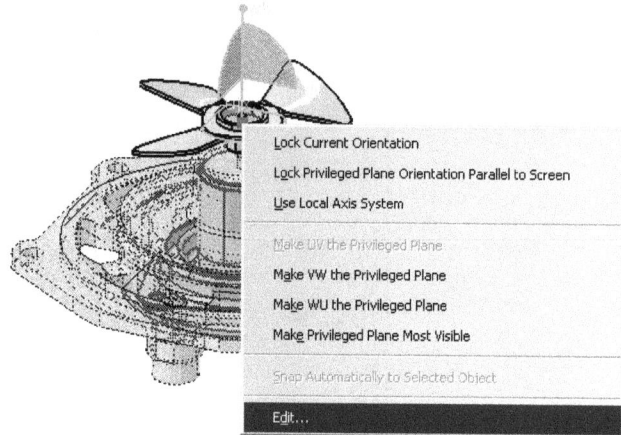

Lock Current Orientation

Lock Privileged Plane Orientation Parallel to Screen

Use Local Axis System

Make UV the Privileged Plane

Make VW the Privileged Plane

Make WU the Privileged Plane

Make Privileged Plane Most Visible

Snap Automatically to Selected Object

Edit...

Figure 15–22

4. The Parameters for Compass Manipulation dialog box opens. Enter **25deg** in the field shown in Figure 15–23, and rotate the compass once in the negative direction.

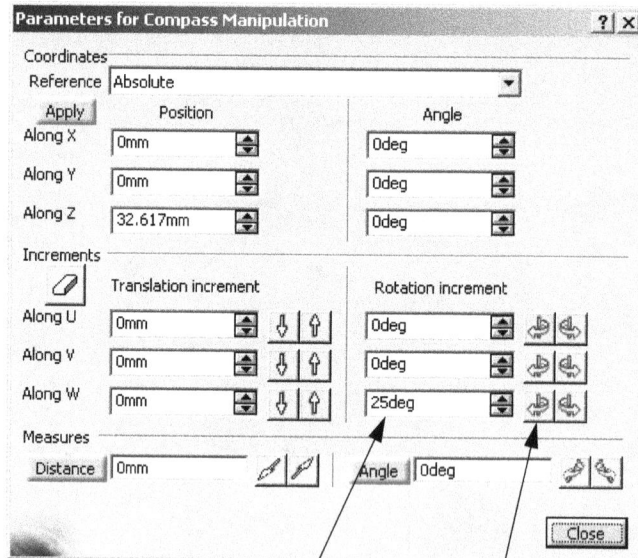

Parameters for Compass Manipulation

Coordinates
Reference Absolute

Apply	Position		Angle	
Along X	0mm		0deg	
Along Y	0mm		0deg	
Along Z	32.617mm		0deg	

Increments

	Translation increment			Rotation increment		
Along U	0mm			0deg		
Along V	0mm			0deg		
Along W	0mm			25deg		

Measures

Distance 0mm   Angle 0deg

Close

Enter 25deg here   Rotate the compass once
                        in the negative direction

Figure 15–23

5. Click the [Record icon] (Record) icon in the Recorder toolbar to take a shot of the current view.

6. Rotate the compass once more in the negative direction and take another shot of the view.

7. Repeat step 6. three more times to take an additional 3 shots.

8. Close the Parameter for Compass Manipulation dialog box.

9. Enter **1m_s** in the *Speed* field of the Track dialog box.

10. Click the [Skip to Begin icon] (Skip to Begin) icon in the Player toolbar to rewind the model to its initial position.

11. Click the [Play icon] (Play) icon in the Player toolbar to play the animation.

12. Click **OK**. The **Track** branch displays in the specification tree as shown in Figure 15–24.

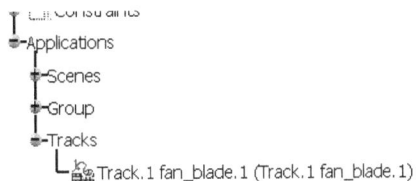

Figure 15–24

Task 3 - Add color actions.

1. Click the [Color Action icon] (Color Action) icon in the **SimuActionsIconBox** flyout menu of DMU Generic Animation toolbar. The Color Action dialog box opens, as shown in Figure 15–25.

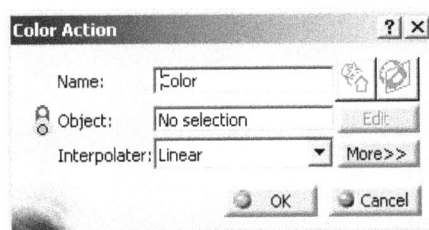

Figure 15–25

2. Select **fan_blade** in the specification tree as the object to which to add color actions. The Color Action dialog box updates with the selected option and the part highlights on the model.

3. Click **Edit** in the Color Action dialog box.

4. The Properties dialog box opens. Select the *Graphic* tab and set the color of the model to red.

5. Click **OK** and click the (Record) icon to take a shot of the view.

6. Repeat steps 3. to 5. for colors blue and green.

7. Click the (Skip to Begin) icon in the Player toolbar to rewind the model to its initial position.

8. Click the (Play) icon in the Player toolbar.

9. Click **OK**. The **Color Actions** branch displays in the specification tree as shown in Figure 15–26.

Figure 15–26

Task 4 - Create a Sequence.

1. Click the ▦ (Edit Sequence) icon in the DMU Generic Animation toolbar. The Edit Sequence dialog box opens, as shown in Figure 15–27.

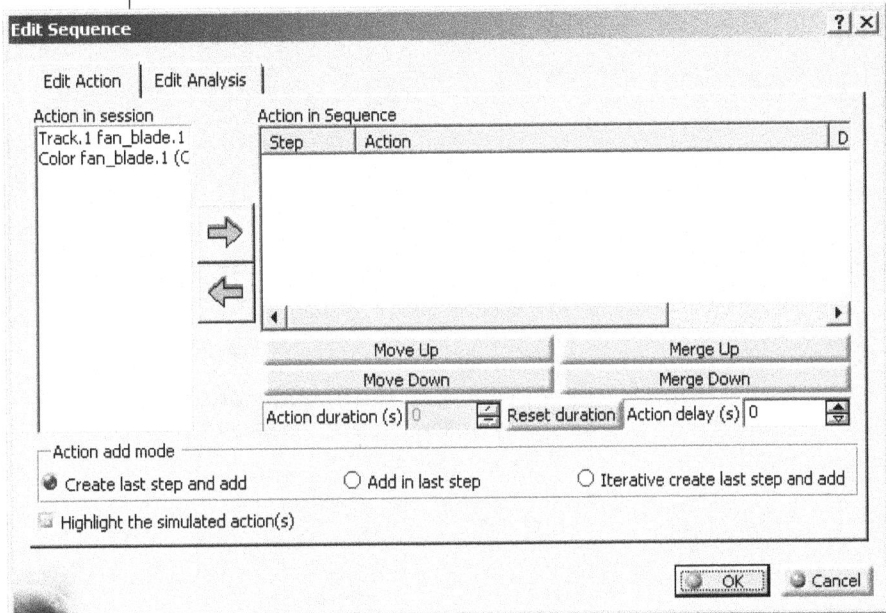

Figure 15–27

2. Select **Track.1 fan_blade.1** in the *Action in Session* column and use ⇨ to move it to the *Action in Sequence* column.

3. Select **Color fan_blade.1** in the *Action in Session* column and use ⇨ to move it to the *Action in Sequence* column.

4. With the **Color fan_blade.1** row selected, click **Merge Up** to run both actions at the same time.

5. Select the **Track.1 fan_blade.1** row and enter **10** in the *Action duration(s)* field.

6. Select **Color fan_blade.1** row and enter **10** in the *Action duration(s)* field. The Edit Sequence dialog box opens, as shown in Figure 15–28.

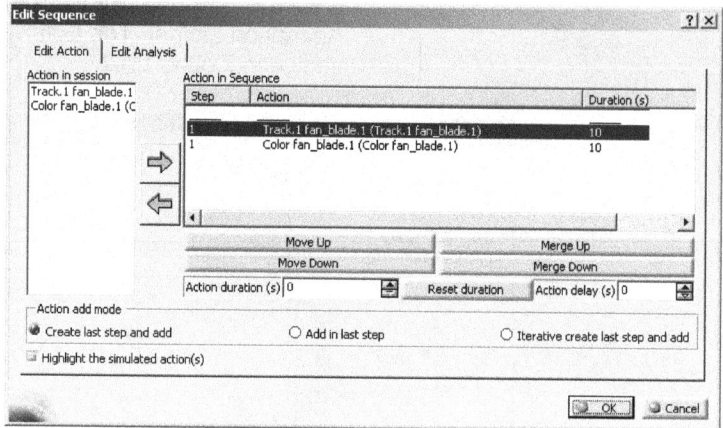

Figure 15–28

7. Click **OK**. The **Sequences** branch displays in the specification tree, as shown in Figure 15–29.

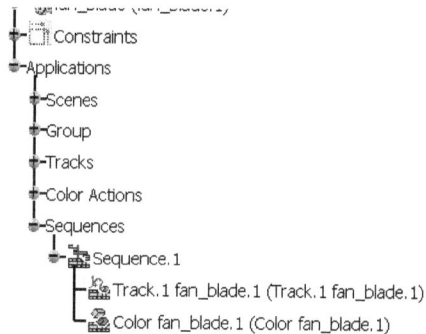

Figure 15–29

Task 5 - Play the animation.

1. Select **Sequence.1** in the specification tree and click the
   (Simulation Player) icon.

2. The Player toolbar displays. Click the (Play) icon.

3. Save the file and close the window.

Practice 15b	# Animation with Clash Detection

Practice Objective

- Detect clash during an animation.

In this practice, you will use the Clash detection tool to locate clash interferences between assembly components during an animation.

Task 1 - Open the assembly.

The files for this practice can be found in the CVJoint directory.

1. Open **CageBall.CATProduct**. The assembly displays as shown in Figure 15–30. Ensure that the DMU Navigator workbench is active.

Figure 15–30

Task 2 - Record a Track.

1. Click the (Track) icon in the DMU Generic Animation toolbar. The Track dialog box opens, as shown in Figure 15–31.

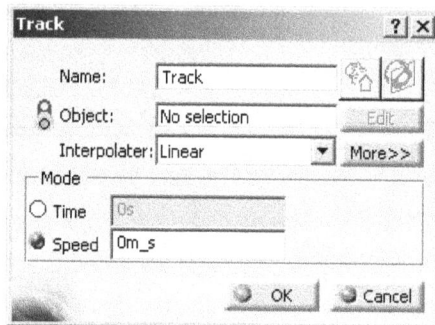

Figure 15–31

2. Select **Cage** in the specification tree as the object to track. The compass snaps to the center of the Cage component. The model and the Track dialog box appear as shown in Figure 15–32.

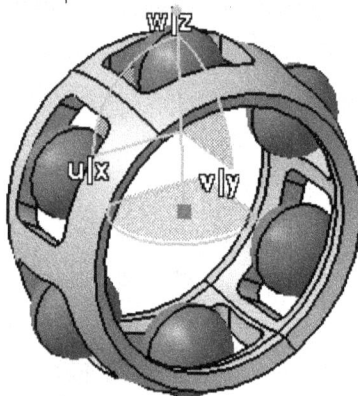

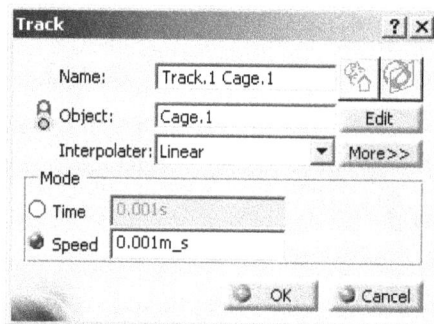

Figure 15–32

3. Move the cursor over the red dot on the compass until the move handles appear. Right-click over the red dot and select **Edit** as shown in Figure 15–33. The Parameters for Compass Manipulation dialog box opens.

Lock Current Orientation
Lock Privileged Plane Orientation Parallel to Screen
Use Local Axis System
Make UV the Privileged Plane
Make VW the Privileged Plane
Make WU the Privileged Plane
Make Privileged Plane Most Visible
Snap Automatically to Selected Object
Edit...

Figure 15–33

1. Enter **30** mm in the Along Y field, as shown in Figure 15–34, and click **Apply**.

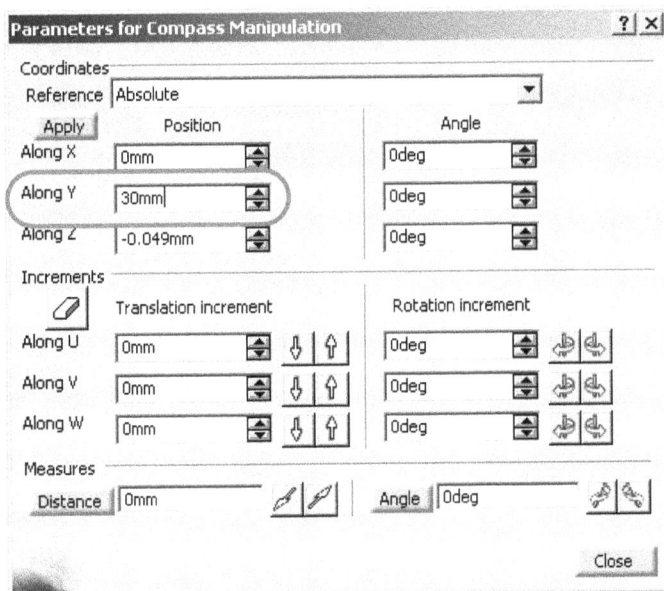

Figure 15–34

2. Close the Parameters for Compass Manipulation dialog box. The model displays as shown in Figure 15–35.

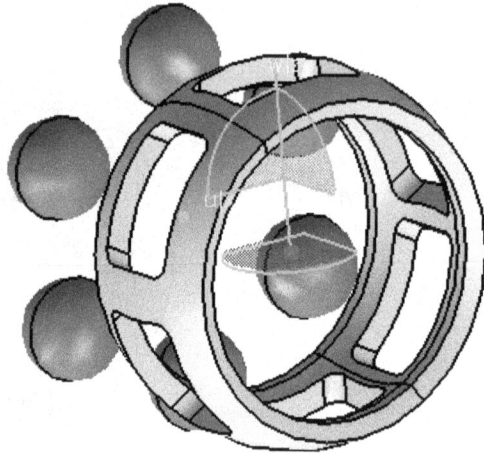

Figure 15–35

3. Click the (Record) icon in the Recorder toolbar to take a shot of the current view.

4. From the Track dialog box, change the speed to **0.01m_s**.

5. Click **OK** in the Track toolbar.

Task 3 - Play the animation and detect clash.

---

1. Select **Track.1 Cage.1** in the specification tree and click the (Simulation Player) icon.

2. The Player toolbar displays. Click the (Skip to Begin) icon to rewind the model back to its original position.

3. Click the (Clash Detection Off) icon in the **Clash Mode** flyout menu of the DMU Generic Animation toolbar.

4. Click the (Play) icon. The animation plays without any clash. Rewind the animation.

5. Click the ▨ (Clash Detection On) icon.

6. Play the animation. As it plays, some areas on the model highlight in red indicating the occurrence of clash at those points, as shown in Figure 15–36.

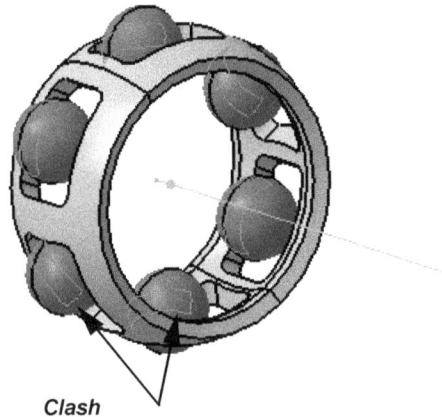

Clash

Figure 15–36

7. Rewind the animation.

8. Click the ▨ (Clash Detection Stop) icon.

You can click the

▶ *(Play) icon again to continue playing the animation. The animation stops again at the next clash.*

9. Play the animation. The animation stops after 1 second due to the **(Clash Detection Stop)** option. This option is used to stop the animation as soon as the first clash is detected.

10. Close the model without saving.

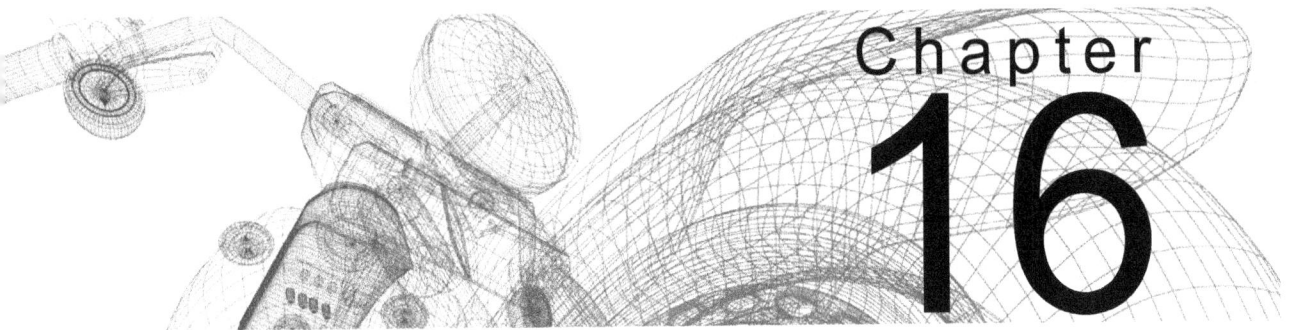

Viewing a Drawing

The 2D workbench is used to view drawings. It provides tools that enable you to take measurements, compare drawings and create annotations. The annotations can be published to an HTML report that can be used for reference and presentations.

Learning Objectives in this Chapter

- Learn how to work with 2D documents.
- Measure, compare, and publish 2D documents.

16.1 Working with 2D Documents

2D documents can be opened inside the ENOVIA DMU 2D Viewer and they can be annotated in the same way as 3D documents. The following formats can be opened inside the 2D Workshop:

- cgm
- dxf, dwg
- GL, GL2
- HPGL
- CATIA V5 Drawings (*.CATDrawing)
- CATIA V4 drawings (*.model)

2D documents can be created or opened. To open a 2D document click the [Open icon] (Open) icon in the standard toolbar, and select the 2D document. The file opens automatically in the 2D Viewer, as shown in Figure 16–1.

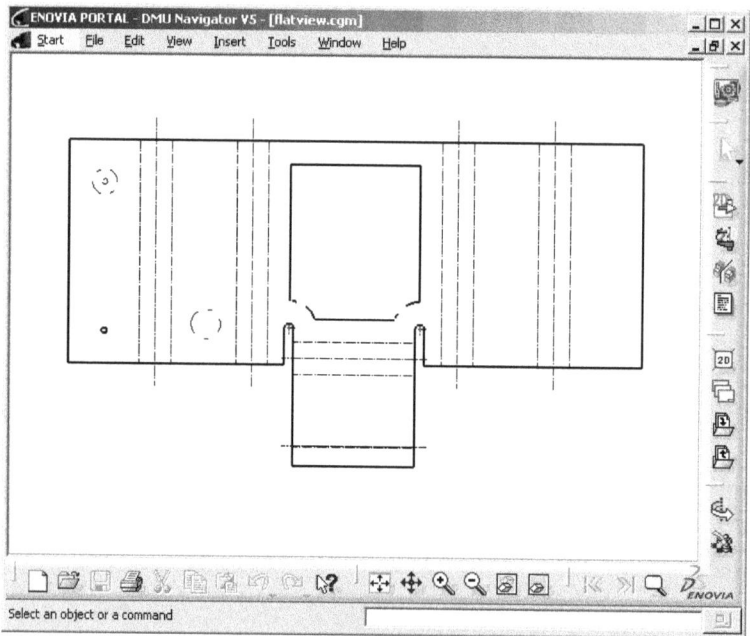

Figure 16–1

You can also open an empty 2D document by clicking the

 (New) icon in the Standard toolbar and selecting **cgm** in the New dialog box, as shown in Figure 16–2.

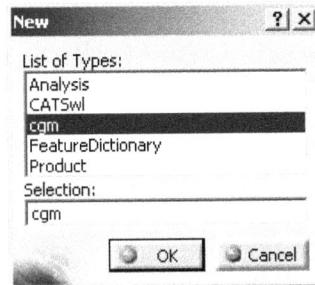

Figure 16–2

Although many formats can be opened to the 2D Workshop, not all of them have full functionality. The file must be in cgm format for full functionality. If it is not in cgm format, it is best to insert the document into a cgm file.

Inserting Documents

Whether you have created a new empty document or opened an existing file you can insert another document into the open one

by clicking the (Insert 2D document) icon in the DMU 2D Tools toolbar and selecting the document in the Select 2D Document box, as shown in Figure 16–3.

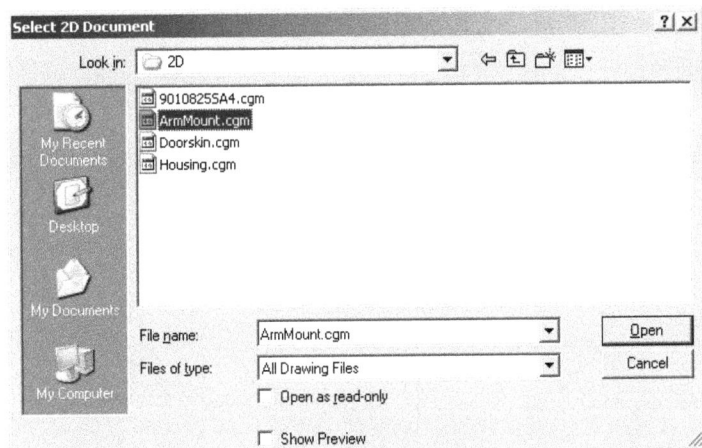

Figure 16–3

Manipulating 2D Documents

You can translate, rotate and zoom 2D documents. To translate a document, select it and, while holding the middle mouse button down, drag the view as shown in Figure 16–4. Views can be resized by holding the left mouse button on a handle and dragging the view. To zoom, hold the middle mouse button, right-click and move the cursor up or down.

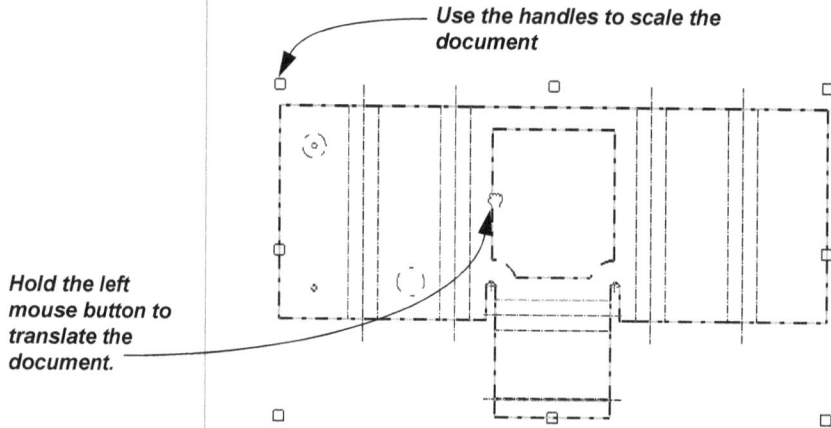

Use the handles to scale the document

Hold the left mouse button to translate the document.

Figure 16–4

To rotate the document click the (Free Rotation) icon in the 2D Move toolbar and select the document to be rotated. Green manipulators appear on the border of the document. Hold the left mouse button over one of the manipulators, as shown in Figure 16–5, and drag the document to rotate.

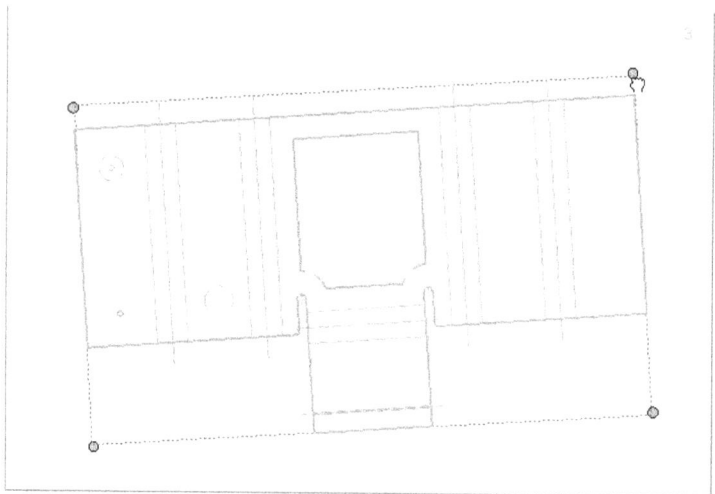

Figure 16–5

Movements can be controlled more accurately using the 2D Move dialog box. To access 2D Move, click the  (Translate or Rotate) icon in the 2D Move toolbar and select the document to move. The 2D Move dialog box opens as shown in Figure 16–6. Use the Coordinates fields to translate and rotate based on the origin of the document. Use the Increments fields to translate and rotate the document relative to its current position.

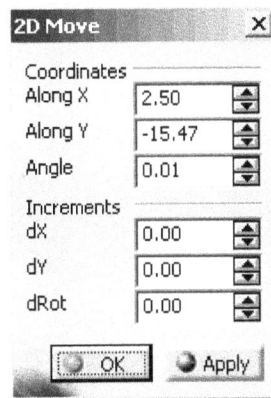

Figure 16–6

Annotation

Annotation can be created inside 2D documents using Annotated Views. To create an Annotated view, click the

[2D] (Annotated View) icon in the DMU 2D Annotated Views toolbar. The DMU 2D Marker toolbar displays, as shown in Figure 16–7. Options available in the toolbar are the same as those in a 3D document. Toggle between Annotated views using

the [2D] (Manage Annotated Views) icon. This also behaves the same as in the DMU Navigator workbench.

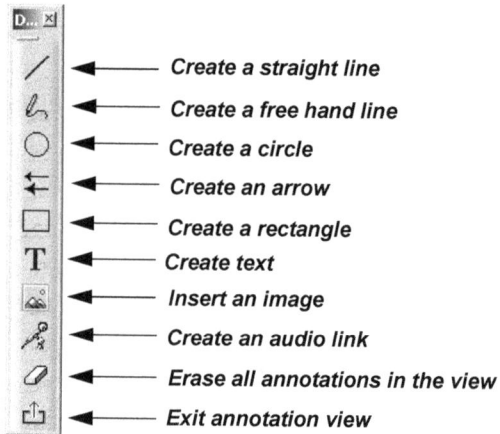

Create a straight line
Create a free hand line
Create a circle
Create an arrow
Create a rectangle
Create text
Insert an image
Create an audio link
Erase all annotations in the view
Exit annotation view

Figure 16–7

Annotated views can be exported and imported into the workshop. To export the 2D Annotated Views select the

 (Annotated Views file export) icon in the DMU 2D Annotated Views toolbar. The Annotated Views file export dialog box opens, as shown in Figure 16–8. Browse to the correct directory and save the file with a meaningful name. Click **Save** to save the annotated view as an xml file.

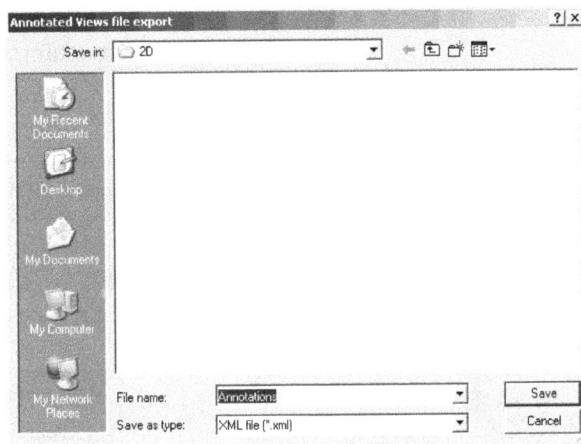

Figure 16–8

Annotated views can also be imported into the document by

clicking the (Annotated Views file import) icon in the DMU 2D Annotation toolbar. This is useful if more then one file containing notes exists. The notes can be combined into one file.

16.2 Measure 2D Documents

2D documents can be measured for distance, angles, and radii. Both vector and pixel documents, including cgm, hpgl, jpeg, and bmp, can be measured.

General Steps

Use the following general steps to measure a 2D document:

1. Access the 2D Measure dialog box.
2. Calibrate the measurement.
3. Take the measurement.

Step 1 - Access the 2D Measure dialog box.

Click the ![icon] (2D Measure) icon in the DMU 2D Tools toolbar to open the 2D Measure dialog box, as shown in Figure 16–9.

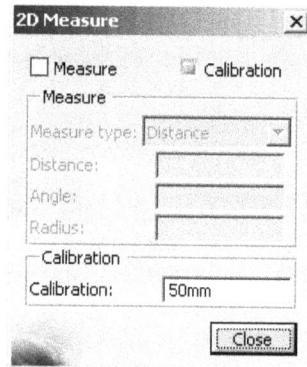

Figure 16–9

Step 2 - Calibrate the measurement.

For pixel formats, such as jpg, tif or bmp, the 2D Measure dialog box opens to the **Calibration** option. Since no vector geometry is in the document, ENOVIA needs to know the distance between two references to calibrate the 2D measuring tool.

Select two references on the image and enter the known distance between the selected references to calibrate the tool, as shown in Figure 16–10.

Since there is no vector geometry in a pixel image for the cursor to snap to, the measurements can only be approximate.

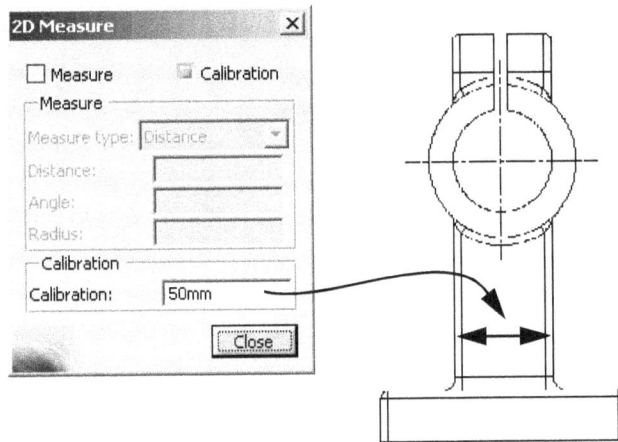

Figure 16–10

For vector formats, an automatic calibration based on the width of the document is already calculated. View the reference for calibration by selecting **Calibration** in the 2D Measure dialog box. If required, calibration can be adjusted by overriding the calibration value. You can also select two new reference points and enter the distance between them in the calibration field.

Step 3 - Take the measurement.

Select **Measure** in the 2D Measure dialog box to begin taking measurements. Select the type of measurement in the Measure type drop-down list, as shown in Figure 16–11.

Figure 16–11

The different measurement types are described as follows:

Description	Image	Resultant Dialog box
Distance Measures the distance between two reference points.	 ***Cursor changes to indicate where you are in the measurement.***	
Angle Measures the angle as defined by three points		
Arc Measures the angle and radius of an arc that is fitted through three points.		

Once you have finished taking measurements, click **Close** to close the measurement tool.

16.3 Compare 2D Documents

The Compare Drawings tool compares two cgm format documents to detect differences between them. This is useful when comparing the same document at different stages in a design or when looking at the differences in a design when changes are made.

General Steps

Use the following general steps to compare drawings:

1. Activate the Compare Drawings tool.
2. Review the results.
3. Close the Compare Drawings tool.

Step 1 - Activate the Compare Drawings tool.

To compare two documents, have one open and the other closed. In the open document, click the [Compare Drawings icon] (Compare Drawings) icon in the DMU 2D Tools toolbar. In the File Selection dialog box navigate to the file to be compared, highlight it and click **Open**, as shown in Figure 16–12.

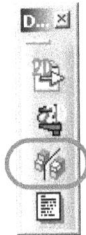

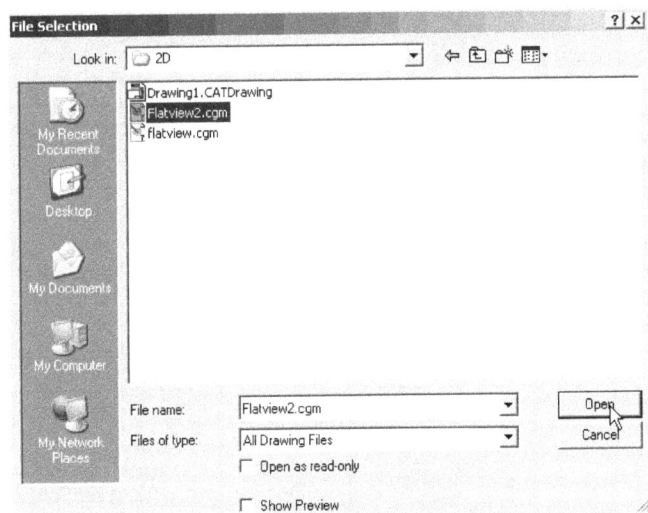

Figure 16–12

Step 2 - Review the results.

The 2D Measure tool can be used while in the Compare Drawing tool.

Once the second document is selected, it is compared to the first and the results display. The Compare Drawings dialog box opens, as shown in Figure 16–13. The Compare Drawings dialog box indicates the selected drawings. By default, elements that appear only in Drawing 1 appear in red, elements that appear only in the Drawing 2 appear in green and elements that are common to both appear in blue.

Click to display only the 1st drawing.

Click to display only the 2nd drawing.

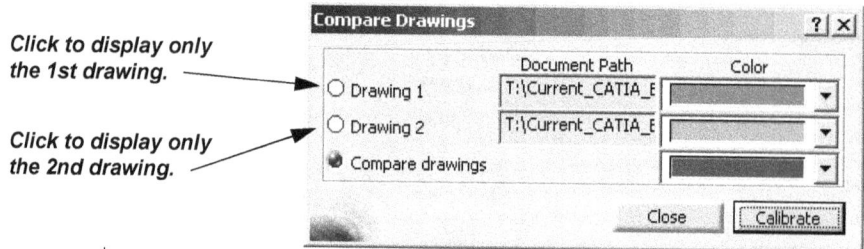

Figure 16–13

Calibration

If the documents are not lined up correctly, as shown in Figure 16–14, they can be moved by clicking **Calculate**. The Calibrate dialog box opens as shown in Figure 16–14.

Lines should be aligned.

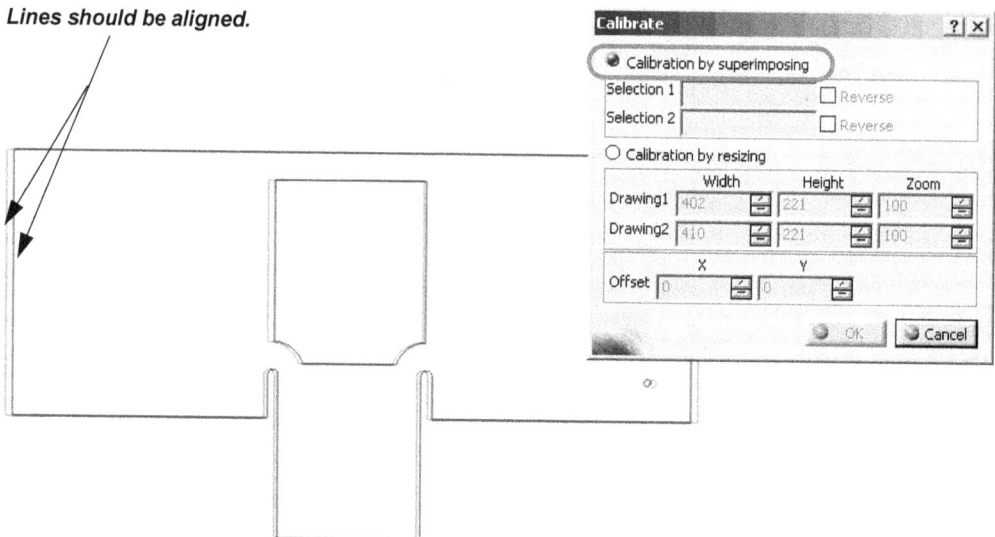

Figure 16–14

Ensure that the **Calibration by Superimposing** option is selected, and select a reference line or axis on each drawing to align. Click **OK** to return to the Compare Drawings dialog box. The documents shift so that the references are aligned, as shown in Figure 16–15.

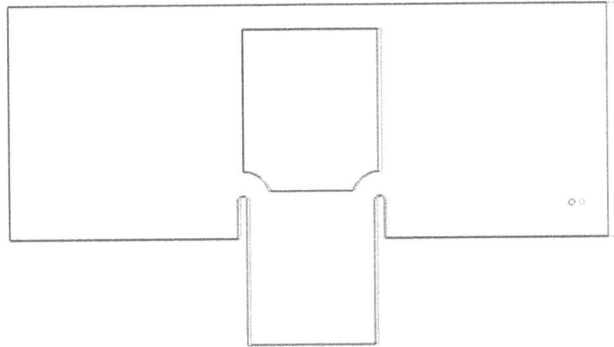

Figure 16–15

Calibration can also be done by resizing the documents. If one of the documents is not scaled correctly, click **Calibrate**, select **Calibration by Resizing** in the Calibrate dialog box, and change the drawing sizes using the fields as shown in Figure 16–16.

Use offset to move the 2nd document vertically or horizontally a known distance. This can be used in place of superimposing if no two references align.

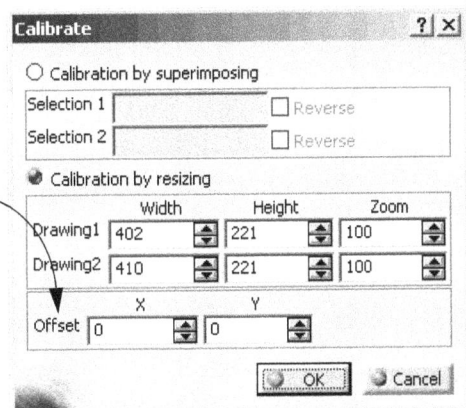

Figure 16–16

Step 3 - Close the Compare Drawings tool.

Once you have finished reviewing the differences, click **Close** to close the Compare Drawings dialog box. The second drawing disappears from the display.

16.4 Publish 2D Documents

You can publish 2D documents in HTML format for use by others. The publishing tools enable you to take snapshots and add comments to the report. You need a web browser to view an HTML file. An example of a published 2D document is shown in Figure 16–17.

Published Report

Directional Control Valve

Image 1

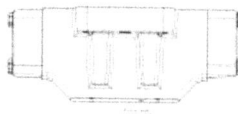

Creation date: 07/28/2004
Created by: rsamra

Figure 16–17

General Steps

Use the following general steps to create a published report of your results.

1. Activate the Publishing tool.
2. Select the elements to include in the report.
3. Save the published report.

Step 1 - Activate the Publishing tool.

To begin publishing, click the  (Start Publish) icon and the select Publish File dialog box opens. Enter a meaningful name in the *File Name* field and identify the path in which to save the file. Click **Save** to create the HTML file. The Publishing Tools toolbar displays as shown in Figure 16–18.

Figure 16–18

Step 2 - Select the elements to include in the report.

Inside the report, you can take snapshots of your model, publish findings, and enter comments.

Snapshots

Snapshots are used to create an image of everything inside the ENOVIA window. This includes comparison results, annotations, comments, etc. Any floating toolbars are also included in the snapshot. To use a snapshot, place the elements on the screen in the required positions and click the 📷 (Snapshot) icon. The image is added to the HTML file. A snapshot created of the front view of a model is shown in Figure 16–19. The image can be enlarged in the HTML viewer by clicking on it.

Published Report

Image 1

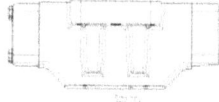

Click on the image to enlarge.

Date HTML file was created and the publisher of the file are included at the bottom of the page.

Creation date: 07/28/2004
Created by: rsamra

Figure 16–19

Feature Publish

Results of Clash calculations, Hyperlinks, Simulations, and Replays can be published to the report. To add results to the report, click the 𝒫 (Feature Publish) icon and select the feature to publish. Published results are placed at the end of the HTML page.

Text

The $\mathbf{T}$ (Text) icon is used to add additional comments to the report. If the text is created after a snapshot is taken, it displays below the image. If the text is created first and then the snapshot is taken, it displays above the image.

Step 3 - Save the published report.

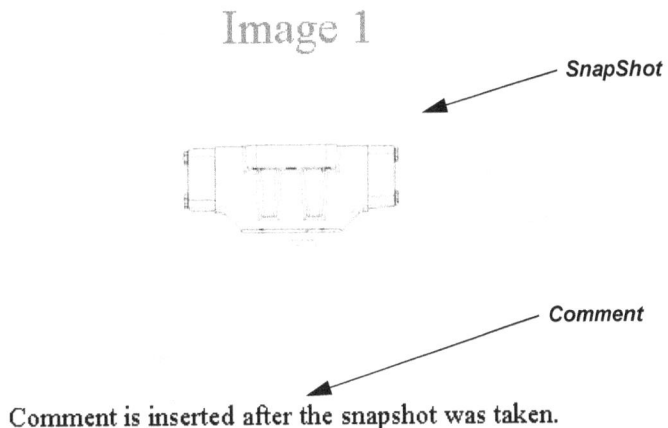

Once all of the required elements have been added to the report, click the (Stop Publish) icon. The HTML file is created and saved to the specified directory. An example of a published report is shown in Figure 16–20.

Published Report

Image 1

SnapShot

Comment

Comment is inserted after the snapshot was taken.

Creation date: 07/28/2004
Created by: rsamra

Figure 16–20

Practice 16a	# Measuring a 2D Document

Practice Objectives

- Insert 2D documents.
- Take Measurements.

In this practice, you will insert a 2D document into the workshop and take distance, angle, and arc measurements. You will need to calibrate the Measurement tool first to set the distance between two points, which will be used by ENOVIA to take further measurements.

Task 1 - Insert a 2D drawing.

1. Select **File>New**. Select cgm in the New dialog box as shown in Figure 16–21.

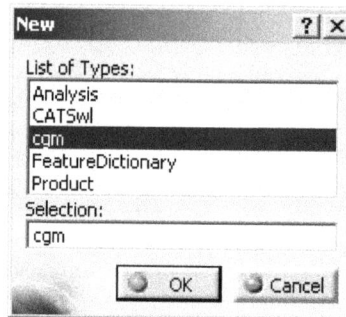

Figure 16–21

2. Click **OK**. The 2D drawing workbench opens with all of its standard toolbars.

3. Click the 🖼 (Insert 2D Document) icon in the DMU 2D Tools toolbar. The Select 2D Document dialog box opens. Browse to the FrontWheel directory and select Arm.cgm to open, as shown in Figure 16–22.

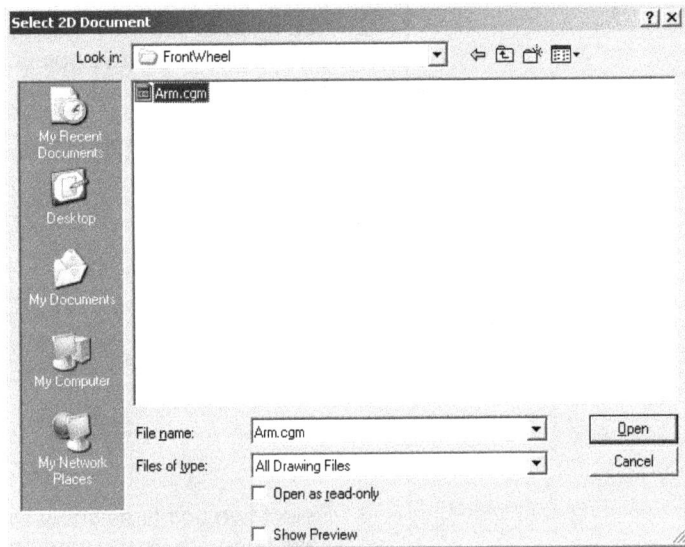

Figure 16–22

4. If required, click the ⊕ (Fit All In) icon to fit the drawing in the window as shown in Figure 16–23.

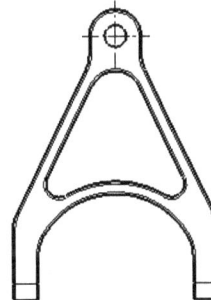

Top view
Scale:1:1

Front view
Scale:1:1

Figure 16–23

Task 2 - Take measurements.

1. Click the ![icon] (2D Measure) icon in the DMU 2D Tools. The 2D Measure dialog box opens.

2. You need to calibrate the measuring tool by defining a known distance between two points. Select **Calibration**, as shown in Figure 16–24.

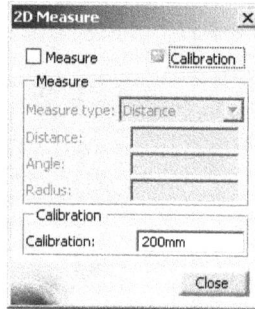

Figure 16–24

3. Select two points as shown in Figure 16–25. Ensure that the selections are on the same horizontal line.

4. Enter **200** in the *Calibration* field of the 2D Measure dialog box. This sets the distance between the selected points to be 200mm. Any further measurements are taken relative to this value.

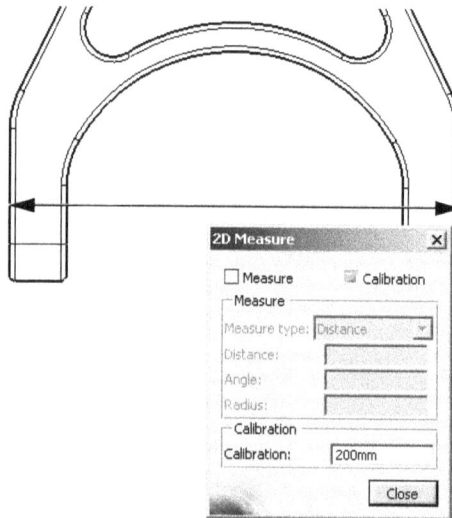

Figure 16–25

5. Select **Measure**.

6. Select **Distance** in the Measure type drop-down list.

7. Zoom in on the model and measure the distance between the two points as shown in Figure 16–26. It should be approximately 150mm.

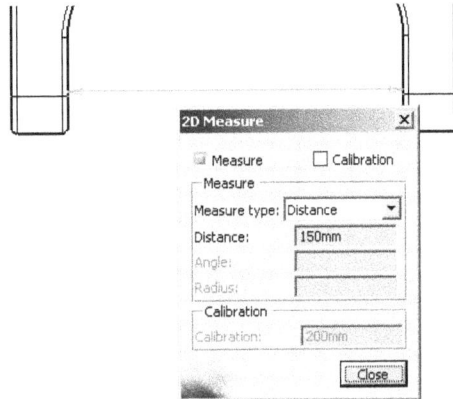

Figure 16–26

8. Select **Angle** in the Measure type drop-down list.

9. Figure 16–27 shows the three points to be selected. The angle dimension should be approximately 160deg.

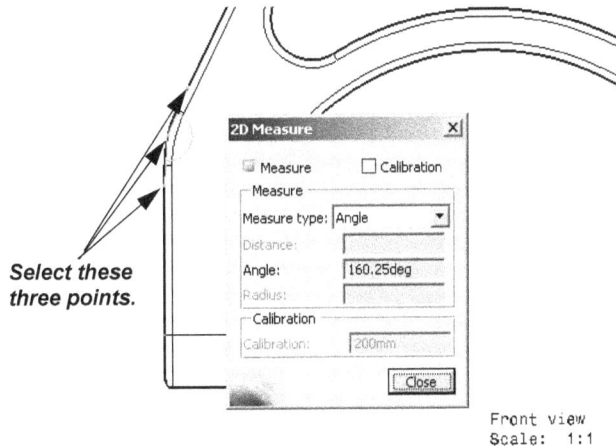

**Select these
three points.**

Front view
Scale: 1:1

Figure 16–27

10. Select **Arc** in the Measure type drop-down list.

Your measurements might be slightly different depending on where the points are selected.

11. Figure 16–28 shows the three points to be selected. The *Angle* and *Radius* of the arc should be approximately **180deg** and **25mm** respectively.

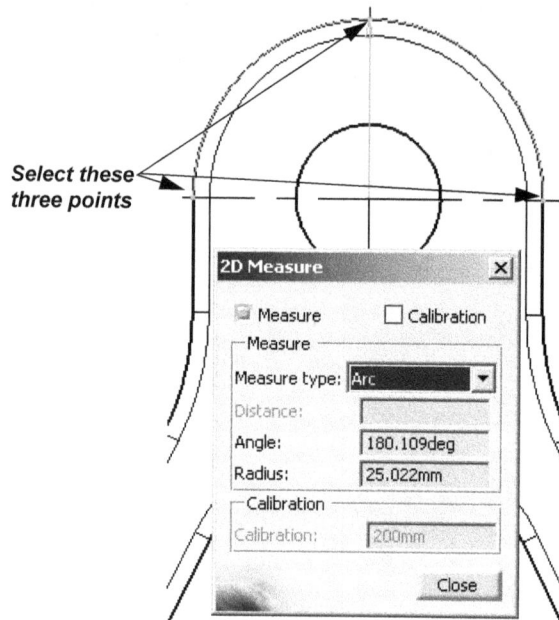

Figure 16–28

12. Close the 2D Measure dialog box.

13. Save the cgm file as **Arm2D** in the FrontWheel folder, and keep it open. This part is used in the next practice.

Practice 16b	# Annotate and Publish a 2D Document

Practice Objectives

- Insert Annotations.
- Publish 2D Documents.

In this practice, you will insert and import annotations into a 2D document. You will then publish the document along with all of its annotations for viewing by other users.

Task 1 - Import an annotation.

The files for this practice can be found in the FrontWheel directory.

1. Open **Arm2D.cgm**.

2. Click the (Annotated Views file import) icon.

3. Browse to the FrontWheel directory and open **Annotations.xml**.

4. While the annotation is successfully imported, it is not displayed in the model. You need to toggle to the Annotated view to see it. Click the (Manage Annotated Views icon).

5. Select **View.2** in the Annotated Views dialog box and click **OK**. Figure 16–29 shows the imported annotation.

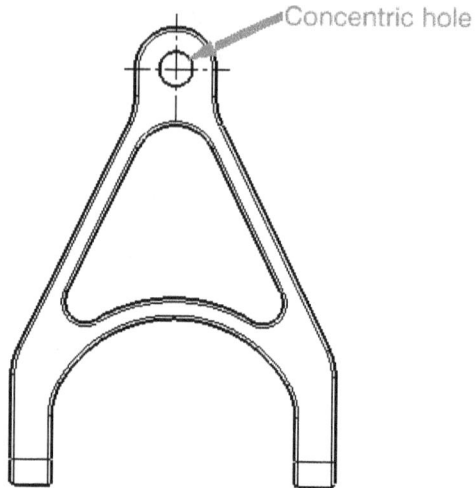

Concentric hole

Front view
Scale:1:1
Figure 16–29

Task 2 - Insert an annotation.

1. Click the **T** (Add Annotation Text) icon.

2. Select a location underneath the Front view. The Annotation Text dialog box opens.

3. Enter **All holes 20mm diameter**, as shown in Figure 16–30.

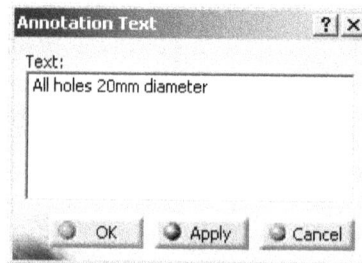

Figure 16–30

4. Click **OK**. Figure 16–31 shows the annotation as it displays
    on the drawing.

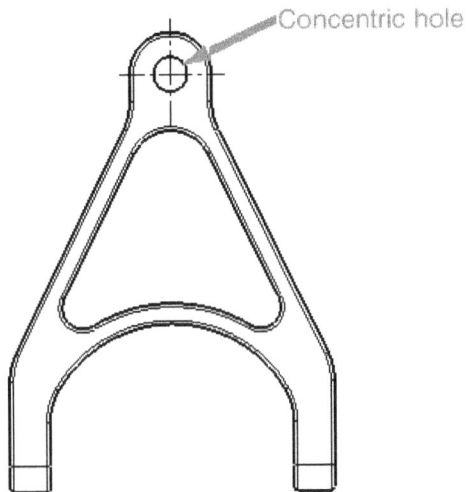

Figure 16–31

Task 3 - Publish the document.

1. Click the ▦ (Start Publish) icon.

2. Save the report as **Arm.html** in the FrontWheel directory.

3. Click the 📷 (Snapshot) icon to take a screen shot of the
    document.

4. Click the ▦ (Stop Publish) icon to end the publish.

5. Exit the annotated view by clicking the ⬆ (Exits from the
    Annotated View) icon.

6. Save the model and close the file.

7. Use Windows Explorer to browse to the *C:\DMU Navigator and SpaceAnalysis Class Files\FrontWheel* directory and open **Arm.html**. The report opens in your internet browser, as shown in Figure 16–32.

Published Report

Image 1

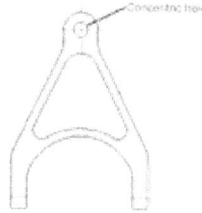

Top view
Scale: 1:1

Concentric hole

Front view
Scale: 1:1
All holes 20mm diameter

Creation date: 07/27/2004
Created by: rsamra

Figure 16–32